SEA URCHIN DEVELOPMENT: Cellular and Molecular Aspects

Louis W. Stearns
CALIFORNIA STATE UNIVERSITY,
LOS ANGELES

Dowden, Hutchinson & Ross, Inc.
Stroudsburg, Pennsylvania

Library of Congress Cataloging in Publication Data

Stearns, Louis W
    Sea urchin development.

    Bibliography: p.
    1. Sea urchin embryo. I. Title. [DNLM: 1. Sea
urchins--Embryology. QL958 S839s 1973]
QL958.S83   593'.95   73-18054
ISBN 0-87933-026-0

Manufactured in the United States of America.

Exclusive distributor outside the United States and Canada:
John Wiley & Sons, Inc.

Dedication

To Professor G. Arthur Brown,
with affection and appreciation
and
To Norma Anne Stearns, whose contributions in time,
ideas, and criticism have been of
major significance in the writing of this book and
whose encouragement and patience
have made the task a pleasant one.

L. W. S.

PREFACE

This book is a survey of some of the important problems in sea urchin development and of some of the research that has been devoted to them. We have addressed ourselves to this single developmental system with only rare allusion to parallel problems in development in other animals, and we have considered all developmental stages, from oogenesis to pluteus. Although we have given ourselves at times to descriptions of developmental events in order to guide the discussion, we have assumed that the reader has a knowledge of basic embryology. Our concern is not with the description of development in the animal, but rather with the findings of research on the mechanisms of development and with the significance of such findings. It is our hope and expectation that this survey will be of service to the senior biologist or the graduate student who anticipates undertaking investigations on sea urchin development or who wishes to acquaint himself with the progress of work in this field of experimental endeavor.

The embryology of the sea urchin is not an exotic subject. The sea urchin is one of the three principal animals to which we normally find recourse in the study of general embryology. A bibliography of publications on the sea urchin egg and embryo would include titles numbering into the thousands, although a substantial fraction of these would be found not to be directly concerned with the phenomena of development. The sea urchin has received attention in reviews on selected aspects of development such as fertilization. These have usually been comparative studies which have surveyed events in a variety of organisms. A few reviews have been devoted exclusively to the sea urchin but have considered only limited aspects of its development. In the past several decades only two or three surveys have confined themselves solely to the embryology of echinoids and at the same time considered all developmental stages through pluteus.

One of these works, *The American Arbacia and Other Sea Urchins* by Ethel Browne Harvey, has included a bibliography and a very brief summary of research on the echinoid egg and embryo extending back into the previous century. In the fifteen years that have elapsed since the publication of *The American Arbacia,* experimentation on the sea urchin has given rise to a bibliography larger than the comprehensive bibliography compiled by Harvey. We have not set before us the objective of writing a supplement to this excellent book, nor have we in any way attempted to use its contents as a base point or point of departure in our discussions. Our interests are different from those which characterize the work, and our approach and emphasis have been different as well. We have tended, however, to concentrate our efforts on the consideration of the work performed in those intervening fifteen years, primarily because we wished to discuss the more recent studies in the field and found that this time span was a very natural and convenient one in which to work. The very nature of our discussion, however, would disallow our being harnessed to this temporal restriction, and where necessary, we have departed from it. We have not attempted a comprehensive coverage, but rather, have elected to survey selected areas of research.

The omission of any recent reference constitutes neither a judgment on the worth of the publication nor a judgment on the importance of the subject with which it deals. In the selection of references we have considered only the balance and direction of the discussion. If a reference that is directly germane to the subject under consideration has been omitted, we are guilty of an oversight and our apologies are tendered to its author. With regard to the older work, we have found it necessary to exercise some selectivity in the interests of brevity, but we have striven to do so without biasing the discussion. We refer the reader in quest of a more comprehensive background in this early work to the bibliography and résumé of Harvey in *The American Arbacia and Other Sea Urchins.*

We have dedicated the first half of this work to a consideration of cellular mechanisms and biochemical problems associated with sea urchin development and have included a description of many of the visible aspects of each developmental stage. In the second half, we have accented problems primarily associated with the molecular biology of echinoid embryogenesis, in particular those involved with the regulation of the biosynthesis of proteins and with differentiation. The final chapter deals with an assortment of problems that are currently the focus of considerable research activity. All the problems discussed have a direct bearing on the developmental process. We have omitted altogether the examination of studies wherein the sea urchin has been used as a system to investigate problems in physiology, pharmacology, and other disciplines when such problems have not been directly concerned with development. Such an omission carries a risk, which must be accepted, that we are slighting some findings which may ultimately prove to be of significance in the explanation of developmental phenomena.

We recognize the fact that it is equivocal as to whether our omission of the subject of investigations on interspecific hybrids is justifiable. We did not include it because we thought it to be somewhat peripheral to the trend of the discussion. We have referred the reader to reviews on the subject.

We should like to express our appreciation to Dr. Peter Gray of the University of Pittsburgh for his reading of the manuscript and for his advice and criticism. We are grateful also for the help that we have received from the staff of California State University at Los Angeles, in particular to Dr. Dudley Thomas and to Jennie Nelson for their assistance in the preparation of the manuscript. We should like to thank Drs. Richard Allen and William Hanson for their advice and encouragement. The gracious assistance of Audrey Hawk, Arline Bock, and Cornelia Balogh of the Science and Technology Department of the Library has been invaluable and is deeply appreciated. We should like to thank Jerry Batagliotti for his work on the illustrations and Gilbert Weingourt for his work on photographic reproductions. We are grateful also for the assistance we have received from Elsie Robinson and Kathleen Moore of the staff of the Biology Department.

Finally, we should like to express our thanks to Paul Hanson, MEDLARS Search Analyst at the University of California, Los Angeles, for his help and cooperation in our search for bibliographical material.

L. W. S.

Contents

CHAPTER I

The Sea Urchin as a System for the Study of Development

GENERAL CONSIDERATIONS

The sea urchin is never an animal to evoke much interest or attention from society. Its eggs may on occasion find their way to the table in some gourmet specialty. It may capture a small headline on the back pages of the newspapers when, after a period in which food supplies are bountiful and climatic conditions are favorable, it multiplies to the extent that it can, and does, make alarming incursions into the offshore kelp beds. Mankind is generally content, however, to ignore this little echinoderm in favor of animals that are more dramatic in their appearance or behavior, more lovable, or more annoying. However little this creature has stimulated the curiosity of the masses, it has proved to be anything but unexciting to scholars who devote themselves to the study of reproduction and development. More knowledge about development has been accumulated from eggs and embryos of the sea urchin than from those of any other animal.

It is not difficult to account for the prodigious amount of study that has centered upon the sea urchin egg; the list of reasons for the repeated selection of this developmental system for investigation by embryologists is quite long, and only a few of these reasons need be discussed here. The eggs are usually very easy to obtain in amount.

1

A single female may produce eggs up into the millions in a reproductive season. Certain species are extremely prolific, and adequate numbers of adult individuals of such species may be harvested readily. Depending upon species and geographical regions, one can frequently obtain sufficient numbers of adults for experimental work in the intertidal zone at very low tides. Adults of some species commonly used in experimentation, however, have become scarce in certain localities. There has been considerable depletion in the beds of *Arbacia punctulata* in the New England region in recent years, for example.

The fact that the eggs and embryos are microscopic means that enormous numbers of individuals may be contained in a small volume, and thus enough individuals may be involved in a single experiment to provide an excellent statistical base. The amount of yolk with which the egg is endowed is sufficiently small usually not to introduce difficulties into analytical procedures. The embryo undergoes virtually no growth and shows no obligate dependence on exogenous precursors up to the formation of the pluteus. These circumstances, coupled with the paucity of yolk, make it urgent for the animal to develop into a feeding larva in a very short period of time. The process may require less than 48 hours. This brief time span represents a great convenience to the experimenter.

The extent of synchrony of development among embryos that occurs following the fertilization of a batch of eggs tends to produce a situation in which the metabolic processes of large numbers of cells are running in phase with one another. Added to this happy circumstance stands the fact that within an individual embryo the cells normally divide in synchrony with one another for the first few cleavages, although this synchrony begins to wane at the 16-cell stage.

Many other characteristics of the sea urchin embryo have often proved, in one way or another, to be a blessing to the researcher. The eggs and embryos of many species are relatively transparent. The jelly coat may be removed with relative ease. Movements of pigments often serve as indicators of developmental events. Embryos are conveniently permeable to a wide variety of substances. Blastomeres may be dissociated from one another without great difficulty. The layers of blastomeres formed by radial cleavage, layers that play a significant role in morphogenesis, may be conveniently isolated from one another. Finally, by low-speed centrifugation fertilized eggs may be separated into halves or quarters, which retain some degree of function despite the fact that they may lack some of the major components of a cell. Such halves and quarters represent a very valuable type of experimental medium.

The period during which embryogenesis in the sea urchin has been under intensive study spans well over 100 years. It is not to be imagined, however, that embryologists represent the only group of biologists who have been preoccupied with the eggs and embryos of this animal during this time. The egg, fertilized or unfertilized, is a single cell. It is a fairly large cell with a diameter that may run to 10 times that of a red blood cell. Cytologists and cell physiologists have found it an excellent medium for a wide variety of experiments: the isolation and investigation of the mitotic apparatus, investigations in osmometry, radiation studies, experiments in electrophysiology, and measurements of cytoplasmic viscosity, to name a few. Some of the electron microscope studies made in recent years, particularly on the oocyte, clearly are oriented more in the direction of cytology than of embryology. A batch of eggs represents a population of cells, all of the same type. Such populations, whose individuals are expected to be quite similar to one another as regards the nature of their components and of the reactions in which their components participate, often prove difficult to isolate from organisms and are at a premium for experimental work. Thus it has come about that biochemists, physical chemists, molecular biologists, pharmacologists, and other nonembryologists have also found the eggs and embryos to be useful in their experimentation and have made extensive additions to the already voluminous literature on the animal.

It is interesting that among the publications on sea urchin morphogenesis, numbering into the thousands, which have appeared in this century, relatively few have been devoted to the period of metamorphosis following the pluteal stage. Hyman has reviewed the descriptive aspects of postpluteal echinoid development in her major work on the invertebrates. We shall confine our discussions to sea urchin development prior to metamorphosis.

The study of oogenesis and the maturing of the egg in the sea urchin has been somewhat neglected also. Much of the modest body of information on sea urchin oogenesis that does exist is the result of cytological studies, which have relied heavily on the use of biological stains. The last decade has been marked by an ever-increasing application of electron microscopy to the purely morphological aspects of oogenesis. The discovery in recent years that the sea urchin produces m-RNA during oogenesis for translation after fertilization may be expected to serve as a stimulus to a protracted study of the events of oogenesis by the molecular embryologist and the biochemist. Up to the present, however, investigations on sea urchin development have largely concentrated on the period beginning with the mature unfertilized egg and extending through fertilization to the pluteus stage.

In the previous century, much of the study of embryogenesis in the sea urchin was of a descriptive nature. Observations, often very thorough, were made on visible changes, especially in the period from fertilization to the formation of the pluteus, in a wide variety of species. The beginning of the twentieth century saw an increase of interest in the problems of experimental embryology. The sea urchin became the experimental medium for some elegant studies in which the egg or embryo was subjected to some type of systematic abuse to determine the effect on development of such abuse. Such experiments were doubtless aimed at the explanation of the visible phenomena of development, but they often afforded an insight into the basic mechanisms of development which suggested a picture infinitely more complicated than that implied by the visible phenomena. In the face of growing emphasis on molecular embryology, interest in problems of experimental embryology is still moderately strong among those concerned with sea urchin development. There are, in fact, broad areas in which molecular embryology and experimental embryology overlap or complement one another. Among the more important contributions of the experimental embryologist to the field of echinoid development have been studies of artificial parthenogenesis, of the physiology and behavior of half-eggs and merogones, and of morphogenetic gradients.

The beginning of the present century also marked the beginning of serious study of the nature of fertilization. Papers on fertilization in the sea urchin have been incredibly numerous. In the period from 1935 to 1955, preoccupation with the phenomenon reached its zenith. Work in this field has tapered off rather sharply in the last few years. Fertilization, however, represents an extremely involved interplay of events, and the years of intensive investigation raised many problems, few of which have been resolved satisfactorily.

As might be expected, the sea urchin egg and embryo represent an unparalleled medium for experiments in respirometry, and the literature over a period of at least 60 years is richly endowed with reports of such experiments. The results of such work have been confusing at times and have been subject to some misinterpretation. In recent years, biochemical studies of the activity of respiratory cycles have shed considerable light on the problems, but many of the early findings on respiration in embryogenesis should be reexamined experimentally. It is probable that embryologists have overemphasized the correlation between curves for respiratory rates and curves for rates of synthesis to the extent of viewing respiration as more of a control element in synthesis than it really is.

The years since World War II have seen the development of highly sophisticated experimental techniques and intricate instrumentation and equipment. Developments in the realms of electron microscopy, autoradiography, immunological methodology, radioisotope detection and counting, analytical and preparative ultracentrifugation, electrophoresis, and chromatography have introduced new dimensions into analytical work. Such developments have paid off handsomely in the study of the embryology of the sea urchin. The growth curve for information obtained has been exponential.

In the past decade, the major emphasis in developmental studies in the urchin has been on the exploration of mechanisms of flow of genetic information. Interest has centered around the problem of how and why the spectrum of active information comes to vary from one cell type to another as new cell types emerge in development, in other words, the problem of differentiation. Inherent in the problem is the necessity for investigation of the mechanisms controlling the transcription and translation of coded molecules in protein biosynthesis. Of particular importance is the study of the timing of the activity of such control mechanisms. One major goal of such work is to gain the first faint glimpses of the command sequences on the molecular "master tape" that controls the entire developmental program. These problems are of no small magnitude.

To date, knowledge of the mechanics of differentiation in the sea urchin, or in any other system, is meager in the extreme. Even the detection of the occurrence of differentiation at the molecular level in the sea urchin has proved to be difficult. One can point to a few findings of change in the spectrum of proteins or of change of an undetermined nature in message content as the end result of the not insignificant amount of time and effort that has been devoted to observing molecular differentiation in action up to the present moment.

The problem of differentiation probably deserves to be considered the most important single problem confronting the molecular or cellular biologist. Concern with differentiation is by no means the exclusive territory of the sea urchin embryologist, nor of any other type of embryologist or developmental biologist. Because differentiation proceeds so rapidly and plays such a dominant role in development, however, the embryologist may be expected to remain in the forefront of those who study it. Actually, sea urchin embryologists were investigating the problems of differentiation long before molecular biology appeared on the scene. An approach to the problem that has focused on animal–vegetal polarity and chemical and physiological gradients has been in existence for four or five decades. This work will be discussed at a later point. It has often led to results that are difficult to interpret. It has been careful work, performed by competent investigators; and as Leigh-Mallory noted of Mount Everest, it is *there* and cannot be ignored. It has been subject to the limitations that are often imposed where the necessity of resorting to histochemical techniques exists. The view that it affords of differentiation is one seen "through a glass darkly." There is a question as to how much promise this experimental approach may hold with respect to yielding a substantial amount of valuable information in the future. The answer may perhaps lie in another question: Does the inadequacy of techniques constitute the real barrier to the understanding of differentiation through the study of polarity and gradients? Given substantial improvements in methodology, can we expect any great enhancement of our understanding of differentiation through intensive investigation of polarity and gradients? We are partial to the view that these phenomena are superficial manifestations of the molecular processes of differentiation too remote from such processes to provide any significant insight into their nature and, more importantly, into their interrelationships. Implicit in this view, of course, is the idea that the best approach to an appreciation of differentiation lies in understanding the molecular events that cause it.

Despite the amount of research being concentrated on the flow of information in sea urchin embryos, very little is known about the Mendelian genetics of the creatures. Apart from the problems of discovering mutant traits in a species, the sea urchin would doubtless be an unfortunate choice as a system for genetic study because of the difficulties involved in rearing the embryos to adulthood, particularly with regard to the metamorphic stages.

SPECIES OF SEA URCHINS COMMONLY USED IN EXPERIMENTATION

Although a great many species of sea urchin are used in experimental work, certain species tend to be favored over others for a variety of reasons, such as availability, length of breeding season, yield of eggs, ease of maintaining the adult animal in the laboratory, and the like. Workers in laboratories along the Mediterranean appear commonly to use *Paracentrotus lividus, Sphaerechinus granularis,* and *Arbacia lixula,* with some use of *Psammechinus microtuberculatus* and *Echinocardium mediterraneum.* Laboratories with access to more northly European waters employ *Psammechinus miliaris, Echinus esculentus,* and less often *Brissopsis lyrifera.* In Japanese laboratories, *Hemicentrotus pulcherrimus, Pseudocentrotus depressus,* and *Anthocidaris crassispina* are commonly used experimental animals.

In the United States, *Arbacia punctulata* is a traditional experimental animal on the Atlantic Coast, particularly in New England. *Echinarachnius parma* and *Strongylocentrotus dröbachiensis* are also used to a degree in laboratories near North Atlantic waters. Along the South Atlantic Coast and in the West Indies the experimental animals are frequently *Lytechinus variegatus, Mellita quinquiesperforata,* or *Echinometra lucuntur.* Here on the West Coast *Strongylocentrotus purpuratus* and *Lytechinus pictus* are favored. *Strongylocentrotus franciscanus* is a good experimental animal in many respects, but finds less frequent use than *Strongylocentrotus purpuratus.* It has frequently been our experience to find *Strongylocentrotus franciscanus* in great numbers in collecting beds at some times, and virtually lacking at others, thus constituting an undependable source of supply. If beds are too easily accessible, they tend to be depleted of this species by those who find eggs of the animal to be a delicacy. *Dendraster excentricus* finds occasional use, perhaps because its breeding season begins at about the time when that of *Strongylocentrotus purpuratus* begins to wane.

It would be fortunate if the distribution of experimental species were such that a given species might be available to principal centers of sea urchin study in widespread areas of the world so that related experiments could conveniently be performed on the same animal. Nature has generally not been that obliging. The spatangid *Echinocardium cordatum* is found in the waters on the coasts of England, Sweden, Italy, and Japan, in all of which countries are located major centers of research in sea urchin development. Distribution does not necessarily equate with availability or convenience, and although *Echinocardium cordatum* is used to a degree in experimentation, it is not heavily used in all these regions. There does appear to be an increasing trend toward shipping sea urchin eggs from one region to another so that biologists working on similar problems can compare their results on the same species.

It cannot be emphasized too strongly that one must give heed to differences among species in evaluating and interpreting research on sea urchin embryos. Cells may vary from one species to another as to their structures and their chemical content. Overall rates of development differ among species, as do rates of synthesis of individual compounds along with timing of changes in rate of synthesis and of activation and deactivation of synthesis. Although the biochemist has a natural reticence toward testing a given group of findings on one species after another, more information needs to be garnered on the validity of applying certain experimental data gathered from one, two, or a few species across the board to species in general. Any inherent danger in such extrapolation is obviously increased when the extrapolation is applied to taxonomic groupings above the genus level.

Data on breeding seasons of sea urchins have been presented in a review by Boolootian in 1966. There is, or course, inconvenience involved in working with experimental animals that have as short a reproductive season as do some sea urchins. Actually both the number of months in a reproductive season and the month in which the season begins vary with individual species. In some regions, workers may be fortunate enough to have living material available for a respectable portion of the year simply by being able to obtain different species whose spawning periods do not coincide.

LABORATORY PROCEDURES

Harvey (1956) and Tyler and Tyler (1966) have discussed techniques for obtaining and culturing eggs and sperm and preparing them for experimental work. Spawning may be induced by the use of KCl solutions or by mild electrical shock. Where a species is abundant and easy to obtain, some workers prefer to kill the animal and extract the gonads. In the past, filtered seawater was commonly used in culturing eggs, but artificial seawater is finding increasing use in experimental work. It reduces the possibility of contaminants or of artificial environmental parameters being introduced into the culture.

The rate of development, particularly of cleavage, is strongly temperature sensitive in many species. It is desirable to culture embryos at a constant temperature and to indicate that temperature in the publication of experimental results. The designation of the stage of development by the hours in age of the embryo may prove to be an annoyance to the reader unless the culture temperature is given to indicate developmental rate. Even then, such usage presupposes enough familiarity with the species to be able to relate age and stage of development. It is a convenience to the reader to be appraised of the approximate developmental stage under consideration. It goes practically without saying that, in addition to controlling the temperature, one should exert all possible efforts to prevent the concentration of the medium by evaporation. Cultures must normally also be aerated by one means or another.

Except in instances where the actual number of gametes needs to be estimated, the size of a batch is normally reported in terms of volume. Obviously, the seminal fluid accounts for a good amount of the volume of a batch of sperm before dilution. Dilution of sperm is not performed until immediately before fertilization, since dilution markedly shortens the life span of sperm. The degree of dilution is often standardized, standard sperm solutions being prepared in a prescribed manner so that the number of sperm per unit volume which they contain is expected to fall within a definite range.

Fertilizability of eggs is normally checked before fertilization. It is desirable, where possible, to obtain eggs that range from 98 to 100 percent fertilizable. A variety of parameters appears to affect fertilizability, of which a very important one may be the nature of the food supply, although other environmental conditions in the beds from which the animals are harvested may also be critical. It has been our experience in the instance of *Strongylocentrotus purpuratus* that pronounced variation in fertilizability may be found in specimens from beds only a few hundred yards apart. Virtually nothing is known about the genetic aspects of the problem. Before fertilization of the culture, one must check for premature fertilization by contaminating sperm, and it may also be of advantage to search for the presence of immature cells or contaminating debris of one sort or another.

One may not wish to have to contend with the mucopolysaccharide of the jelly coat in the preparation of homogenates or in other experimental procedures. To this end, the jelly coats may be removed readily by mechanical methods or by subjecting the eggs to a drop in pH. The removal may be performed prior to fertilization.

REFERENCES

Boolootian, R. A., 1966. Reproductive physiology. In R. A. Boolootian (ed.), *Physiology of the Echinodermata*. John Wiley & Sons, Inc. (Interscience Division), New York, 561–613.

Harvey, E. B., 1956. *The American Arbacia and Other Sea Urchins*. Princeton University Press, Princeton, N.J.

Hyman, L. H., 1955. *The Invertebrates: Echinodermata. The Coelomate Bilateria. Vol. IV*. McGraw-Hill Book Company, New York.

Tyler, A., and B. S. Tyler, 1966. The gametes; some procedures and properties. In R. A. Boolootian (ed.), *Physiology of the Echinodermata*. John Wiley & Sons, Inc. (Interscience Division), New York, 639–682.

CHAPTER II

Sea Urchin Gametes and Early Developmental Processes

SEA URCHIN SPERM

Several studies with the electron microscope (including those of Afzelius, 1955a: Afzelius and Murray, 1957; Takashima and Takashima, 1960; Bernstein, 1962) have described the ultra structure of the sea urchin sperm and in doing so have considered several different species. J. C. Dan and her co-workers have made extremely thorough studies of sperm structure, concentrating heavily on the structure of the acrosome.

Deprived as it is of a cytoplasm, a spermatozoon may be regarded more conveniently as a highly organized cluster of organelles than as a cell. Its prospects for an appreciable longevity as an independent entity in the absence of a cytoplasm are about as bleak as those of a mule for fertility. A diagrammatic sketch of the sperm of *Arbacia punctulata* is seen in Fig. 1. The spermatozoon of the sea urchin does not differ markedly in structure from the conventional picture of an animal sperm. The head is usually wedge-shaped. The nucleus in most species is marked by a depression at its anterior tip over which sits a rounded acrosomal granule. In *Echinocardium cordatum,* how-

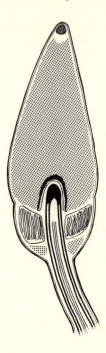

Figure 1

Semidiagrammatic sketch of the sperm of *Arbacia punctulata*. The acrosomal granule is seen in front of the depression in the nucleus. Note that the nuclear envelope is visible only in the region of the posterior nuclear depression, where it underlies a basal plate of undetermined nature. The distal mass is seen on either side of the flagellum, immediately posterior to the ring-shaped mitochondrion, which is shown in cross section. Darkened area at the anterior tip of the flagellum represents the approximate position of the proximal centriole. [From Bernstein (1962); by permission.]

ever, the acrosomal granule is located at the anterior end of a long projection extending from the sperm head. Nucleus and acrosome of the sea urchin sperm are surrounded by a plasma membrane.

There is also a depression in the posterior edge of the nucleus. In this depression, in line with the axis of the sperm, lies a single (proximal) centriole, from which the filaments of the flagellum arise. Early accounts of sperm ultrastructure describe this as the only centriole in the sperm. Franklin (1965), Longo and Anderson (1969), and others have shown that the sea urchin sperm, like the sperm of most animals, possesses two centrioles. The second (distal) centriole lies to one side of the sperm axis between the nucleus and the mitochondrion. It is believed that the sperm donates this centriole to the egg to organize the formation of the aster and the mitotic spindle for the first cleavage. The unfertilized egg lacks any visible evidence of a centriole. In 1961, however, Dirksen showed in an electron-microscope study that cytasters will form in parthenogenetically activated eggs. This finding demonstrates that the egg can provide centrioles under unusual conditions, but not that it does so under normal conditions. It does raise the question as to how the centriole, normally a self-duplicating system, can arise *de novo*. The electron microscope reveals the centriole to consist of microtubules, and cytoplasmic pools of microtubule precursors clearly exist, as will be discussed at a later point. It remains to be resolved which forces would organize the *de novo* formation of a microtubular organelle that in itself organizes the formation of microtubular structures.

The outstanding component of the midpiece of the sea urchin sperm is a single, large, ring-shaped mitochondrion in most species. Through the center of this mitochondrion passes the sperm flagellum. The mitochondrion is held in intimate contact with the posterior surface of the nucleus, probably by the plasma membrane, which surrounds the midpiece and flagellum as it does the head. Medially, the mitochondrion adheres closely to the proximal region of the flagellum. In *Arbacia* the cristae are oriented in an anterio-posterior direction. Bernstein (1962) has described in the sperm of *Arbacia* a homogeneous, electron-dense body associated with the posterior surface of the mitochondrion. He has designated this structure, the function of which is unknown, as the *distal mass*.

It has been well established that the midpiece and the tail of the sea urchin sperm enter the egg along with the head. Franklin (1965) has produced some striking electron micrographs of the sperm mitochondrion and flagellum in the cytoplasm in experiments in which he inseminated oocytes of *Arbacia punctulata*. Because mitochondria, carry genetic information, the fate of the sperm mitochondrion in the egg cytoplasm is of considerable interest. Anderson (1968a) addressed himself to the problem in an electron-microscope study of the fertilization of the egg of *Paracentrotus lividus*. In the electron micrographs, he was able to distinguish the large mitochondrion of the sperm from the small mitochondria of the egg with great ease. He found that the sperm mitochondrion undergoes a gradual disintegration and dispersion. It is not beyond the realm of possibility that prior to its disappearance it may exert some influence on the early metabolism of the fertilized egg, although there is no direct evidence to that effect. It forms transitory associations with egg mitochondria, and it is certainly a matter for further investigation as to whether it may transfer metabolites, or even informational molecules, to them. (Molecular cytologists and geneticists are close to unanimity in the opinion that, to the extent that the mitochondrion is independent of nuclear control, the inheritance of its genetic information is maternal and non-Mendelian.) Anderson also reported that the sperm mitochondrion makes what look to be transitory contacts with the rough endoplasmic reticulum, a phenomenon of which the significance is uncertain.

The flagellum of the sea urchin sperm is generally similar in structure to those of sperm of other species and shows the nine peripheral and two central filaments. A few explanatory comments might facilitate further discussion of the subject throughout this work: The term *filaments* or *fibers* as used to describe the components of the axoneme of the flagellum or cilium represents common, but somewhat loose, usage. The term *microtubules* is more appropriate. In the axoneme of typical sperm flagella, with which the flagellum of the sea urchin sperm conforms, the outer nine microtubules are doublets, and the central microtubules are singlets. The perpendicular to a line passing through the centers of the central singlets cuts only one peripheral doublet. That doublet is often used as a reference, and the doublets are numbered 1 to 9, proceeding in a circle from it in the direction in which a pair of arms on one microtubule of each doublet extends. The doublet microtubule with the arms is designated *subtubule A*. The doublet microtubule without arms is designated *subtubule B*. The central singlets lack arms. The walls of each microtubule are made up of spherical subunits 70 Å in diameter. A cross section of each shared in the cross section of a common wall.

Stephens et al. (1967), Stephens (1968), and Bibring and Baxandall (1968) noted strong similarities between the properties of the outer-doublet fibers of sperm flagella and those of the microtubules of the mitotic apparatus in sea urchins. In the years since these findings were published, widespread investigations have made it evident that there are identities or very strong similarities among microtubule proteins in sperm flagella, flagella from other cell types, cilia, mitotic apparatuses, and cytoplasmic microtubules. It is obvious that problems involving the nature of microtubules extend beyond the cells of developmental systems to cells in general. During this period in which knowledge of microtubules has been broadening, the component molecules of these structures have been isolated, purified, and partially characterized.

In 1968, Mohri isolated from the 9 + 2 fibers of *Pseudocentrotus depressus* and *Anthocidaris crassispina* a protein that he called *tubulin*. He found it to contain 2.5S and 3.5S subunits with amino acid composition similar to that of comparable proteins in the mitotic apparatus. Stephens, in 1970, isolated a B-tubulin from the B subtubules and an A-tubulin from the A subtubules of *Strongylocentrotus dröbachiensis* sperm. Tryptic peptide mapping showed that the two proteins are very similar, but they did prove to have some differences in amino acid composition, mobility on polyacrylamide gels, and solubility. On the basis of evidence from peptide mapping, they bear little resemblance to muscle actin.

In the consideration of microtubules and their component proteins, one must distinguish between studies in which the structure containing them is being used as a system with which to study microtubules and their proteins for their own sake and studies that seek to describe the production and/or function of microtubules in the cell. Despite the complete legitimacy and recognized value of the former type of work, we feel compelled to give it but limited attention throughout our discussions, because it is not actually germane to our objective. We are concerned rather with the latter experimental approach, the study of microtubules and their proteins in the light of their function in development and of the mechanism of their production in development. In this respect there is little to be said of flagellar microtubules. Their function is the propulsion of the sperm, and little is known of the mechanics of flagellar movement. They cannot be studied in the embryo, and they have not been studied in the gonad. As a result, all the information that we have on their production is found in a few electron micrographs of the phenomenon of spermatogenesis. We know nothing of the synthesis of their constituent proteins or of the flow of genetic information that implements it.

STRUCTURAL ASPECTS
OF THE ACROSOME REACTION

Experimental studies of the acrosome reaction have produced such a bonanza of information on the phenomenon relative to that available on many other processes involved in fertilization that there is some danger of overestimating not so much the importance, perhaps, but at least the magnitude of its role in the scenario of fertilization. The acrosome is no walk-on player with one or two lines, but it is by no means the star of the production. The acrosome is a product of the activity of the Golgi apparatus in the young spermatid. Longo and Anderson (1969) in investigations of spermatogenesis in *Arbacia punctulata* and *Strongylocentrotus purpuratus* found that at the time of formation of the acrosomal granule the rough endoplasmic reticulum is poorly represented in the spermatid. This may suggest that at least part of the proteins of the granule may be being made on free polysomes and incorporated into the Golgi apparatus by mechanisms other than those involved in the interchange between endoplasmic reticulum and Golgi apparatus, which is the more common channel for the accumulation of protein by the latter. They also found that the fibrous precursor material of the axial core of the acrosome does not arise from the vesicles of the Golgi network. They speculate that it originates by the aggregation of a floccular material which is seen to be dispersed throughout the cytoplasm in the spermatid. In the mature sperm, the fibrous precursor material lies in a cavity formed by the posterior region of the acrosomal granule and a cave in the tip of the nucleus, which has been described above.

The acrosomal granule in the sea urchin is not vesiculated as it is in the sperm of many invertebrates. Cytochemical tests show that it is PAS-positive and contains some basic protein and some lipid material. One might speculate that the lipid material represents, at least in part, precursor for the formation of the membrane of the acrosomal process.

The eversion of the acrosomal filament in the sea urchin is not the result of an active change in form of the acrosomal granule, but rather the result of the production of a lumen bound by the acrosomal process membrane, which creates a progressively expanding indentation in the acrosomal granule.

In normal fertilization, the principal stimulus to the eversion of the acrosomal filament lies in the interaction between fertilizin, a mucopolysaccharide from the jelly coat of the egg, and complementary substances on the surface of the sperm. Under experimental conditions, the reaction can be elicited by the use of seawater in which eggs have been standing and into which fertilizin has diffused (egg water).

For a more detailed description of the acrosome reaction than giv-
en here and for descriptions of the reaction in the sperm of other organisms, the reader is referred to reviews by Austin (1968) and Dan
(1970).

A series of diagrams of the acrosome reaction in *Pseudocentrotus
depressus* and *Heliocidaris crassispina* from Dan et al. (1964) is shown
in Fig. 2 and illustrates some of its salient structural characteristics:
stages A through D represent 1-second fixations. Stage E is a 2-sec-
ond fixation, and stage F is an 8-second fixation. In stage A, the
plasma membrane (e), which in the unreacted sperm lies in close association with the acrosomal granule (g), has begun to lift in the region above the granule, exposing its surface (s). The lifting action is
purported to be caused by the expansion and disintegration of an
osmiophilic substance that caps the granule. This substance is held by
Dan and her co-workers to be a trigger substance activated by fertilizin directly or indirectly. The precursor material for the formation
of the fibrous axial core lies in the nuclear indentation. An electron-
dense material lying under the plasma membrane in the region (d)
has broken down and disappeared. Dan proposes that this material
enters the cavity under the acrosome and provides osmotic properties for the expansion of the lumen of the acrosomal process by
hydrostatic pressure.

In stage B, the apical plasma membrane has all but disintegrated,
probably as a result of the disintegration of the osmiophilic substance described above. An indentation has appeared under the acrosomal granule, and this heralds the beginning of the formation of the
acrosomal process. Laminate precursor material associated with the
granule in the region of the indentation begins to form process membrane and simultaneously yields to pressure from below to bulge inward.

In stage C, a blind tubule, the nascent acrosomal process, delim-
ited by process membrane (i), pushes inward at the center of the
acrosomal granule. In the region (i'), the process membrane unites
with, and becomes continuous with, the plasma membrane where it
girdles the base of the process. In stage D the fibrous material in the
nuclear indentation has begun to organize itself into the fibrous axial
core (f) of the process. In the remaining stages, both the process and
its axial core undergo extensive elongation, and the material of the

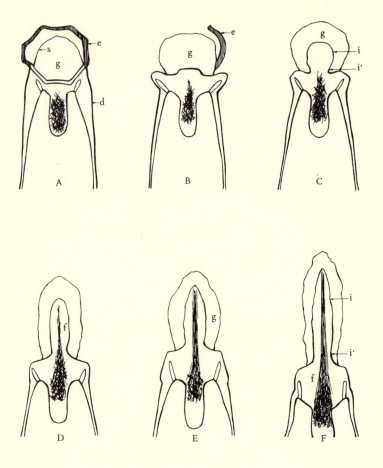

Figure 2

Diagram showing course of acrosome reaction. For explanation, see text. Stages A through D are 1-second fixations. Stage E is a 2-second fixation. Stage F is an 8-second fixation.

d   Region of plasma membrane which is underlaid with an electron-dense material that is degraded in the course of the reaction.
e   Plasma membrane with postulated underlying trigger material.
f   Axial core of fibrous material.
g   Acrosomal granule.
i   Process membrane.
i′   Process membrane.
s   Surface of acrosomal granule.

[Redrawn from Dan et al. (1964); by permission.]

acrosomal granule spreads over the surface of the process. The elongation of the lumen of the acrosomal process is clearly not caused by its being pushed outward by the extension of the axial core, since the profile of the tip of the process shows no sign of stress being exerted upon it. The most logical explanation of the phenomenon is that it is caused by hydrostatic pressure.

FUNCTIONAL ASPECTS OF THE ACROSOME REACTION

Despite the profusion of data on the mechanics of the elaboration of the acrosome filament, attempts to describe the reaction in its natural setting, the process of fertilization, and to determine its function, as well as the forces that control it in the fertilization of the sea urchin egg, have met with but partial success.

The ability of the sperm to evert its acrosome decreases with age, gradually with "dry sperm" and rapidly in sperm preparations diluted with seawater. The acrosome reaction is inhibited by lowering the pH of the medium or by removing calcium ions from the medium. In three species of sea urchin from Japanese waters (see Dan, 1956), the ability of egg water to agglutinate sperm—that is, of fertilizin to complex with complementary molecules on the surface of the sperm—was not lost when the acrosome reaction was blocked by a medium low in calcium. Here we have the activation of the appropriate stimulus without the elicitation of the customary response. With calcium acting as a *sine qua non* for acrosome eversion, it is more reasonable to suppose that the ion is serving as an instrument for the stimulus, directly or indirectly, than that it is merely a requisite environmental parameter for sensitivity to the stimulus. The reaction of fertilizin with substances on the sperm membrane can be postulated to cause distortion of the membrane, thus altering its permeability to ions in the medium and allowing an influx of calcium ion, which is capable of activating, or participating in, an enormous variety of reactions, and of modifying the behavior, and sometimes the structure, of many molecules. The phenomenon is sufficiently familiar to cell physiologists in instances where it involves activity of molecules other than fertilizin that it needs no further elaboration here.

Dan is prone to ascribe the loss of the apical plasma membrane to just such an influx of calcium ion, and postulates that the ion may react with the osmiophilic trigger layer lying atop the acrosomal granule. There are two other phenomena, or systems of phenomena, in which we might speculate that forces associated with calcium influx could be at work. One of these is the production of osmotic changes that allow the buildup of hydrostatic pressure to distend the acrosomal process. The other is the swelling of the midpiece that accompanies the acrosomal reaction. There is generally assumed to be an extensive interaction between fertilizin and the sperm surface in the region of the midpiece, although Tyler and Tyler (1966) have proposed that the events that occur at the midpiece upon acrosomal activation could be explained by a stretching of the plasma membrane caused by acrosome eversion.

Bernstein (1962) has described the reaction in the midpiece in *Arbacia* as an explosive expansion that destroys the ordered arrangement of the membranes of the mitochondrion. If this disarrangement destroys or impairs the activity of the mitochondrion, however, it does so within a few seconds of the time when the requirement for a mitochondrion by the sperm has terminated. The swelling is probably due to osmotic changes produced by ion influx. Calcium ion may react with materials in the midpiece to produce permeability changes in the mitochondrial membrane(s). Mitochondria are normally very active accumulators of calcium ion.

Although Bernstein has described the midpiece as being distorted, the distortion is less pronounced than in some other classes of echinoderm in which the flagellum is violently flipped around so that it comes to lie at almost 90 degrees to the axis of the sperm. If a distortion of such violence did occur in the sea urchin sperm, its visibility would simplify the task of trying to determine the moment in sperm penetration when the acrosome reaction occurs. As will be discussed at a later point, it is virtually impossible so to determine at present.

There is actually no experimental proof that the acrosome reaction is an absolute requisite for fertilization, beyond the fact that substances or parameters that inhibit the reaction also inhibit fertilization. It is not unequivocal that they inhibit fertilization because they inhibit the acrosome reaction. The function of the acrosome reaction in fertilization has not been decisively settled by experimentation. Since the reaction occurs in almost all instances of interspecific hybridization (although not necessarily with 100 percent of the sperm involved), it cannot be seriously implicated in maintaining species specificity.

The contribution of the acrosome reaction to the block to polyspermy has not been ascertained. Some of the early workers observed that the contact of the tip of the acrosomal fiber with the egg surface initiates the cortical reaction (which is involved in blocking polyspermy) when the tip of the sperm head is still the length of the acrosomal process away from the egg surface. It is doubtful that any advantage is served, however, by this slight advancing of the time of establishment of the block relative to the arrival of the sperm head at the egg surface. It is the acrosomal filament, and not the sperm head, that initiates penetration of the egg by the sperm.

Dan, Bernstein, and others have described a stimulus to acrosome eversion other than the reaction with fertilizin. In control sperm solutions, which contain sperm without egg water, many sperm have often been seen with everted processes. The eversion has been ascribed to contact with the glass container, in other words, to a nonspecific contact stimulus. Dan has further shown that the acrosomal filaments give evidence of actually adhering to the glass surface. From this observation, one can extrapolate to the idea that the acrosome filament functions to attach the sperm to the surface of the egg.

Over the years many workers have expressed the conviction that the acrosome filament contracts to pull the sperm into the egg. It is unwise to give any credence to this postulate where the sea urchin sperm is concerned. The fibers of the axial core, although they have received little study from a molecular approach, show no evidence of being contractile, and they lack the precision in array that usually characterizes the fibers of contractile structures. There is a strong likelihood that they impart rigidity to the acrosomal process. It is less easy to dismiss the concept that the acrosomal process serves to afford a purchase for forces in the egg cytoplasm to pull the sperm into the egg. It is difficult either to prove or to disprove that such a pull exists, but its existence has been proposed to explain sperm entry in forms in which the flagellum of the sperm gives evidence of being immobilized by the jelly coat. If the entry of the sperm into the sea urchin egg is facilitated by a cytoplasmic pull on its acrosomal filament, the facilitation is not mandated by incapacitation of its flagellum. The jelly coat offers no visible opposition to sperm movement in the sea urchin, and there is no indication that it hampers flagellar activity (see Colwin and Colwin, 1957).

The thesis that a principal function of the acrosome reaction is to provide lysins for the breakdown of materials of the membrane barriers of the egg, particularly the vitelline membrane, is extremely appealing. Lysins that degrade the substance of the vitelline membrane have been found in the sperm of many animals, but there is no direct proof of their existence in the sea urchin. Certain experimental findings have been construed as indirect evidence that lysins may be present. Runnström et al. (1944) found that methanol extracts of sperm cause eggs to shrink in hypertonic seawater without wrinkling, suggesting some damage to the membrane, possibly by a lysin in the extract. Tyler and Tyler (1966) have presented an electron micrograph that reveals a hole in the vitelline membrane through which the head of the sperm of *Lytechinus pictus* has entered. The hole has the appearance of resulting from the dissolution of the membrane, but there is no actual proof that it did not arise from mechanical causes (see Fig. 3).

Actually there is no definite evidence that the vitelline membrane is the sole barrier against which the sperm might require a lysin to effect entry. Enzymes that lyse carbohydrates have been reported in sea urchin sperm by Hultin and Lundblad in 1952 and by Takashima et al. in 1955. It is interesting to speculate that they may serve to break down the mucopolysaccharide of the jelly coat, but the site of their activity in nature has not been determined. Hathaway and his co-workers (see, for example, Hathaway and Warren, 1961) have demonstrated the presence in sea urchin sperm of what appears to be a sulfatase that is able to disperse the jelly coat. Brookbank (1958) has reported the existence of a comparable enzyme in the sand dollar. Should these sulfatases turn out to be bona fide sperm lysins for jelly-coat breakdown, or should any other enzymes in the sperm prove to have that function, we are confronted with a paradox. If existing theories of the nature of fertilization are correct, then we must assume that as the sperm passes through the jelly coat molecules on its surface react with the fertilizin of the jelly coat. It is difficult to

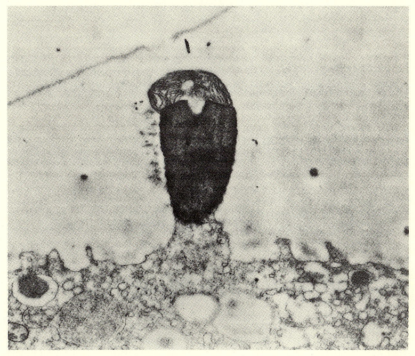

Figure 3

Thin section of the egg of *Lytechinus pictus,* 45 seconds after insemination. Magnification: 20,000 ×. OsO_4. Hole in elevated vitelline membrane through which sperm has penetrated may be seen. Entrance cone where egg plasma membrane joins that of the sperm is shown. Some microvilli of the egg surface are visible. [From Tyler and Tyler (1966); by permission.]

envision this reaction occurring with the jelly coat being broken down around the sperm by lysins. Even if it should prove to be possible, some revision of our thinking would be necessary, because the theories presume that the structural array of fertilizin molecules in the jelly coat in some way plays a role of importance in the sperm–jelly coat interactions. It is to be expected that lysins would destroy or damage this array. To the extent that comparisons with sperm of other invertebrates are valid, it may be expected that if acrosomal lysins exist in the sea urchin they are directed against the vitelline membrane. The findings on enzymes postulated to be jelly-coat lysins may reflect the existence of sperm enzymes once active in the gonad and perhaps reactivated by extraction procedures.

Dan submits that it is inferential that the acrosomal granule contains egg-membrane lysins

> because 1. Following the acrosome reaction, it is exposed at the sperm apex, where it should be if it is to be effective. 2. It dissipates rapidly, which demonstrates that it is labile. 3. It resembles the lytic substances of other invertebrate spermatozoa. 4. There is no other obvious role for it.

SPERMATOGENESIS

Spermatogenesis (spermiogenesis) has been studied in a wide variety of organisms, but up until very recently the sea urchin has not been included among them. In 1969, Longo and Anderson explored the problem of sperm differentiation and metamorphosis in *Arbacia punctulata* and *Strongylocentrotus purpuratus* with the electron microscope.

The pentamerous gonads of the male sea urchin each contain a single gonoduct that opens to the exterior aborally through an orifice in the genital plate. Longo and Anderson found that a section through the acinus of a gonad reveals three layers: an outer, perivisceral coelomic epithelium resting on a basement membrane as is normal with epithelia, a middle layer of smooth muscle and connective tissue, and an inner layer of sperm cells at various stages of differentiation. Sperm cells are interspersed with interstitial tissue. The lumen of the acinus is filled with sperm. The interstitial cells are found in intimate association with spermatids and are presumed to be nurse cells. They contain aggregates of glycogen scattered throughout their cytoplasm.

Spermatogonia have a cytoplasm richly endowed with polysomes, a circumstance certainly to be construed here as a sign of active protein synthesis. Rough endoplasmic reticulum, however, is but poorly represented in these cells. The nucleus of the spermatogonium contains a nucleolus-like body that disappears as differentiation proceeds. The future proximal and distal centrioles are already present in the cytoplasm of the spermatogonium, and the proximal centriole has begun to produce the flagellum.

The spermatids likewise have a cytoplasm rich in polysomes and poor in rough endoplasmic reticulum. Glycogen aggregates are dispersed throughout this cytoplasm. The spermatids are connected by intercellular bridges, broad continuities of cytoplasm between adjacent cells. The apical and posterior indentations of the mature sperm nucleus are formed in the spermatid. As the spermatid matures, the chromatin of the nucleus, which existed as heterogeneous clusters in the nucleus of the spermatogonium, begins to compact, and thereupon the nucleus elongates. At this time, the cytoplasm begins to be sloughed off. The jettisoned cytoplasm still contains a fairly large amount of glycogen.

The formation of the acrosome in the spermatid has been discussed above. The mechanism of formation of the mitochondrion has not been completely resolved. Mitochondria aggregate in the region of the prospective midpiece in tight apposition to the nuclear envelope. They reduce in number and increase in size, events which probably bespeak mitochondrial fusion, although there is no firm proof that fusion does occur. Finally, one large mitochondrion surrounds the proximal region of the flagellum. Its close association with the proximal centriole has led to the assumption that the structural alliance may represent a mechanism for channeling to the flagellum of ATP needed for motility.

SPERMATOZOAN MOTILITY

The problem of spermatozoan motility, its nature, and control has been studied extensively and can be considered but briefly here. Excellent surveys of the problem exist, for instance those of Bishop (1962) and Nelson (1967). Over and above the problem of the mechanism of the motility of the flagellum *per se,* which may be one with the problem of the mechanism of motility of cilia and flagella in general, there exists a variety of problems involving the energy sources for motility and the parameters affecting the intensity and duration of motility. The term *fertilizable life span* is applied to the period during which an actively motile sperm is capable of entering and activating an egg. Dilution of the seminal fluid by seawater, as occurs in spawning, decreases the fertilizable life span of the sperm; the more extensive the dilution, the greater the decrease in fertilizable life span.

Upon dilution by seawater, sea urchin sperm also become intensely motile. Some early workers, such as Hayashi (1945), have asserted that sperm are motile in the seminal fluid, and hence that dilution increases rather than initiates sperm motility. Rothschild (1948a) has claimed that sperm are motionless in the undiluted semen of *Echinus esculentus*. Be it increased or initiated, the motility seen upon dilution is transitory, and after a short period of time begins a gradual decline. The spermatozoa of sea urchins normally have a requirement for oxygen and will usually become immobile very rapidly under anaerobic conditions. The ultimate decline in motility following dilution, however, occurs in the presence of what is presumably an adequate supply of oxygen.

Still another effect of dilution is to produce a substantial increase in the respiratory activity of sperm, which is reflected in an increased consumption of oxygen. This increase is known as the *respiratory dilution effect*. Like the increase in motility, it is transitory. There is no necessary cause–effect relationship between the increase in oxygen consumption in the respiratory dilution effect and the increase in motility, since agents that abolish the former may allow the latter to occur. Whatever may cause the ultimate cessation of respiration upon sperm aging, it is not attributed to exhaustion of substrates in energy cycles. Rothschild (1948b) noted that after the cessation of respiration and motility, the presence of oxidizable substrates and of the necessary dehydrogenases may be demonstrated in the spermatozoa of sea urchins. Hultin, moreover, observed in 1958 that ATP resources are relatively undiminished after aging and loss of motility in the sperm of *Brissopsis lyrifera*.

Assuming Hultin's findings to be valid, one could speculate that if ATP evolution through respiration and ATP utilization through the mechanism of motility were coupled or were rather closely balanced, and if they were halted at about the same time or fell off at about the same rate, then Hultin's undiminished ATP resources would represent the level of an untapped reserve of ATP; but such a speculation smacks of the simplistic. It would appear that if motility could continue for an appreciable period of time after the cessation of respiration it would cause a diminution in the levels of ATP, but it is pointless to speculate on this point until more is known of the actual causes for the loss of both respiration and motility. In this regard, Rothschild's findings are important in that they cut the ground out from under the concept that the sperm "burns itself out," exhausts its fuel supplies, upon dilution. At the time, however, when Rothschild performed his experiments, we had not gained a full comprehension of the complexity of the energy cycles, of the intricate interplay between their reactions and peripheral reactions, of the kinetics of their enzymes, of the behavior of their coenzymes and cofactors, and of many other important aspects of their activity. In future search for the cause of the demise of respiratory activity in senescent sperm, we should not overlook the possibility among all the others that should be explored, that some critical participant in energy metabolism has indeed been exhausted.

The gradual loss of motility and the loss of fertilizable life span are symptoms of the acceleration of senescence of sperm by dilution. The two phenomena are separate and distinct. Motility is no guarantee of the ability to fertilize, and sperm may continue to be motile after the fertilizable life span has terminated. They may occasionally be viable after motility has ceased. Where the sea urchin sperm is concerned, the terms *life span* and *fertilizable life span* are not synonymous. Regardless of the degree of dependence, the fertilizable life span of a sperm is related to respiration and motility. The ability of a sperm to fertilize, relates to more than these two phenomena alone. It will be recalled, for example, that the acrosome reaction and the molecules (antifertilizin) on the sperm surface which react with fertilizin are critical for successful fertilization.

Certain agents that tend to abolish the respiratory dilution effect may increase the fertilizable life span of the sperm. Among such agents are materials that bind cations. The sea urchin sperm has a considerable affinity for such cations as Cu^{2+} and Zn^{2+}, which have the ability to shorten the fertilizable life span and which are present in seawater. Chelating agents such as ethylenediaminetetraacetic acid, which remove these cations from sperm, materially increase the fertilizable life span by so doing. Tyler in 1950 and 1953 and Tyler and Rothschild in 1951 found that various amino acids and peptides will increase the fertilizable life span and the motility of the sperm and in many instances also prevent the respiratory dilution effect. The amino acids do not appear to be utilized metabolically in these experiments, but, rather, to exert their effect through their ability to bind cations. At the time of his initial studies on these agents, Tyler (see Tyler, 1953) proposed that a partial explanation for their effect might be that they reflect the activity of proteins in the seminal fluid which may bind the cations to prevent them from exerting toxic effects on the sperm. In later years he was attracted by the idea that chelating agents and other cation-binding agents may operate by increasing the efficiency of utilization of respiratory substrates through the removal of ions of copper and zinc, which quite possibly hold phospholipid substrate captive in a lipoprotein complex (see Tyler and Tyler, 1966). The response of sea urchin sperm to Zn^{2+} and Cu^{2+} is not precisely the same as that of sperm of other echinoderms, particularly asteroids (see Utida and Nanao, 1956; Mizuno, 1956).

Cation-binding agents, then, clearly have the capacity to increase the probability of fertilization of the egg by counteracting some of the adverse effects of dilution upon the sperm, particularly by decreasing the curtailment by dilution of the time period in which the sperm can fertilize, that is by increasing fertilizable life span. The question arises as to whether this benefit is available to the sperm in nature after dilution by seawater has occurred or whether post-dilution cation-binding effects are merely experimental curiosities. The answer is not known at present, but it is possible that fertilizin may be able to enhance the probability of fertilization by binding copper and zinc ions that are associated with molecules of the sperm. That egg water increases both the motility and fertilizable life span of sea urchin sperm has long been recognized by scholars in the field of sperm motility. Hathaway in 1963 observed that this effect still occurs if the eggs used to make egg water have had their jelly coats removed. Whether the fertilizin of the egg proper is involved in such an instance or whether the effect is produced by residual jelly-coat fertilizin remains to be determined.

If, as has been found frequently in the instance of other animals, there is a glycolyzable sugar in the seminal fluid, the sperm is certain to be freed of it upon being spawned into seawater. The sea urchin sperm is forced to depend upon endogenous (intramitochondrial) fuel. The nature of such fuel has been examined by Rothschild and Cleland (1952) and by Mohri and his co-workers (see, for example, Mohri, 1959, 1961, and 1964). The endogenous substrates for respiration appear to be a variety of phospholipids. The breakdown of the phospholipids liberates glycerylphosphoryl compounds and fatty acids, with the latter serving as the fundamental source of energy. Anderson (1968b), through the use of electron microscopy, however, has shown that small aggregates of glycogen are present within the sperm mitochondrion in *Paracentrotus lividus*. He has also demonstrated the presence of intramitochondrial glucose-6-phosphatase.

His experimental approach dictated reliance on cytochemical reagents and techniques, lead citrate, amylase extracts, and the like. He
found the glycogen in dense aggregates with subunits 40 Å in diameter. It is his contention that the mitochondrion of the sea urchin
sperm contains glycolytic sequences.

Preliminary experiments in the realm of the biochemistry of motility in the flagellum have been performed in the sea urchin by Stephens et al. (1967) and Yanagisawa et al. (1968). They made determinations on nucleotide content of whole sperm, isolated flagella,
and isolated microtubules. The highlight of their results was the finding that nucleotides of guanine, and not of adenine, are bound to the
microtubules in the ratio, as far as could be determined, of 1 mole of
nucleotide to 1 mole of microtubule subunit (molecular weight,
60,000).

In the whole sperm, the adenine nucleotide content was found to
be very high, two thirds or more of the total nucleotide content (Stephens et al.). The Yanagisawa group also reported large amounts of
creatine phosphate. Isolation of flagella brought about the loss of
the mitochondria and the rupture of flagellar membranes with concomitant loss of nucleotides of adenine. The result was an extremely
low content of adenine nucleotides in the isolated flagella. Isolated
microtubules contained guanine nucleotides exclusively. The guanine nucleotides present were found to be principally GTP and GDP.
They could not be removed from the microtubules by dialysis, and
there was no exchange of label with radioactive GTP in the medium.
There were believed to be nucleotides of guanine in the flagellum in
excess of the amount bound to the microtubules, but conclusive evidence to this effect was not obtained. In the interpretation of the results of these experiments, a tentative hypothesis can be made that
ATP in amount is to be found in the cytoplasm surrounding the
microtubules.

The nucleotides of guanine doubtlessly play a role in flagellar
motility here. It is not altogether surprising to find nucleotides of
guanine implicated in motility. In the polysome, GTP is probably
involved in the movement of the messenger molecule relative to the
ribosome and in the translocation of t-RNA from one binding site to
another in peptide elongation. These events must be classified as
species of motility in the sense that motility is organized movement
associated with a structure. There is no reason to assume, however,

that the mechanism of action of GTP in the polysome is in any way comparable to what it will be found to be in the flagellum.

The Yanagasawa group see in the association of guanine nucleotides with microtubules a possible analogue to the relationship of ATP to actin in muscle, where ATP reacts with G-actin to form F-actin and ADP in a polymerization process. Their results point to the possibility of extensive transphosphorylation activity in the flagellum between GTP and ADP. The system would require an enzyme to hydrolyze ATP. Claybrook and Nelson (1968) demonstrated the presence of an ATPase activated by both magnesium and calcium ions in flagella of *Arbacia punctulata*. They speculated that it might be a major component of the mechanism for motility.

SOME ASPECTS OF OOGENESIS

The physiology and biochemistry of sea urchin oogenesis, primarily because of vexatious problems in experimental handling, have not received a great amount of study in the past, but some descriptions of the morphological changes that occur have appeared from time to time. For a general view of these morphological aspects of oogenesis, the reader is referred to Tennent and Ito (1941), Raven (1961), and to two recent histological studies by Holland and Giese (1965) and Chatlynne (1969).

The five arborescent ovaries of the sea urchin are suspended by mesenteries in the body cavity. They are covered by an epithelium, which was considered by Tennent and Ito to be the germinal epithelium and hence the source of the oogonia. There is some doubt from the evidence of more recent work that this layer actually is the germinal epithelium. Holland and Giese have suggested that oogonia probably arise largely from previous oogonia. The ultimate origin thus would remain something of a mystery, since little, if anything, is known of the source of primordial germ cells in the sea urchin.

Beneath the covering epithelium is a layer of collagenous connective tissue containing some smooth muscle. Between the connective tissue layer and the lumen is found a region made of two cell types, the sex cells and a species of cell that has been described as either a nurse cell or a phagocyte, and which in point of fact is probably both. Chatlynne has termed these cells *nutritive phagocytes*. This region has been designated by Holland and Giese as the *germinal layer* (not to be confused with the germinal epithelium).

The nutritive phagocyte appears to be fundamentally a follicle cell or a follicle-cell analogue. It is characterized by the cyclic appearance and disappearance of globules within its cytoplasm. The globules are largely polysaccharide and lipid in nature. There is some evidence that the nutritive phagocytes may transfer some of the materials from these globules to the sex cells. There is also evidence to suggest that these accessory cells phagocytize some sex cells, perhaps those which have failed to achieve proper development, and may recirculate their components to other sex cells.

The problem of the transfer of materials to the sex cells from accessory cells, or from whatever other sources may exist, is in need of further study. It is desirable, for example, to know what the status of the transfer of small molecules from accessory cells to sex cells may be. As will be discussed later, newly fertilized sea urchin eggs have enzymes for the transport to their interior of exogenous metabolic precursors such as nucleotides and amino acids. Such precursors are not required by the fertilized egg, and their regular occurrence in amount in its natural environment has not been demonstrated. The fertilized egg has thus little need for transport enzymes. In oogenesis, however, such enzymes could play an important role in transferring small molecules from the accessory or follicle cell to the oocyte.

The question of the transfer of macromolecules is also of interest. Of particular interest is the question of whether proteins and other large molecules are transferred from accessory cells to oocytes to produce yolk or whether yolk is produced entirely by the activities of the oocyte. Should transfer occur, one might expect to observe pinocytotic activity in the sex cell. Such pinocytotic activity is observed from time to time in the sex cells of other animals. Tsukahara (1970) has reported that in *Anthocidaris crassispina, Pseudocentrotus depressus,* and other sea urchins from Japanese waters such activity may be seen in the oocyte, at the time of vitellogenesis. He has noted that one type of pinosome formed was seen in number around immature yolk granules, although the nature of the contents of this pinosome has not been established. Another type of pinosome was shown to contain glycogen-like granules, and he has suggested that it may participate in the formation of cortical granules.

An interesting aspect of the problem of the transfer of macromolecules is the fact that toward the end of oogenesis, and apparently also of vitellogenesis, at a point when they have become quite large, the oocytes free themselves from the investing nutritive phagocytes, at least in some species of sea urchin, and come to lie in the lumen of the ovarian acinus. Transfer of macromolecules from accessory cells would appear unlikely after this detachment.

With respect to sex-cell content, the region of the germinal layer that abuts the connective tissue layer consists primarily of oogonia, whereas the region near the lumen of the ovary is made up primarily of large oocytes. Oocytes are recognizable by the presence of a large germinal vesicle (nucleus) and a very large, densely staining nucleolus. In addition, smaller or "minor" nucleoli may be present. Oogonia, by contrast often have a pair of small, dense nucleoli. In the ootid, which is normally found in the lumen of the ovary, the germinal vesicle has been lost, and a small female pronucleus has replaced it. Ootids may be more basophilic than oocytes, because of the amount of yolk that has formed in their cytoplasm.

An oocyte is characteristically a cell that is very active in synthesis. Synthesis during oogenesis must produce large supplies of materials that will support the metabolism of the embryo from fertilization until the time when it becomes an independent feeder at pluteus, although, of course, such supplies are enormously augmented by the even greater amount of synthesis that occurs after fertilization. Included in the spectrum of synthesis that occurs at oogenesis are the extensive production of RNA, protein production, and the manufacture of some, if not all, of the materials for yolk. The bulk of the RNA synthesized would appear to be ribosomal, although Gross et al. (1965) have reported that there is a substantial synthesis of both t-RNA and m-RNA. The status of DNA is somewhat obscure, since workers have often found it difficult to demonstrate thymidine incorporation at these early stages. Vitellogenesis appears to be a rather late development in oogenesis, according to Esper (1962, 1965) and Cowden (1962). It is observed primarily in the large oocytes.

As the ootid approaches maturity, syntheses in general fall to a very low level of activity. The mature unfertilized egg is essentially a resting cell. Nakano and Monroy (1958a, 1958b), for example, found that labeled exogenous amino acids are incorporated readily into the acid-soluble pools of the unfertilized egg, but that very little amino acid is incorporated into proteins. An event that very quickly follows fertilization is the recrudescence of synthetic activity, particularly with respect to proteins. Much of the synthetic activity that occurs immediately after fertilization is implemented by informational molecules produced at oogenesis.

ASPECTS OF ORGANELLES OF THE SEA URCHIN EGG

The usual point of departure in a discussion of organelles is a consideration of the nucleus. From a morphological standpoint the nucleus of the sea urchin egg is somewhat uninteresting. It reveals little in the way of structural features in electron micrographs. As is common with animal eggs, it is converted from a large germinal vesicle to a small pronucleus prior to the maturing of the ootid into an unfertilized ovum. There have been many misunderstandings about its DNA content in the past because of its recalcitrance in responding to the Feulgen stain. There has been no extensive cataloging of chromosome numbers in sea urchins, but some figures are available. Auclair (1965), for example, sets the haploid number in *Arbacia punctulata* at 22.

The nucleolus has excited considerable interest because of its involvement in r-RNA synthesis. The very active nucleolus of the oocyte undergoes a considerable increase in size, which to a degree is correlated with the tremendous increase in size experienced by the oocyte itself. When the germinal vesicle disappears, the nucleolus disappears likewise, not to reappear until gastrula. The disappearance and reappearance of the nucleolus purportedly correspond to the cessation and resumption of the synthesis of r-RNA. The nucleolus may not disappear in its entirety. Millonig et al. (1968) have reported the existence of small agranular "nucleoli" during cleavage and blastula. As of the moment, however, evidence suggests that a nucleolus functional in r-RNA production probably does not exist between oogenesis and gastrula. This point is controversial and will be discussed in a later chapter.

The sea urchin is somewhat unusual among animal groups in that the entire maturation process occurs in the ovary. The eggs are shed after the polar bodies have been extruded and the germinal vesicle has been lost. This means that a spawned egg has lost its nucleolus. The sea urchin can be induced to spawn prematurely to provide oocytes with nucleoli for experimental purposes. It is common for various species of asteroid to shed their eggs in the germinal vesicle stage, thus providing a nucleolus available for study. Problems of nucleolar function in the sea urchin will be considered at a later point. A comprehensive survey of studies on the nucleolus, including some work on the sea urchin oocyte that we shall discuss below, is to be found in Vincent and Miller (1967). Since its publication, there has been a magnificent burgeoning of studies on the nucleolus of various cell types in many species. Many of these have been reviewed in a monograph by Busch and Smetana (1970). The work gives an excellent picture of the progress in experimentation on the nucleolus; however, it treats but little of work on the sea urchin egg.

We come now to a consideration of the role of cytoplasmic organelles in sea urchin oogenesis, and the fog begins to roll in. First, the sea urchin oocyte, like many other oocytes, contains special organelles of which the function is unknown or uncertain. Second, familiar organelles take on new functions in oogenesis, and there is often perplexity as to whether we are looking at new functions or old functions in new guises, as well as difficulty in deciding which organelle is performing a given function. Third, if evidence from the recent findings on oogenesis is valid, there is a lack of uniformity among organisms as to the way in which the events of oogenesis come about through organelle activity. This is particularly true with respect to the formation of yolk spherules.

Although the mature unfertilized sea urchin egg is so depleted of polysomes that it is difficult to obtain enough polysome material from them to produce density gradient centrifugation data that can be interpreted, oocytes, particularly young oocytes, are well endowed with polysomes. They may occur either free in the cytoplasm or attached to membranes, such as the nuclear envelope or the rough endoplasmic reticulum. The oocyte has very little rough endoplasmic reticulum and virtually no smooth endoplasmic reticulum. The function of the rough endoplasmic reticulum in oocytes has not been clearly demonstrated. It is probable that it provides some protein, including the protein moieties of mucopolysaccharides, for various vesicles, such as cortical granules produced by the Golgi apparatus, and that it provides membranes for yolk spherules, although some yolk spherules appear to form in vesicles produced by the Golgi apparatus.

Yolk formation in oocytes of the sea urchin is not well understood. The problem is complicated by the fact that there are two basic types of yolk, fatty yolk and proteid yolk. Gross et al. (1960) and others have reported that fatty yolk may be formed from lipid droplets originating in the mitochondria and later becoming scattered throughout the cytoplasm. Proteid yolk is found in dense, membrane-enclosed aggregates called *yolk platelets* or *yolk spherules,* the latter term being more appropriate in view of their spherical contour. Nørrevang (1968), who has classified mechanisms of origin of yolk spherules in various organisms into five distinct categories, places the sea urchin yolk spherule in the class that is formed within preexisting vesicles. The question arises as to the origin of such vesicles. There are two plausible answers: (1) they originate from the endoplasmic reticulum, and (2) they originate from the Golgi apparatus. The best argument for an origin from the rough endoplasmic reticlum lies in the existence of a special cluster of organelles in the oocyte known as the yolk nucleus or nucleus of Balbiani (Nørrevang, 1968, has discussed the yolk nucleus). This structure in the sea urchin definitely appears to produce yolk; in fact, yolk spherules are often seen in association with it. Its principal component is rough endoplasmic reticulum. Although the rough endoplasmic reticulum has in association with it polysomes that might be postulated as the source of yolk protein, if the vesicles operate in the same manner as those in certain other animal species which form yolk spherules from preformed vesicles, they probably acquire most of their contents by micropinocytosis.

Apart from the assertions of some of the early electron microscopists, Afzelius, for example, that their micrographs suggest a Golgi-apparatus origin for the preformed vesicles, the fact that yolk spherules have a moderately high glycoprotein content points to a possible Golgi-apparatus origin, although this argument is not very compelling. Doré and Cousineau (1967) assayed acid phosphatase activity in fractions of homogenates from *Arbacia punctulata,* with p-nitrophenyl phosphate as a substrate. They found that the activity was contained almost exclusively in the yolk fraction in unfertilized eggs and that it underwent a shift to the microsome fraction following blastula. They formed from their results the hypothesis that either a yolk spherule is a modified lysosome or may be converted to a lysosome following the utilization of its contents. Acid phosphatase activity characterizes lysosomes, and lysosomes originate, to the best of our present knowledge, from the Golgi apparatus. It is best to reserve judgment on this argument. The attributes of a lysosome coincide with the needs of a yolk spherule in the sense that it is appropriate that the hydrolytic enzymes that break down yolk be isolated from the cytoplasm. Yolk spherules in many animals, however, are not vesiculated by the Golgi apparatus; hence other avenues must exist for their acquisition of hydrolytic enzymes. The verification of the thesis that a yolk spherule is converted into a lysosome would, of course, reinforce the idea that it was modified from one originally. The degradation of yolk spherules followed by, or accompanied by, the formation of new lysosomes from the Golgi apparatus could reveal itself in a similar shift of acid phosphatase from one fraction to another in embryogenesis in the absence of interconversion. If the spherule is not vesiculated by the Golgi apparatus, the means by which hydrolytic enzymes are incorporated into it remain to be described.

It has been reported that yolk spherules contain DNA (see, for example, Tyler, 1967). Celi et al. (1967) have described aggregates of ribonucleoprotein in yolk spherules. Dubois et al. (1971) have isolated a 9S and a 12S RNA by polyacrylamide electrophoresis, and have found that these two RNA particles exist exclusively in the yolk spherule fractions of homogenates, disappearing at the time in embryogenesis when yoke spherules disappear. Assuming that these particles are not contaminants which adhere to yolk spherules and that the 9S peak is not in reality a component of the 9–10S peak, which has been associated with histone production as will be discussed in a later chapter, it can be said that their presence in spherules along with DNA is consistent with the idea that the yolk spherule is an independent center for protein synthesis. The nature of the proteins synthesized is conjectural, but hydrolytic enzymes are a logical candidate. The mystery as to how the yolk spherule acquires DNA remains to be unraveled. The simplest explanation is that DNA is transferred to the spherule from the mitochondrion. Mitochondria are frequently seen in association with yolk nuclei, vesicles produced by the Golgi apparatus, and the endoplasmic reticulum. In the language of criminology, however, mitochondria appear to have the opportunity, but it is doubtful that they have the motive. It is possible but unlikely that mitochondria and yolk spherules would use an identical DNA to synthesize identical proteins. Poor as it is in information content, it is improbable that mitochondrial DNA carries extra and different information to provide for protein synthesis in the spherule. The nucleus has the requisite broad spectrum of information content so to provide, but we have no knowledge that it is the source, let alone knowledge as to how the transfer might be effected.

Afzelius (1955b) observed and described annulate lamellae in sea urchin oocytes. These organelles take the form of tapering stacks of fenestrated double membranes that are proliferated by, and sloughed or blebbed off from, the nuclear envelope. Their fenestrations contain a ring-like (annular) structure (see Fig. 4). Kessel (1968) has published an excellent review and commentary on the nature of annulate lamellae. Annulate lamellae are not limited to sex cells but

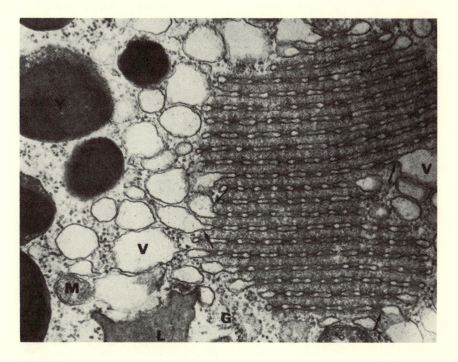

Figure 4

Stack of annulate lamellae from oocyte of *Rana pipiens*. Magnification: 34,000×. OsO₄. Large vesicles (V) surround the stack and are continuous with the ends of the lamellae in some instances (arrows). Micrograph also shows lipid globule (L), granules (G), mitochondrion (M), and yolk platelets (Y). [From Kessel (1968); by permission.]

are common in cells that are either in a state of rapid proliferation or in a state or rapid differentiation. Their function is not known. They frequently have RNA (believed to be ribosomal) associated with them in sea urchin oocytes, although such an association is not found in all animal forms. The presence of RNA does imply an involvement with protein synthesis. Kessel has proposed that annulate lamellae may carry nuclear information out into the cytoplasm and there serve as a locus of nuclear control of cytoplasmic activity, a nuclear substation as it were. There is little evidence to substantiate this at present. Tilney and Marsland (1969) have recommended the exploration of the possibility that the organelle may be implicated in the initiation of the cleavage mechanism, since annulate lamellae disappear shortly before the first cleavage.

Electron-microscope studies of the sea urchin oocyte reveal the presence of organelles characterized as *heavy bodies* by Afzelius (1957) and as *dense bodies* by certain other workers. The use of either term is unfortunate, since the term *dense bodies* is frequently applied to primary lysosomes. Heavy bodies in the sea urchin oocyte are made up of dense aggregates of ribonucleoprotein, which may be of nucleolar origin. Much of the work devoted to them has been performed with cytochemical techniques, and some of the results are not particularly convincing. Harris (1967) has expressed disbelief in the nucleolar origin of heavy bodies and submits that they probably contain masked m-RNA. The work of Mano, which will be discussed later, describes vesiculated RNA presumed to be masked template in the unfertilized egg. The membrane of a heavy body is usually a single annulate lamella. Heavy bodies are quite numerous and are scattered throughout the cytoplasm.

The Golgi apparatus undergoes division in oogenesis. The number of individual apparatuses may be quite high at times in sea urchin oocytes, although both the number and distribution may vary widely as a function of time. Although its traditional role in secretion may be lacking in the egg, the organelle is quite versatile, and its function in generating vesicles and in producing mucopolysaccharides is highly important. E. Anderson (1968) has demonstrated that the Golgi apparatus is involved in the production of cortical granules, which later feature prominently in fertilization and in the artifical activation of the egg.

Very little work has been done on the activity of mitochondria in oogenesis. Some studies have been made on mitochondrial behavior in the mature ovum. Although it is not completely appropriate to consider them under the subject of oogenesis, we shall discuss these studies briefly. They have been reviewed by Monroy and Maggio (1964).

Early workers found that, as revealed by oxygen consumption, the activity of oxidative phosphorylation is high in mitochondria in oogenesis. Such activity is normal in view of the brisk synthesis of RNA and protein at this time. In the mature unfertilized egg, oxygen consumption drops to a very low level, as does synthetic activity. As will be discussed in a later chapter, however, the attenuation of total protein synthesis is probably not due to diminished supplies of ATP here. The status of mitochondrial DNA synthesis before fertilization is unknown. Anderson (1969) has reported that there is a surge of mitochondrial DNA synthesis shortly after fertilization.

Some experiments were performed nearly a decade and a half ago which argue that protein synthesis within the mitochondrion is repressed in the unfertilized egg and reactivated after feritilization. These experiments are important historically, but they must be viewed in the light of the existing knowledge and techniques, since today the more sophisticated methods of molecular embryology have shown the activities of the protein synthesizing machinery of the sea urchin mitochondrion to be somewhat obscure, and workers have not yet succeeded in describing them. These early experiments raise the question as to whether the forces that suppress the synthesis of mitochrondrial proteins in the unfertilized sea urchin egg are intrinsic or extrinsic to the organelle. Nakano and Monroy (1958b) and Giudice and Monroy (1958) labeled fertilized and unfertilized sea urchin eggs with ^{35}S-methionine and found that there was no incorporation into protein of mitochondrial fractions of homogenates of unfertilized eggs, but that incorporation did occur by the time the eggs reached cleavage. They found that the label in the unfertilized eggs was almost completely recoverable from the acid-soluble pools, suggesting that little protein synthesis of any sort was occurring. Giudice (1960) demonstrated that isolated mitochondria from unfertilized and fertilized eggs incorporate amino acids equally well into their proteins in vitro. This finding implies that in vivo the synthesis of mitochondrial protein is being suppressed by forces external to the organelle.

Monroy in 1957 studied the swelling of mitochondria isolated from fertilized and unfertilized sea urchin eggs and suspended in various concentrations of sucrose. The phenomenon is familiar to cell physiologists. The two mitochondrial membranes have different permeabilities to sucrose. The sucrose penetrates the outside membrane to find itself facing an inner membrane that is relatively impermeable to it. It raises the osmotic pressure in the space between the two membranes. Water then flows in and elevates the outside membrane without damaging the matrix. Monroy found that this swelling was much greater in mitochondria from unfertilized eggs than in those from fertilized eggs. These results suggested to him that structural alterations, which were responsible for the change in permeability, had occured in the membrane of the mitochondria of the unfertilized egg. The question arises as to whether such changes might be produced by the mitochondrion itself.

The idea that the increase in swelling is due to increased permeability of the external membrane, and thus more likely to be the result of external effects, is appealing, but as with the cause for swelling of sperm mitochondria in the acrosome reaction, one can but speculate. Mitochondria *within cells* are known to possess the *intrinsic* capability to change their shape (swell, for example) or to maintain their shape in the face of forces that would alter it, in response to changes in their environment. Control of shape is thought to occur in relation to their respiratory activity. Surely much more study is needed, however, to determine whether structural alterations in the membrane are caused by external reactions that directly turn off mitochondrial activity, or result from the mitochondrion turning itself off in response to external influences, or arise from some entirely unrelated mechanism.

Although pigment granules do not properly qualify for the status of organelle, it is appropriate to discuss them at this time. The eggs and embryos of some species of sea urchin are richly endowed with them. Most commonly they are either naphthoquinones or carotenoids. A modicum of work has been done in the isolation, characterization, and assay of pigments (see, for example, Monroy and De Nicola, 1952; De Nicola and Monroy-Oddo, 1952; De Nicola, 1954; De Nicola and Goodwin, 1954), but little is known of the physiological activity or developmental function of pigments. Fluctuations in the pigment content of the embryo over the course of development have suggested to some workers that pigment may play some type of morphogenetic role. In experimentation, pigments are often useful as markers to show movements of materials within the egg. This is particularly true in centrifugation experiments. One of the naphthoquinone pigments, echinochrome, excited some interest when it was believed to be involved in sperm–egg interactions. It has been demonstrated that there is no justification for this belief. Among the echinoderms, only the echinoids possess echinochrome. Its function remains unknown.

CORTICAL GRANULES

Cortical granules have received a great deal of attention from sea urchin embryologists because of the role these granule play in fertilization, particularly with respect to the elevation of the fertilization membrane. Runnström in 1966 published a comprehensive review of the work that has been done on cortical granules and on the cortical reaction. The cortical granules are manufactured during oogenesis. At that time, they are randomly distributed throughout the cytoplasm and are freely movable upon centrifugation. Upon maturation of the egg, the granules are transported to the cortex to become organized into a layer immediately below the plasma membrane, actually in contact with it in some instances. Having formed this layer, they cease to be freely movable upon centrifugation. E. Anderson (1968) has described the formation of the granules from vesicles pinched off from the Golgi apparatus with the Golgi apparatus apparently producing both the membrane and contents of the granules. An electron micrograph of the cortical granules may be seen in Fig. 5.

Many cytologists (including McCulloch, 1952; Cheney and Lansing, 1955; Afzelius, 1956; Balinsky, 1960; Endo, 1961; Wolpert and Mercer, 1961; Pasteels, 1965) have studied the ultrastructure of the cortical granules. These studies have involved several different species of sea urchin. Apart from the membrane, there are three important structures in the granule. The first of these is an electron-transparent material perhaps best thought of as matrix material. Endo (1961) assesses this material with the responsibility for the swelling that the granule undergoes prior to opening at fertilization. It probably also increases the osmotic pressure in the space between the plasma and vitelline membranes to facilitate the elevation of the pro-

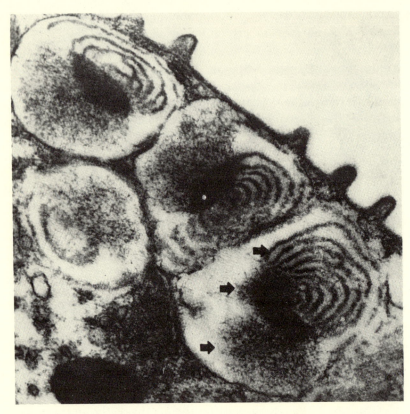

Figure 5

Cortical particles of *Strongylocentrotus purpuratus.* Magnification: 50,000×. Lowest arrow, extralamellar body; middle arrow, basal region of lamella; uppermost arrow, lamellar filaments. [From Runnström (1966); by permission.]

spective fertilization membrane. The second is an electron-dense lamellar structure, which ultimately plays a role in the formation of the fertilization membrane. The third is a smaller, compact, sometimes granular, electron-dense structure, which may be involved in the formation of the hyaline layer. Afzelius (1956) showed that there is great variation in the morphology of the electron-dense substances from one species of sea urchin to another. The cortical granules are rich in mucopolysaccharides, as is the cortical region in general.

Much has been made of the fact that the cortical granules do not migrate upon centrifugation, whereas other cytoplasmic particles and organelles do so migrate. The phenomenon has been related to the nature of the cortex itself. Since the migration of particles in a centrifugal field does not affect the structure of the pluteus, it has been asserted often that the polarity of the egg and the orientation of the precursors of the future germ layers must be housed in the area of the cytoplasm which does not move in a centrifugal field, that is, the cortex. This picture assumes a gel-like cortex, a cortex undisturbed by mild centrifugal force, a cortex that in a sense anchors the materials contained within it during centrifugation.

Evidence for a gel-like cortex with the ability to organize the future pluteus may be seen in the experiments of Hörstadius et al. (1950) in which they sucked out the "fluid" cytoplasm of an egg with a micropipette and were able to develop from the remainder of the egg a pluteus that was normal in everything but size. Further evidence is seen in the fact that Allen (1955) was able to isolate cortical strips from eggs of the sea urchin. The electron microscope, however, does not show any inner layer to the cortex of the sea urchin egg, and Mercer and Wolpert (1962) and others have questioned the existence of a gel-like cortex. One theory offered to explain the immovability of the cortical granules under centrifugation is that they may possibly be attached to the plasma membrane. Electron micrographs show that the granules lie very close to the plasma membrane, and that in some species they are clearly in contact with it. Mercer and Wolfpert found that in both fertilized and unfertilized eggs in a centrifugal field cytoplasmic particles could move freely in and out of the cortical region.

When the cortical granules open to discharge their contents, their membrane unites with the plasma membrane. Endo (1961) and Wolpert and Mercer (1961) have produced evidence to the effect that the two membranes fuse to form a mozaic membrane, with each cortical granule membrane becoming an integral part of the surface membrane of the egg. The new surface membrane should then be characterized as a mozaic with respect to the origins of its components, portions being part of the original plasmalemma and portions being derived from the Golgi network. It may also be a mozaic with respect to structural makeup. Many molecular cytologists dispute the unit-membrane theory and would assert that the two membranes under consideration here differ in dimensions and in molecular construction. The membranes do not differ enough in structure to prevent their mating, and numerous examples of such mating are known. It is seen repeatedly in secretory cells and has been noted above in the instance of the union of the acrosomal process membrane with the plasmalemma in the sperm.

The critical question here in the cortical reaction is whether we have a mozaic with respect to function, whether the membrane produced by the Golgi apparatus possesses the ability to perform all the functions of a plasma membrane. There has been no loss of plasmalemma, but there has been a decrease in area of plasmalemma per unit area of surface membrane. Whether this circumstance contributes to a decrease in efficiency of surface activities is not known. In the instance of secretory cells, some cytologists have proposed that there is a process of membrane flow, with the alien membrane being degraded and translocated to the Golgi apparatus, where it is recycled.

The details of the role of the cortical granules in fertilization will be discussed at a later point.

INVESTMENTS OF THE EGG

The investments of the unfertilized egg consist of a plasma membrane, a vitelline membrane, and a jelly coat. The plasma membrane appears to be typical of plasma membranes of cells in general. It is thrown up into a moderate number of microvilli.

The vitelline membrane is in direct contact with the plasma membrane and appears to be a primary membrane, that is, one made by the egg itself. The vitelline membrane is very delicate and is often difficult to see with the electron microscope. It appears to be fibrous in nature, although it is by no means certain that it does not contain nonfibrous components. The fact that it shows a marked sensitivity to proteolytic enzymes suggests that it is probably protein in nature. Runnström (1966) has proposed that it is probably somewhat elastic in nature and that its lack of birefringence may bespeak a lack of orientation in its fibrous components. It is the vitelline membrane, of course, that rises to become the fertilization membrane.

The jelly coat of the sea urchin egg has received an enormous amount of attention from embryologists. It appears to be a product of the egg and is formed during oogenesis. It may vary considerably in thickness among various species of sea urchin. It swells when the eggs are spawned and then slowly dissolves as the eggs stand in seawater. The diffusion of the jelly coat material, fertilizin, as noted above, produces egg water. Fertilizin in egg water reacts with molecules of antifertilizin on the surface of the sperm to agglutinate sperm suspensions. This agglutination reaction has been the keystone in most major studies of the characteristics of fertilizin–antifertilizin reactions and of the parameters that control them. Sperm agglutination, however, is probably not involved in normal fertilization.

Solutions of antifertilizin have the capacity to neutralize the sperm-agglutinating activity of fertilizin. They have also the property of agglutinating a suspension of homologous eggs and producing a preciptation membrane on the surface of the egg in the process. Since the index of refraction of the jelly-coat is very close to that of seawater, the jelly-coat is invisible under ordinary light microscopy. One is aware of its presence, of course, because of the regular spacing between eggs that are packed closely together, and lost jelly coats can be detected by aberrations from this regularity. In Fig. 6 are seen a fertilized egg and an unfertilized egg that have been suspended in a solution of antifertilizin. The precipitation membrane that was formed in the reaction has rendered the jelly coat visible. In the fertilized egg the precipitation membrane is seen outside the fertilization membranes.

The jelly coat is easily removed by a great variety of techniques, including lowering of pH, washing and agitation, straining through bolting silk, and treating with proteolytic enzymes. It is often desirable to remove it in experimentation, particularly to avoid having to contend with the mucopolysaccharide in analytical procedures.

Tyler (1948, 1949, 1956) reported that the jelly coat is essentially homogeneous with respect to the mucopolysaccharide, fertilizin, a substance that plays a prime role in sperm–egg interactions. Tyler and Vasseur, in particular, made circumspect studies of the chemical and physical nature of fertilizin (see Vasseur, 1947, 1948, 1950 1952). Fertilizin from the jelly coat was shown to be a polymer having a molecular weight estimated at 300,000 for *Arbacia punctulata*, with some variation among species. Sedimentation constants, determined for several species tended to run from 4.5 to 6.5. The fact that the sedimentation velocity of fertilizin increases with dilution gives one to suspect that it is an elongate molecule. The axial ratio has been determined as being 20:1. The molecule has a high sulfate content, about 25 percent on the average among several species of sea urchin.

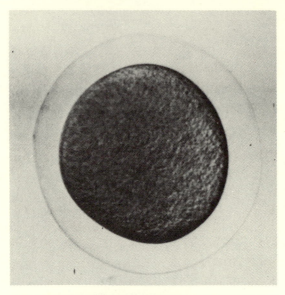

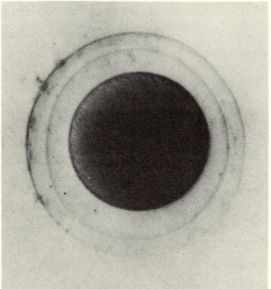

Figure 6

Photomicrographs of an unfertilized egg (top) and a fertilized egg (bottom) of *Lytechinus pictus* in a solution of antifertilizin. Magnification: unfertilized egg, 300×; fertilized egg, 250×. Agglutination produces a visible precipitation membrane on the surface of the jelly coat. In the unfertilized egg, the fertilization membrane is seen inside the precipitation membrane. [From Tyler and Tyler (1966); by permission.]

The monosaccharides of fertilizin vary among species and include fructose, galactose, fucose, glucose, mannose, and xylose, among which fucose appears to be the most common. In these early studies, attempts to dissociate the protein and polysaccharide moieties were unsuccessful. Tyler (1949, 1956) suggested a degree of interlocking of sugar and amino acid groups.

One group of workers has presented substantial evidence that the jelly coat is not homogeneous (see Hotta et al., 1970; Isaka et al., 1970). These workers have isolated several sialopolysaccharides from the jelly, and they conceive the jelly coat to consist of many types of glycoproteins and polysaccharide–protein complexes. The sialopolysaccharides show strong sperm-agglutinating power.

There is no reason to assume that the molecular interactions between egg and sperm are limited to fertilizin–antifertilizin reactions during the process of fertilization. Sperm lysin reactions with egg substrates, if they exist in the sea urchin, represent an exception. The reactions responsible for the fusion of the plasma membrane with the acrosomal process membrane may represent an exception, and there may be other exceptions. Fertilizin–antifertilizin reactions are extremely important in fertilization, however. They are responsible for a variety of events, and it is probable that the variety is achieved through a variety of specificities. *Antifertilizin* is a generic term for what may be several different compounds in an individual sperm. A meaningful picture of the extent and nature of heterogeneity in either fertilizin or antifertilizin is not available at persent.

The agglutination and precipitation reactions that mark the combining of fertilizin and antifertilizin are envisioned as being analogous to antigen–antibody reactions, with fertilizin constituting the analogue of the antibody. The fertilizin of the sea urchin has been demonstrated to be multivalent with respect to its active sites. The mechanism of agglutination and precipitation is postulated to follow the lattice hypothesis that has been proposed to explain the nature of comparable reactions between antigens and antibodies. The structural aspect of fertilizin responsible for the interaction with antifertilizin has not been determined. Metz (1954) has presented evidence to eliminate free S-S, SH, phenolic, and amino groups from involvement. Without any apparent destruction of active sites, fertilizin can be converted to a univalent form by such agents as proteolytic enzymes, X-rays, ultraviolet light, or hydrogen peroxide (see Tyler,

1941, 1948, Metz, 1942, 1957). Studies on the univalent form have been reviewed briefly by Metz (1967). The fragmentation that produces the univalent form is ostensibly nonrandom and gives rise to several subunits, although to date there are no findings to show which of these subunits are active.

In experiments wherein sea urchin sperm are agglutinated with homologous fertilizin, univalent fertilizin forms spontaneously, eliminating the agglutinated state after a brief time period. The sperm, with univalent fertilizin attached to its antifertilizin molecules, is incapable of fertilizing the egg, presumably because active sites have been occluded.

Antifertilizin from sperm has not received an extensive amount of study, particularly in recent years. It has been revealed to be protein, probably acidic protein, in nature. Immunological studies have demonstrated that it contains four or more antigens. It had been thought to be composed of molecules with molecular weights of less than 10,000, but studies in which it has been extracted by freeze–thaw techniques have shown it to consist of large particles sedimenting between 20,000 and 30,000 × g.

Fertilizin shows a remarkably high degree of species specificity in the agglutination of sperm, and the maintenance of species specificity is considered a function of fertilizin–antifertilizin reactions in fertilization. This specificity is highly effective in preventing interbreeding among species of sea urchin, but on occasion its protection fails to extend to broader taxonomic groups. Sperm of certain worms and mollusks, such as *Cerebratulus* and *Mytilus* have been shown to attach to sea urchin eggs, sometimes penetrate them, and in rare instances activate them to give rise to a pluteus (see Kupelwieser, 1909).

Tyler and Metz (1955) showed that eggs deprived of their jelly coat can still be fertilized and that in such instances there is a reaction between antifertilizin and the egg surface. The reaction may be due to residual jelly-coat material or alternatively to the presence of a fertilizin distinct from that of the jelly coat and known to be produced by the egg. Motomura (1950) isolated this compound, known as *cytofertilizin*, from eggs by boiling them or by ageing them in seawater. Gregg and Metz (1966) compared it with jelly-coat fertilizin by immunodiffusion tests. Both fertilizins showed differences in precipitin bands, although they do have at least one band in common. Cyto-fertilizin agglutination of sperm shows spontaneous reversal and species specificity, and cytofertilizin increases sperm motility. The two fertilizins may react with at least some common sites of the sperm surface.

Tyler (1940) and Monroy and Runnström (1952) isolated an antifertilizin that is produced by the egg. It makes its presence known by the fact that cytolysis of eggs neutralizes the activity of fertilizin in egg water. The function in fertilization of this substance which exists in the interior of the egg but ostensibly reacts with fertilizin on the surface of the egg, is quite unknown.

Fertilizin–antifertilizin reactions will be discussed further in the following chapter.

REFERENCES

Afzelius, B. A., 1955a. The fine structure of sea urchin spermatozoa as revealed by the electron microscope. *Z. Zellforsch., 42,* 134–138.

Afzelius, B. A., 1955b. The ultrastructure of the nuclear membrane of the sea urchin oocyte as studied with the electron microscope. *Exp. Cell Res., 8,* 147–158.

Afzelius, B. A., 1956. The ultrastructure of the cortical granules and their products in the sea urchin egg as studied with the electron microscope. *Exp. Cell Res., 10, 257 –.* 285.

Afzelius, B. A., 1957. Electron microscopy of the basophilic structures of the sea urchin egg. *Z. Zellforsch., 45,* 660–675.

Afzelius, B. A., and A. Murray, 1957. The acrosomal reaction of spermatozoa during fertilization or treatment with egg water. *Exp. Cell Res., 12,* 325–337.

Allen, R. D., 1955. The fertilization reaction in isolated cortical material from sea urchin eggs. *Exp. Cell Res., 8,* 397–399.

Anderson, E., 1968. Oocyte differentiation in the sea urchin, *Arbacia punctulata,* with particular reference to the origin of cortical granules and their participation in the cortical reaction. *J. Cell Biol., 87,* 514–539.

Anderson, W. A., 1968a. Structure and function of the paternal mitochondrion during early embryogenesis of *Paracentrotus lividus. J. Ultrastruct. Res., 24,* 311–321.

Anderson, W. A., 1968b. Cytochemistry of sea urchin gametes. 1. Intramitochondrial localization of glycogen, glucose-6-phosphatase, and adenosine triphosphastase in spermatozoa of *Paracentrotus lividus. J. Ultrastruct. Res., 24,* 398–411.

Anderson, W. A., 1969. Nuclear and cytoplasmic DNA synthesis during early embryogenesis of *Paracentrotus lividus. J. Ultrastruct. Res., 26,* 95–110.

Auclair, W., 1965. The chromosomes of sea urchins, especially *Arbacia punctulata;* a method for studying unsectioned eggs at the first cleavage. *Biol. Bull. Mar. Biol. Lab., Woods Hole, 128,* 169–176.

Austin, C. R., 1968. *Ultrastructure of Fertilization.* Holt, Rinehart, and Winston, Inc., New York.

Balinsky, B. I., 1960. The role of cortical granules in the formation of the fertilization membrane of fertilized sea urchin eggs. *Symposium on Germ Cells and Development, Institut. Intern. d'Embryologie and Fondazione A. Baselli,* 205–219.

Bernstein, M. H., 1962. Normal and reactive morphology of sea urchin spermatozoa. *Exp. Cell Res., 27,* 197–209.

Bibring, T., and J. Baxandall, 1968. Mitotic apparatus: the selective extraction of protein with mild acid. *Science, 161,* 377–379.

Bishop, D. W. (ed.), 1962. *Spermatozoan Motility.* American Association for the Advancement of Science, Washington, D.C.

Brookbank, J. W., 1958. Dispersal of the gelatinous coat material of *Mellita quinquiesperforata* eggs by homologous sperm and sperm extracts. *Biol. Bull. Mar. Biol. Lab., Woods Hole, 115,* 74–80.

Busch, H., and K. Smetana, 1970. *The Nucleolus.* Academic Press, Inc., New York.

Celi, A. D., L. D'Este, and D. Teti, 1967. La vitellogenesi in *Arbacia lixulae e Sphaerechinus granularis (Echin. Echin.). Experientia, 23,* 433–434.

Chatlynne, L. G., 1969. A histochemical study of oogenesis in the sea urchin *Strongylocentrotus purpuratus. Biol. Bull. Mar. Biol. Lab., Woods Hole, 136,* 167–184.

Cheney, R. H., and A. I. Lansing, 1955. Caffein inhibition in *Arbacia.* Electron microscopy. *Exp. Cell Res., 8,* 173–180.

Claybrook, J. R., and L. Nelson, 1968. Flagellar adenosine triphosphotase from sea urchin sperm: properties and relation to motility. *Science, 162,* 1134–1136.

Colwin, A. L., and L. H. Colwin, 1957. Morphology of fertilization: acrosome filament formation and sperm entry. In A. Tyler, R. C. von Borstel, and C. B. Metz (eds.), *The Beginnings of Embryonic Development.* American Association for the Advancement of Science, Washington, D.C.

Cowden, R. R., 1962. RNA and yolk synthesis in growing oocytes of the sea urchin *Lytechinus variegatus. Exp. Cell Res., 28,* 600–604.

Dan, J. C., 1956. The acrosome reaction. *Int. Rev. Cytol., 5,* 365–393.

Dan, J. C., 1970. Morphogenetic aspects of acrosome formation and reaction. *Advances in Morphogenesis, Vol. 8.* Academic Press, Inc., New York, 1–39.

Dan, J. C., Y. Ohori, and H. Kushida, 1964. Studies on the acrosome reaction VII. Formation of the acrosomal process in sea urchin spermatozoa. *J. Ultrastruct. Res., 11,* 508–524.

De Nicola, M., 1954. Further investigation on the change in the pigment during embryonic development in echinoderms. *Exp. Cell Res., 7,* 368–373.

De Nicola, M., and T. W. Goodwin, 1954. Carotenoids in the developing eggs of the sea urchin *Paracentrotus lividus. Exp. Cell Res., 7,* 23–31.

De Nicola, M., and A. Monroy-Oddo, 1952. The distribution of carotenoids in the eggs, ovaries, and testicles of *Paracentrotus lividus. Experientia, 8,* 187–189.

Dirksen, E. R., 1961. The presence of centrioles in artificially activated sea urchin eggs. *J. Biophys. Biochem. Cytol., 11,* 244–247.

Doré, D., and G. H. Cousineau, 1967. Acid phosphatase analysis in sea urchin eggs and blastulae. *Exp. Cell, Res., 48,* 179–182.

Dubois, R., M. Dugré, I. Deuker, S. Inoue, and G. H. Cousineau, 1971. 12S and 9S RNA species. Localization and fate during development of *Strongylocentrotus purpuratus* eggs. *Exp. Cell Res., 68,* 197–204.

Endo, Y., 1961. Changes in the cortical layer of sea urchin eggs at fertilization as studied by the electron microscope. I. *Clypeaster japonicus. Exp. Cell Res., 25,* 383–397.

Esper, H., 1962. Incorporation of C^{14}-glucose into oocytes and ovarian eggs of *Arbacia punctulata. Biol. Bull. Mar. Biol. Lab., Woods Hole, 123,* 476.

Esper, H., 1965. Studies on the nucleolar vacuole in the oogenesis of *Arbacia punctulata. Exp. Cell Res., 38,* 85–96.

Franklin, L. E., 1965. Morphology of gamete membrane fusion and of sperm entry into oocytes of the sea urchin. *J. Cell Biol., 25,* 81–100.

Giudice, G., 1960. Incorporation of labeled amino acids into the protein of mitochondria isolated from the unfertilized eggs and developmental stages of *Paracentrotus lividus*. *Exp. Cell Res., 21,* 222–225.

Giudice, G., and A. Monroy, 1958. Incorporation of S^{35}-methionine in the proteins of the mitochondria of developing and parthenogenetically activated sea urchin eggs. *Acta Embryol. Morphol. Exp., 2,* 58–65.

Gregg, K. W., and C. B. Metz, 1966. A comparison of fertilizin and cytofertilizin from eggs of *Arbacia punctulata. Assoc. Southeast. Biol. Bull., 13,* 34.

Gross, P. R., L. I. Malkin, and M. Hubbard, 1965. Synthesis of RNA during oogenesis in the sea urchin. *J. Mol. Biol., 13,* 463–481.

Gross, P. R., D. E. Philpott, and S. Nass, 1960. Electron microscopy of the centrifuged sea urchin egg, with a note on the surface of the ground cytoplasm. *J. Biophys. Biochem. Cytol., 7,* 135–142.

Harris, P., 1967. Structural changes following fertilization in the sea urchin eggs. Formation and dissolution of heavy bodies. *Exp. Cell Res., 48,* 569–581.

Hathaway, R. R., 1963. Activation of respiration in sea urchin spermatozoa by egg water. *Biol. Bull. Mar. Biol. Lab., Woods Hole, 125,* 486–487.

Hathaway, R. R., and L. Warren, 1961. Further investigations of egg jelly dispersal by *Arbacia* sperm extract. *Biol. Bull. Mar. Biol. Lab., Woods Hole, 121,* 416–417.

Hayashi, T., 1945. Dilution medium and survival of the spermatozoa of *Arbacia punctulata*. I. Effect of the medium on fertilizing power. *Biol. Bull. Mar. Biol. Lab., Woods Hole, 89,* 162–179.

Holland, N. D., and A. C. Giese, 1965. An autoradiographic investigation of the gonads of the purple sea urchin (*Strongylocentrotus purpuratus*). *Biol. Bull. Mar. Biol. Lab., Woods Hole, 128,* 241–258.

Hörstadius, S., L. J. Lorch, and J. F. Danielli, 1950. Differentiation of the sea urchin egg following reduction of inner cytoplasm in relation to the cortex. *Exp. Cell Res., 1,* 188–193.

Hotta, K., H. Hamazaki, M. Kurokawa, and S. Isaka, 1970. Isolation and properties of a new sialopolysaccharide-protein complex from the jelly coat of sea urchin eggs. *J. Biol. Chem., 245,* 5434–5540.

Hultin, E., and G. Lundblad, 1952. Degradation of starch, hydroxyethyl cellulose ether, and chitosan by enzymes in spermatozoa and sperm fluid from *Psammechinus* and *Modiola. Exp. Cell Res., 3,* 427–432.

Hultin, T., 1958. The contents of nucleotide pyrophosphate in ageing sea urchin sperm. *Exp. Cell Res., 14,* 633–634.

Isaka, S., K. Hotta, and M. Kurokawa, 1970. Jelly coat substances of sea urchin eggs. 1. Sperm agglutination and sialopoly-saccharides in the jelly. *Exp. Cell Res., 59,* 37–42.

Kessel, R. G., 1968. Annulate lamellae. *J. Ultrastruct. Res., Suppl. 10,* 1–82.

Kupelwieser, H., 1909. Entwicklungserrugung bei Seeigeleiern durch Molluskensperma. *Wm. Roux Entwicklsmech. Org., 27,* 434–462.

Longo, F. J., and E. Anderson, 1969. Sperm differentiation in the sea urchins *Arbacia punctulata* and *Strongylocentrotus purpuratus. J. Ultrastruct. Res., 27,* 486–509.

McCulloch, D., 1952. Note on the origin of the cortical granules in *Arbacia punctulata* eggs. *Exp. Cell Res., 3,* 605–607.

Mercer, E. H., and L. Wolpert, 1962. An electron microscope study of the cortex of the sea urchin egg. *Exp. Cell Res., 27,* 1–13.

Metz, C. B., 1942. The inactivation of fertilizin and its conversion to the "univalent" form by X-rays and ultraviolet light. *Biol. Bull. Mar. Biol. Lab., Woods Hole, 82,* 446–454.

Metz, C. B., 1954. The effect of some protein group reagents on the sperm agglutinating action of *Arbacia* fertilizin. *Anat. Rec., 120,* 713–714.

Metz, C. B., 1957. Specific egg and sperm substances and activation of the egg. In A. Tyler, R. C. von Borstel, and C. B. Metz (eds.), *The Beginnings of Embryonic Development.* American Association for the Advancement of Science, Washington, D.C.

Metz, C. B., 1967. Gamete surface components and their role in fertilization. In C. B. Metz and A. Monroy (eds.), *Fertilization.* Vol. I. Academic Press, Inc., New York, 163–236.

Millonig, G., M. Bosco, and L. Giambertone, 1968. Fine structure analysis of oogenesis in sea urchins. *J. Exp. Zool., 169,* 293–313.

Mizuno, T., 1956. Relation between zinc and sperm motility in some marine forms. *J. Fac. Sci., Univ. Tokyo. Sec. IV., 7,* 477–487.

Mohri, H., 1959. Enzymic hydrolysis of phospholipids in sea urchin spermatozoa. *Sci. Pap. Coll. Gen. Educ. Univ. Tokyo, 9,* 269–278.

Mohri, H., 1961. Column chromatographic separation of phospholipids in sea urchin spermatozoa. *Sci. Pap. Coll. Gen. Educ. Univ. Tokyo, 11,* 109.

Mohri, H., 1964. Phospholipid utilization in sea urchin spermatozoa. *Pubbl. Staz. Zool. Napoli, 34,* 53–58.

Mohri, H., 1968. Amino acid composition of "tubulin" constituting microtubules of sperm flagella. *Nature* (London), *217,* 1053–1054.

Monroy, A., 1957. Swelling properties of the mitochondria of unfertilized and newly fertilized eggs. *Experientia, 13,* 398–399.

Monroy, A., and M. De Nicola, 1952. The pigment granule of the egg and embryo of the sea urchin, *Paracentrotus lividus. Experientia, 8,* 29–30.

Monroy, A., and R. Maggio, 1964. Biochemical studies on the early development of the sea urchin. *Advances in Morphogenesis,* Vol. 3. Academic Press, Inc., New York, 95–145.

Monroy, A., and J. Runnström, 1952. A cytoplasmic factor acting on the surface layers of *Arbacia punctulata* eggs. *Exp. Cell Res., 3,* 10–18.

Motomura, I., 1950. On the secretion of fertilizin in the eggs of a sea urchin, *Strongylocentrotus pulcherrimus. Sci. Rep. Tohoku Univ., Ser. 4, 18,* 554–560.

Nakano, E., and A. Monroy, 1958a. Some observations on the metabolism of S^{35}-methionine during development of the sea urchin egg. *Experientia, 14,* 367–371.

Nakano, E., and A. Monroy, 1958b. Incorporation of S^{35}-methionine in the cell fractions of sea urchin eggs and embryos. *Exp. Cell Res., 14,* 236–244.

Nelson, L., 1967. Sperm motility in fertilization. In C. B. Metz and A. Monroy (eds.), *Fertilization.* Vol. I. Academic Press, Inc., New York, 27–97.

Nørrevang, A., 1968. Electron microscopic morphology of oogenesis. *Int. Rev. Cytol., 23,* 113–186.

Pasteels, J. J., 1965. Aspects structuraux de la fécondation vus au microscope electronique. *Arch. Biol.* (Liège), *76,* 463–509.

Raven, C. P., 1961. *Oogenesis: the Storage of Developmental Information.* Pergamon Press, Inc., Elmsford, N.Y.

Rothschild, Lord, 1948a. The physiology of sea urchin spermatozoa. Lack of movement in spermatozoa. *J. Exp. Biol., 25,* 344–352.

Rothschild, Lord, 1948b. The physiology of sea urchin spermatozoa. Senescence and the dilution effect. *J. Exp. Biol., 25,* 353–368.

Rothschild, Lord, and K. W. Cleland, 1952. The physiology of sea urchin spermatozoa; the nature and location of the endogenous substrate. *J. Exp. Biol., 29,* 66–71.

Runnström, J., 1966. The vitelline membrane and cortical particles in sea urchin eggs and their vital function in maturation and fertilization. *Advances in Morphogenesis,* Vol. 5. Academic Press, Inc., New York, 221–235.

Runnström, J., S. Lindvall, and A. Tiselius, 1944. Gamones from the sperm of sea urchin and salmon. *Nature* (London), *153,* 285–286.

Stephens, R. E., 1968. On the structural proteins of flagellar outer fibers. *J. Mol. Biol., 32,* 277–283.

Stephens, R. E., 1970. Thermal fractionation of outer doublet microtubules into A- and B- subfiber components A- and B- tubulin. *J. Mol. Biol., 47,*353–363.

Stephens, R. E., F. L. Renaud, and I. R. Gibbons, 1967. Guanine nucleotide associated with the protein of the outer fibers of flagella and cilia. *Science, 156,* 1606–1608.

Takashima, R., S. Mori, M. Kawano, and T. Itatani, 1955. Beta glucuronidase in semen. *Bull. Exp. Biol., 5,* 119–121.

Takashima, R., and Y. Takashima, 1960. Electron microscopical observations on the fertilization phenomenon of sea urchin with special reference to the acrosomal filament. *Tokushima J. Exp. Med., 6,* 334–339.

Tennent, D. H., and T. Ito, 1941. A study of the oogenesis of *Mespilia globulus* (Linné). *J. Morphol., 69,* 347–404.

Tilney, L. G., and D. Marsland, 1969. A fine structural analysis of cleavage induction and furrowing in the eggs of *Arbacia punctulata. J. Cell Biol., 42,* 170–184.

Tsukahara, J., 1970. Formation and behavior of pinosomes in the sea urchin during oogenesis. *Develop. Growth Differ.* (Nagoya), *12,* 53–64.

Tyler, A., 1940. Agglutination of sea urchin eggs by means of a substance extracted from the eggs. *Proc. Nat. Acad. Sci., U.S.A., 26,* 249–256.

Tyler, A., 1941. The role of fertilizin in the fertilization of eggs of the sea urchin and other animals. *Biol. Bull. Mar. Biol. Lab., Woods Hole, 81,* 190–204.

Tyler, A., 1948. Fertilization and immunity. *Physiol. Rev., 28,* 180–219.

Tyler, A., 1949. Properties of fertilizin and related substances of eggs and sperm of marine animals. *Amer. Nat., 83,* 195–219.

Tyler, A., 1950. Extension of the functional life span of spermatozoa by amino acids and peptides. *Biol. Bull. Mar. Biol. Lab., Woods Hole, 99,* 324.

Tyler, A., 1953. Prolongation of life span of sea urchin spermatozoa and improvement of the fertilization by treatment of spermatozoa and eggs with metal-chelating agents (amino acids, versene, DEDTC, oxine, cupron). *Biol. Bull. Mar. Biol. Lab., Woods Hole, 104,* 224–239.

Tyler, A., 1956. Physico-chemical properties of the fertilizins of the sea urchin, *Arbacia punctulata* and the sand dollar *Echinarachnius parma. Exp. Cell Res., 10,* 377–386.

Tyler, A., 1967. Masked messenger RNA and cytoplasmic DNA in relation to protein synthesis and the processes of fertilization and determination in embryonic development. *Develop. Biol., Suppl. 1,* 170–226.

Tyler, A., and C. B. Metz, 1955. Effects of fertilizin treatment of sperm and trypsin treatment of eggs on homologous and cross-fertilization in sea urchins. *Pubbl. Staz. Zool. Napoli, 27,* 128–145.

Tyler, A., and Lord Rothschild, 1951. Metabolism of sea urchin spermatozoa and induced anaerobic motility in solutions of amino acids. *Proc. Soc. Exp. Biol. N.Y., 76,* 52–58.

Tyler, A., and B. S. Tyler, 1966. Physiology of fertilization and early development. In R. A. Boolootian (ed.), *Physiology of the Echinodermata.* John Wiley & Sons, Inc., (Interscience Division), New York, 683–747.

Utida, S., and S. Nanao, 1956. Effects of zinc and 2,4-dinitrophenol on the oxygen uptake of the spermatozoa of sea urchin and other marine animals. *J. Fac. Sci., Univ. Tokyo Sec. IV., 7,* 505–514.

Vasseur, E., 1947. Sulphuric acid content of the egg coat of the sea urchin, *Strongylocentrotus droebachiensis. Ark. iv. Kemi., 25B,* No. 6, 1–2.

Vasseur, E., 1948. Chemical studies on the jelly coat of the sea urchin egg. *Acta Chem. Scand., 2,* 900–913.

Vasseur, E., 1950. L-Galactose in the jelly coat of *Echinus esculentus* eggs. *Acta Chem. Scand., 4,* 1144.

Vasseur, E., 1952. Periodate oxidation of the jelly coat substance of *Echinocardium cordatum. Acta Chem. Scand., 6,* 376–384.

Vincent, W. S., and O. L. Miller (eds.), 1967. The nucleolus. Its structure and function. *National Cancer Institute Monograph 23.* U.S. Government Printing Office, Washington, D.C.

Wolpert, L., and E. H. Mercer, 1961. An electron microscope study of fertilization of the sea urchin egg, *Psammechinus miliaris. Exp. Cell Res., 22,* 45–55.

Yanagisawa, T., S. Hasegawa, and H. Mohri, 1968. The bound nucleotides of the isolated microtubules of sea urchin sperm flagella and their possible role in flagellar movement. *Exp. Cell Res., 52,* 86–100.

CHAPTER III

Fertilization and Some Associated Events

PENETRATION OF THE SPERM

It is probable that the advent of the sperm to the immediate vicinity of the sea urchin egg is a purely random event. No one to date has unearthed any viable evidence that chemotaxis is involved in the phenomenon or that the sperm is attracted to the egg in any way, although the existence of chemotaxis is often more difficult to disprove than to demonstrate in living systems. As one author puts it, chemotaxis frequently "wins by default" when its existence is in question. At the perimeter of the jelly coat the first fertilizin–antifertilizin reactions must certainly occur, most importantly on initial contact of sperm with jelly coat, but perhaps to some degree in a gradient of fertilizin molecules diffusing from the jelly coat. It is extremely difficult to assess the importance of a diffusion effect. It is from this effect that fertilizin should be expected to increase fertilizable life span, if this service is to be useful to the sperm. Once a sperm contacts the jelly coat, it requires but a few seconds to penetrate it and activate the egg. If there is no enhancement of fertilizable life span, laboratory studies suggest that a sperm has from ½ to perhaps 2 hours after being spawned before its fertilizing power is lost, depending on a variety of circumstances. The increasing of sperm motility by diffusing fertilizin has been observed frequently since first reported by F. R. Lillie in 1913. Again an increase in motility would appear to be more useful to a sperm (to increase the probability of its reaching the egg) while it is in the medium than after it has made contact with the jelly coat. Existence of egg water attests to the reality of diffusion of fertilizin from the jelly coat. There is a question, however, as to whether diffusion is rapid and extensive enough to maintain a sufficient concentration of fertilizin in the vicinity of the egg to produce these effects in the natural marine environment of the egg as opposed to laboratory glassware.

At the surface of the jelly coat, the sperm finds itself in the company of a multitude of its fellows. This aggregation of sperm on the surface of the jelly coat is held by many authorities to be the result of a trapping action, with the sperm becoming "stuck" to the jelly coat as a result of fertilizin–antifertilizin reactions. We have no certain knowledge as to what happens here, but analogies between the jelly coat and flypaper or a miring ooze are doubtless extreme. We might speculate that a more reasonable analogy might be made between the first reaction of sperm surface and jelly coat and the first reaction between molecules and the resin at the top of an ion-exchange column. These are bondings that can be broken and remade repeatedly. The idea of repeated making and breaking of bonds between fertilizin and antifertilizin during the passage of the sperm through the jelly coat may be inaccurate, but it is a useful idea in formulating theories as to the nature of the journey through the jelly coat that would include the results of findings of experiments on sperm in egg water and that would see that journey as involving more than a simple contest between flagellar motility and forces of viscous resistance in the jelly coat once initial attachment of the sperm to the jelly coat has been made.

Whatever the form of entrapment may be, the hordes of sperm may be seen by the light microscope as a thin halo outlining the jelly coat. At this point in time, the important fertilizin–antifertilizin reaction is probably a recognition reaction, the reaction that determines species specificity in fertilization. It is an appealing hypothesis that the mechanism of rejection lies in the fact that antifertilizin that is not homologous will not react with the jelly-coat fertilizin, and hence the sperm of the alien species cannot attach to the jelly coat. A varying degree, usually very small, of interspecific hybridization is usually possible, depending on the nature of the cross. There is evidence that a second stage of screening to prevent the entry of alien sperm into the egg exists at the egg surface. Tyler and Metz (1955) found that in eggs treated with trypsin, which ostensibly destroys the vitelline membrane, cross fertilizability between species is markedly increased.

Dan *et al.* (1964) have reported that the excursion of the sperm through the jelly coat requires but 2 or 3 seconds in the sea urchin *Hemicentrotus pulcherrimus* on the basis of microscopical observation. If the time is comparable in *Arbacia punctulata,* then the velocity required for the traverse of a 32 μm jelly coat is very close to the 16–17 μm/sec speed of the sperm in the seawater medium that has been reported for this species (see Harvey, 1956). One cannot rely very heavily on such figures, but there is a suggestion here that the viscosity or drag of the jelly coat is not exerting an enormous braking effect on the sperm. It is possible, however, that the sperm mitochondrion may have to increase its energy output for the sperm to maintain a given speed in one medium versus the other. Observations by early workers of protozoa swimming in the jelly coat point to the probability of its viscosity not being a severe impediment to sperm movement.

It is impossible at present to evaluate directly the status or importance of any effect on sperm motility, such as that produced by chelation of copper and zinc ions, that the jelly coat may have on the sperm as it passes through it. It is possible, however, to envision the jelly coat having an effect on the rate of movement of the sperm through successive making and breaking of bonds between fertilizin and antifertilizin, which might either facilitate progress by allowing a series of temporary attachments or moorings to give the sperm purchase in its movement or hinder progress by slowing down the sperm through repeated snagging and dragging actions. Such an effect would assume some species of fixed structural array of the fertilizin molecules, an array not excessively rigid, witness the swimming protozoa, but rigid enough to provide a stable base for sperm attachment. A definite structural organization would be expected also to orient the sperm and decrease the randomness of its movements on the way to the egg surface. Electron micrographs of the jelly coat show it to be largely electron transparent and not to have much in the way of distinct structure apart from some finely fibrous masses and large flocs of low electron density. The jelly coat, of course, has a very high degree of hydration, and its fertilizin content is probably low relative to its volume. Early light microscopy studies with vital stains showed a birefringence in the jelly coat, attributed to a lining up of the dye molecules tangentially to the surface of the egg, a phenomenon that suggests the existence of an ordered structure in the jelly coat, but which has never been interpreted satisfactorily in terms of the fundamental organization of the fertilizin molecules.

Experimental findings show that the jelly coat does indeed affect the progress of the sperm to the egg surface, but they shed little light on the nature of the mechanism, and they are mutually contradictory. Hagström (see, for example, Hagström, 1956) has been a strong proponent of the concept that the jelly coat hinders the movement of the sperm. He sees the jelly coat as a mechanism for the prevention of polyspermy in the sense of its preventing too many sperm from reaching the egg surface before the appropriate barriers for the prevention of polyspermy have been established. He found that if jelly coats are removed with care, at a pH of 5.5, there occurs an increase in the *rate* of fertilization, the number of eggs fertilized per unit time.

Tyler, by contrast, saw the jelly coat as an instrument in increasing the fertilizability of the egg. Tyler and Metz (1955) showed that when sea urchin eggs have been treated with trypsin to remove the jelly coat, an increased percentage of sperm is needed to fertilize a given percentage of eggs in a definite time period. Tyler and O'Melveny (1941) had previously removed antifertilizin from sperm and found that the sperm sustained a reduced fertilizing capacity. They cited the fact that respiration was not impaired as an indication that the sperm was uninjured by the experimental treatment. It is difficult to determine the validity of this assumption, because of the lack of data on the effect of the experimental treatment on the flagellar mechanism and on the machinery that delivers ATP to it. It has been the contention of Hagström that the techniques used by Tyler for jelly-coat removal definitely injure the egg. Basically, Hagström's findings relate jelly-coat function to the speed with which sperm can fertilize eggs, rather than to the probability that they will fertilize them. Metz (1967) attributes Hagström's finding of sperm retardation by the jelly coat to viscosity effects. In the last analysis, we do not know how strong the effect of viscosity is here nor have we evidence that bonds between fertilizin and antifertilizin can be broken and remade in the jelly. The mechanism of action of the jelly coat in affecting the rate of sperm movement is still unknown after three decades of experimentation.

As has been mentioned previously, the exact time when the stimulus for acrosome eversion occurs is not known. It is generally thought to take place when the sperm is passing through the jelly coat. Afzelius and Murray (1957) have demonstrated that the sperm in contact with the egg surface almost invariably has an everted acrosome.

Electron micrographs of gamete fusion and penetration of the sperm have been produced by Afzelius and Murray (1957), Takashima and Takashima (1960), and Franklin (1965). A composite sketch by Franklin of stages in sperm penetration assembled from observations on insemination of sea urchin eggs and oocytes, which are deemed to be generally comparable in behavior with respect to the mechanics of engulfment per se, is shown in Fig. 7. The stubby acrosomal filament pierces the vitelline membrane whereupon its tip fuses with the plasma membrane of the egg. This fusion spreads upward around the sperm, rapidly effecting a union of the two plasma membranes, even in the region of the flagellum. Membrane fusion is accompanied by a rising of egg cytoplasm around the sperm to form a fertilization cone. The sperm is engulfed—head, mitochondrion, and flagellum. There follows a dissolution of the fused membranes, leaving the organelles of the sperm in contact with egg cytoplasm. Flagellum and mitochondrion are degraded shortly after sperm entry, leaving the nucleus and the centrioles, of which only the distal centriole appears ultimately to survive. The significance of the formation of a fertilization cone is uncertain. In some species it appears that the fertilization cone forms after the sperm has been engulfed.

In normal fertilization of the mature egg, the cortical granules rupture within 20 seconds of contact of the acrosome and the egg plasma membrane, pouring their contents into the space between plasma and vitelline membranes. Elevation of the fertilization membrane begins almost immediately. The cortical reaction spreads in a wave around the egg from the point of sperm entry.

The various visible phenomena that characterize the arrival of a sperm at the surface of the egg, and some of the invisible phe-

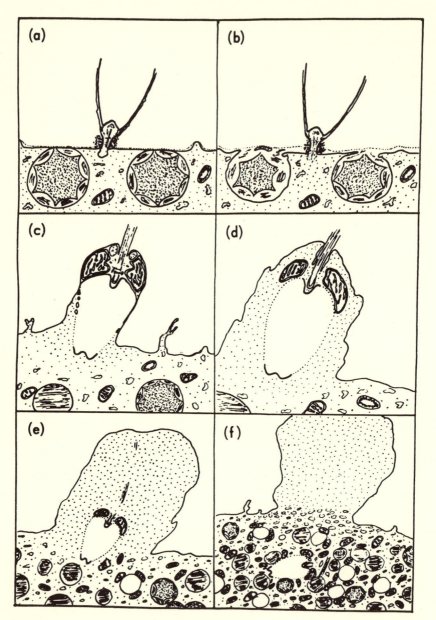

Figure 7

Diagrammatic representation of stages of gamete contact and fusion and of sperm entry. Figures (a) and (b) represent mature eggs, and figures (c) through (f) represent oocytes. See description in text. (a) Contact of the everted acrosomal tubule of the spermatozoon with the surface of the mature egg. (b) Fusion of the acrosomal process membrane with the egg plasma membrane. (c) Early stage of incorporation of the sperm nucelus into an oocyte. (d) Incorporation of the sperm middle piece and tail into an oocyte. (e) and (f) Migration of the spermatozoon into the organelle region of the oocyte cytoplasm. [From Franklin (1965); by permission.]

nomena as well, are for the most part induced by or attended by specific interactions between molecules on the sperm surface and molecules on or near the egg surface. These interactions must at the very least be associated with

> 1. Recognition reactions, probably occurring at the vitelline membrane, which offer additional safeguards against interspecific hybridization.
> 2. Lysis of the vitelline membrane if acrosomal lysins exist.
> 3. Attachment of the acrosomal tip to the plasma membrane.
> 4. Reactions implicated in the activation of the egg, which may be said to begin with the initiation of the cortical reaction and which probably is triggered as a result of the attachment of the tip of the acrosome.
> 5. The progressive lateral fusion of the acrosomal process membrane and the plasma membrane of the sperm with the plasma membrane of the egg.

An immediate question arises as to whether, apart from the obvious instance of lysins, these interactions take the form of bondings between fertilizin and antifertilizin. Tyler (see Tyler and Tyler, 1966) was of the opinion that all of them could be so explained. He envisioned the lateral fusion of the membranes as a zipper-like union of fertilizin and antifertilizin on their surfaces, which he thought to be responsible for drawing the sperm into the egg. He believed that a fertilizin–antifertilizin reaction was the stimulus to activation, and proposed that activation in artificial parthenogenesis might be explained in terms of a triggering reaction between surface fertilizin and the antifertilizin of the egg. Perlmann, whose work will be discussed below, was doubtful, on the basis of studies with antisera against the jelly coat, that the activation of the egg is triggered by fertilizin–antifertilizin reactions. The problem remains unsolved.

With the exception of the retardation of sperm by the jelly coat, if Hagström's concept be correct, and of reactions that monitor against the penetration of the egg by sperm of alien species, all the interactions between substances on the two gametes that we have considered have operated to promote the successful entry of the egg by a homologous sperm. The sea urchin egg, however, can accept but a single sperm. If more than one sperm succeeds in entering, cleavage and subsequent development are almost invariably irregular. The successful sperm gives the stimulus to activation, which sets in motion the machinery to ensure that all other sperm will be denied admission.

There is little doubt that the formation of the fertilization membrane is the principal mechanism involved in the prevention of polyspermy in the sea urchin, although it may not be the only mechanism so involved. The fertilization membrane is the result of the elevation and modification of the vitelline membrane produced by the cortical reaction. The cause for membrane elevation has not been completely established. The vitelline membrane, in some species at least, may pull away from the cell surface before the cortical granules open. This aspect of elevation is ascribed by Isaka and Aikawa (1963) to the rupture of hydrogen bonds that hold the vitelline membrane firmly bound to the egg surface. They note that several substances which are capable of breaking hydrogen bonds will initiate membrane elevation.

Many earlier workers believed the elevation to be due to properties inherent in the membrane itself, but the concept most favored in recent years holds that elevation follows from the influx of water caused by the presence of a substance (or substances) in the perivitelline space which establishes an osmotic gradient, a substance that originates in the cortical granules. It is commonly associated with the electron-transparent material of the granules. One of the foremost proponents of the osmotic theory is Hiramoto (1945, 1955a, 1955b). He has also asserted that once the membrane has elevated there exist structural elements in the perivitelline space that maintain the circumferences of the fertilization membrane and of the egg concentric to one another.

It has been shown that the vitelline membrane becomes thickened and toughened as it is converted to the fertilization membrane. This reinforcement appears to arise from the electron-dense lamellate structures of the cortical granules. Runnström (1966) has given a comprehensive discussion of the problem. The reinforcement of the membrane appears to be responsible for its effectiveness in preventing polyspermy. Tyler, Monroy, and Metz (1956) demonstrated that upon removal of the fertilization membrane, *Lytechinus* eggs can be refertilized within a time limit. Bryan (1970a) isolated what appears to be a principal constituent of the lamellate structures. He found it to be precipitable by calcium into large aggregates of tubular structures.

Some workers have reported that the fertilization membrane does not constitute the sole block to polyspermy. The membrane requires as much as 2 minutes for completion of elevation in some species. There is a latent period of perhaps 20 seconds between the moment of sperm attachment to the egg surface and the beginning of elevation. It has been proposed that during this latent period a rapid block to polyspermy, a block of unknown nature, is established. Rothschild and Swann (1951a, 1951b, 1952) have studied the problem. One of their approaches involved subjecting sperm and eggs to conditions, such as an increase in sperm concentration, that would increase the probability of polyspermy, and then determining the number of polyspermic eggs as a function of time, beginning with the moment of initial exposure of eggs to sperm. Their results suggest a rapidly established partial block occurring in the first few seconds of the latent period discussed above, followed by a complete block established after about 60 seconds and occurring during the time of membrane elevation.

Very recently, Tegner and Epel (1973) have reported that during a period of 25 seconds between insemination and the inception of the cortical reaction many sperm attach themselves to the vitelline membrane of the egg. From the moment of initiation of the cortical reaction, there occurs a progressive detachment of the excess sperm, probably caused by the release of a protease by the cortical granules. These workers have photographed this attachment–detachment phenomenon through the use of the scanning electron microscope. Their micrographs also reveal a "dense array of regularly spaced projections" on the outer surface of the vitelline membrane. Such projections may be presumed to be impressions of the microvilli of the egg.

The cortical reaction, once elicited by the activation of the egg, does not limit its contribution to development to the prevention of polyspermy, but produces a structure that plays a key role in morphogenesis. This is the hyaline layer, which is derived from the electron-dense hyaline material of the cortical granules. Microvilli of the plasma membrane extend into this layer. The hyaline layer is an elastic layer that holds the blastomeres together. It is probably responsible to a large degree for the maintaining of the spherical shape of the blastula, and certainly features importantly in invagination at gastrula. It maintains its integrity when the fertilization membrane is broken down by the hatching enzyme during blastula. There is little evidence to show that it participates in fertilization under normal physiological conditions. It has been demonstrated to be able to exclude supernumerary sperm, that is, to participate in the prevention of refertilization, when the fertilization membrane has been removed. This phenomenon has been demonstrated by Hagström and Hagström (1954) and by Nakano (1956). Tyler and Tyler (1966) have suggested that the time span mentioned above, during which refertilization in *Lytechinus* is possible, represents a period before the hyaline layer has developed to the extent of occluding sperm receptors on the egg. Following activation the fertilization membrane is not indispensable for development, and it is conceivable that fertilization membranes may be lost on occasion in nature. There appears, however, no justification for the idea that protecting eggs which have lost their fertilization membrane from being refertilized is an important or even natural function of the hyaline layer.

Somewhat more is known about the molecular aspects of the hyaline layer than about those of other derivatives of the cortical granules. The contents of the cortical granules can be isolated, as can the material of the hyaline layer, by the fractionation of homogenates. Cortical granule material can also be isolated by activating the egg and breaking down the vitelline membrane as it elevates, so that the cortical granules discharge their contents into the medium. Hyaline material has been isolated by Kane and Hersh (1959), Yazaki (1968), Vacquier (1969), Bryan (1970b), Stephens and Kane (1970), and others.

The principal component of the hyaline layer and a major component of the cortical granules is a calcium-precipitable protein originally isolated by Kane and Hersh in 1959. Yazaki (1968) found by immunofluorescence techniques that this protein is located in the cortical granules before fertilization and in the hyaline layer after fertilization. Stephens and Kane (1970) found it to be extremely high in acidic amino acid content and almost completely lacking in basic amino acids. Virtually all the cysteine is present in the disulfide form. The minimal subunit molecular weight appears to be in the magnitude of 100,000. Bryan (1970b) found the S_{20w} for this protein to be 9.5. Calcium causes the protein to gel and become birefringent.

ACTIVATION OF THE EGG

The activation of the egg is a difficult phenomenon to describe and evaluate, principally because of the problem of distinguishing among the processes that are a part of it, the processes that are a consequence of it, and the processes that accompany it or immediately precede it but are independent of it.

The stimulus to activation in normal fertilization is purported to be the surface interactions that occur between the gametes when the tip of the acrosome touches the plasma membrane of the egg. Colwin and Colwin (1967) have noted that it is the substance of the acrosomal granule, rather than the acrosome process, that makes the contact, and that the substance which the sperm contributes to the interaction should be found in the granule.

One possible avenue of investigation in viewing activation against the total process of fertilization is the study of the insemination of oocytes, a situation in which the male gamete is in a state of preparedness for fertilization, and the female gamete is not. Here the process of sperm entry is visibly similar to that seen in the mature unfertilized egg, showing that the gamete surface components which promote penetration of the jelly coat and entry into the egg are functional. Superficially, this fact would appear to separate the activity of these components from that of those associated with activation. Activation does not occur in any of its visible forms. There is no membrane elevation nor block to polyspermy. Polyspermy is normally seen in inseminated oocytes, a fact that increases the probability of obtaining electron micrographs showing the sperm within the egg. The nuclei will not unite; the sperm will not form asters; and development will not proceed. There is a basic difficulty here in distinguishing between the failure of sperm–egg interactions to occur and a general state of cytoplasmic immaturity as the cause of the absence of activation. It is equivocal as to whether the interactions have or have not occurred. One species of sperm–egg interaction in inseminated oocyte shows activity below the level of that seen in normal fertilization of the mature unfertilized egg. Franklin (1965) found that oocytes of *Arbacia punctulata* inseminated by sperm from the sand dollar *Mellita quinquiesperforata* allow an abnormally high amount of sperm entry relative to the amount of crossing obtainable with the mature unfertilized egg, where failure to hybridize may be considered a manifestation of the failure of sperm to enter. One can surmise that in these oocytes the site of gamete interaction which is operating below par in its effectiveness in maintaining species specificity is the one located at the surface of the egg as opposed to the surface of the jelly coat. It remains to be demonstrated however, that in the insemination of oocytes there is not to be found a situation in which the signal for activation is given, but the system cannot respond. A fertilization membrane, for example, cannot be raised because the cortical granules are scattered throughout the cytoplasm and may not be in a state of full maturity.

Hiramoto (1962) injected a live sperm into an unfertilized egg. Its flagellum was seen to make spasmodic movements as has been observed in normal fertilization, but nothing happened. There was no activation, and it is reasonable to assume that the failure was due to the lack of interaction between specific substances on the gametes which normally give the stimulus at the surface of the egg for activation to occur. When the egg was fertilized, however, the injected sperm formed an aster in a high percentage of the experiments performed, and the cleavage pattern took on the irregularity seen when polyspermy occurs. Comparable results were obtained when a sperm was injected into a newly fertilized egg. It is to be supposed that the activation of the centriole of the sperm occurs concomitantly to the sequence of reactions which ensues from the gamete interaction at the surface of the egg that is responsible for activation of the egg, but that the activation of the centriole does not have the prerequisite that its sperm participate in such interaction at the surface.

Fertilization is a complex of stimuli and responses. The task still remains of determining which stimulus–response relationships and how many stimulus–response relationships characterize activation. The problem also remains of finding the dividing line between the phases of activation and the initial events in embryogenesis.

Artificial parthenogenesis elicits activation in the absence of gamete interaction. Its mechanisms are entirely unknown, and it has not been studied in recent years. The agents that will produce it are legion. They include acids, bases, tissue extracts, alkaloids, proteins, heat, cold, ultraviolet irradiation, X-rays, treatment with hypertonic solutions, shaking, pricking, organic solvents, detergents, and so on. It is difficult to understand what such agents have in common—if there need be a common feature—to produce activation. Many of them have the potential of altering the permeability of the plasma membrane of the egg by one means or another. Harvey (1956) has reviewed the work on artificial parthenogenesis up to that date. For 40 years, the most widely used technique for activating sea urchin eggs and half-eggs has been treatment with butyric acid followed by treatment with hypertonic seawater.

The immunological experiments of the Perlmann and the Baxandall groups (see Perlmann, 1956, 1957; Perlmann and Perlmann, 1957; Baxandall et al., 1964a, 1964b) have cast some light on the nature and possible location of some of the specific substances that may be involved in activation reactions. Some of these experiments have revealed antigens, surface antigens in particular, which when reacted against antisera prepared against jelly-free egg homogenates cause activation of the egg or some aspect of it. Two or three of these antigens merit particular consideration. One antigen (termed the A antigen), located primarily on the surface of the egg, was reported to react with the antiserum to produce activation as manifested by the formation of a fertilization membrane, the activation of the nucleus, monaster formation, and sometimes cell division. The reaction was dependent to a degree on the state of maturity of the egg, and results could be improved by the removal of the jelly coat. This antigen was found to be a mucopolysaccharide with glucose and mannose as sugar moieties. Another antigen (the C antigen), believed to be a protein, caused abortive membrane elevations and a series of abnormal cortical changes, indicating an association with the cortical reaction. A third antigen (the F antigen) showed a disposition to inhibit the rate of fertilization severely. It is difficult to pinpoint a specific role for this antigen in fertilization, and it could well represent a group of antigens. Immunological tests showed that the A, C, and F antigens bear no identity to jelly-coat fertilizin.

These experiments tend to associate different aspects of activation with separate receptor substances in the egg, to separate, for example, the master stimulus to activation from the stimulus to the cortical reaction. Considerable caution should be exercised in accepting the conclusions from these experiments, however. It is not always patent that an antibody is actually reacting with the actual egg receptor that is involved in a particular sperm–egg interaction. Suppose one were to asssume that a decrease in fertilization caused by an antibody is being caused by a sperm being denied access to receptor sites on the egg. The possibility exists that the interference with sperm–egg binding is due not to the reaction of the antibody with the receptor site, but to the fact that the antibody (bound to some unknown antigenic group) is merely serving as a physical barrier between the sperm and the receptor site. It is not, in other words, completely safe to assume that antibodies are actually identifying participants in gamete interactions.

Baxandall et al. (1964a, 1964b) attempted to locate the sites of the A, C, and F antigens by electron microscopy with the use of ferritin-labeled antisera. The label was seen in a thin layer lying just outside the egg plasma membrane, with very little antigen activity being associated with the plasma membrane itself. Baxandall was able to produce very high percentages of eggs activated by antisera. Other workers (see, for example, Tyler, 1959, 1963) have been unsuccessful in attempts to produce antisera that would induce activation of the egg, at least to the extent of leading to cell division.

Activation reactions are assessed with two basic responsibilities that are not completely separable. The first is to initiate the processes of embryogenesis, to set in motion the activities that will lead to the union of the pronuclei, the generation of the mitotic figure, and the initiation of cleavage. The second is to accelerate to a high level of activity the synthesis and metabolic reactions that have been severely depressed in the unfertilized egg. The events and/or sequelae of activation manifest themselves by membrane elevation, changes in permeability to ions and to small organic molecules, including nucleotides and amino acids, ion movements that generate electrical potential, changes in respiratory metabolism, changes in pH, activation of synthesis of proteins and nucleic acids, possibly the activation of certain enzymes, and changes in activity of some cytoplasmic organelles. Some of these processes will be discussed next.

CHANGES IN RESPIRATORY METABOLISM ASSOCIATED WITH FERTILIZATION

Respiratory activity probably has been studied more extensively in sea urchin eggs and embryos than in other developmental systems. Respirometry studies were being performed on sea urchin eggs at the beginning of the century. As the various cycles of respiratory metabolism were discovered, these too were given considerable study with regard to their activity in sea urchin embryogenesis. The changes in respiratory activity associated with fertilization have attracted particular interest.

In the unfertilized egg, metabolism in general is at a low ebb. Cleland and Rothschild (1952a, 1952b) and Ycas (1954) have shown that most of the enzymes of the respiratory cycles are present in the unfertilized egg, but it is apparent that they are under inhibition. Inhibition of respiratory metabolism does not imply that a supply of ATP (or of other molecules containing high-energy phosphate) is lacking in the egg. Upon fertilization, respiratory activity and certain synthetic activities are "turned on" or released from inhibition. It is to be assumed that the new respiratory activity will ultimately provide energy for the new synthetic activity. It is not proper to assume within the limits of present knowledge that the turning on of respiratory activity is *responsible* for the turning on of synthetic activity or that in the unfertilized egg the depression of respiratory activity is directly responsible for the depression of synthetic activity. MacKintosh and Bell (1969) demonstrated that the availability of ATP and GTP for synthesis in vivo does not change upon fertilization.

Studies in respirometry, including polarographic analysis of oxygen consumption, made during fertilization by Laser and Rothschild (1939), Ohnishi and Sugiyama (1963), and others show that there is a transitory burst of oxygen consumption within a few seconds after sperm entry. The duration of this activity is usually not more than 2 or 3 minutes, whereafter the rate of oxygen consumption drops to a value just slightly higher than that of the unfertilized egg. It then starts to rise again at a much slower rate of climb. This rise continues until gastrula. The transitory increase in oxygen consumption occurs during the period in which the cortical reaction, membrane elevation, and other surface changes are taking place. Whether it is associated with these changes is not known. This transitory metabolic effect is possibly not unique to the sea urchin, but it is not seen in animal species in general.

Various theories as to the cause of the inhibition of respiratory activity in the unfertilized egg have been proposed. One theory holds that the block may be due to the lack of availability of phosphate acceptors such as ADP. Monroy (1965) quotes Rossi et al. as finding that the concentration of ATP in the unfertilized egg is high relative to that of ADP, which is quite low, whereas shortly after fertilization the ratio of ATP to ADP returns to a value consistent with those of actively growing cells in general.

A somewhat more attractive theory proposes that the block to respiration in unfertilized eggs is caused by the scarcity of hexose phosphates. The activation process is purported to trigger phosphorylase activity, which in producing glycogenolysis relieves the shortage. Aketa et al. (1964) have found that glucose-6-phosphate is in low supply in the unfertilized egg and begins to increase rapidly after fertilization. Örström and Lindberg (1940) and Monroy and Vitorelli (1960) have shown that moments after fertilization the breakdown of a polysaccharide occurs. If this theory is valid, it might well be of interest to explore the question of possible similarities between sperm –egg interactions and the behavior of many hormones that activate a cyclase to produce 3,5-AMP, which, in turn, activates a kinase, which turns on phosphorylase activity, resulting in the breakdown of glycogen. It might be noted that Castañeda and Tyler (1968) identified adenyl cyclase in plasma membrane preparations from sea urchin eggs. The activity of the enzyme appeared to increase after fertilization. If the enzyme is involved in changes in respiratory metabolism after fertilization, it is of interest to know the extent to which it is involved.

Cyclic AMP is quite versatile. It is able, for instance, to facilitate protein biosynthesis. Protein biosynthesis is indeed facilitated following fertilization. It must be borne in mind that there *are* hormones present in the egg. The general relationship between sperm–egg interactions, hormone activity, and the activity of 3,5-AMP is well worth exploring in the sea urchin embryo.

Some attempts to explore the role of cyclic AMP in sea urchin development have been made. In 1971, Hand tried to activate sea urchin eggs with it but was unsuccessful. Bergami et al. (1968) studied glycogen phosphorylase activity in the unfertilized and fertilized egg. The enzyme was found largely in the active form, and significant quantitative differences were not found in its activity between unfertilized eggs and embryos. In the unfertilized egg it was found, however, that some enzyme appears to exist in an inactive form bound to particulate material of undetermined nature. Activation of the egg releases the enzyme into the cell-sap fraction from differential centrifugation. Cyclic AMP does appear to increase the activity of the enzyme (presumably through the kinase), but the process is pH sensitive and appears not to be effective above a pH of 6.5, which is slightly below the pH of the unfertilized egg. One might speculate that the transitory drop in pH at fertilization may stimulate some phosphorylase activity, but the problem should be investigated further.

The pentose phosphate pathway is generally recognized as playing an extremely important role in the respiration of sea urchin embryos. There is evidence that the activity of this pathway is blocked in the unfertilized egg. Krane and Crane (1960) and Epel (1964a, 1964b) have shown that reduced NADP, the production of which is a characteristic of the pathway, begins to increase markedly in amount at fertilization, even before the transitory increase in oxygen consumption. Isono (1963), Isono et al. (1963), Bäckström (1963), and Ishihara (1957) have shown increases in activity of such enzymes of the pentose phosphate pathway as glucose-6-phosphate dehydrogenase, 6-phosphogluconate dehydrogenase, and aldolase immediately upon fertilization.

Aketa (1957) reported that there is some anaerobic activity in *Hemicentrotus pulcherrimus* during the first 2 to 5 minutes after fertilization. Ten to twenty minutes later, the lactic acid formed is apparently oxidized. Several other workers have failed to repeat this finding, but there is a distinct possibility that species differences are involved here.

OTHER PHENOMENA
ASSOCIATED WITH FERTILIZATION

A transient acid production is found to occur moments after fertilization in sea urchin embryos. It does not appear to be attributable to the elaboration of lactic acid (see Rothschild, 1958). Mehl and Swann (1961) have reported that this acid production can probably be explained by two phenomena: (1) an ion-exchange reaction between groups of molecules within the egg and the seawater, and (2) the evolution of a strong acid. Aketa (1961a, 1961b, 1962, 1963) has reported that the strong acid involved is sulfuric acid, possibly split off from a mucopolysaccharide or mucopolysaccharides. One might speculate that such splitting may occur in transformations of mucopolysaccharide molecules during the cortical reaction, but there is no evidence to reinforce this speculation. Actually the cortex of the egg is rich in mucopolysaccharides and glycoproteins, which could be involved in a variety of reactions at fertilization.

Certainly one of the most important aspects of activation is the switching on of the synthesis of DNA, RNA, and proteins. The triggering of these syntheses is a subject that has excited intense interest and is currently the focus for an enormous amount of experimentation, which will be the subject of subsequent discussions. DNA synthesis is associated with the mitotic cycle, and its inception subsequent to development heralds the initiation of the first cleavage. Shifts in the activity of the deoxyribonucleotide pools are triggered as a prelude to this DNA synthesis. The studies of Scarano (1958) and Scarano and Maggio (1959a, 1959b) reveal that enzymes involved with the metabolism of dUMP and dCMP are particularly active at this time. Protein synthesis, occurring on preexisting maternal message, may start almost immediately upon activation. The question of the timing of the first RNA synthesis (m-RNA) is still somewhat controversial, but it follows quickly on the heels of activation. Definite changes occur among the proteins of the egg upon sperm entry. Mirsky (1936), for instance, noted changes in solubility of certain proteins in $1M$ KCl. Other workers (see, for example, Monroy, 1950; Monroy and Monroy-Oddo, 1951; D'Amelio, 1955) have cited alterations in the electrophoretic mobility of proteins or in their sensitivity to the action of trypsin. In a very important series of papers, Lundblad (see, for example, Lundblad, 1950, 1952, 1954) demonstrated that there is an increase in proteolytic activity in the sea urchin egg upon fertilization. This finding provided a beachhead for a series of studies by later workers on mechanisms of triggering biosynthetic activity. Of particular interest among these later papers is a report by Mano (1966) of the activation of a protease at fertilization, which he speculated might be responsible for releasing maternal m-RNA from a complex with protein that, in the unfertilized egg, had prevented its being translated. These later studies will be discussed elsewhere. Krischer and Chambers in 1970 reexamined the problem of activation of proteases at fertilization. They reported that they could find no change in either protease activity or distribution of proteases between unfertilized and newly fertilized eggs.

Upon activation of the egg, the cell membrane undergoes drastic alterations in its permeability to small organic molecules, important among which are precursors to protein and nucleic acid synthesis. The problem of permeability to such molecules will be considered in a later chapter under the heading of relationships between uptake and incorporation in synthesis of macromolecules during early development. There also occur changes in the electrical potential across the membrane and modifications in the intracellular concentration of ions. The literature on the subject of membrane permeability to ions and of accumulation of ions in the egg is extensive and cannot be reviewed here. It is of interest that Tyler and Monroy (1959) were able to show that the ability of the unfertilized egg to accumulate radioactive potassium ions is altered upon fertilization, when an increased amount of potassium ion becomes exchangeable with the outside medium. Monroy (1965) has pointed out that this alteration could reflect a transition of the ions from a bound to a free state or a change in intracellular compartments. There appear to be also significant modifications of intracellular concentration of magnesium and calcium ions.

If fluctuations in the amount of binding of ions or redistribution of ions within the cell occur subsequent to activation of the egg, it is difficult to appraise the meaning of such changes. It is obvious that ions can be called upon to play roles as cofactors or can be released from such roles. It is known that certain ions may be required to maintain some particulates or organelles in an active or an inactive state. Ribosomes, for example, require magnesium ions and possibly calcium ions to remain intact. The exact extent to which the activity of ions may affect synthesis within the egg remains to be determined.

REFERENCES

Afzelius, B. A., and A. Murray, 1957. The acrosomal reaction of spermatozoa during fertilization or treatment with egg water. *Exp. Cell Res., 12,* 325–337.

Aketa, K., 1957. Quantitative analyses of lactic acid and related compounds in the sea urchin egg at the time of fertilization. *Embryologia, 3,* 267–268.

Aketa, K., 1961a. Studies on the production of the fertilization acid in sea urchin eggs. I. Acid production at fertilization and activation and the effect of some metabolic inhibitors. *Embryologia, 5,* 397–405.

Aketa, K., 1961b. Studies on the production of the fertilization acid in sea urchin eggs. II. Experimental analysis of the production mechanism. *Embryologia, 5,* 406–412.

Aketa, K., 1962. Studies on the production of the fertilization acid in sea urchin eggs. III. Cytochemical exploration of the possible role of mucopolysaccharide compounds in the acid production. *Embryologia, 7,* 223–227.

Aketa, K., 1963. Studies on the acid production at fertilization of sea urchin eggs. *Exp. Cell Res., 30,* 93–97.

Aketa, K., R. Bianchetti, E. Marre, and A. Monroy, 1964. Hexose monophosphate levels as a limiting factor for respiration in unfertilized sea urchin eggs. *Biochim. Biophys. Acta, 86,* 211–215.

Bäckström, S., 1963. 6-Phosphogluconate dehydrogenase in sea urchin embryos. *Exp. Cell Res., 32,* 566–569.

Baxandall, J., P. Perlmann, and B. A. Afzelius, 1964a. Immuno-electron microscope analysis of the surface layers of the unfertilized sea urchin egg. II. Localization of surface antigens. *J. Cell Biol., 23,* 629–650.

Baxandall, J., P. Perlmann, and B. A. Afzelius, 1964b. Immuno-electron microscope analysis of the unfertilized sea urchin egg. I. Effects of the antisera on the cell ultrastructure. *J. Cell Biol., 23,* 609–628.

Bergami, M., T. E. Mansour, and E. Scarano, 1968. Properties of glycogen phosphorylase before and after fertilization in the sea urchin egg. *Exp. Cell Res., 49,* 650–655.

Bryan, J., 1970a. On the reconstruction of the crystalline components of the sea urchin fertilization membrane. *J. Cell Biol., 45,* 606–614.

Bryan, J., 1970b. The isolation of a major structural element of the sea urchin fertilization membrane. *J. Cell Biol., 44,* 635–645.

Castañeda, M., and A. Tyler, 1968. Adenyl cyclase in plasma membrane preparations of sea urchin eggs and its increase in activity after fertilization. *Biochem. Biophys. Res. Commun., 33,* 782–787.

Cleland, K. W., and Lord Rothschild, 1952a. The metabolism of the sea urchin egg. Anaerobic breakdown of carbohydrate. *J. Exp. Biol., 29,* 285–294.

Cleland, K. W., and Lord Rothschild, 1952b. The metabolism of the sea urchin egg. Oxidation of carbohydrate. *J. Exp. Biol., 29,* 416–428.

Colwin, L. H., and A. L. Colwin, 1967. Membrane fusion in relation to sperm-egg association. In C. B. Metz and A. Monroy (eds.), *Fertilization.* Vol. I. Academic Press, Inc., New York, 295–367.

D'Amelio, V., 1955. Trypsin sensitivity of some proteins of the sea urchin egg before and after fertilization. *Experientia, 11*, 443.

Dan, J. C., Y. Ohori, and H. Kushida, 1964. Studies on the acrosome reaction. VII. Formation of the acrosomal process in sea urchin spermatozoa. *J. Ultrastruct. Res., 11*, 508–524.

Epel, D., 1964a. A primary metabolic change of fertilization. Interconversion of pyridine nucleotides. *Biochem. Biophys. Res. Commun., 17*, 62–68.

Epel, D., 1964b. Simultaneous measurement of TPNH formation and respiration following fertilization of the sea urchin. *Biochem. Biophys. Res. Commun., 17*, 69–73.

Franklin, L. E., 1965. Morphology of gamete membrane fusion and of sperm entry into oocytes of the sea urchin. *J. Cell Biol., 25*, 81–100.

Hagström, B. E., 1956. The effect of removal of the jelly coat on fertilization in sea urchins. *Exp. Cell Res., 10*, 740–743.

Hagström, B. E., and B. Hagström, 1954. Refertilization of the sea urchin egg. *Exp. Cell Res., 6*, 491–496.

Hand, G. S., Jr., 1971. Stimulation of protein synthesis in unfertilized sea urchin and sand dollar eggs treated with trypsin. *Exp. Cell Res., 64*, 204–208.

Harvey, E. B., 1956. *The American Arbacia and Other Sea Urchins.* Princeton University Press, Princeton, N.J.

Hiramoto, Y., 1954. Nature of the perivitelline space in sea urchin eggs. *Jap. J. Zool., 11*, 227–243.

Hiramoto, Y., 1955a. Nature of the perivitelline space in sea urchin eggs. II. *Jap. J. Zool., 11*, 333–334.

Hiramoto, Y., 1955b. Nature of the perivitelline space in sea urchin eggs. III. On the mechanism of membrane elevation. *Annot. Zool. Jap., 28*, 183–193.

Hiramoto, Y., 1962. Microinjection of the live spermatozoa into sea urchin eggs. *Exp. Cell Res., 27*, 416–426.

Isaka, S., and T. Aikawa, 1963. Separation of the fertilization membrane in *Urechis* and sea urchin eggs as a phenomenon caused by breakage of hydrogen bonds. II. Action of carboxylic acids. *Exp. Cell Res., 30*, 150–159.

Ishihara, K., 1957. Release and activation of aldolase at fertilization in sea urchin eggs. *J. Fac. Sci., Univ. Tokyo Sect. IV, 8*, 71–93.

Isono, N., 1963. Carbohydrate metabolism in sea urchin eggs. IV. Intracellular localization of enzymes of the pentose phosphate cycle in fertilized and unfertilized eggs. *J. Fac. Sci., Univ. Tokyo Sect. IV, 10*, 37–53.

Isono, N., A. Tsusaka, and E. Nakano, 1963. Glucose-6-phosphate dehydrogenase in sea urchins. *J. Fac. Sci., Univ. Tokyo Sect. IV, 10*, 55–66.

Kane, R. E., and R. T. Hersh, 1959. The isolation and preliminary characterization of a major soluble protein of the sea urchin egg. *Exp. Cell Res., 16*, 59–69.

Krane, S. M., and R. K. Crane, 1960. Changes in the level of triphosphopyridine nucleotide (TPN) in marine eggs subsequent to fertilization. *Biochim. Biophys. Acta, 43*, 369–373.

Krischer, K. N., and E. L. Chambers, 1970. Proteolytic enzymes in sea urchin eggs. Characterization, localization, and activity, before and after fertilization. *J. Cell Biol., 76*, 23–35.

Laser, H., and Lord Rothschild, 1939. The metabolism of eggs of *Psammechinus miliaris* during fertilization. *Proc. Roy. Soc.* (London) *Ser. B, 126*, 539–557.

Lillie, F. R., 1913. Studies in fertilization. V. The behavior of the spermatozoa of *Nereis* and *Arbacia* with special reference to egg extractives. *J. Exp. Zool., 14*, 515–574.

Lundblad, G., 1950. Proteolytic activity in sea urchin gametes. *Exp. Cell Res., 1,* 264–271.

Lundblad, G., 1952. Proteolytic activity in sea urchin gametes. II. Activity of extracts and homogenates of eggs subjected to different treatments. *Arkiv. Kemi., 4,* 537–565.

Lundblad, G., 1954. Proteolytic activity in sea urchin gametes. III. Further investigation on the proteolytic enzymes of the egg. *Arkiv. Kemi., 7,* 127–157.

MacKintosh, F. R., and E. Bell, 1969. Labeling of nucleotide pools in the sea urchin. *Exp. Cell Res., 57,* 71–73.

Mano, Y., 1966. Role of a trypsin-like protease in "informosomes" in a trigger mechanism of activation of protein synthesis by fertilization in sea urchin eggs. *Biochem. Biophys. Res. Commun., 25,* 216–221.

Mehl, J. W., and M. M. Swann, 1961. Acid and base production in the sea urchin. *Exp. Cell Res., 22,* 233–245.

Metz, C. B., 1967. Gamete surface components and their role in fertilization. In C. B. Metz and A. Monroy (eds.), *Fertilization,* Vol. I. Academic Press, Inc., New York, 163–236.

Mirsky, A. E., 1936. Protein coagulation as a result of fertilization. *Science, 84,* 333–334.

Monroy, A., 1950. A preliminary electrophoretic analysis of proteins of protein fractions in sea urchin eggs and their changes on fertilization. *Exp. Cell Res., 1,* 92–104.

Monroy, A., 1965. *Chemistry and Physiology of Fertilization.* Holt, Rinehart and Winston, Inc., New York.

Monroy, A., and A. Monroy-Oddo, 1951. Solubility changes of proteins in sea urchin eggs upon fertilization. *J. Gen. Physiol., 35,* 245–253.

Monroy, A., and M. L. Vittorelli, 1960. A glycoprotein of the sea urchin egg and its changes following fertilization. *Experientia, 16,* 56–57.

Nakano, E., 1956. Physiological studies on the refertilization of the sea urchin egg. *Embryologia, 3,* 139–165.

Ohnishi, T., and M. Sugiyama, 1963. Polarographic studies of oxygen uptake of sea urchin eggs. *Embryologia, 8,* 367–384.

Örström, A., and O. Lindberg, 1940. Über den Kohlenhydratstoffwechsel des Seeigeleies. *Enzymologia, 8,* 367–384.

Perlmann, P., 1956. Response of unfertilized sea urchin eggs to antiserum. *Exp. Cell Res., 10,* 324–353.

Perlmann, P., 1957. Analysis of the surface structure of the sea urchin egg by means of antibodies. I. Comparative study of the effects of various antisera. *Exp. Cell Res., 13,* 365–390.

Perlmann, P., and H. Perlmann, 1957. Analysis of the surface structure of the sea urchin egg by means of antibodies. III. The C- and F-antigens. *Exp. Cell Res., 13,* 475–487.

Rothschild, Lord, 1958. Acid production after fertilization of sea urchin eggs. A re-examination of the lactic acid hypothesis. *J. Exp. Biol., 35,* 843–849.

Rothschild, Lord, and M. M. Swann, 1951a. The conduction time of a block to polyspermy in the sea urchin egg. *Exp. Cell Res., 2,* 137.

Rothschild, Lord, and M. M. Swann, 1951b. The fertilization reaction in the sea urchin. The probability of a successful sperm-egg collision. *J. Exp. Biol., 28,* 403–416.

Rothschild, Lord, and M. M. Swann, 1952. The fertilization reaction in the sea urchin. The block to polyspermy. *J. Exp. Biol.*, *29*, 469–483.

Runnström, J., 1966. The vitelline membrane and cortical particles in sea urchin eggs and their function in maturation and fertilization. *Advances in Morphogenesis*, Vol. 5. Academic Press, Inc., New York, 221–235.

Scarano, E., 1958. 5'-Deoxycytidylic acid deaminase. Enzymic production of 5'-deoxyuridylic acid. *Biochim. Biophys. Acta*, *29*, 459–460.

Scarano, E., and R. Maggio, 1959a. The enzymatic deamination of 5'-deoxycytidylic and of 5-methyl-5'-deoxycytidylic acid in the developing sea urchin embryo. *Exp. Cell Res.*, *18*, 333–346.

Scarano, E., and R. Maggio, 1959b. Enzymatic deamination of 5-methyldeoxycytidylic acid to thymidylic acid. *Arch. Biochem. Biophys.*, *84*, 22–31.

Stephens, R. E., and R. E. Kane, 1970. Some properties of hyalin, the calcium-insoluble protein of the hyaline layer. *J. Cell Biol.*, *44*, 611–617.

Takashima, R., and Y. Takashima, 1960. Electron microscopical observations on the fertilization phenomenon of sea urchin with special reference to the acrosomal filament. *Tokushima J. Exp. Med.*, *6*, 334–340.

Tegner, M. J., and D. Epel, 1973. Sea urchin sperm-egg interactions studied with the scanning electron microscope. *Science*, *179*, 685–688.

Tyler, A., 1959. Some immunobiological experiments on the fertilization and early development in sea urchins. *Exp. Cell Res., Suppl. 7*, 183–189.

Tyler, A., 1963. The manipulation of macromolecular substances during fertilization and early development of animal eggs. *Amer. Zool.*, *3*, 109–126.

Tyler, A., and C. B. Metz, 1955. Effects of fertilizin treatment of sperm and trypsin treatment of eggs on homologous and cross-fertilization in sea urchins. *Pubbl. Staz. Zool. Napoli*, *27*, 128–145.

Tyler, A., and A. Monroy, 1959. Changes in the rate of transfer of potassium across the membrane upon fertilization of eggs of *Arbacia punctulata*. *J. Exp. Zool.*, *142*, 675–690.

Tyler, A., A. Monroy, and C. B. Metz, 1956. Fertilization of fertilized sea urchin eggs. *Biol. Bull. Mar. Biol. Lab., Woods Hole, 110*, 184–195.

Tyler, A., and K. O'Melveny, 1941. The role of antifertilizin in the fertilization of sea urchin eggs. *Biol. Bull. Mar. Biol. Lab., Woods Hole, 81*, 364–374.

Tyler, A., and B. S. Tyler, 1966. Physiology of fertilization and early development. In R. A. Boolootian (ed.), *Physiology of the Echinodermata*. John Wiley & Sons, Inc., (Interscience Division), New York, 683–747.

Vacquier, V. D., 1969. The isolation and preliminary analysis of the hyaline layer of sea urchin eggs. *Exp. Cell Res.*, *54*, 140–142.

Yazaki, I., 1968. Immunological analysis of the calcium precipitable protein of sea urchin eggs. *Embryologia*, *10*, 131–141.

Ycas, M., 1954. The respiratory and glycolytic enzymes of sea urchin eggs. *J. Exp. Biol.*, *31*, 208–217.

CHAPTER IV

Cleavage and Associated Phenomena

UNION OF THE PRONUCLEI

The central fact of the cleavage stage is cell division, division so rapid as to be able to have produced a thousand cells by 8 hours after fertilization in the sea urchin embryo. The central fact of cell division is DNA replication and the equal distribution of genetic information between the two daughter cells. All this begins after fertilization with the union of two haploid pronuclei to form a diploid nucleus.

The mechanisms that cause the pronuclei to unite in the sea urchin egg have excited little interest in the last three decades. Rothschild (1956) and Allen (1958) have reviewed the problem very briefly. The movement of the male pronucleus and the formation of the sperm aster are purported to depend on a successful cortical reaction, but the phenomena responsible for this dependence are not known. The egg and the sperm have no fixed orientation with respect to one another when the process of rendezvous begins. The sperm may penetrate the egg at any point on its surface and the egg pronucleus has no determined location in the cytoplasm. They meet to fuse at the approximate center of the egg. The early cytologists described the path of the male pronucleus toward the center of the egg as curved, the curve being the resultant of two separate paths, a penetration path at right angles to the surface of the egg and a copulation path, which causes the male pronucleus to veer toward the female pronucleus. The studies of Chambers (1939) led him to the conclusion that the concept of the copulation path was erroneous and that the sperm travels straight along the line of a radius of the egg to the center. The propulsive force is thought to be the elongation of the rays of the developing aster pushing against the inside surface of the egg, although some workers have described protoplasmic streaming in association with the movement of the male pronucleus in other animal types.

The female pronucleus gives every indication of being attracted to the male pronucleus as the latter moves on its path to the center of the egg. Chambers noted an instance of a female pronucleus, originally located at the center of the egg, moving away from that position toward the male pronucleus. The path taken by the female pronucleus depends on its original position at the time of sperm entry. The nature of the attractive force, as well as that of the force propelling the female pronucleus, is unknown. When the female pronucleus contacts the sperm aster, it moves toward the male pronucleus along a radius of the circle formed by the perimeter of the aster. Even when eggs are activated parthenogenetically, there is a centering of the female pronucleus. The pronuclei may fuse before centering is complete in normal fertilization. The pronuclei swell prior to fusion. Swelling is even noted in the pronucleus in artificial parthenogenesis. After the pronuclei have united, the rays of the aster spread through the egg to produce what is known as the *monaster stage*. The astral rays soon vanish, and the centrioles divide, with the daughter centrioles assuming polar positions with respect to the nucleus. A curved disk is seen extending across the top of the nucleus, possibly the first sign of condensation of the spindle. This configuration characterizes the *streak stage*. The asters reappear (probably their disappearance should be regarded as a state of becoming less conspicuous under light microscopy rather than a going out of existence), and a full-blown spindle develops. The nucleus undergoes an enormous enlargement followed by the rupture and dissolution of the nuclear membrane. Mitosis thereupon proceeds.

MITOTIC APPARATUS

The term *mitotic apparatus* is applied to an isolable structure that participates in the distribution of chromosomes between daughter cells in the process of cell division. The term is applied to an array, which really includes three distinct structures: the centrioles, the asters, and the spindles. All these entities are characterized by the presence within them of an organized system of microtubules. The microtubule is essentially a contractile structure, although it is not known that the microtubules exhibit contractility in all structures in which they are found.

The formation of the mitotic apparatus of the first cleavage, as noted above, begins with a single centriole donated by the sperm. This centriole replicates to form a pair. During mitosis, each member of the pair replicates to pass a pair of centrioles to each daughter cell. In the centrioles of most animals the replication occurs as a budding process with the daughter centriole forming from the side of the parent centriole. It is common practice to speak of the centrioles as organizing the mitotic apparatus. From a morphological view this concept is accurate enough. The centrioles represent centers with respect to the positioning of the spindles and the astral rays in the architecture of the mitotic apparatus. In normal division the centrioles assume polar positions on opposite sides of the nucleus with the fibers of the spindle extending between them. The centrioles are surrounded by large numbers of microtubules, which radiate outward from them like the spokes of a wheel to form the asters. The number of astral microtubules may vary considerably in the course of a cell cycle in most animal forms. The centrioles themselves appear in electron micrographs as hollow cylinders walled by microtubules arranged in nine sets of triplets, which show a paddlewheel configuration in cross section.

Some reservations are in order, however, to the traditional view of the centrioles organizing the mitotic apparatus, when organizing the apparatus is considered synonymous to producing it. It has been clearly established that centrioles replicate to form basal bodies which generate the axial cores of cilia and flagella. In many species the fibers of the axonemes may be seen to be in actual contact with such basal bodies, which are in essence centrioles. An example of such contact is seen in the proximal centriole of the sperm flagellum. No such connection exists between the centrioles and the fibers of the spindle or between the centrioles and the astral rays. One cannot discount the possibility of the fibers of asters and spindle being generated by the centrioles on this basis alone, but if they are so generated here, the centriole ought at least not to be viewed as an analogue to a spinnerette.

Dietz (1966) has succeeded in removing the asters and centrioles from cells in the process of successive divisions. The cells without centrioles form spindles that are essentially normal and divide normally. It has been known for many years that the spindles of angiosperms lack centrioles. It can, of course, be argued that in the animal kingdom under rare circumstances spindles can arise *de novo* just as centrioles can occasionally arise *de novo* (as we have discussed with regard to parthenogenetically activated anucleate half-eggs), but that under normal circumstances centrioles arise from other centrioles by replication and spindles are generated by centrioles. The problem clearly needs further investigation.

Dietz has suggested—and the idea is by no means new—that the deployment of the centrioles in the polar position in mitosis is primarily a mechanism for ensuring that each daughter cell in division receives a pair of centrioles to make provision for possible future needs for the production of cilia and/or flagella. This position is reinforced to some extent by the fact that many workers have found that, as with the microtubules of cilia and flagella, many agents which disrupt the spindle leave the centriole intact, in other words, from a molecular standpoint, the microtubules of the centriole may bear more affinities to the microtubules of cilia and flagella than to microtubules of the mitotic apparatus. The problem of molecular relationships between various categories of microtubules is still under study in the sea urchin.

Instances of *de novo* origin of centrioles are sufficiently scarce to cause many cytologists to categorize the centriole as an autonomous replicating structure and to seek evidence of its having genetic control of its functions independent of the nucleus. Electron micrographs reveal no DNA, and attempts to detect incorporation of tritiated thymidine in centrioles of metazoa have been largely fruitless, and at the best, inconclusive.

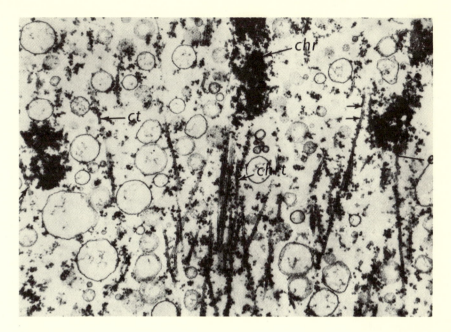

Figure 8

Longitudinal section through a mitotic apparatus. Magnification: 25,000×. Note chromosomes (chr) and the microtubules running directly to the chromosomes (chrt). One microtubule (e) is seen to end at the surface of a chromosome. Other microtubules are seen to pass between the chromosomes and appear to represent elements of continuous fibers (ct). Arrows show ribosome-like particles, which appear to be associated with microtubules. (From Goldman and Rebhun, 1969. The structure and some properties of the isolated mitotic apparatus. *Journal of Cell Science, 4.* Reprinted by permission.)

Mazia et al. (1960) studied the replication of centrioles in the sea urchin. Their observations were consistent with those made on many animal species, including the demonstration of the existence of the bud or procentriole in the formation of daughter centrioles and of the fact that the timing of replication coincides with the formation of the interphase nucleus.

The ultrastructure of the isolated mitotic apparatus and of the apparatus *in situ* has been studied by Harris (1961), Kane (1962), Goldman and Rebhun (1969), and others (see Fig. 8). The apparatus has been revealed to contain microtubules, ribosomes, vesicles, membranous fragments, which are probably elements of rough endoplasmic reticulum, and a matrix material that is electron-lucent. Chromosomes, of course, show in some sections of the spindle. In electron micrographs made on other animal species, small vesicles and ribosomes are observed lying among the microtubules of the asters, a circumstance that probably applies in the sea urchin in view of the remarkable uniformity found in the apparatus among various animal types.

At present it is virtually impossible to determine which of the particulate inhabitants of the mitotic apparatus are bona fide components of the stucture and which are transient occupants, moving in and out, or alien particulates captured during the condensation of the spindle. Bibring and Cousineau (1964), for example, found that particulate material labeled with radioactive amino acids was lost from the apparatus over a period of time and that some of the labeled material moved in and out of the apparatus in a cyclic fashion, being most strongly localized there at metaphase.

Autoradiography (see Gross, 1967) reveals active labeling of protein within the apparatus that does not represent label within the microtubules. This discovery poses the question as to whether the ribosomal material in the apparatus is contained to any extent on polysomes engaged in active protein synthesis. Hartmann and Zimmerman (1968) extracted large amounts of ribosomal material from the mitotic apparatus of *Strongylocentrotus purpuratus* and were unable to demonstrate the presence of polysomes in it with the use of RNAase. The RNAase test is considered a valid criterion for detecting the presence of polysomes, but the question of whether there is active protein synthesis within the apparatus is too critical to the understanding of the function of the organelle not to call for continued investigation.

In other animal species, the cross sections of microtubules of the mitotic apparatus show quite consistently a circle made up of 13 subunits. The microtubules of the apparatus are generally considered to be structurally rigid. The idea of a rigid microtubule harmonizes with the hypothetical role of the asters in the movement of the male pronucleus and in the induction of cleavage furrow formation. Obviously, the fibers of the spindle are flexible enough to bend in the shallow arc that describes the contour of the spindle. The spindle microtubules are clearly contractile, being responsible for at least part of the movement of chromosomes in cell division. Studies on the chemistry of the nucleotides of the mitotic apparatus lag behind those made on the sperm flagellum. As with the flagellum, an ATPase (dynein) has been shown to be present in the mitotic apparatus of other animal species.

The isolation of the mitotic apparatus by Mazia and Dan (1952) made possible intensive and extensive investigation of the molecular biology of the organelle. As we have suggested previously, many studies on the molecular biology of the mitotic apparatus have used the apparatus as a system for the investigation of the nature of its molecules without giving any conspicuous amount of attention to the relationship of these molecules to the biology of the cell. Without discounting the importance or necessity of such investigations —as one cannot—we shall attempt to minimize our discussion of them to the extent possible, in favor of a consideration of studies addressed to the problem of the mechanisms by which the mitotic apparatus is produced in embryogenesis.

The investigation of the proteins of the mitotic apparatus and of the circumstances surrounding the synthesis of those proteins in the sea urchin embryo presents some unique advantages that are not attendant upon the study of this organelle in other types of cells. The sea urchin embryo undergoes little, if any, growth from fertilization to pluteus. The amount of protein per embryo is essentially invariant; that is, there is no net synthesis of protein during development. Some proteins are synthesized, and other proteins, presumably yolk proteins in particular, are degraded to maintain the levels of precursors in the pools of free amino acids. The amount of protein synthesized to increase the mass of the embryo in early development is insignificant. The net result is that there is no sythesis of proteins for growth to obscure the synthesis of protein that is peculiar to, or characteristic of, the developmental process itself. Any type of protein synthesis that is a particularly prominent component of the development process should therefore be revealed in all its splendor.

During early cleavage, the objective of the developmental program is the production of an immense supply of cells. This supply must be large enough to provide for the formation of tissues and of organs when these cells and their progeny differentiate in the period fellowing gastrulation. For the production of large numbers of cells, two categories of protein synthesis must be predominant: protein synthesis to provide for the production of nuclei, and protein synthesis to support cell division. The first category involves primarily the production of histones and other types of nuclear proteins. This synthesis must keep pace with the synthesis of a fixed amount of DNA per cell in a population of cells that is increasing exponentially, so that each new cell will have its proper chromosome complement. Histone production will be discussed in another chapter. The second category is concerned primarily with the elaboration of a new mitotic apparatus for each cell division. During cleavage in the sea urchin embryo, these two types of protein synthesis are thus stellar events, unobscured by other types of protein synthesis to any degree. The synthesis of the major type of mitotic apparatus protein, the tubulins or proteins of the microtubules, is linked also to the production of microtubules for cilia and for cytoplasmic microtubules. It is not patent that all these species of microtubules can be constructed from common monomers, but the evidence is beginning to mount that it may be possible.

It is probable that at some time during each cleavage cycle, protein is produced to provide for the production of the mitotic apparatus. This synthesis is known to occur in at least the first cleavage cycle. Gross (1964) and Stafford and Iverson (1964) found that amino acids are incorporated at that time into 'the mitotic apparatus. It is inferential from the work of Raff et al. (1972) that this type of protein synthesis persists throughout the entire cleavage period. Hultin (1961) demonstrated that protein synthesis is obligate for the elaboration of the mitotic apparatus. His study was directed at the phenomenon of cleavage itself rather than at the formation of the mitotic apparatus in particular. He was able to block cleavage through the use of puromycin, an agent that halts protein synthesis. In the first two cleavage cycles the block was found to occur at the time of the migration of the centrioles to polar positions in the streak stage, just as the spindle was beginning to condense. The formation of the organelle was halted at that point, as was cleavage as a whole. The nature of the critical protein or proteins of which the synthesis is requisite here is not known. If parallels may be drawn between the formation of the mitotic apparatus and the regeneration of cilia, it may be considered unlikely that the protein is a constituent of the microtubules.

The mitotic apparatus is a complicated organelle, more complicated, for example, than cilia. More than a single major category of protein may be expected to constitute it and to participate in its formation. It is certain that at least two major categories of mitotic apparatus protein exist. One of these is, of course, the tubulins, which have already been the focus of considerable study in sea urchins and other organisms. The other is the matrix protein, with which one protein fraction isolated from the mitotic apparatus has been tentatively identified. A third category may consist of proteins that catalyze the reactions involved in the assembly of the mitotic apparatus. Such catalysis may not necessarily involve the polymerization of tubulin subunits into microtubules. We have no direct evidence linking specific catalytic proteins to mitotic apparatus production. The mitotic apparatus is formed at a predictable time in the cleavage cycle; its appearance is one event in a predictable sequence of events in the cycle. Such predictability bespeaks an elaborate system of controls, and such controls may involve the production of specific proteins. It is possible that there exist proteins which are not components of the apparatus and which do not participate in its assembly, but which are nonetheless a *sine qua non* for its elaboration.

To date, only one protein has been identified with the matrix of the mitotic apparatus. This protein was originally thought to be a major component of the microtubules. In the isolation of the proteins of the organelle, workers have repeatedly described a protein with a sedimentation coefficient of 22S (see Stephens, 1967; Kane, 1965, 1967; Sakai, 1966). Kane has isolated this protein not only from the mitotic apparatus, but also from the cytoplasm of the unfertilized egg, which lacks a mitotic apparatus. The S-value of this protein was revised to 27S, and several investigators have expressed the belief that it is identical to a 27S protein found in yolk by Malkin et al. (1965). There has been a general tendency to continue to use the original 22S designation for the protein, and to avoid confusion we shall so designate it. The 22S protein appeared to be unable to bind to colchicine, a fact which suggested that it is unlike microtubule protein. Bibring and Baxandall (1969), through the use of ferritin-labeled antibody to the 22S protein were able to demonstrate by autoradiography that this protein is not a microtubule protein but is rather a component of the matrix of the mitotic apparatus. It takes the form of an amorphous substance that embeds the particles within the organelle and that lines the walls of the microtubules.

The presence of the 22S protein in the cytoplasm of the unfertilized egg, as well as its possible location in the yolk, points to the fact that the assembly of thé mitotic apparatus can be fed by reserve pools of protein in the cytoplasm. Historically, the existence of such reserve pools was suggested by the work of Went (1959a, 1959b, 1960), who demonstrated the presence in the cytoplasm of the unfertilized egg of two antigens that were immunologically identical to antigens found in the isolated mitotic apparatus. The actual nature of the antigens is unknown. Reserve pools of protein for microtubule production were ultimately discovered in the cytoplasm of the embryo, and these pools have been investigated to determine the manner in which they function and the manner in which they are formed. They can be isolated for study from 150,000 $\times g$ supernatants by the use of precipitants specific for the tubulins. It has also been demonstrated that there exist in the cytoplasm reserve pools of protein for the formation of cilia. The activity of these pools has also been studied, although by indirect methods rather than by direct isolation of the tubulins (see Auclair and Meismer, 1965; Auclair and Siegel, 1966). It has not been determined that all microtubules arise from a single pool, but it would not be suprising if this were found to be true.

Rebhun and Sawada (1969) treated fertilized eggs of *Lytechinus pictus* with a variety of agents, such as hexylene glycol and dimethylsulfoxide, which cause the dissolution of the microtubules of mitotic apparatus. If the exposure was not too lengthy, the microtubules reformed quickly when the agent was removed. This phenomenon has been demonstrated in other animal cells, and it has been shown that the spindle can be made to disappear and reform by the application and removal of physical agents as well as chemical. Puromycin does not interfere with the reconstitution of the microtubules. It would appear that microtubules are formed by some type of rapid polymerization process which may be fed by pools of tubulin subunits. The nature of the parameters that effect the polymerization is not known, but polymerization does not appear to require protein synthesis. A theory of the mechanism of movement of spindle fibers has been based on this polymerization. The theory assumes an equilibrium between monomers in the pools and polymers in the microtubules and proposes that the microtubule can be shortened or elongated by the assembly or disassembly of the polymer at localized regions along its length (see Inoué and

Sato, 1967). There appears no reason to construe the ability of a spindle to reform in the absence of protein synthesis, following its dissolution by artificial means, as a refutation of Hultin's finding that protein synthesis is necessary for the formation of the mitotic apparatus during the cleavage cycle. One can see an urgency, however, for study of aspects of the formation and function of the mitotic apparatus that do not directly involve the behavior of the microtubules in order to attain a clearer picture of the mechanics of formation of the organelle.

Early studies on the structure of the microtubule proteins of the mitotic apparatus were extremely misleading, perhaps because the work was beset with some vexatious technical difficulties. Although the microtubules of the mitotic apparatus are quite susceptible to dissolution compared to those of cilia and flagella, the agents used by early workers to solubilize the microtubule proteins were usually quite unsatisfactory. They tended to fracture microtubules in unlikely places, producing in the literature a wide assortment of S-values and giving rise to isolates that gave little insight into the nature of the parent compound. Another irritation was found in the fact that the yield of one protein isolate versus another would tend to vary with the extractant. Perhaps the most serious difficulty encountered was that the extractants used were not specific for the tubulins. It was usually found that the bulk of the proteins extracted from the microtubules by a given reagent were not microtubule proteins. When an extractant specific for the tubulins was finally found, they were extracted in what appears on the basis of comparison with flagellar tubulins to be their proper physicochemical form, by Bibring and Baxandall.

In 1971, Bibring and Baxandall discovered that through the use of meralluride sodium, an organic mercurial, they could bring about the selective dissolution of the microtubules of the mitotic apparatus, while leaving the remainder of the organelle intact. The effects of the reagent on the morphology of the organelle were confirmed by electron microscopy. As the microtubules disappeared, the mercurial was revealed to be extracting specifically proteins which resembled those of the outer doublet fibers of the sperm tail (see Stephens, 1970). The resemblance to the flagellar tubulins was seen in properties considered typical, such as precipitability with calcium ion and with vinblastine sulfate, binding with colchicine, S-value, electrophoretic mobility on polyacrylamide gels, molecular weight, and (according to preliminary investigations) probably amino acid composition. Bibring and Baxandall had also had some success with the selective extraction of tubulins from the apparatus in 1968, with the use of mild HCl at pH 3.

The organic mercurial isolated two very closely related species of protein from the mitotic apparatus. Their S-value, after dialysis with meralluride at acid pH, was 4.9S and at alkaline pH was 8.9S. These correspond to values found by Stephens (1970) for flagellar outer-doublet fibers. Bibring and Baxandall postulated the two S-values to represent different association states of the proteins, with the 4.9S value probably representing a dimer of a subunit with a molecular weight of about 52,000. This subunit may correspond to the 2.5S protein described for the mitotic apparatus by Sakai (1966) and Miki-Noumura (1968) and for the outer-doublet fibers of the flagellum by Mohri (1968). The authors, however, had reservations about the value obtained by Sakai, who produced his 2.5S protein by reduction of a 3.5S protein with bisulfite. Their extimated molecular weight did not vary after they had submitted their proteins to treatment essentially identical to that used by Sakai. They did speculate that their proteins would prove to be identical to the colchicine-binding protein found in the mitotic apparatus by Borisy and Taylor (1967), and that, as with sperm-tail tubulins, they would be shown to contain one guanine nucleotide bound to each monomer molecule. They found the yield of mitotic apparatus tubulins to be low, running maximally to 15 percent of the total mitotic apparatus proteins.

The existence of A- and B-tubulins in the flagellum and cilium corresponds to the presence of two types of outer-doublet fibers. Since this dichotomy has not been observed in the mitotic apparatus, the rationale for its possessing two tubulins is not known. Bibring and Baxandall have suggested two possible explanations: (1) the microtubules are constructed of two types of tubulin (supposedly as a matter of necessity) and (2) perhaps only one type is needed for the construction of the microtubule, but the other type is produced (and can be used in the construction) in anticipation of cilia production. Such flexibility should provide for the feeding of mitotic apparatus production and cilia production from a common pool and provide for the perpetuation of the system in cells where mitotic activity ceases and cilia or flagellar production becomes necessary.

Raff et al. (1971, 1972) have examined the activity of the cytoplasmic pools of tubulin subunits of the microtubules by isolating the tubulins from the 100,000×g supernatants (cell sap) of homogenates of eggs and embryos by precipitation with vinblastine sulfate. The organisms studied were *Arbacia punctulata* and *Strongylocentrotus purpuratus*. These investigators determined the incorporation of radioactive amino acids into the tubulins as an index of the extent of tubulin synthesis. Their outstanding discovery was that the tubulins of the cytoplasmic pool are synthesized on maternal message made at oogenesis. Incubation of embryos in the presence of actinomycin D, which inhibits transcription of nuclear genes, had no effect on the incorporation of amino acids into the tubulins. They found also that tubulin synthesis occurs in anucleate half-eggs and cannot be ascribed to transcription from genetic information contained in cytoplasmic organelles. Their results suggest that the synthesis begins immediately after fertilization and continues throughout cleavage and through the hatching period. A very low level of synthesis was found in the unfertilized egg. Both species of tubulin were labeled.

The level of tubulins in the pools was found to change but little in the period from fertilization to hatch. Chase experiments in which incubation with radioactive amino acids was followed by incubation with the same precursors without label revealed a loss in specific activity in the pools. The most logical explanation for the loss is that tubulins are being withdrawn from the pools to form microtubules. It is conceivable that some tubulin may be lost from the pools by degradation. The constancy of level in the pool is probably maintained largely by replenishment through synthesis to compensate for loss through withdrawal. Dissolution of the mitotic apparatus when it has discharged its cytological function may also be supposed to replenish the pools.

There is no proof offered in this study that the tubulin pool for mitotic apparatus production also supports cilia production, but it appears likely that it does so. One may expect there to be some difference in activity with relation to the pool, between microtubules of cilia and those of the mitotic apparatus. Tubulins may be expected to move from pool to organelle and back again in the instance of the mitotic apparatus, whereas tubulins entering cilia may be expected to remain in them for extended periods of time. The removal from the pool of tubulins to provide for the formation of cilia, moreover, is likely to occur under some special morphogenetic controls, witness excessive ciliation in animalized embryos, whereas the mitotic apparatus is formed under control systems governing the cleavage cycle.

The Raff group found that the increment of increase in rate of tubulin synthesis, at least in the first few cleavage cycles, equals or exceeds that of total protein synthesis. This essentially corroborates a similar finding by Meeker and Iverson (1971). Historically, this finding was anticipated by Gross and Cousineau (1963), Bibring and Cousineau (1964), and Stafford and Iverson (1964), who reported that isotope incorporation into the mitotic apparatus in early cleavage exceeds in rate the total protein synthesis in the embryo. Mangan et al. (1965) anticipated the finding of the Raff group that tubulin synthesis begins almost immediately after fertilization, although they were looking at proteins of the mitotic apparatus as a whole in their experiments.

Although some evidence points to an identity between the tubulins of cilia and flagella, on the one hand, and of the mitotic apparatus, on the other, the problem is still somewhat controversial. Much is made of the fact that many agents that disrupt the mitotic apparatus leave the outer-doublet fibers intact and that there are differences in response to fixatives and to certain stains between the outer-doublet fibers and the microtubules of the mitotic apparatus. The outer-doublet fibers of cilia and flagella do indeed give every appearance of being the more stable of the two categories of microtubule, and it is not illogical that they should be. Mitotic apparatuses are ephemeral. They come and go with each cleavage cycle. Cilia and flagella, on the whole, endure. They may be changed or destroyed and regenerated, but generally they have a quasi-permanent status in the cell. It may be postulated that the cell may have to build certain characteristics into the microtubules of all these organelles to provide for these functional differences.

Tilney and Gibbins (1968) have proposed that should the microtubules of cilia and of the mitotic apparatus be constructed of the same tubulins (as evidence intimates that they are) the stability of ciliary microtubules could be increased relative to that of microtubules of the mitotic apparatus by the addition of material to the microtubule or by increasing the strength of bonding or number of bonds between adjacent tubulin molecules within the microtubule. Behnke and Förer (1967), who have made extensive comparative studies of microtubules of various organisms, have proposed that in the sea urchin differences in properties of microtubules may reflect the action of the cell upon the microtubule rather than differences in the component tubulins. Such concepts do not appear unrealistic when one considers differences in properties of collagen fibers that are wrought by variations in binding and by interaction with mucopolysaccharide ground substance.

Fulton et al. (1971) have made immunological investigations on cross reactions of tubulins and various microtubular structures in the sea urchin embryo with antisera to axonemes of sea urchin sperm tails. Their conclusion is that tubulins of microtubules of various types are immunologically similar, but not identical. Their antisera look to have been purified with considerable thoroughness. The antigen materials representative of various species of microtubule, which were compared by immunodiffusion as to their tendencies to cross react with the antiserum, consisted for the most part of extracts from various organelles (with the exception of purified outer-doublet-fiber tubulins). There is a question here as to how much these tests really reveal about differences between the tubulins contained in the extracts. The authors are quite explicit, however, in acknowledging the limitations of their experiments.

CLEAVAGE

The basic scheme of cleavage in the sea urchin embryo is shown in Fig. 9. Cleavage patterns are quite similar in most species of sea urchin, and they can be followed readily in terms of their relationship to the basic pattern of the egg in species like *Paracentrotus lividus,* which possess a band of pigment that comes to lie just under the equator of the egg after fertilization. This pigment band divides the egg into three zones and serves to delineate a natural fate map. The uppermost of these three zones is the animal hemisphere, at the pole of which the polar bodies were extruded. This zone represents prospective ectoderm. The middle zone is, of course, the pigmented zone, which will ultimately give rise to the

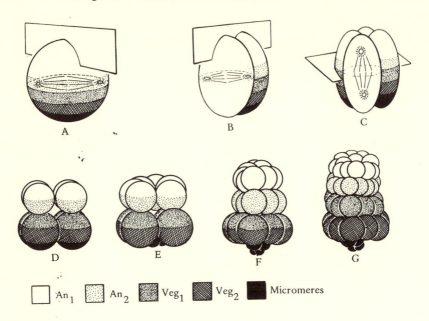

Figure 9

Cleavage in the sea urchin embryo. A, B, and C show positions of the spindle in the 1-, 2-, and 4-cell stages, respectively. D, E, F, and G show 8-, 16-, 32-, and 64-cell stages resulting from the third, fourth, fifth, and sixth cleavages, respectively. (Redrawn from J. W. Saunders, Jr., *Patterns and Principles of Animal Development,* New York, Macmillan, 1970, adapted from C. H. Waddington, *Principles of Embryology,* New York, Macmillan, 1966; by permission.)

gut and its derivatives, including coelomic pouches and secondary mesenchyme and which may be characterized as being prospectively endodermal and mesendodermal. Surrounding the vegetal pole the third zone represents the site of formation of future primary mesenchyme.

The first cleavage furrow is meridional, passing through both poles and dividing the egg into two daughter cells, approximately equal in size. The second cleavage furrow is likewise meridional, lying at right angles to the first. The third is latitudinal and cuts through the four blastomeres just above the equator of the original egg.

There are thus formed eight blastomeres in two tiers of four blastomeres each, with the cells of the lower tier being just slightly larger than those of the upper. At the fourth cleavage, the cells of the upper tier divide meridionally to produce eight cells of approximately equal size. The bottom tier, however, pinches off four minute cells in the region of the vegetal pole. These diminutive cells are appropriately called *micromeres*. They are the source of the primary mesenchyme and the future pluteal skeleton. Their large sister cells are called *macromeres* and will become the gut as well as part of the epidermis of the pluteus. The middle-sized cells of the animal region are known as *mesomeres*.

The cleavage is holoblastic, since not enough yolk is present to prevent the cleavage furrows from bisecting the entire egg. The cleavage is also radial, in fact, a classical example thereof. Radial cleavage is achieved by the proper timing and synchrony of formation of meridional cleavage planes versus cleavage planes parallel to the equator. The direction of these planes depends upon whether the spindles are positioned horizontally or vertically with respect to the polar axis of the egg. The cleavage plane, of course, forms at right angles to the long axis of the spindle. The net result is that as cleavage advances, cells become arranged symmetrically with respect to the polar axis of the egg and lie in tiers or rings parallel to the equator.

The formation of the macromeres and micromeres is an exception to the normal perpendicular formation of cleavage planes. Here, the spindles come to lie in an oblique position, and the small cells are split off from the lower inner sides of the large cells.

Up to the 8-cell stage, there is synchrony of cleavage. After that stage, asynchronies develop with respect to the embryo as a whole, even though cells may divide in synchrony within given regions of the embryo. On occasion a 12-cell stage preceding the 16-cell stage has been seen in some species. Macromeres and micromeres normally divide out of synchrony, resulting in a 20-cell stage and a 28-cell stage being formed prior to the 32-cell stage.

Official designations have been given to the tiers for convenience in discussion. In the formation of the 32-cell stage, the 8 mesomeres are cleaved horizontally to form two tiers, an_1 and an_2, with the former being nearer to the animal pole. At this cleavage, the 4 macromeres are cleaved meridionally to double in number. In the following cleavage, the macromeres are cleaved horizontally to form two tiers veg_1 and veg_2, with veg_2 being nearer the vegetal pole. It is veg_2 that will give rise to the gut, with veg_1 becoming pluteal epidermis. At the 64-cell stage, there are 16 micromeres, 16 macromeres, and 32 mesomeres. At the 128-cell stage, the embryo has begun to show signs of the spherical shape characteristic of the blastula.

The cleaving cells are held together to quite an extent by the hyaline layer. This layer depends upon calcium ion for its integrity. Immersing the embryo in calcium-free seawater will cause the dissociation of the blastomeres. Vacquier in 1968 was able to effect a physical separation without complete dissociation of the blastomeres in calcium-free seawater by weakening the hyaline layer without destroying it. The blastomeres were found to be interconnected by filopods. Time-lapse cinematography revealed bulbous swellings moving along the walls of the filopods, and at advanced stages of cleavage the movement became more active. The significance of the filopodal interconnections among cells is not known. Vacquier has suggested that the filopods may represent another mechanism for holding blastomeres together or that they may provide a means of establishing cytoplasmic continuity among the blastomeres.

It is appropriate at this time to mention some of the findings of the experimental embryologists with respect to the cleavage period.

Twinning is a subject that has traditionally been of interest to the embryologist. Studies on twinning in the sea urchin hearken back to Driesch (1892). If blastomeres of the 2-cell stage or the 4 cell stage are separated, they can give rise to two or four plutei, respectively, which are normal in all respects except that their size is reduced. This phenomenon normally does not occur beyond the 4-cell stage. The problem of potency is, of course, involved here. After the 4-cell stage the embryo appears to lose the initial totipotency in its individual cells.

The original work of Driesch involved separation of the blastomeres by shaking. He later discovered that blastomeres can be separated through the use of calcium-free seawater, a technique, as noted above, still in use after 70 years. Twinning can also be achieved by dividing a fertilized egg in half surgically. Here the results may be different from those attained by dissociation and may reflect the organization of the egg.

If the division is made through the polar axis of the egg, the halves survive to produce two normal, but undersized plutei. If the concept of the cortex as the site of the basic organization of the egg be valid, it can be speculated that the division has produced halves that contain adequate samples of cortically located precursors to all three germ layers. If the division is made across the polar axis of the egg, that is through the equator, the vegetal half will give rise to an incomplete larva with some ectoderm, a gut of sorts, and a skeleton. The animal half will develop into an excessively ciliated permanent blastula or dauerblastula (see Fig. 10), which may swim about for several days, but will develop no further and will perish. In each half, some of the germ layer material requisite for normal morphogenesis is lacking. The experiment gives evidence of a definite distribution of material in the egg along the polar axis. It specifies neither what materials are distributed nor where the critically distributed materials are located. The results of the experiment are not inconsistent with the concept that the materials in question may be located in the cortex, however.

It is interesting that by aligning their axes, it is possible to fuse sea urchin embryos in early development. The result is a giant pluteus, properly proportioned and showing no duplication of organs.

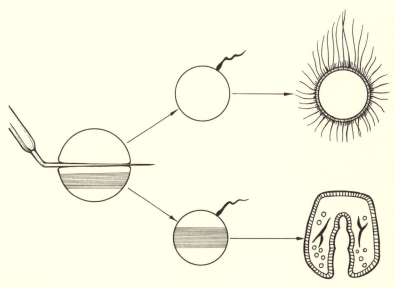

Figure 10

Development of animal and vegetal halves of the sea urchin egg. The egg is cut in half through the equator. The animal half develops into a dauerblastula upon being fertilized. The vegetal half after fertilization forms an incomplete embryo with some degree of archenteron formation and limited skeletal development. (From *Modern Embryology* by Charles W. Bodemer. Copyright © 1968 by Holt, Rinehart and Winston, Inc. Redrawn by permission of Holt, Rinehart and Winston, Inc.)

Let us now proceed to the consideration of experiments involving the surgical manipulation of the embryo in the process of cleavage. Such experiments tell us little of the phenomenon of cleavage itself, but they do reflect on the state of cells in cleavage with respect to their developmental future.

It has proved feasible to divide embryos through the equator or in planes parallel to the equator by making the division between the tiers or rings of cells described above. An 8-cell embryo can thus be divided into animal and vegetal halves. The vegetal half gives rise to an incomplete larva, which lacks a stomodaeum and ciliary tufts and bands, but otherwise contains a complete complement of organs. The animal half does not gastrulate. It does not accordingly produce an archenteron or a skeleton. It does produce an apical tuft and ciliary bands as well as a stomodaeum. Weiss (1939), in discussing this experiment, has pointed out that the results are reminiscent of the mozaic development of the ascidian. Each half appears to be contributing its own quota of organs to the animal.

The sea urchin egg is, however, normally and rightfully considered a regulative egg. There is overwhelming evidence of its plasticity. Hörstadius (1928 and 1935) was able to separate embryos in advanced stages of cleavage and in blastula into meridional halves. Larvae developing therefrom were perfectly normal although of reduced size. If an animal half was grafted to a meridional half so that the embryo came to possess an enormous excess of animal material, the embryo developed normally, suggesting the conversion of some animal cells into cells with vegetal tendencies. Embryos divested of their micromeres, which exclusively give rise to the skeleton in normal development, were shown by Horstadius to develop normally with the presumptive endoderm of veg_2 presumably taking over the function of skeleton formation.

A truly dramatic phenomenon is seen when a vegetal half is isolated and divested of its micromeres. It develops into a pluteus with a normal complement of organs, including ciliary bands, apical tuft, and stomodaeum. As Weiss has suggested, the evidence here is that the vegetal half does not really lack the ability to organize a normal embryo despite its apparent mozaic proclivities. Its potential for organizing the animal half appears to be overridden by the presence of the micromeres. This phenomenon relates to certain aspects of the gradient theory, which will be discussed in a later chapter.

Micromeres grafted to an animal half result in the production of a nearly normal pluteus. This is apparently the result of induction, the evoking of specific activities in one tissue by another, a picture quite familiar to the student of vertebrate embryology. Further evidence of the inductive capacity of micromeres is seen when they are grafted onto a normal embryo. If removed by an adequate distance from the vegetal pole, the graft organizes a second center of invagination with the formation of a second gut and extra skeletal elements. These events call to mind the organizing tendencies of the amphibian dorsal blastopore lip.

Macromeres also have inducing ability. They can produce partial or complete larvae when grafted to an animal half. The more macromeres grafted, the more complete the larva. The relative inducing ability of micromeres and macromeres appears to represent further evidence of gradient design in embryos.

For further general information on the work of the experimental embryologists not only in the sea urchin, but in other organisms as well, the reader is referred to Weiss (1939), Kuhn (1965), and Czihak (1971). We shall not venture further into the subject because it is ground already familiar to many embryologists and because, if treated with the thoroughness it deserves, it could easily bury our present discussions. It is a subject not completely appropriate to a chapter on cleavage. We have considered here the type of experiment in which the work is done on embryos in cleavage, but the observations are made on, and the results proceed from, things which happen to those embryos in later development. The experimenter is much more often interested in the experiences undergone by the embryo in later development than in the conditions existing at cleavage that predisposed to those experiences. It is axiomatic, however, that those conditions do exist in cleaving embryos, and it is important to reflect upon them. They are reminders that cleavage is more than a period in which cells undergo a population explosion, and that when one looks away from the mitotic events of cleavage one is not likely to see barren ground for exploration. These experiments make the particularly important revelation that cleavage is a period in which differential distribution within the zygote of materials critical for morphogenesis is being translated into meaningful, organized differential distribution of those same materials among a population of cells.

Up until the beginning of the last decade, sea urchin embryologists found great preoccupation with the rate of cleavage and with agents and reagents that are capable of altering it. An almost interminable list of compounds that affect the rate of cleavage attests, if nothing else, to the ease with which the rate of cleavage may be altered. Probably the bulk of experiments that have given birth to this list are not particularly important to sea urchin embryology, except in instances where the actual mechanism of inhibition or acceleration of cleavage can be described. Of these, the more interesting ones are those which reflect informatively on the normal metabolism or other activities of the egg or embryo. The consideration of inhibitors and accelerators of cleavage (the former are much more numerous) is beyond the scope of this discussion. Harvey has summarized the work done prior to 1956. The numerous publications of Lallier in recent years are of considerable interest, where pharmacological aspects of sea urchin research are concerned and will serve to expand the summary presented by Harvey to quite a degree.

It is extremely important to bear in mind that cleavage rates vary with temperature and with species. Harvey (1956) has compiled data on the time required for the first cleavage in a dozen different species and on the time required for the first cleavage as a function of temperature in *Arbacia punctulata*. The variation with species in all probability reflects genetic variations in basic rates of synthesis in these species. The first cleavage requires a much longer time for completion than subsequent cleavages. Harvey cites a period of 50 minutes and 28 minutes for the first and second cleavages, respectively, at 23°C in *Arbacia*.

Various types of radiation affect the rate of cleavage and other aspects of sea urchin development. This circumstance has on occasion made radiation a valuable tool in sea urchin research. It is also of interest to know that there are agents which appear to affect the rate of cleavage of sea urchin embryos in their natural environment. The products of dinoflagellates in red tides, for example, are purported to slow down cleavage rates (see Cornman, 1947). The effects of pesticides and pollutants from industrial wastes on sea urchin development have not received any great amount of study and might be worthy of investigation.

Culture media used in experimentation on sea urchin embryos, if not carefully controlled, can cause alterations from the normal rate of cleavage. Tonicity of the medium, content of particular ions, and pH are of particular importance in this regard. Timourian et al. (1963) and Timourian and Denny (1964) have shown that calcium and magnesium ions are required for cleavage. Potassium at high concentrations may inhibit cleavage. Since protein synthesis is similarly affected by these ions, the effect on cleavage may possibly be attributable, at least in part, to the facilitation or inhibition of protein synthesis (see, for example, Meeker, 1971).

One would normally expect a most intimate relationship between nuclear division and cleavage. It is therefore surprising to find that Harvey (1935) discovered that artificially activated anucleate half-eggs produced by centrifugation will undergo cleavage, albeit the cleavage is abnormal. In the process, cytasters appear; and when a pair of asters form, the cleavage plane cuts between them. Obviously, such cleavage occurs without the concomitant transcription of genes. The "embryo" does not develop beyond blastula. The question arises as to whether development fails at this point because supplies of critical materials that cannot be replaced without transcription have been exhausted, or because some *new species* of molecule is needed that cannot be provided without activation and transcription of genes. In the special case of the anucleate half-egg being produced by the constriction occurring across the equator, conditions prevail, which have been described above, of the loss of germ-layer material. Gastrulation would not be expected to occur in a proper manner if activation be by fertilization (which would otherwise produce a half-sized pluteus) rather than by artificial parthenogenesis. Harvey has noted the frequent occurrence of dauerblastulae in her experiments.

As has been mentioned, the orientation of the spindle is of cardinal importance in determining cleavage patterns. Hörstadius (1928) was able to delay the rate of cell division by such techniques as shaking the eggs or diluting the medium. If he delayed the first cleavage until the time when control eggs were in the third, the spindle would orient in a position perpendicular to the normal for the first cleavage, and the division would be equatorial rather than meridional. The following division would occur with normal cleavage planes of the fourth cleavage, that is, planes identical to those of the controls, and the result would be a T-shaped configuration with two mesomeres, one macromere, and one micromere. This experiment demonstrates the concept that the orientation of the spindle is probably due to cytoplasmic forces and that it is independent of the number of divisions that have previously occurred. In this instance, the first cleavage may be assumed to have behaved like a third cleavage, having occurred at the time in the developmental program at which the third cleavage was destined to occur.

CLEAVAGE MECHANISM

The problem of the forces that cause cleavage to occur has been under continual study for the last half century and had received some attention in earlier times, but many questions that pertain to it remain unanswered. The major problem concerning the nature of cleavage is obviously that of the elicitation of furrow formation. This problem falls naturally into five subdivisions:

1. The question of the locus at which the stimulus to furrow formation originates.
2. The problem of the nature of the stimulus, a problem that can best be approached by determining the nature of the response.
3. The question of the nature of transfer of the stimulus to the locus at which it excites the effector mechanisms, a locus that, prior to experimentation, cannot be assumed to coincide with the site at which the response (furrow formation) occurs.
4. The problem of the nature of the response.
5. Problems directly associated with the locus of the response.

Such a categorization is an oversimplification in view of the complexity of cleavage, but it is helpful in sorting out and interpreting some of the results of experimentation.

It has been reasonably well established that furrow formation in the sea urchin embryo results from a stimulus originating in the mitotic apparatus and that normally the mitotic apparatus stipulates the site at the surface of the egg where the furrow will form. Once the stimulus has been given, a point in time occurs (usually by anaphase), following which no component of the mitotic apparatus needs to be present for the furrow to form. Beams and Evans (1940) and Swann and Mitchison (1953) have shown that the disruption of the mitotic apparatus through the use of colchicine does not interfere with cleavage once the furrow has started to form. Hiramoto (1956) removed spindles from eggs of *Clypeaster japonicus* by micromanipulation and showed that in their absence the formation of the cleavage plane was unmodified. When both asters and spindles were removed, however, cleavage did not occur. This finding is in harmony with the contention of many workers that the aster is the region of the mitotic apparatus that is primarily important in giving the signal for furrowing. In polyspermy, furrows form between supernumerary sperm asters (caused by the presence of extra centrioles donated by the extra sperm) or between a supernumerary sperm aster and aster of the mitotic apparatus (see Hiramoto, 1962, and Sugiyama, 1951), so that mutiple furrowing comes to be a common feature of polyspermic development in the sea urchin.

Perhaps the most convincing demonstration that the aster possesses the ability to elicit furrow production is found in the work of Rappaport (1961). He was able to convert a normal spherical sand dollar fertilized egg into a torus-shaped egg. The first cleavage produced a horseshoe-shaped egg with a nucleus in each end of the horseshoe. At the second cleavage, two of the four asters were produced in the arms of the horseshoe. Spindles formed between these asters and those in the ends of the horseshoe, and cleavage planes cut the spindles. The unusual aspect of this cleavage, however, was that in the bend (toe) of the horseshoe a third cleavage plane *was formed between the aster of each arm, where no spindle was present*. The result was, of course, the formation of four cells, which is the normal number at this stage of development.

The work of Dietz (1966) with anastral spindles, which has been cited in this chapter, suggests that the spindle has the capability of substituting for the aster in producing the stimulus to furrowing. In the sea urchin, at least two instances of cleavage occurring in the absence of any formed component of the mitotic apparatus have been claimed. Lorch (1952) has reported that such cleavage may occur upon the enucleation of blastomeres, and Harvey (1960) has shown that it may occur on artificial parthenogenesis followed by centrifugation. These unusual situations merit further investigation.

Many workers have envisioned the stimulus as a diffusible substance that originates in the asters and that, upon reaching some critically sensitive region of the cell, causes regional change, either through alterations in physical properties or through activation of a contractile system. Such change is thought to engender the furrow. Speculation as to the nature of such a substance will become more meaningful once the nature of the response mechanism is understood to some extent.

Timourian and Watchmaker (1971) have suggested that it may be extremely difficult, if not impossible, to isolate and characterize such a substance. They devised an experiment that was hoped might prompt a diffusible stimulus to reveal its presence. Through the use of two techniques, polyspermy and treatment with mercaptoethanol, they stimulated sea urchin eggs to produce tetrapolar division in the first cleavage, when normal cells produce bipolar division. Their hypothesis was that since the asters are closer to the surface in the tetrapolar division, the distance over which the stimulating substance must diffuse is shorter; hence tetrapolar division should precede bipolar division in time. Tetrapolar division produced by mercaptoethanol treatment did indeed precede bipolar division. When tetrapolar division was produced by polyspermy, however, its occurrence coincided with that of bipolar divsion. They postulated that in polyspermy a time period is required for the asters participating in tetrapolar division to assume polar positions, a circumstance which would account for the lag relative to the timing of the division in mercaptoethanol treatment in which the asters were already in position.

The stimulus need not be postulated to travel by diffusion *in strictu sensu.* Cytoplasmic streaming has been postulated as a means of transfer. Such streaming, which in this instance is sometimes termed *fountain streaming,* probably because it is envisioned as pouring out from the aster like jets from a fountain, is not likely to be the vehicle that transports the stimulating substance. Rappaport (1960, 1961, 1970) extruded eggs through a constriction, put them under stretch, and cut notches in them, all in a fashion calculated to interfere with fountain streaming, and found cleavage to be unaffected.

In a review in 1971, Rappaport has elaborated on the theory that the stimulus to cytokinesis, be it chemical or physical, is associated with the microtubules of the aster. The mechanism by which the astral microtubules might perform this function remains obscure. One might envision them as serving as pathways for the movement of substances and/or as physical tools for the manipulation of materials, bearing in mind the fact that they are both rigid and potentially contractile structures. Nothing in the recent investigations of the nature of microtubules, however, has been uncovered to lend support to this idea. The theory is consistent with the fact that there are observable relationships between the position of the astral microtubules or the number of astral microtubules in a given region and the ease with which cleavage can occur. The theory is also consistent with the findings that the subsurface organization of the egg is not seriously involved in cleavage-furrow induction. Rappaport (1966) stirred up the cytoplasm of the egg with a needle and found that this abuse did not disrupt cleavage.

There is no differentiated region on the surface of the egg that is designated for furrow production. A furrow can be induced at any point on the surface of the egg experimentally. The polarization of the egg in terms of the positioning of the mitotic apparatus stipulates that the cleavage plane will cut across the equator established by that polarization, but the position of the mitotic apparatus can be varied without violating this principle. Rappaport and Ebstein (1965) showed that new furows can be elicited by shifting the position of the mitotic apparatus in the egg. Such an effect occurred in principle in the centrifugation experiments of Harvey (see Harvey, 1956). In that instance the eggs could be expected to elongate under centrifugation in almost any plane bisecting the egg, although the probability of any particular planes being favored because of the distribution of particles relative to their mass appears never to have been investigated. Regardless of the plane, when an elongated egg was fertilized, the first mitotic apparatus formed came to lie parallel to the long axis of the egg, and the cleavage plane cut it equatorially. Presumably any point on the surface of the egg was fair game for the site of furrow formation.

The question arises as to the site on the surface of the polarized egg at which the stimulus will act. Wolpert (1960) and Swann and Mitchison (1958) postulated that site to be located at the poles. The former saw a polar relaxation giving rise to a tension at the equator to cause furrowing. A stimulus to the equator that would cause tension could be conceived to produce the same effect. The latter visualized a stimulus to polar expansion as causing a passive infolding at the equator. The concept of polar expansion is refuted by the work of Hiramoto (1968). He showed that the furrow forms by an active stretching of the equatorial surface. His measurements of tension at the surface showed this tension to be much higher latitudinally at the equator than longitudinally at the equator or at the poles. The concept of furrowing as an elastic response to a stimulated relaxation at the poles is superficially more reasonable, but there is considerable evidence that the stimulus does not act at the poles. The concept for the polar site of stimulation arose from the observation of the closer proximity of the asters to the poles than to the equator. The equator was deemed to be out of range of the stimulus and thus not stimulated. Rappaport (1971) has noted that it should be possible to produce extra areas too far away from the poles to receive a stimulus and, like the equator, susceptible to furrowing. Such an area exists in the toe of the horseshoe resulting from the first cleavage of the torus-shape cell discussed above. A cleavage plane does not form there in the first cleavage.

In 1965, Rappaport flattened cells so that the polar regions were farther away from the aster than was the equator, but the furrow formed in the equatorial region. In previous experiments (1964) he had constricted sand dollar eggs so that all points on the surface were equidistant from the astral centers, and likewise had produced equatorial cleavage. In 1969, he isolated equatorial regions with incipient furrows and found that the cleavage plane continued to form even in the complete absence of poles. These experiments provide strong evidence for the equatorial region as the site of stimulation.

Rappaport in a review of cytokinesis in 1971 discusses a theory, which he has expressed in previous writings, that there may be some importance to the ratio of the interastral distance to the distance to the surface of the egg from a line cutting the astral centers (spindle-to-surface distance) in determining whether furrows will or will not be generated. He cites as evidence the fact that when the mitotic apparatus is reduced in size by chemicals to the extent that cleavage is blocked, it is possible to restore cleavage, if concentration of the chemical involved is not excessive, by pushing the surface inward toward the mitotic apparatus.

Zimmerman and Marsland in 1960 were able to induce furrowing to occur before its normal time by subjecting eggs to centrifugal forces of 40,000 × g or more under high hydrostatic pressure. The plane of the furrows was found invariably to be perpendicular to the axis of centrifugation. They assumed that the effect of hydrostatic pressure is to solvate gel structures, allowing for increased movement of cellular components. Their conclusion was that the induction of the cleavage furrow is caused normally by the transport of cellular materials to the cell cortex in the polar regions. They speculated that the mitotic apparatus might act as a transporting agency. This is a description of a stimulus. If subsequent interpretations (see Rappaport, 1971) are correct, it implies a polar stimulus in normal cleavage and an equatorial stimulus under these experimental conditions. The gel solvation is assumed to occur in the cortex, and it purportedly releases cell components and facilitates their movement. There appears to be no assumption here that all of the migrating cell components had initially a cortical location. The solvation also produces a loss in cortical strength, which may be supposed to figure in furrow induction from a physical-property standpoint. It has not been demonstrated that changes in cortical strength in normal cleavage mirror those seen under these experimental conditions. Finally, there remains the question as to the nature of the cellular components that constitute this stimulus. No answer has been forthcoming apart from the suggestion by Tilney and Marsland (1969) that annulate lamellae may be involved. Although these organelles are found in situations where cells are undergoing rapid proliferation, their function is unknown.

Actually, evidence as to the nature of the stimulus is extremely sketchy. It appeared at one time (see Moore, 1938) that a stimulatory substance had revealed itself when it was shown that eggs subjected briefly to high-speed centrifugation to elongate them and then stimulated parthenogenetically developed asters and a cleavage furrow at their centrifugal end, while no mitotic apparatus developed in association with the nucleus, which was located at the opposite end. The nucleus, of course, did not divide. Kojima (1959) associated this phenomenon with the movement of granules having special staining characteristics. Such granules migrating to the centrifugal pole were visualized as stimulating a cleavage that could not function in conjunction with the abandoned nucleus. Whether the stimulus was housed in these granules or not, it is clear that it elicited the production of both asters and furrows. It can be postulated that the centrifugable substance was a stimulus not to cytokinesis, but to the formation of the mitotic apparatus. Results in the study of this problem, moreover, were conflicting, since Harvey (1951) had reported cleavage occurring in both ends of the egg when the particulates were patently stratified (see Rappaport, 1971).

The most appealing theory as to the nature of the stimulus at present is that it is a substance which activates a contractile system. Such a system may well be involved in cleavage. Mercer and Wolpert (1958) described a profusion of small tubules underlying the whole surface of the egg of *Psammechinus miliaris*, but occurring most densely in the furrow region. In 1968, Harris discovered filaments extending from microvilli down into the cortical region of the egg. Tilney and Marsland (1969) found such filaments to be imbedded in an amorphous material. The filaments are described as being 50 Å in diameter. It is probably premature to assume any kinship between these filaments and cytoplasmic microtubules. Miki-Noumura and Kondo (1970) have proposed that these filaments may contain actin and may participate in furrow productions in a contractile role.

An actin-like substance that binds to vertebrate myosin has been found in the sea urchin egg by Miki-Noumura (1969), Miki-Noumura and Oosawa (1969), and Hatano et al. (1969). Some studies that center on the activity of this substance and that may offer some clues as to the nature of the stimulus have been performed on sea urchin embryos by Kinoshita (1968, 1969, 1971) and Kinoshita and Yazaki (1967). They employed a system that involves treatment of glycerinated eggs with relaxing granules, ATP, and divalent cations, and that has been shown to induce furrow production in differentiated cells of other animal types. Glycerination is thought to destroy the activity within the egg of a relaxing system that promotes contraction. Exogenous relaxing granules are presumed to restore this activity. They provide the experimenter with the means of activating the contractile system.

Relaxing granules consist largely of vesicular elements of the sarcoplasmic reticulum of vertebrate striated muscle. They have been postulated to release an inhibitor, variously termed the *relaxing factor* or the *Marsh–Bendall factor,* that is thought to block the acitvity of an ATPase in order to prevent the hydrolysis of ATP prior to the stimulation of the muscle fiber. When the action potential reaches the fiber, the inhibiting activity is withdrawn, and the reactions promoting contraction proceed. Sarcoplasmic-reticulum vesicles have the ability to release, retrieve, and store calcium ion. The inhibition of actinomyosin ATPase is calcium dependent, but it depends also on the concentration of magnesium ion. Despite the fact that relaxing granules produce a contractile effect in sea urchin eggs, there is considerable room for reservation as to whether their activity there parallels that in vertebrate skeletal muscle.

The Kinoshita group used fluorescent antibody to follow the movements of the relaxing granules where furrowing was induced. The granules associated with the asters and spindle of the mitotic apparatus. Their distribution suggested to Rappaport (1971) that they would exert their stimulating effect at the poles. Kinoshita found that this system caused variations in the heparin content of the embryo, and submitted that the granules may release heparin to vary the calcium ion content at the surface of the egg. Apart from the role that calcium ion plays in contractility, it has been known for years to cause sol-gel transformations in the cortex. Such transformations might be postulated to relate in some way to the gel-solvation concept of Zimmerman and Marsland where the facilitation of stimulus propagation is concerned, and the work of Hiramoto described below appears not to rule out the possibility of their being directly involved in the formation of the furrow.

Rappaport (1971) points out the contractile protein of Sakai (see Sakai, 1968) as a possible contractile mechanism in furrow formation, but rightfully suggests that judgment should be reserved on the likelihood that it so serves, pending further investigation. This protein was discovered by Sakai about a decade ago. It has been studied extensively *in vitro*. Its contractility has been shown to depend upon redox activity centering around sulfhydryl groups. In at least one form in which it is isolated, it appears to bear resemblance to the tubulins. This protein has not yet been put into proper perspective with regard to its function in the cell.

The problem of the locus of the response to stimulus in cytokinesis deals with the extent of participation of various districts of the equatorial region in furrowing. Hiramoto (1968) has reviewed the subject. He has essentially ruled out active involvement of the endoplasm, that is, the cell fluid inside the cortex, which he has found to be moderately viscous. Although the internal pressure of the cell, which reflects the participation of the endoplasm in the overall effort of the cell to resist deformation, builds up before cleavage and drops markedly during cleavage, it is uniform throughout the cell. If the endoplasm were actively engaged in promoting the development of the furrow, one would expect to find local variations in the internal pressure. Hiramoto proposes that the generation of the furrow involves structural changes of an unknown nature in the cortex of the equatorial region of the cell. He has noted a thickening of the cortex in the region of the incipient furrowing.

Hiramoto has observed the movement through the gap between advancing furrows of cellular particulates and of an iron filing introduced into the cell and manipulated by a magnetic field. The ease with which they move back and forth implies that no membrane is in the process of forming between the furrows. As the cleavage plane comes to completion by the closure of a constricting ring, the plasma membrane and its underlying cortex are stretched the entire distance across the constriction. It is generally held, however, that new membrane is ultimately synthesized. This synthesis certainly must occur when the cell begins to grow to replace its lost volume, a phenomenon that does not occur to any great extent during cleavage. The timing in development of new membrane production and the site(s) on the cell surface at which it occurs have not been investigated in the sea urchin embryo.

REFERENCES

Allen, R. D., 1958. The initiation of development. In W. D. McElroy and B. Glass (eds.), *The Chemical Basis of Development.* The Johns Hopkins Press, Baltimore, 17–72.

Auclair, W., and D. Meismer, 1965. Cilia development and associated protein synthesis in the sea urchin embryo. *Biol. Bull. Mar. Biol. Lab., Woods Hole, 129,* 397.

Auclair, W., and B. W. Siegel, 1966. Cilia regeneration in the sea urchin embryo: evidence for a pool of ciliary proteins. *Science, 154,* 913–915.

Beams, H. W., and T. C. Evans, 1940. Some effects of colchicine upon the first cleavage of *Arbacia punctulata. Biol. Bull. Mar. Biol. Lab., Woods Hole, 79,* 188–198.

Behnke, O., and A. Forer, 1967. Evidence for 4 classes of microtubules in individual cells. *J. Cell. Sci., 2,* 169–191.

Bibring, T., and J. Baxandall, 1968. Mitotic apparatus: the selective extraction of protein with mild acid. *Science, 161,* 377–379.

Bibring, T., and J. Baxandall, 1969. Immunochemical studies of 22S protein from isolated mitotic apparatus. *J. Cell. Biol., 41,* 577–590.

Bibring, T., and J. Baxandall, 1971. Selective extraction of the isolated mitotic apparatus. *J. Cell. Biol., 48,* 324–339.

Bibring, T., and G. H. Cousineau, 1964. Percentage incorporation of leucine labeled with C-14 into isolated mitotic apparatus during early development of sea urchin eggs. *Nature* (London), *204,* 805–807.

Borisy, G. G., and E. W. Taylor, 1967. The mechanism of action of colchicine. Colchicine binding to sea urchin eggs and the mitotic apparatus. *J. Cell Biol., 34,* 535–548.

Chambers, E. L., 1939. The movement of the egg nucleus in relation to the sperm aster in the echinoderm egg. *J. Exp. Biol., 16,* 409–424.

Cornman, I., 1947. Retardation of *Arbacia* egg cleavage by dinoflagellate-contaminated sea water (red tide). *Biol. Bull. Mar. Biol. Lab., Woods Hole, 93,* 295.

Czihak, G., 1971. Echinoids. In G. Reverberi (ed.), *Experimental Embryology of Marine and Fresh Water Invertebrates.* American Elsevier Publishing Company, Inc., New York, 363–506.

Dietz, R., 1966. The dispensability of the centrioles in the spermatocyte divisions of *Pales ferruginea.* In C. D. Darlington and K. R. Lewis (eds.), *Chromosomes Today,* Vol. I. Plenum Publishing Corporation, New York, 161–166.

Driesch, H., 1892. Entwicklungsmechanische Studien. 1. Der Werth der beiden ersten Furchungszellen in der Echinodermentwicklung. Experimentelle Erzeugung von Theil- und Doppelbildungen. *Z. Wiss. Zool., 53*, 160–178.

Fulton, C., R. E. Kane, and R. E. Stephens, 1971. Serological similarity of flagellar and mitotic microtubules. *J. Cell Biol., 50*, 762–763.

Goldman, R. D., and L. I. Rebhun, 1969. The structure and some properties of the isolated mitotic apparatus. *J. Cell. Sci., 4*, 179–209.

Gross, P. R., 1964. The immediacy of genomic control during early development. *J. Exp. Zool., 157*, 21–41.

Gross, P. R., 1967. Protein synthesis, mitosis, and differentiation. *Can. Cancer Conf., 7*, 84–110.

Gross, P. R., and G. H. Cousineau, 1963. Synthesis of spindle-associated proteins in early cleavage. *J. Cell. Biol., 19*, 260–265.

Harris, P., 1961. Electron microscope study of mitosis in sea urchin blastomeres. *J. Biophys. Biochem. Cytol., 11*, 419–431.

Harris, P., 1968. Cortical fibers in fertilized eggs of the sea urchin, *Strongylocentrotus purpuratus*. *Exp. Cell Res., 52*, 677–681.

Hartmann, J. R., and A. M. Zimmerman, 1968. The isolated mitotic apparatus. Studies on nucleoproteins. *Exp. Cell Res., 50*, 403–417.

Harvey, E. B., 1935. Parthenogenetic merogeny or cleavage without nuclei in *Arbacia punctulata*. *Biol. Bull. Mar. Biol. Lab., Woods Hole, 69*, 332.

Harvey, E. B., 1951. Cleavage in centrifuged and in parthenogenetic merogones. *Ann. N.Y. Acad. Sci., 51*, 1336–1348.

Harvey, E. B., 1956. *The American Arbacia and Other Sea Urchins*. Princeton University Press, Princeton, N.J.

Harvey, E. B., 1960. Cleavage with nucleus intact in sea urchin's eggs. *Biol. Bull. Mar. Biol. Lab., Woods Hole, 119*, 87–89.

Hatano, S., H. Kondo, and T. Miki-Noumura, 1969. Purification of sea urchin egg actin. *Exp. Cell Res., 55*, 275–277.

Hiramoto, Y., 1956. Cell division without mitotic apparatus in sea urchin eggs. *Exp. Cell Res., 11*, 630–636.

Hiramoto, Y., 1962. Microinjection of the live spermatozoa into sea urchin eggs. *Exp. Cell Res., 27*, 416–426.

Hiramoto, Y., 1968. The mechanics and mechanism of cleavage in the sea urchin egg. *Symp. Soc. Exp. Biol., 22*, 311–327.

Hörstadius, S., 1928. Über die Determination des Keimes bei Seeigeln. *Acta Zool., 9*, 191.

Hörstadius, S., 1935. Über die Determination im Verlaufe der Eiachse bei Seeigeln. *Pubb. Staz. Zool. Napoli, 14*, 251–479.

Hultin, T., 1961. The effect of puromycin on protein metabolism and cell division in fertilized sea urchin eggs. *Experientia, 17*, 410–411.

Inoué, S., and H. Sato, 1967. Cell motility by labile association of molecules. *J. Gen. Phys., 50*, 259–292.

Kane, R. E., 1962. The mitotic apparatus. Fine structure of the isolated unit. *J. Cell Biol., 15*, 279–287.

Kane, R. E., 1965. Identification and isolation of the mitotic apparatus protein. *Biol. Bull. Mar. Biol. Lab., Woods Hole, 129*, 396.

Kane, R. E., 1967. Identification of the major soluble component of the glycol-isolated mitotic apparatus. *J. Cell. Biol., 32*, 243–253.

Kinoshita, S., 1968. Relative deficiency of intracellular relaxing system observed in furrowing reaction in induced cleavage in the centrifuged sea urchin egg. *Exp. Cell Res., 51*, 395–405.

Kinoshita, S., 1969. Periodical release of heparin-like polysaccharide within cytoplasm during cleavage of sea urchin egg. *Exp. Cell Res., 56,* 39–42.

Kinoshita, S., 1971. Heparin as a possible initiator of genomic RNA synthesis in early development of sea urchin embryos. *Exp. Cell Res., 64,* 403–411.

Kinoshita, S., and I. Yazaki, 1967. The behavior and localization of intracellular relaxing system during cleavage in the sea urchin egg. *Exp. Cell Res., 47,* 449–458.

Kojima, M. K., 1959. Relation between the vitally stained granules and cleavage activity in the sea urchin egg. *Embryologia, 4,* 191–209.

Kuhn, A., 1965. *Vorlesungen über Entwicklungsphysiologie,* 2nd ed. Springer-Verlag New York, Inc., New York.

Lorch, I. J., 1952. Enucleation of sea urchin blastomeres with or without removal of asters. *Quart. J. Microscop. Sci., 93,* 475–486.

Malkin, L. I., J. Mangan, and P. R. Gross, 1965. A crystalline protein of high molecular weight from cytoplasmic granules in sea urchin eggs and embryos. *Develop. Biol., 12,* 520–542.

Mangan, J., T. Miki-Noumura, and P. R. Gross, 1965. Protein synthesis and the mitotic apparatus. *Science, 147,* 1575.

Mazia, D., and K. Dan, 1952. The isolation and biochemical characterization of the mitotic apparatus of dividing cells. *Proc. Nat. Acad. Sci. U.S., 38,* 826–838.

Mazia, D., P. J. Harris, and T. Bibring, 1960. The multiplicity of the mitotic centers and the time course of their duplication and separation. *J. Biophys. Biochem. Cytol., 7.* 1–20.

Meeker, G. L., 1971. Intracellular potassium requirement for protein synthesis and mitotic apparatus formation in sea urchin eggs. *Exp. Cell Res., 63,* 165–170.

Meeker, G. L., and R. M. Iverson, 1971. Tubulin synthesis in fertilized sea urchin eggs. *Exp. Cell Res., 64,* 129–132.

Mercer, E. H., and L. Wolpert, 1958. Electron microscopy of cleaving sea urchin eggs. *Exp. Cell Res., 14,* 629–632.

Miki-Noumura, T., 1968. Purificaiton of the mitotic apparatus protein of sea urchin eggs. *Exp. Cell Res., 50,* 54–64.

Miki-Noumura, T., 1969. An actin-like protein of the sea urchin eggs. II. Direct isolation procedure. *Develop. Growth Differ.* (Nagoya), *11,* 219–231.

Miki-Noumura, T., and H. Kondo, 1970. Polymerization of actin from sea urchin eggs. *Exp. Cell Res., 61,* 31–41.

Miki-Noumura, T., and F. Oosawa, 1969. An actin-like protein of the sea urchin eggs. I. Its interaction with myosin from rabbit striated muscle. *Exp. Cell Res., 56,* 224–232.

Mohri, H., 1968. Amino acid composition of "tubulin" constituting microtubules of sperm flagella. *Nature* (London), *217,* 1053–1054.

Moore, A. R., 1938. Segregation of "cleavage substance" in the unfertilized egg of *Dendraster excentricus. Proc. Soc. Exp. Biol. Med., 38,* 162–163.

Raff, R. A., H. V. Colot, S. E. Selvig, and P. R. Gross, 1972. Oogenetic origin of messenger RNA for embryonic synthesis of microtubule protein. *Nature* (London), *235,* 211–214.

Raff, R. A., G. Greenhouse, K. W. Gross, and P. R. Gross, 1971. Synthesis and storage of microtubule proteins by sea urchin embryos. *J. Cell Biol., 50,* 516–527.

Rappaport, R., 1960. Cleavage of sand dollar eggs under constant tensile stress. *J. Exp. Zool., 144,* 225–231.

Rappaport, R., 1961. Experiments concerning the cleavage stimulus in sand dollar eggs. *J. Exp. Zool., 148,* 81–89.

Rappaport, R., 1964. Geometrical relations of the cleavage stimulus in constricted sand dollar eggs. *J. Exp. Zool., 155,* 225–230.

Rappaport, R., 1965. Geometrical relations of the cleavage stimulus in invertebrate eggs. *J. Theoret. Biol.*, *9*, 51–66.

Rappaport, R., 1966. Experiments concerning the cleavage furrow in invertebrate eggs. *J. Exp. Zool.*, *161*, 1–8.

Rappaport, R., 1969. Division of isolated furrows and furrow fragments in invertebrate eggs. *Exp. Cell Res.*, *56*, 87–91.

Rappaport, R., 1970. An experimental analysis of the role of cytoplasmic fountain streaming in furrow establishment. *Develop. Growth Differ.* (Nagoya), *12*, 31–40.

Rappaport, R., 1971. Cytokinesis in animal cells. *Int. Rev. Cytol.*, *31*, 169–213.

Rappaport, R., and R. P. Ebstein, 1965. Duration of stimulus and latent periods preceding furrow formation in sand dollar eggs. *J. Exp. Zool.*, *158*, 373–382.

Rebhun, L. I., and N. Sawada, 1969. Augmentation and dispersion of the *in vivo* mitotic apparatus of living marine eggs. *Protoplasma*, *68*, 1–22.

Rothschild, Lord, 1956. *Fertilization*. Methuen and Company Ltd., London.

Sakai, H., 1966. Studies on sulfhydryl groups during cell division of sea urchin eggs. 8. Some properties of mitotic apparatus proteins. *Biochim. Biophys. Acta*, *112*, 132–145.

Sakai, H., 1968. Contractile properties of protein threads from sea urchin eggs in relation to cell division. *Int. Rev. Cytol.*, *23*, 89–112.

Stafford, D. W., and R. M. Iverson, 1964. Radioautographic evidence for the incorporation of leucine carbon-14 into mitotic apparatus. *Science*, *143*, 580–581.

Stephens, R. E., 1967. The mitotic apparatus, physical chemical characterization of the 22S protein component and its subunits. *J. Cell Biol.*, *32*, 255–275.

Stephens, R. E., 1968. On the structural proteins of flagellar outer fibers. *J. Mol. Biol.*, *32*, 277–283.

Stephens, R. E., 1970. Thermal fractionation of outer doublet microtubules into A- and B-subfiber components A- and B-tubulin. *J. Mol. Biol.*, *47*, 353–363.

Sugiyama, M., 1951. Re-fertilization of the fertilized eggs of the sea urchin. *Biol. Bull. Mar. Biol. Lab., Woods Hole*, *101*, 335–344.

Swann, M. M., and J. M. Mitchison, 1953. Cleavage of sea urchin eggs in colchicine. *J. Exp. Biol.*, *30*, 506–514.

Swann, M. M., and J. M. Mitchison, 1958. The mechanism of cleavage in animal cells. *Biol. Rev.*, *33*, 103–132.

Tilney, L. G., and J. R. Gibbins, 1968. Differential effects of antimitotic agents on the stability and behavior of cytoplasmic and ciliary tubules. *Protoplasma*, *65*, 167–169.

Tilney, L. G., and D. Marsland, 1969. A fine structural analysis of cleavage induction and furrowing in the eggs of *Arbacia punctulata*. *J. Cell. Biol.*, *42*, 170–184.

Timourian, H., and P. C. Denny, 1964. Activation of protein synthesis in sea urchin eggs upon fertilization in relation to magnesium and potassium ions. *J. Exp. Zool.*, *155*, 57–70.

Timourian, H., P. C. Denny, and A. Tyler, 1963. Protein synthesis and development of sea urchin embryos in relation to potassium and magnesium. *Amer. Zool.*, *3*, 485.

Timourian, H., and G. Watchmaker, 1971. Bipolar and tetrapolar cleavage time in sea urchin eggs. *Exp. Cell Res.*, *68*, 428–430.

Vacquier, V.D., 1968. The connection of blastomeres of sea urchin embryos by filopodia. *Exp. Cell Res.*, *52*, 571–581.

Weiss, P., 1939. *Principles of Development*. Holt, Rinehart and Winston, Inc., New York.

Went, H. A., 1959a. Some immunochemical studies on the mitotic apparatus of the sea urchin. *J. Biophys. Biochem. Cytol.*, *5*, 353–356.

Went, H. A., 1959b. Studies on the mitotic apparatus of the sea urchin by means of antigen-antibody reactions in agar. *J. Biophys. Biochem. Cytol., 6,* 447–455.

Went, H. A., 1960. Dynamic aspects of mitotic apparatus protein. *Ann. N.Y. Acad. Sci., 90,* 422–429.

Wolpert, L., 1960. The mechanics and mechanisms of cleavage. *Int. Rev. Cytol., 10,* 163–216.

Zimmerman, A., and D. Marsland, 1960. Experimental induction of the furrowing reaction in eggs of *Arbacia punctulata. Ann. N.Y. Acad. Sci., 90,* 490–485.

CHAPTER V

Later Stages of Development

BLASTULATION

The blastula is usually considered as the stage at which the embryo is poised to begin the cellular movements of gastrula. In the sea urchin and other animals that have a small amount of yolk, blastulation is commonly characterized by the organization of the cells of the embryo into a hollow sphere. In the sea urchin, blastula is the stage at which the animal hatches. It ciliates, it digests its fertilization membrane through the activity of a hatching enzyme, and it becomes free swimming, with the cilia providing motility. Blastula is also a time at which respiratory activity and various types of synthetic activity level off in rate after a steep climb that began at fertilization. The rates of these activities will begin another steep climb at gastrula, ostensibly to support morphogenesis. At blastula, the sea urchin embryo is polarized with respect to morphogenetic tendency, and biochemical activity has become graded along the axis formed by this polarization, yet blastula is a time at which biochemical differentiation, as manifested by the synthesis of new chemical species, has not gained much momentum.

The embryo begins to take on a rounded form as early as the 128-cell stage, but it may be said to have attained the status of blastula only after it has undergone about 10 cleavages and acquired approximately 1000 cells. Hatching may occur at 7 or 8 hours after fertilization, depending upon the species and upon the temperature and other parameters. At blastula the cells come to form a single layer that encloses the blastocoel, a fluid-filled cavity. The fluid of the blastocoel has been shown by Monné and Hårde (1951) to contain a colloid substance, which may be largely mucopolysaccharide in nature. Wolpert and Mercer (1963) have demonstrated by electron microscopy the presence of fibrous material in the blastocoel.

Berg and Akin (1971) devised a means of isolating the blastocoel fluid by pressing it out through the use of centrifugation. When this fluid is applied externally to embryos, it reversibly blocks gastrulation, although the ingression of micromeres to form a mesenchyme blastula does occur. If this effect is not the result of alteration of the fluid by the extraction process, it is difficult to explain other than in terms of a difference in chemical behavior between the inside and outside of the blastula cells and/or an interference by some substance in the fluid with interactions between the external surface of the cells and the hyaline layer that are necessary for gastrulation.

The mechanism that causes the blastula to assume the form of a hollow sphere is not known. It is conceivable that osmotic forces within the blastocoel, due to the presence of colloid, may inflate the blastula. Gustafson and Wolpert (1963) have discounted the effect of osmotic forces. They have postulated that the outstanding force in blastula formation is the strong tendency for cells to adhere to the hyaline layer, even to the extent of sending out microvilli to increase surface contact with it. They visualize a force of cell movement, engendered by the magnitude of this affinity for the hyaline layer relative to the magnitude of forces that cause cells to adhere to one another, as packing the cells into a single layer.

The cilia, which develop as the embryo blastulates, rotate the animal within the fertilization membrane before it is freed of that investment. Those cilia at the animal pole become longer and coarser than their brethren and form into a tuft. Cilia are retained throughout early development and serve as the mechanism of motility for the pluteus larva. The number, length, and location of cilia, at least during blastulation, are under the control of biochemical gradients within the embryo. Forces that alter the complexion of these gradients often produce profound changes in the pattern of ciliation. More, however, may be involved in the induction of cilia formation than the distribution and concentration within a cell of substances significant in biochemical gradients. Amemiya (1971) has demonstrated that deciliated blastomeres that have been dissociated from swimming blastulae, as well as blastomeres dissociated from blastulae just prior to ciliation, will not regenerate cilia or form cilia, as the case may be, if reaggregation is prevented. This finding implies that cellular interactions are a prerequisite for cilia formation.

Auclair and Meismer (1965) isolated cilia during the ciliation period in development and studied the incorporation of amino acids into them. They found that there was incorporation into ciliary protein and that the blocking of transcription of nuclear genes by actinomycin D had a repressive effect on this incorporation. Auclair and Siegel (1966) reexamined the problem. They investigated the synthesis of proteins in regenerating cilia of *Paracentrotus lividus* following deciliation at late gastrula. They found that actinomycin D did *not* affect the synthesis of ciliary protein but that this synthesis was blocked by puromycin, which inhibits total protein synthesis in the cell. In the presence of puromycin, however, the cilia could be regenerated readily.

These experiments show that there are reserve pools—probably large ones—of proteins for cilia production present in the cells of the embryo. Since cilia form when protein synthesis is severely repressed, the reserve pools probably contain *all* types of protein necessary to produce cilia. Auclair and Siegel concluded that the synthesis of ciliary protein which feeds these pools occurs on maternal m-RNA. This work was done with whole cilia, and the experiments say nothing about the kinds of ciliary protein that are being labeled or are not being labeled. In particular, they provide no specific information on tubulin synthesis.

The hatching enzyme, which is responsible for the dissolution of the fertilization membrane, was discovered by Ishida in 1936. Yasumasu (1960 and 1963) found that it is contained in a particulate system that precipitates upon centrifugation at $10,000 \times g$ for 30 minutes. The nature of the particulate is not known. There is a possibility that it is a secretory vesicle responsible for delivering the enzyme into the perivitelline space. The hatching enzyme shows evidence of being synthesized after fertilization, at least in part on message transcribed from maternal genes at oogenesis. Barrett, and Angelo (1969) found that the enzyme has a different sensitivity to manganese ions in *Strongylocentrotus purpuratus* than in *Strongylocentrotus fran-*

ciscanus. In reciprocal crosses between the two species, the sensitivity of the enzyme to the manganese ion is invariably that of the maternal species. Such evidence relates to some degree also to the time of expression of maternal versus paternal genes. Protein synthesis before blastula has not been shown to occur on paternal genes, although some workers, particularly in the field of interspecific hybridization, have some reservations as to whether it cannot so occur.

Another type of synthesis occurs during blastula that may be of morphogenetic significance in the immediate future of the embryo at this stage, although there is no proof that it is not merely a maintenance synthesis. Citkowitz (1971) has demonstrated that protein is being synthesized and deposited in the hyaline layer. Autoradiography shows a uniform distribution of grains in this layer at blastula when embryos are incubated with labeled amino acids. As the animal goes into gastrula there is a reduction of labeling in the vegetal region of the layer. The hyaline layer is believed to play an important role in invagination. It can be postulated that this synthesis may alter the structural makeup or physical properties of the hyaline layer to adapt it to its function in gastrulation.

MESENCHYME BLASTULA

After hatching, the blastula swims about for 6 or 7 hours depending on the variables discussed above, maintaining the while its spherical shape. It then flattens and thickens at the vegetal pole, and there occurs an ingression to the blastocoel of the micromeres to produce primary mesenchyme. This ingression marks the mesenchyme blastula stage. Gastrulation follows shortly thereafter. At the time of ingression the micromeres show considerable pulsation of their surfaces. Balinsky investigated the problem of ingression in 1959 by electron microscopy. His work suggests that the ingression may occur because the cells lose their ability to adhere to one another and to the hyaline layer. About 40 or 50 cells enter and accumulate initially at the vegetal polar region. They become amoeboid, and the movement of their filopods or pseudopods, coupled with the contacts which these processes make with surrounding cells, is probably responsible for their distribution at a given time in later development. Primary mesenchyme cells before and after ingression are seen in Figs. 11 and 12.

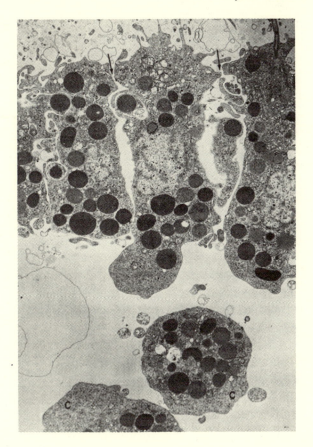

Figure 11

Section cut through the vegetal pole of a late blastula. Magnification: 11,000×.
Lobes that have been associated by some authors with pulsatory pseudopods may
be seen projecting from the basal surfaces of the ectodermal cells. The appearance
of such lobes is a prelude to the ingression of these cells to the blastocoel. The lobes
have a high ribosome content and are richly endowed with rough endoplasmic
reticulum. The contents of these lobes appear to remain segregated in primary
mesenchyme cells in the form of a ribosome-rich cap (C), which may be seen on
the two primary mesenchyme cells. Arrows indicate loci of desmosomes, which are
disappearing or have disappeared. The outer surface of the ectodermal cells is
thrown up into projections that extend into the hyaline layer. [From Gibbins et al.
(1969); by permission.]

Hagström and Lonning (1969) demonstrated by light and electron
microscopy that micromeres will at times form a syncytium with one
another and with macromeres. They will likewise form a syncytium
with mesomeres when implanted in animal halves. This same ten-

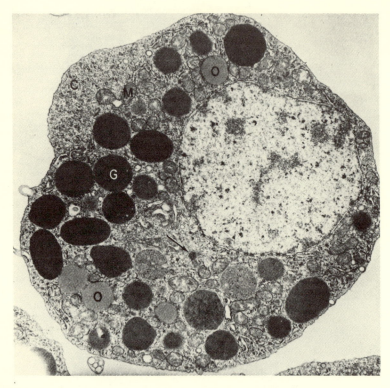

Figure 12

Low-power electron micrograph of a section cut through an entire primary mesenchyme cell. Magnification: 16,000×. Yolk granules (G), oil droplets (O), and mitochondria (M) are shown in sharp detail. Arrow indicates a centriole. A golgi apparatus with two stacks of cisternae is seen to one side of the centriole. Note that the cap (C) contains primarily ribosomes. The cap region is postulated to give rise to the pseudopod, which participates in the formation of cables for skeleton production. [From Gibbins et al. (1969); by permission.]

dency for syncytium formation was observed among primary mesenchyme cells. Pucci-Minafra et al. (1968) found that micromeres also form syncytia when isolated and cultured. It is tempting to identify the union of cytoplasm between micromere and macromere with the inductive function of the micromeres and with the transmission of information from cell to cell in order to direct morphogenetic reactions. The formation of syncytia between micromere and micromere and between one primary mesenchyme cell and another is more difficult to assess. The formation of temporary syncytia is seen under a variety of circumstances in living systems, not all of which appear to reflect the establishment of a mechanism for passing information from cell to cell. Further research on this problem is needed.

The mesenchyme blastula stage in the sea urchin is of considerable interest. In embryonic systems the gastrula is generally the stage at which one sees an accelerated appearance of new protein species associated with the process of differentiation, changes in the ratio of translational to transcriptional control, and probably the first expression of the paternal genes. In the sea urchin there may be the beginnings at mesenchyme blastula of some of the chemical events that characterize the gastrula. This stage corresponds to some aspects of gastrulation in many other animal species.

GASTRULA AND PRISM STAGES

The events described immediately below are illustrated in the sketches in Fig. 13 of the various stages in development from mesenchyme blastula to the pluteus larva. Gastrulation in the sea urchin embryo has been studied by time-lapse cinematography and other methods, so that a fairly complete description of it is available (see Gustafson and Kinnander, 1956; Trinkhaus, 1965). It occurs in two principal phases: The first is characterized by the partial invagination of the archenteron, involving its elongation into the interior of the embryo to the extent of one quarter to one third of its final length. This movement is autonomous, resulting from forces inherent to the cells of the vegetal region. The second phase results from the activity of secondary mesenchyme cells, which are produced by the archenteron. These cells put out filopods, which are very fine pseudopods. These make repeated contacts with the roof of the bastocoel until stable contacts have been achieved. When a number of these lasting contacts have been made, the filopods contract to pull the archenteron to full invagination.

The tip of the archenteron then bends ventrally and fuses with the stomodaeal region of the ectoderm, a region situated laterally just below the animal pole. Here, a breakdown of the fused tissues will form the future mouth. A small invagination occurs in the stomo-

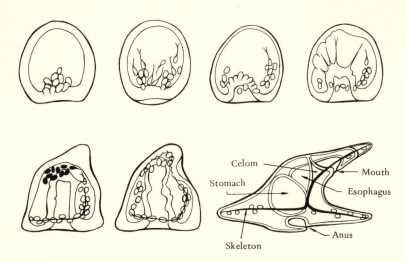

Figure 13

Some stages in the early development of *Psammechinus miliaris*. Top row shows, from left to right, the flattening of the vegetal region to form the vegetal plate, the ingression of primary mesenchyme and its initial deployment in skeleton formation, the formation of the rudiment of the primitive gut by invagination, and the formation of filopods by secondary mesenchyme on the roof of the archenteron. Bottom row left shows the beginnings of skeleton formation by primary mesenchyme. Secondary mesenchyme cells are shown in black. Bottom row center reveals the invagination in the region of the future mouth. The pluteus is shown at bottom row right. (Redrawn from Gustafson and Toneby, 1971. Reprinted by permission, *American Scientist,* journal of The Society of the Sigma Xi.)

daeal ectoderm by a mechanism not yet determined, but possibly similar to that responsible for the first (autonomous) phase of the invagination of the archenteron.

The archenteron gradually differentiates an esophagus and a stomach. The original opening (blastopore) of the invaginating archenteron becomes differentiated into an anus in accordance with the normal pattern of deuterostome development. A coelomic rudiment forms from the archenteron near the mouth region. Two coelomic sacs are ultimately produced, one of which sends an extension to the dorsal ectoderm to become the primary pore canal. The anlage of the hydropore, the opening of this canal to the surface, forms even when a coelomic rudiment is lacking, showing that it is independent of coelomic differentiation. The archenteron of the coelomic rudiments, like that of the archenteron proper, produces secondary mesenchyme cells. These secondary mesenchyme cells remain for the most part within the walls of the coelomic rudiment, but send out filopods. The filopods become differentiated into muscular elements, associating with the esophagus to promote swallowing or with the coelom to produce pumping activity (see Gustafson and Toneby, 1971). Figure 14 shows the detail of these coelomic filopods. For convenience in photography, the picture was taken, not from a normal development, but from one in which the gastrula was partially evaginated by experimental treatment. The filopods may be assumed to be undamaged.

The skeleton, formed by primary mesenchyme cells, starts as a pair of triradiate spicules. As more spicules are produced, they are consolidated into skeletal bars. The growth of the skeletal structure pushes out the ectoderm in the direction of elongation of skeletal elements and determines to quite a degree the ultimate shape of the

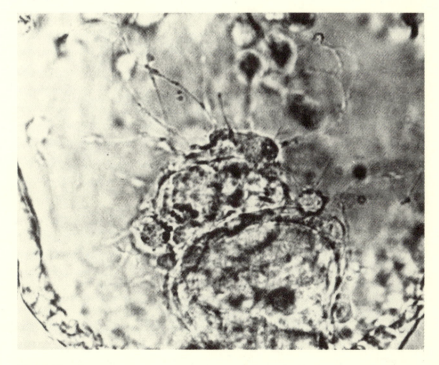

Figure 14

Pseudopods of secondary mesenchyme radiating from the unpaired coelom of a vegetalized partial exogastrula of a sea urchin. See the text. [From Gustafson and Wolpert (1963); by permission.]

pluteus. In the very early stages of skeletal formation the embryo becomes flattened in the oral and anal regions and assumes a triangular shape. The animal pole and surrounding region are raised into an apex, which tips ventrally to face in the same direction as the future mouth. This produces a change of axis. The future mouth and the apical tuft are now facing anteriorly, and the blastopore or anal region opens ventrally. The gut thus assumes a J shape. At approximately the time when the embryo embarks on this change of axis it is termed a *prism larva*. It will not be considered a pluteus until it develops arms (pushed out by its skeletal rods) and loses its ciliary tuft.

The mechanisms involved in the first stage of invagination at gastrula are not well understood. Gustafson and Wolpert (1963) have propounded an interesting theory to explain them. The theory has to do with the relative tendency of cells in a sheet (as in the instance of the single layer of the blastula) to adhere to an elastic supporting layer (such as the hyaline layer) compared to their tendency to adhere to one another (see Fig. 15). Some of the points of the theory are as follows:

1. In a given region, if in a sheet of cells the individual cells gain contact with one another and lose some contact with the supporting membrane they will become columnar (grow taller). Such an effect may possibly explain the thickening of the vegetal region at mesenchyme blastula.

2. If the cells increase contact with one another but do *not* lose contact with the supporting membrane, the sheet will curve. If the supporting membrane will yield, the curve will represent an evagination (viewed from the standpoint of gastrular invagination). If the elastic forces in the supporting membrane are strong so that it will not yield, the curve will be an invagination. It is doubtful, nonetheless, that gastrulation occurs by this mechanism.

3. If the elastic forces in the membrane are strong, and the cells *lose* considerable contact with one another and with the membrane, there will be a rounding up of the cells and an *extensive* invagination. This appears to be the premise most applicable to gastrulation.

It is known that the cells of the vegetal plate round up, evincing pulsating movements as they do so. They do not lose complete contact with one another nor do they lose a great deal of contact with the hyaline layer. The rounding-up process causes the rupture of desmosomal connections that exist between adjacent cells in the blastula. The notion that the cells of the vegetal plate assist the invagina-

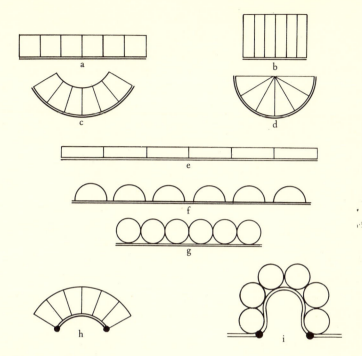

Figure 15

Models to illustrate the effect of changes in contact between cells, and between cells and a supporting membrane, in the form of a cell sheet. The cross-sectional area of the cells is fixed. (a) Moderate contact between cells and between cells and the supporting membrane. (b) Increased contact between the cells and loss of contact with the supporting membrane. (c) Increased contact between the cells and no change in degree of contact of cells with supporting membrane. (d) The effect of a further increase in contact between the cells, compared to that in (c), with no loss in contact with the supporting membrane. (e) The effect of stretching the supporting membrane if the cells are able to increase their contact with it. (f) The effect of stretching the supporting membrane if the cells are able to increase their contact with the membrane, but not to the same extent as in (e), and lose contact with one another. (g) The effect of the cells in (a) rounding up. The sheet becomes longer. (h) The effect of the cells in (b) reducing their contact with one another if the ends of the sheet are fixed. The sheet becomes curved. (i) The effect of the cells in (b) rounding up if the ends of the sheet are fixed. For further details, see text. [Redrawn from Gustafson and Wolpert (1963); by permission.]

tion by increasing in number must be rejected. There is little or no cell division in the region during the period of autonomous invagination.

The loss of contact with one another and with the hyaline layer by the cells of the plate is not sufficient in itself to produce invagination. Another condition must apply. The area in which this special cellular behavior occurs must be anchored at its perimeter. The invagination must have a force to oppose it. It is not certain whether the cells of the perimeter of the invagination offer a passive resistance to the pull of the invaginating archenteron or whether they generate forces which actively pull against the archenteron.

In 1939 and 1941, Moore performed experiments on *Dendraster excentricus* in which he excised the vegetal plate just prior to the beginning of gastrula. The results were spectacular. The central portion of the isolated plate demonstrated the movements characteristic of invagination. The edges of the plate then rolled upward and closed together to form a miniscule gastrula. Surgical incisions made in the plate while the invaginating movements were in progress tended to widen, their edges pulling apart. This widening would appear to reflect a situation in which the whole plate is under tension. The cells of this isolated vegetal plate, however, have been deprived of what might be conceived to be a very powerful system for opposing the forces exerted by the invaginating archenteron, that is, the vector of the forces exerted by the cells of the sphere of the blastula, the elasticity of the hyaline layer surrounding them, and probably to some degree the hydrostatic pressure of the blastocoel fluid. The cells at the perimeter of the invagination, nonetheless, manage to resist the invagination to the extent of generating considerable tension. It is possible to visualize these cells as offering a passive resistance to invagination, perhaps by being compressed into a ring like the bricks in a rounded arch by the elastic forces in the hyaline layer of the plate; but, intuitively, they may be suspected of generating active forces of resistance, particularly in the light of the rolling upward of the outer edges of the isolated plate.

A finding that may figure importantly in theories of the mechanism of invagination at gastrula was made by Citkowitz in 1971. She developed a technique for isolating the hyaline layer of the sea urchin embryo in a nearly intact form. The hyaline layer so isolated at blastula had the form of a hollow sphere. That isolated at gastrula had similarly the form of a hollow sphere, but it contained an indentation or inpocketing, supposedly in the region of the invaginated archenteron. Beyond pointing to the fact that the hyaline layer enters the blastocoel with the archenteron, the finding raises the question as to why the inpocketing persists after the removal of the hyaline layer. It could either have been stiffened or lost elasticity so that it was unable to snap back out. It is also possible that the residual intrinsic forces which maintain in a spherical form the empty hyaline layer that formerly surrounded the ectoderm are operating to preserve this portion of a smaller sphere. Protein synthesis at late blastula was revealed by autoradiography to be less in amount in the region over the vegetal plate than in the region surrounding the future ectoderm. One might speculate that the protein produced could contribute to a difference in physical properties between the two regions.

In summary, the theory of Gustafson and Wolpert proposes that the first step of gastrulation may be attributed to the interaction between at least three major forces: the degree at any time of contact of the cells of the vegetal plate with one another, the degree at any time of their contact with the hyaline layer, and the degree of elasticity in the hyaline layer. Whether this theory proves ultimately to be valid or not, it is at present a useful basis for visualizing the forces involved in the first phase of gastrulation in the sea urchin embryo.

Where the second phase of invagination is concerned, it is tempting to speculate that there may exist on the surface of the cells of the blastocoel roof and on the surface of filopods, substances that react with one another with varying free energies of binding. The stable contact may represent a situation at which the energy characteristics of the bonds are optimal. The direction in which the archenteron is pulled is definite, not random. It is possible that the favorable sites for filopod attachment are most numerous in the stomodaeal region. Gustafson and Wolpert submit that attachments with the dorsal roof in the region of the animal pole are probably made because this is the nearest region to the tip of the archenteron, where the preponderance of the secondary mesenchyme cells exist.

The pulsation of cells and/or the formation of filopods are seen in the majority of visible morphogenetic events leading to the formation of the pluteus. Pulsation is seen in the ingression of micromeres, in primary mesenchyme cells, in cells of the vegetal plate prior to invagination, in cells of the forming coelomic rudiment, and in the formation of neuron-like cells in the pluteus. Filopods form on the archenteron tip for the second stage of gastrulation, in the attachment of the archenteron to the stomodaeal invagination, on the coelom for the production of muscle elements, and in primary mesenchyme for motility and skeleton formation. Each new morphogenetic event is initiated by the activation of mechanisms of motility in cells. Filopodal function reflects the activity, in one way or another, of a contractile system, and it is probable that pulsatility does also, although the cause of pulsatility has not been established. The preponderance of cells that show pulsatile activity in morphogenesis ultimately develop filopods, and it is possible that pulsation is the outward sign of a series of changes that leads to the organization of a contractile system for filopods, apart from any contribution to morphogenesis that pulsation may make by breaking association between cells. Ultrastructural studies of filopods and of cells containing them reveal the presence of cytoplasmic microtubules and of 50 Å filaments reminiscent of those seen in the cortex of cleaving cells.

Gibbins and Tilney (1965) and Tilney and Gibbins (1969a, 1969b) have studied the filaments and microtubules of the filopods of secondary mesenchyme by electron microscopy. They have observed that the filopods are filled with filaments 50 Å in diameter and have large numbers of microtubules at their bases. Microtubules are also found in the regions of the cytoplasm near the filopods. These microtubules appear to have been formed from a centriole near the center of the cell, and they radiate outward from this centriole. Yolk granules and mitochondria are numerous at the base of the filopods. Both colchicine and hydrostatic pressure, which cause the dissolution of the microtubules of secondary mesenchyme, will cause the cessation of the second phase of invagination of the archenteron. These workers believe that the microtubules figure in the *formation* of the filopods, whereas the filaments are involved in their *contraction.*

Gibbins et al. (1969) have investigated the ultrastructure of primary mesenchyme and find a somewhat similar picture. Upon ingression, the cilia of the erstwhile micromeres are lost, and immediately prior to this loss, microtubules are seen radiating in all directions from the basal body. In the primary mesenchyme cells inside the blastocoel, one observes the same pattern of radiating microtubules as in secondary mesenchyme, also emanating from a centriole in the center of the cell. It is probable that this centriole, which produces the cytoplasmic microtubules, was derived from the ciliary basal body. The cytoplasmic microtubules enter filopods as they form, and once skeleton formation has begun, the microtubules of the filopod lose connection with their centriole.

Understanding of the mechanisms of filopodal activity is likely to be improved as the work on the nature of microtubules and filaments progresses. More knowledge is needed on the relationship between the microtubules and the filaments. Although the dimension of the cross section of a filament is not greatly disparate from the thickness of the wall of a microtubule, it would appear likely that the filaments may be components of an actin-like contractile system, similar to that which has been described in connection with cleavage furrow formation. The microtubule, however, is also a contractile fiber. Although it may well be responsible for the formation of the filopod as suggested by Tilney and Gibbins, one may suspect that it may function in primary mesenchyme in a manner similar to that suggested for neurotubules in the axon, to transport materials along the length of the filopod. Such transport would serve to support skeleton formation. Studies now in progress with filopods of heliozoa and tentacles of suctorians may, however, ultimately demonstrate that microtubules, as opposed to filaments, may be responsible for the contraction of filopods.

Gustafson and Toneby (1971) have proposed that the cellular movements which characterize the onset of gastrulation may be triggered by serotonin, accumulated in the vegetal regions of the blastula. Serotonin levels, however, appear to fall off after early gastrula and may become too low for the substance to be involved as a trigger for cellular movements in the later phases of this developmental stage. Gustafson and Toneby postulate that an acetylcholine–cholinesterase system may be responsible for stimulating the filopodal contractions of secondary mesenchyme in the second phase of gastrulation. Buznikov et al. (1964, 1968, 1970) have determined that significant levels of serotonin and acetylcholine may be found at various developmental stages. The overall picture that is emerging from such studies is that neurohumors may prove not only to trigger the initiation of motility that characterizes different phases of morphogenesis, but also to be responsible for such activities as the stimulation of ciliary movement in swimming blastulae.

It is virtually impossible to isolate the subject of gastrulation in a discussion of morphogenesis. Gastrulation occurs because of events that have preceded it, and gastrulation coexists with the beginnings of many of the major events that follow it. It is not, in fact, an isolated phenomenon in morphogenesis. There are, however, many events which occur at gastrulation that make the stage a time of major importance in development. It is a time of extensive physiological change as well as structural change. A definitive nucleolus appears in cells for the first time, and the first significant synthesis after fertilization of r-RNA and of t-RNA occurs at gastrula or soon thereafter. Oxygen consumption increases sharply. Gastrula is usually the time when interspecific hybrids begin to show paternal characteristics. There is a sharp increase in the propensity of the cells of the embryo for differentiative change at this time, and an increased number of new message types are required and produced. Eggs chemically, mechanically, or radiologically enucleated immediately following fertilization rarely, if ever, achieve gastrulation. Mitotic activity is not especially high at gastrula in comparison to previous stages.

PRIMARY MESENCHYME
AND SKELETON FORMATION

Once inside the blastocoel, primary mesenchyme cells move about through the activity of their filopods. The filopods, like those of secondary mesenchyme, establish stable contact with the inner surface of those cells of the blastula which are soon to become ectoderm. The pattern of these contacts, which may show some tendency to change as development proceeds, determines the morphology of the skeleton, and is determined, in turn, by the configuration of sites on the surface of the ectoderm cells that are optimal for the attachment of the filopods. The ectoderm thus participates in the shaping of a mesodermal structure. The deployment of the primary mesenchyme by this means results in the formation of a ring of cells in the vegetal region with a pair of arms extending toward the animal pole. From this structure a pair of triradiate spicules begins to form.

We shall mention only a few details of skeleton formation here, although a great deal is known about the phenomenon. The reader is referred to von Ubisch (1937, 1950), Bevelander and Nakahara (1960), and Okazaki (1956, 1960, 1961, 1962, 1965).

As skeleton formation begins, the filopods of several cells in critical locations combine into a common cable. The cable is believed to produce a syncytium. We have noted above a general tendency for primary mesenchyme to form syncytia, and we see here one aspect of it. Several of these cables may ultimately be formed. The calcite for the skeleton is laid down initially within these cables and then secreted. The chemical and molecular mechanisms of deposition are not known. It has not been determined, to the best of our knowledge, what the mechanism is for producing an organic matrix for deposition, but such a matrix is known to be present here. A triradiate spicule is believed to be initiated at a point where three cables converge. The spicules grow and form arms by further deposition of mineral.

Wolpert and Gustafson (1961) have proposed that two fundamental mechanisms are responsible for skeletal structure. One is a crystallographic mechanism that is responsible for the orientation of the crystals within the skeletal arms, and which is so precise that, as Gustafson and Wolpert (1963) have commented, the skeleton has the appearance of being carved from a single crystal. This mechanism also provides for the initial triradiate shape of the skeleton and for the tendency of skeletal branches to grow in a straight line unless altered in direction by the filopodal cables.

The other mechanism is, of course, the activity of the filopodal cables. They reorient the initial triradiate structure, which is laid down randomly. They are responsible for the various bends and branches in the skeleton. They reorient the overall pattern of the forming skeleton through development until it achieves its final configuration.

The skeleton is a paired structure (see Fig. 16). Each member of the pair possesses three main branches: the body rod, which elongates the larva posteriorly; the oral rod, which elongates one of the two oral arms; and the anal rod, which elongates one of the two anal arms. Anlagen for the arms actually form as buds at four points in a ciliary band at the perimeter of the oral region. They have, however little capacity for autonomous elongation. The arms become longer only when they are pushed forth by the skeleton. The structures being elongated are protected from being punctured by the skeletal rod through the padding effect of a small plug of mesenchyme cells interposed between the elongating tip of each rod and the cells of the ectoderm.

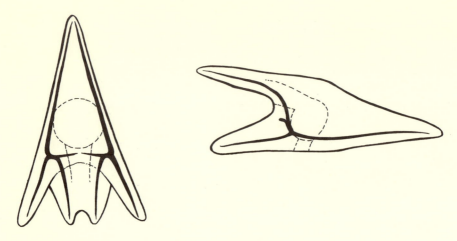

Figure 16

Pluteal skeleton seen from above (left) and from the side (right). The gut is shown in dashed lines. Figure on right shows one member of each pair of rods. The body rod points to the posterior end of the animal. The oral rod extends into an oral arm at the top, and the anal rod extends into an anal arm at the bottom of the figure. The midventral rod is seen as a small projection between oral and anal rods. In the figure on the left, the oral rods are medial and the anal rods lateral. The midventral rods extend transversely. [Redrawn from Gustafson and Wolpert (1963); by permission.]

PLUTEUS

The general morphogenetic steps leading to the formation of the pluteus have been described above. Larvation is swift in the sea urchin. The pluteus is fully formed about 24 hours after fertilization in some species. Actually, the pluteus, while appearing somewhat larger than earlier stages of development, has been stretched by skeletal growth. The sea urchin embryo is not capable of any appreciable growth until it starts to feed. For the first 3 or 4 days after it comes to full development, the pluteus can feed on material normally found in seawater. After that, it requires artificial feeding in the laboratory. It is usually fed diatoms and protozoa.

The pluteus will not develop in water that is deficient in calcium, magnesium, carbonate, and, probably, sulfate ions, since these ions are a prerequisite for the formation of its skeleton. In metamorphosis the pluteal skeletal spines are broken up and discarded. Primary mesenchyme cells form the ossicles of the test, the spines, the lantern, and the teeth in the adult.

The pluteus swims by the movement of its cilia, which cover the surface of its body. Its position in locomotion is with the arms and mouth forward.

Although a multitude of studies have been made on the pluteus in the realm of molecular biology and biochemistry in recent years, there has been very little work done recently on morphogenesis in the larva. Gustafson and Toneby (1971) have reported the beginnings of what may be a rudimentary nervous system in the pluteus. Ciliated epidermal cells round up, pulsate, move into the body cavity, and form into a pattern that has at least the appearance of being a nervous system. They absorb some pigment, which the authors believe to constitute precursor for the formation of neurohumors.

Harvey (1956) has described and photographed the postpluteal development of *Arbacia punctulata*. She has appended to this description a good bibliography of larval and metamorphic development in other species. Hyman (1955) has compiled a great deal of valuable information on metamorphic development in echinoids. A discussion of metamorphosis may also be found in Czihak (1971).

BIOCHEMICAL GRADIENTS IN THE EMBRYO

We have completed our description of the panorama of change in the embryo during development, and the time has come to discuss in detail some of the events occurring at the molecular level that are characteristic of some of the stages of development and/or responsible for them. It is not within the scope of this discussion to consider the entire spectrum of chemical studies that have been made on the sea urchin embryo; we shall limit ourselves primarily to problems of information flow and protein biosynthesis.

The molecular approach to developmental biology begins with the exploration in detail of biochemical events within the embryo in the hope and expectation that when an adequate amount of information has been garnered the events considered in the field of experimental embryology or of descriptive embryology, for example the aspects of morphogenesis revealed by light and electron microscopy, may be explained. That goal has been rarely attained to date, partly because the field to be explored is vast and complicated and partly because the research is not geared to the systematic exploration of all aspects of a problem, but rather, tends to concern itself with major aspects or with isolated, but interesting, aspects. The situation is not unlike one in which when assembling a jigsaw puzzle a person first attempts to assemble the principal figures and, having accomplished this, cannot determine what the figures are doing until the background is filled in.

Before turning to molecular problems, let us consider briefly some important experimental work that has taken essentially the opposite approach, experimental work that began with the microscopist and his microdissection equipment and proceeded to the biochemical laboratory, where workers probed to find direct evidence of biochemical activity reflecting the findings of the microscopist. The problem involved here is that of gradients in the embryo.

The experimental embryologist found that the egg shows a polarity and that regions of the egg responsible for elaboration of structures in the larva are arranged in sequence from animal pole to vegetal pole. He also showed that the region presumptive for the formation of an organ or structure does not necessarily have the capability to ensure that the organ or structure will have a normal size or develop normal morphological characteristics. The animal region is responsible for the development of a certain pattern of ciliation, but it may develop excessive ciliation when separated from the vegetal region. The overall picture that emerged from studies in experimental embryology was that the animal region has a degree of responsibility for the normal development of the vegetal region and vice versa. We can thus speak of a vegetal propensity that controls to a degree the development of structures derived from the animal region and of an animal propensity that exerts control over the genesis and formation of structures derived from the vegetal region. The animal tendency is most powerful at the animal pole, and the vegetal tendency, at the vegetal pole. The strength of the propensities weakens in gradient fashion along the axis of the egg. This is the substance of the double-gradient theory.

Gradients give the initial indication that cells have become heterogeneous with respect to their morphogenetic proclivities. They are viewed as representing gradations in activity between small populations of cells. The properties of one population merge with those of its neighboring population in a manner that is mindful of the way an artist blends one color into another with his brush.

Studies on these tendencies have been aided by various chemical agents that cause development to aberrate from the normal in the direction of one of the two tendencies, usually by suppressing the effects of the other tendency. Lithium salts are the most common vegetalizing agent. Animalization is often achieved with thiocyanate.

The question then arises: One sees here the superficial evidence of a gradient. What is being graded? A number of biochemical features of the embryo have been investigated in search of an answer to this question. This is the simplest problem to solve among those that concern the grading of biochemical activity. It is much more difficult to determine whether graded substances interact and if so to characterize the reaction(s). Most difficult of all is the resolution of the relationship between reactions that occur and the phenomena observed by the experimental embryologists that led to the propounding of the double-gradient theory.

Since interest in gradients reached a peak at a time when many physiologists worshipped at the shrine of the Warburg respirometer, it is not surprising that a great deal of work has been devoted to the study of respiratory gradients. The respirometer, however, is not easily adapted to this type of work, and so investigators often resorted to the use of dyes to detect respiratory activity. Among the important dyes used were tetrazolium dyes, Janus green, or methylene blue, which give a characteristic color change upon *reduction*. Dye reduction reactions were thought to reflect to a large extent the activity of the hexose monophosphate shunt pathway, with the color change purportedly occurring as the direct result of the activity of dehydrogenase enzymes.

Child was working on the problem of reduction gradients as early as 1936. Later investigations of dye reduction were made by Hörstadius (1952, 1955), Lallier (1958), and Bäckström (1959a). Their experiments have shown that there is a gradient of reducing activity in late cleavage and blastula and that it is an animal to vegetal gradient, in other words, is strongest at the animal pole. At about mesenchyme blastula a reduction gradient appears in the opposite direction, from the vegetal to the animal region. This second reduction gradient is purported to develop in association with mesendoderm formation.

The activity of the hexose monophosphate shunt has been studied in the total embryo (as opposed to regions of the embryo) by Bäckström (1959b, 1963). The cycle is very active at cleavage, but levels off at blastula, to increase again during mesenchyme blastula and early gastrula, at a time that coincides with the establishment of the second reduction gradient. As Gustafson (1965) has noted, the correlation between the two periods of shunt activity and the appearance of the two gradients would seem to be important, but it is to be hoped that it is a correlation and not a coincidence.

The studies of Hörstadius on reduction gradients involved some work with animal and vegetal halves. At mesenchyme blastula, the time when both gradients are first seen to be present, he was able to detect remnants of the animal-pole gradient in the vegetal half, but no trace of the vegetal-pole gradient in the animal half. This finding has been offered as an explanation of the fact that vegetal halves can often achieve normal development, whereas animal halves cannot. He also found that the implantation of micromeres in normal embryos establishes on extra reduction center, and that the implantation of micromeres in animal halves reestablishes the lost gradient emanating from the vegetal pole and allows normal development. These studies in 1952 and 1955 do not, of course, suggest how the gradient may have been established, whether by the triggering of synthesis, the activation of enzymes, or other means, but they at least establish the instigation of gradient activity by cellular interaction.

Respiratory gradients appeared to be involved with more than the activity of the shunt, and a great deal of work was done to show evidence of graded activity of other respiratory pathways. Czihak (1963) and Berg (1958) studied the activity of mitochondrial enzymes. Berg investigated the oxidation of reduced cytochrome c in animal and vegetal halves. At the 16-cell stage, both halves showed the same activity, but in later stages the activity was much higher in the animal half. Czihak studied the activity of cytochrome oxidase by the use of the indophenol blue reaction. He observed the existence of the animal-to-vegetal gradient as early as the eight-cell stage. At mesenchyme blastula, he still found the dorsal–ventral gradient, but found that activity in one half the animal region was considerably higher than in the other half. He was able to demonstrate that the site of higher activity was the site of the future oral field.

The question as to whether gradients of respiratory activity are reflected in the distribution of mitochondria in the embryo has been a center for some controversy. Gustafson and Lenicque (1952, 1955) reported that after mesenchyme blastula there are more stainable (with vital stains) mitochondria in the animal region than in the vegetal region. Shaver (1956) failed to observe gradients of mitochondrial distribution and criticized the techniques of Gustafson and Lenicque. Gustafson (1965) has discussed the controversy. Berg et al. (1962) and Berg and Long (1964) examined a variety of developmental stages by electron microscopy for evidence of gradients in mitochrondrial numbers, but could find none. They did find that mitochondria were larger in the vegetal region, a circumstance that suggests a difference in activity. Such a difference may be reflected in a difference in ratios of intramitochondrial to extramitochondrial malate dehydrogenase from vegetal to animal region that has been found by Villee and his co-workers, which will be discussed in another chapter.

Gradients have also been observed in the rate and extent of RNA and protein synthesis in the embryo. It is not known to what extent these gradients are associated with respiratory gradients or dependent upon them. It is usually wise to be cautious about making judgments on dependence or cause–effect relationships between parallel trends in respiration and RNA or protein synthesis. Gustafson (1965) has made the point that hexose monophosphate shunt activity may figure importantly in providing ribose for RNA synthesis. There are active metabolic pathways, the synthesis of inosine monophosphate for example, that contribute to RNA synthesis and that have a demand for ribose, but there is a limited amount of information available as to how much ribose production is actually required to support RNA synthesis in the development of the sea urchin embryo.

Markman (1961a, 1961b, 1961c) separated the 16–32 blastomere stage of *Paracentrotus lividus, Psammechinus miliaris,* and *Psammechinus microtuberculatus* into meridional halves surgically. He found by autoradiographic techniques that the incorporation of ^{14}C-adenine and ^{14}C-leucine in each half varied only slightly from 50 percent of that of the whole embryo. When he separated the embryos into animal and vegetal halves he found by contrast that incorporation into the animal half was considerably greater than 50 percent of that of the whole embryo. During blastula, also, the incorporation of ^{14}C-adenine and ^{14}C-leucine was much greater in the animal than in the vegetal region. At mesenchyme blastula, the incorporation of label into the RNA and protein of the vegetal region began to dominate, and the vegetal dominance grew even stronger at gastrula. This second gradient in RNA and protein synthesis corresponds in time and direction to the second reduction gradient. The overall picture on biochemical gradients is not very informative as to the nature of mechanisms of development. We have gained some idea as to what is graded. Respiratory activity, for example, is graded. Rates of synthesis of RNA and protein may be graded, although Berg (1968) came to believe that differences in amino acid incorporation in animal versus vegetal halves of *Lytechinus anamesus* may be due more to differences in uptake of the amino acids from the medium than to differences in rate of synthesis. Even assuming a gradation of rates of RNA and protein synthesis and a correlation between that gradation and gradation of respiratory activity, it is virtually impossible to give that correlation any meaningful evaluation. Does on increase in protein synthesis exist to provide enzymes for respiratory activity? Does an increase in respiratory activity exist to provide energy or metabolites for protein synthesis? Are both respiratory activity and protein synthesis triggered to provide energy and enzymes for certain reactions, and if so what reactions? These questions are simplistic, of course, but they point up the problem. We do know that certain definite proteins must be, and are, synthesized at certain times, histones for example, but what little we know of this synthesis has not been related to respiratory gradients.

It does not clarify the picture to know that if respiratory activity is not higher at site A than at site B, structure X will not form. Structure X will form because certain reactions will occur to make it possible for it to form, and those reactions will perhaps be qualitatively different from those necessary to form structure Y. Although gradients in respiratory activity may be expected to reflect considerably more than quantitative differences in the amount of ATP produced, it is impossible at the present time to relate quantitative differences in respiratory activity to qualitiative differences in reactions that give rise to structures. There are some morphogenetic events that could conceivably represent correlates to the gradient system. The apparent existence of stable contact regions for filopod attachment in the roof of the blastocoel for secondary mesenchyme and in the sides of the blastocoel for primary mesenchyme are animal and vegetal characteristics, respectively. These could require special synthetic and energetic activity for establishment. Inductive ability, mesendoderm formation, and cellular movement forces, which are all primarily vegetal characteristics, may have similar requirements. The problem is not that of finding where relationships may exist, but of finding ways of determining what the relationships are.

There has been a minimum amount of work done in applying the techniques of molecular biology to the problems related to biochemical gradients or to the problems of the experimental embryologist. Giudice and Hörstadius (1965) treated micromeres with actinomycin D and transplanted them on normal animal halves, as well as transplanting normal micromeres on actinomycin D-treated animal halves. They reported that there was no clear-cut loss of ability to develop normally that might be ascribed to the action of the antibiotic. Their conclusion was that between fertilization and the 16-cell stage, transcription is not required for the establishment of vegetal potentialities, nor is it needed to produce competence in the animal region. They achieved a somewhat low yield of normal embryos, however, and the degree of differentiation achieved where normal micromeres were used was enough less than that achieved with normal animal halves and treated micromeres for the possibility of the difference being due to the effect of actinomycin D to be real.

One outstanding difficulty associated with studies of biochemical gradients is the fact that so many of them have had to be performed with the use of dyes. The use of dyes does not represent the best approach to biochemical experimentation. At times dye studies have nonetheless represented the only feasible method to use for the investigation of important problems. Some dyes are quite specific in their action and generally quite reliable; others are not. The difficulties involved in the use of the Feulgen reaction for the study of nuclear DNA, which will be discussed in the following chapter, are an excellent example of the problems that can be encountered when dyes must be employed in biochemical research.

Workers have been interested in the question of whether natural animalizing or vegetalizing agents exist in the embryo, which might at times enhance one or the other of the tendencies and thereby exert a control over the activity of the double-gradient system. Hörstadius et al. (1967) reported the existence of a potential animalizing agent in the unfertilized egg. It appeared to be a macromolecule, but a somewhat small one, possibly a peptide. Josefsson and Hörstadius (1969) found several different substances in the unfertilized egg that are capable of producing either animalizing or vegetalizing effects. It remains to be demonstrated whether such substances are actually functional in normal development.

REFERENCES

Amemiya, S., 1971. Relationship betwen cilia formation and cell association in sea urchin embryos. *Exp. Cell Res., 64,* 227–230.

Auclair, W., and D. Meismer, 1965. Cilia development and associated protein synthesis in the sea urchin embryo. *Biol. Bull. Mar. Biol. Lab., Woods Hole, 129,* 397.

Auclair, W., and B. W. Siegel, 1966. Cilia regeneration in the sea urchin embryo: evidence for a pool of ciliary proteins. *Science, 154,* 913–915.

Bäckström, S., 1959a. Reduction of blue tetrazolium in developing sea urchin eggs after addition of various substances and phosphopyridine nucleotides. *Exp. Cell Res., 18,* 357–363.

Bäckström, S., 1959b. Activity of glucose-6-dehydrogenase in sea urchin embryos of different developmental trends. *Exp. Cell Res., 18,* 347–356.

Bäckström, S., 1963. 6-Phosphogluconate dehydrogenase in sea urchin embryos. *Exp. Cell Res., 32,* 566–569.

Balinsky, B. I., 1959. An electron microscope investigation of the mechanisms of adhesions of the cells in a sea urchin blastula and gastrula. *Exp. Cell Res., 16,* 429–433.

Barrett, D., and G. M. Angelo, 1969. Maternal characteristics of hatching enzymes in hybrid sea urchin embryos. *Exp. Cell Res., 57,* 159–166.

Berg, W. E., 1958. Distribution of cytochrome oxidase in early cleavage stage of Dendraster. *Exp. Cell Res., 50,* 679–683.

Berg, W. E., 1968. Rates of protein and nucleic acid synthesis in half embryos of the sea urchin. *Exp. Cell Res., 50,* 679–683.

Berg, W. E., and E. J. Akin, 1971. Inhibition of gastrulation by the blastocoel fluid from the sea urchin embryo. *Develop. Biol., 26,* 353–356.

Berg, W. E., and N. D. Long, 1964. Regional differences of mitochondrial size in the sea urchin embryo. *Exp. Cell Res., 33,* 422–437.

Berg, W. E., D. A. Taylor, and W. J. Humphreys, 1962. Distribution of mitochondria in echinoderm embryos as determined by electron microscopy. *Develop. Biol. 4,* 165–176.

Bevelander, G., and H. Nakahara, 1960. Development of the skeleton of the sand dollar. In R. F. Sognnaes (ed.), *Calcification in Biological Systems.* American Association for the Advancement of Science, Washington, D.C., *64,* 41–56.

Buznikov, G. A., I. V. Chudakova, and N. D. Zvezdina, 1964. The role of neurohumors in early embryogenesis. I. Serotonin content of developing embryos of sea urchin and loach. *J. Embryol. Exp. Morphol., 12,* 563–573.

Buznikov, G. A., I. V. Chudakova, and L. V. Berdysheva, 1968. The role of neuro-humors in early embryogenesis. II. Acetylcholine and catecholamine in developing embryos of sea urchin. *J. Embryol. Exp. Morphol., 20,* 119–128.

Buznikov, G. A., A. N. Kost, N. F. Kucherova, A. L. Mndzhoyan, N. N. Suvarov, and L. V. Berdysheva, 1970. The role of neurohumors in early embryogenesis. III. Pharmacological analysis of the role of neurohumors in cleavage divisions. *J. Embryol. Exp. Morphol., 23,* 549–569.

Child, C. M., 1936. Differential reduction of vital dyes in the early development of echinoids. *Wm. Roux Entwicklsmech. Org., 135,* 426–456.

Citkowitz, E., 1971. The hyaline layer, its isolation and role in echinoderm develop-ment. *Develop. Biol., 24,* 348–362.

Czihak, G., 1963. Entwicklungsphysiologische Untersuchungen am Echiniden (Ver-teilung und Bedeutung der cytochrom oxidase). *Wm. Roux Entwicklsmech. Org., 154,* 272–292.

Czihak, G., 1971. Echinoids. In G. Reverberi (ed.), *Experimental Embryology of Marine and Fresh Water Invertebrates.* American Elsevier Publishing Company, Inc., New York.

Gibbins, J. R., and L. G. Tilney, 1965. The distribution of microtubules in primary and secondary mesenchyme in *Arbacia. Biol. Bull. Mar. Biol. Lab., Woods Hole, 129,* 406.

Gibbins, J. R., L. G. Tilney, and K. H. Porter, 1969. Microtubules in the formation and development of the primary mesenchyme in *Arbacia. J. Cell Biol., 41,* 201–206.

Giudice, G., and S. Hörstadius, 1965. Effect of Actinomycin D on the segregation of animal and vegetal potentialities in the sea urchin egg. *Exp. Cell Res., 39,* 117–120.

Gustafson, T., 1965. Morphogenetic significance of biochemical patterns in sea urchin embryos. In R. Weber (ed.), *The Biochemistry of Animal Development,* Vol. I. Academic Press, Inc., New York, 139–202.

Gustafson, T., and H. Kinnander, 1956. Gastrulation in the sea urchin studied by time-lapse cinematography. *Exp. Cell Res., 10,* 733–734.

Gustafson, T., and P. Lenicque, 1952. Studies on mitochondria in the developing sea urchin egg. *Exp. Cell Res., 3,* 251–274.

Gustafson, T., and P. Lenicque, 1955. Studies on mitochondria in early cleavage stages in sea urchin eggs. *Exp. Cell Res., 8,* 114–117.

Gustafson, T., and M. I. Toneby, 1971. How genes control morphogenesis. *Amer. Scientist, 59,* 452–462.

Gustafson, T., and L. Wolpert, 1963. The cellular basis of morphogenesis and sea urchin development. *Int. Rev. Cytol., 15,* 139–214.

Hagström, B. E., and S. Lonning, 1969. Time-lapse and electron microscopic studies of sea urchin micromeres. *Protoplasma, 68,* 271–288.

Harvey, E. B., 1956. *The American Arbacia and Other Sea Urchins.* Princeton University Press, Princeton, N.J.

Hörstadius, S., 1952. Induction and inhibition of reduction gradients by the micro-meres in the sea urchin egg. *J. Exp. Zool., 120,* 421–436.

Hörstadius, S., 1955. Reducing gradients in animalized and vegetalized sea urchin eggs. *J. Exp. Zool., 129,* 249–256.

Hörstadius, S., L. Josefsson, and J. Runnström, 1967. Morphogenetic agents from unfertilized eggs of the sea urchin *Paracentrotus lividus. Develop. Biol., 16,* 189–202.

Hyman, L. H., 1955. *The Invertebrates: Echinodermata. The Coelomate Bilateria.* Vol. IV. McGraw-Hill Book Company, New York.

Ishida, J., 1936. An enzyme dissolving the fertilization membrane of sea urchin eggs. *Annot. Zool. Jap., 15,* 435–459.

Josefsson, L., and S. Hörstadius, 1969. Morphogenetic substances from sea urchin eggs. Isolation of animalizing and vegetalizing substances from unfertilized eggs of *Paracentrotus lividus*. *Develop. Biol., 20*, 481–500.

Lallier, R., 1958. Experimental analysis of embryonic differentiation in echinoderms. *Experientia, 14*, 309–315.

Markman, B., 1961a. Regional differences in isotopic labelling of nucleic acid and protein of early sea urchin development. *Exp. Cell Res., 23*, 118–129.

Markman, B., 1961b. Differences in isotopic labelling of nucleic acid and protein of early sea urchin development. *Exp. Cell Res., 23*, 197–200.

Markman, B., 1961c. Differences in isotopic labelling of nucleic acid and protein in sea urchin embryos developing from animal and vegetal halves. *Exp. Cell Res., 25*, 224–227.

Monné, L., and S. Hårde, 1951. On the formation of the blastocoel and similar embryonic cavities. *Arkiv. Zool., 1*, 463–469.

Moore, A. R., 1941. On the mechanics of gastrulation in *Dendraster excentricus*. *J. Exp. Zool., 87*, 101–111.

Moore, A. R., and A. S. Burt, 1939. On the locus and nature of forces causing gastrulation in embryos of *Dendraster excentricus*. *J. Exp. Zool., 82*, 159–171.

Okazaki, K., 1956. Skeleton formation of sea urchin larvae. I. Effect of calcium concentration on the medium. *Biol. Bull. Mar. Biol. Lab., Woods Hole, 110*, 320–333.

Okazaki, K., 1960. Skeleton formation of sea urchin larvae. II. Organic matrix of the spicule. *Embryologia, 5*, 283–320.

Okazaki, K., 1961. Skeleton formation of sea urchin larvae. III. Similarity of effect of low calcium and high magnesium on spicule formation. *Biol. Bull. Mar. Biol. Lab., Woods Hole, 120*, 177–182.

Okazaki, K., 1962. Skeleton formation of sea urchin larvae. IV. Correlation in shape of spiculae and matrix. *Embryologia, 7*, 21–38.

Okazaki, K., 1965. Skeleton formation of sea urchin larvae. V. Continuous observation of the process of matrix formation. *Exp. Cell Res., 11*, 548–559.

Pucci-Minafra, I., M. Bosco, and L. Giambertone, 1968. Preliminary observations on the isolated micromeres from sea urchin embryos. *Exp. Cell Res., 53*, 177–183.

Shaver, J., 1956. Mitochondrial populations during development of the sea urchin. *Exp. Cell Res., 11*, 548–559.

Tilney, L. G., and J. R. Gibbins, 1969a. Microtubules and filaments in the filopodia of secondary mesenchyme cells of *Arbacia punctulata* and *Echinarachnius parma*. *J. Cell. Sci., 5*, 195–210.

Tilney, L. G., and J. R. Gibbins, 1969b. Microtubles in the formation and development of *Arbacia punctulata*. II. An experimental analysis of their role in development and maintenance of cell shape. *J. Cell Biol., 41*, 227–250.

Trinkhaus, J. P., 1965. Mechanisms of morphogenetic movements. In R. L. DeHaan and H. Ursprung (eds.), *Organogenesis*. Holt, Rinehart and Winston, Inc., New York, 55–99.

von Ubisch, L., 1937. Die normale Skelettbildung bei *Echinocyamus pusillus* und *Psammechinus miliaris* und die Bedeutung dieser Vorgänge für die Analyse der Skelette von Keimblattchimären. *Z. Wiss. Zool., 149*, 402–476.

von Ubisch, L., 1950. Die Entwicklung der Echiniden. *Verhandel. Koninkl. Ned. Akad. Wettenschap. Afdel. Natuurk., Ser. 2*, No. 2, 1–50.

Wolpert, L., and T. Gustafson, 1961. Studies on the cellular basis of morphogenesis in the sea urchin embryo. Development of the pattern. *Exp. Cell. Res., 25*, 311–325.

Wolpert, L., and E. H. Mercer, 1963. An electron microscope study of the development of the sea urchin embryo and its radial polarity. *Exp. Cell. Res., 30*, 280–300.

Yasumasu, I., 1960. Quantitative determination of hatching enzyme activity of the sea urchin blastulae. *J. Fac. Sci. Univ. Tokyo, Sect. IV, 9,* 39–47.

Yasumasu, I., 1963. Inhibition of the hatching enzyme formation during embryogenesis of the sea urchin by chloramphenicol, 8-aza-guanine, and 5-bromo-uracil. *Sci. Pap. Coll. Gen. Educ. Univ. Tokyo, 13,* 211–246.

CHAPTER VI

Nature and Activity of DNA in Sea Urchin Eggs and Embryos

SOME EARLY PROBLEMS

The early history of research on DNA in the sea urchin embryo was marked by a degree of confusion, and as a result, some concepts that were basically fallacious came into being. Although even in the first half of the decade 1950–1960 some sophisticated equipment and techniques for biochemical study were available, this was essentially a pioneer period in research on nucleic acids, at least with respect to its present-day status, and it is perhaps to be expected that some backing and starting and some taking of the wrong road should have occurred. One source of difficulty was what may have been an over-reliance upon staining technique. The Feulgen reaction for the identification or determination of DNA represents a completely adequate technique in many circumstances. In the sea urchin egg, however, it proved to be quite bothersome. It is difficult to get the nucleus of the mature egg to give a positive Feulgen reaction, although Burgos (1955) succeeded in doing so.

Marshak and Marshak (1952, 1953, 1954, 1955, 1956) were unable to detect DNA in the nucleus of the mature unfertilized sea urchin egg. The inadequacies of the Feulgen reaction appear to have been at the root of their problem. Knowing that an egg can be activated parthenogenetically, and assuming that it would then start the development process without any DNA in its nucleus, they reasoned that DNA could not be the sole, or even the primary, component of the genetic material, and proposed that the DNA of embryonic nuclei is a derived, rather than a transmitted, product. This thesis did not gain wide acceptance, perhaps because the concept of DNA as the genetic molecule had taken root rather firmly by that time. It did, however, leave a problem that had to be resolved. The finding by Burgos of a positive Feulgen reaction in the nucleus of the mature egg was helpful in this regard.

Another problem arose, even more difficult to resolve. The earliest workers, through the study of phosphate distribution and through the use of the diphenylamine reaction, found much more DNA in the egg than was expected on the basis of comparisons with the sperm. Some workers reported ratios as high as 100:1. This perplexing finding would not go away. Reports from various laboratories confirmed the existence of this excess of DNA in the egg. It was assumed by many embryologists of the day that the egg nucleus probably contains a haploid amount of DNA and that the excess must be considered to be cytoplasmic. It was not until 1961, however, that Hinegardner performed chemical analyses on isolated nuclei from the sea urchin egg and demonstrated that the egg nucleus does indeed contain the haploid amount of DNA.

As more and more workers verified the existence of cytoplasmic DNA, theories as to its nature began to emerge. Agrell and Persson (1956) and others proposed that during the early embryonic period the animal uses stored cytoplasmic DNA as a source of nuclear DNA and delays DNA synthesis until later in its development, when it is able to obtain its intermediates through *de novo* synthesis. They were led to this belief by what appear to be faulty analytical methods through which they reported that in *Paracentrotus lividus, Psamme-chinus miliaris,* and *Echinus esculentus* the onset of DNA synthesis does not occur until sometime between the 32-cell and 500-cell stage, depending on species. They were given considerable support in this theory by some of the amphibian embryologists, who reported similar findings. Many workers since that time (see, for example, Simmel and Karnofsky, 1961) have shown through the use of labeled thymidine as a precursor that DNA synthesis may begin as early as 20 to 30 minutes after fertilization.

Some of these fallacious ideas have held on to life tenaciously. Until recently, the concept has persisted that the sea urchin embryo and embryos of certain other species possess in early development two DNA's, a metabolic DNA, which is stored in the cytoplasm for the production of nuclear DNA, and a stable DNA, which is synthesized from mononucleotides by the well-known replication process. The stipulation is usually made that metabolic DNA is incorporated into nuclear DNA in a polynucleotide form. The problem of metabolic DNA has been discussed by Roels (1966).

There is no basis for this concept in the light of experimental findings in recent years. The preponderance of cytoplasmic DNA has been shown to be associated with organelles, principally mito-chondria. It has been calculated on the basis of determination of amount of DNA per organelle and numbers of organelles present in the cell that organelle DNA can probably account for all cytoplasmic DNA. Piko et al. (1967) found a small amount of cytoplasmic DNA in supernatants when organelles were thrown down by centrifugation, but they believed that it could be accounted for by organelle break-down. It would be unscientific not to be prepared at any time for the discovery of exceptions to seemingly universal phenomena in nature, and it would be equally unscientific not to preserve a healthy skepti-cism toward such discoveries until they are validated. Replication shows itself consistently to be the mechanism whereby DNA is syn-thesized, but it is also seen consistently in nature as the means where-by DNA is perpetuated, millennium after millennium. If it were wise to have reserved judgment about these old theories on cytoplasmic DNA, there would also appear to be merit in holding some skepticism toward proposed functional systems in eukaryotic cells, which appear to deprive DNA of the ability to perpetuate itself by replication. Such systems include those which envision segments of DNA moving out into the cytoplasm to serve as centers for translation and transcription and would include also yolk DNA, which will be discussed below.

The very high values for the content of cytoplasmic DNA in the egg found in the 1950–1960 decade were gradually shown to be er-roneous. During that decade some workers were able to show more moderate figures (see Elson and Chargaff, 1952; Hoff-Jørgenson, 1954; Whiteley and Baltzer, 1958) the general magnitude of which was corroborated in the 1960s by Sugino et al. (1960), Bibring et al. (1965), and others.

Recently, Piko and his co-workers have revised these figures downward. In 1965 Piko and Tyler, through the use of differential and density-gradient centrifugation, determined the DNA per egg of *Strongylocentrotus purpuratus* to be approximately 8 times the haploid value, and that of *Lytechinus pictus* to be approximately 13 times the haploid value. In 1967, Piko et al. were able to trim these figures still further. Through the use of improved methods that yield a DNA of extremely high purity, they reported a value of DNA per egg of 4.3 times the haploid value for *Strongylocentrotus purpuratus,* and 9.5 times the haploid value for *Lytechinus pictus.* The Piko group proposed that on the basis of the calculations of Shaver (1956), which estimated that mitochondria occupy a volume equal to about 9 percent of that of the egg, cytoplasmic DNA could be considered to be preponderantly mitochondrial.

SOME PROPERTIES OF DNA

The question of the number of chromosomes in the sea urchin that house a haploid value of DNA has been somewhat slow in being resolved. Auclair (1965) has reported a haploid value of 22 for *Arbacia punctulata.* Tyler and Tyler (1966) are of the opinion that the values for other species may be fairly close to that reported by Auclair. Chromosomes are difficult to enumerate in sea urchins, because of problems in achieving good staining intensity and other complications.

The adenine-to-thymine and the guanine-to-cytosine ratios in sea urchin sperm have been calculated by various workers and found to be typical of double-stranded DNA. The ratio of adenine + thymine to guanine + cytosine is quite high in some sea urchin species compared to values determined for many other types of animal. Chargaff (1955) calculated this ratio for several species of sea urchin and found it to be fairly uniform, ranging from 1.58 to 1.85. The DNA content of sperm is also fairly uniform among various species of sea urchin.

Rosencranz (1965), Carden et al. (1965), and Rosenkranz and Carden (1967) isolated DNA from sperm, egg, embryonic, and adult somatic cells of *Arbacia punctulata* and determined its buoyant density in cesium chloride gradients. The DNA isolated from both eggs and sperm was double stranded. Egg DNA and sperm DNA were shown to have identical buoyant densities. In the fertilized egg and during the cleavage period the buoyant density of DNA was the same as in the unfertilized egg (1.700 g/cm³). At blastula the value was 1.701 g/cm³, and at gastrula, pluteus, and in the adult it was 1.702 g/cm³. This difference of 2 mg/cm³ is significant and suggests that DNA undergoes a change in development. Comb (1965) reported that DNA is not methylated until the beginning of gastrula, although this finding is subject to question. These workers, however, were hesitant to attribute the difference in buoyant density to methylation, and the cause of this change in buoyant density value has not been explained.

Bibring et al. (1965) compared the buoyant densities of DNA from whole eggs and nucleate and anucleate half-eggs in *Arbacia lixula*. This amounts to a determination on cytoplasmic DNA in the instance of the anucleate half-egg. The buoyant densities in all instances were the same. Piko et al. (1967), however, found differences in buoyant density values between DNA isolated from nuclei and from cytoplasmic organelles in *Lytechinus pictus*.

The presence of a satellite DNA in the sperm of *Lytechinus variegatus* was reported by Stafford and Guild (1969) and Patterson and Stafford (1970). This DNA was isolated and found to have a buoyant density of 1.722 g/cm³ as compared to 1.695 g/cm³ for the main band. The satellite was detached by a partial denaturation of the main band. This satellite DNA is interesting in that hybridization experiments suggest that it contains nucleotide sequences responsible for the elaboration of ribosomal RNA, and thus may constitute what is sometimes referred to as r-DNA. This DNA might represent a paternal contribution to the DNA of the nucleolar region in cells of the embryo.

DNA SYNTHESIS

The scantiness of our knowledge of DNA synthesis in the sea urchin is not surprising in view of the fact that the mechanism of DNA synthesis in vivo is but poorly comprehended in eukaryotic cells in general.

Much work has been done in vitro with Kornberg's DNA polymerase. This enzyme requires triphosphates of all four major deoxynucleotides, magnesium ions, and a DNA oligonucleotide primer. The enzyme catalyzes the addition of nucleotides to the end of the primer that has a 3′-hydroxyl group on its terminal sugar. Since the other end of the primer has an exposed 5′-phosphate group, the chain may be said to grow in a 5′ to 3′ direction and to require a template with a 3′ to 5′ orientation. DNA synthesis in the cell, however, may differ considerably from the picture obtained of it from a multitude of studies with this enzyme.

Experiments on mammalian cells (see Huberman and Riggs, 1968) have shown that chromosomal DNA probably exists in the form of long fibers made up of many small segments that replicate separately, with replication occurring in both directions from a common origin within the segment. There is evidence that neighboring segments can replicate at different times. The basic nature of DNA replication (semiconservative) requires that the parent chain open up into separate strands. It is not necessary that the entire chain unwind, and it is thought that it does not do so. It is difficult, however, to determine how it does open up to provide for localized replication. One theory, which has several variations, propounds that the parent chain may be broken in places to develop a fork. The daughter strand is thought to grow up one side of the fork and down the other in a 5′ to 3′ direction. Daughter chains are thus held to be formed in segments that are joined together by the intermediation of the enzyme, ligase. Damage to the parent chain is believed to be repaired enzymatically.

The fact that short single-stranded segments of DNA may be isolated from mammalian cells gives some credence to this theory, but workers have consistently failed to isolate such single-stranded segments from certain types of mammalian cells, and other workers have labeled such segments as artifacts of the DNA isolation process.

Rosenkranz et al. (1964) obtained rabbit antisera to several purine- and pyrimidine-albumin conjugants, which antisera would cross react with thermally denatured DNA, but not with native DNA. The antisera were able to penetrate cells of *Arbacia punctulata* and to become fixed therein. Upon doing so they inhibited the development of the embryo. This effect suggests the presence in the embryo of either single-stranded DNA or of double-stranded DNA with partially disrupted base pairs.

A review of some of the problems associated with DNA polymerases may be found in Jansz et al. (1971). DNA polymerases often prove quite difficult to purify, and they sometimes reveal properties that are a result of the method by which they were isolated. DNA polymerases can operate with single-stranded DNA or double-stranded DNA as template, and even with synthetic template. It is a common occurrence that two basic types of polymerase are isolated from eukaryotic cells, one with a preference for native double-stranded DNA, and the other with a preference for denatured or activated DNA, that is, DNA which has been opened up by a DNAase, known as endonuclease, to display single-stranded nicks. It is usually extremely difficult or impossible to determine whether the polymerase involved in DNA replication within the cell is using single-stranded DNA or double-stranded DNA as template.

The question has frequently been raised as to whether DNA polymerase is actually the replicating enzyme in the cell or whether the task is being performed by some enzyme as yet unidentified. The fact has been cited that there are mutant bacteria which produce less than 1 percent of the normal levels of DNA polymerase, yet can divide normally, and there is other evidence which suggests that some other enzyme can, or does, provide for replication. It has been proposed that the polymerase may serve to repair local chromosome damage. The problem has not been resolved.

DNA polymerase has been investigated in the sea urchin by Loeb (1969, 1970), Loeb et al. (1967, 1969), and Fansler and Loeb (1969). They found that in early embryogenesis considerable DNA polymerase is located in the cytoplasm, although the enzyme is primarily active in the nucleus. As development proceeds, more and more enzyme is found in the nucleus. At hatching, as much as 90 percent of the DNA polymerase of the embryo may have a nuclear location. These workers submit that the DNA polymerase active during cleavage is in all probability synthesized during oogenesis. They isolated the enzyme from *Strongylocentrotus purpuratus* and *Strongylocentrotus franciscanus,* finding it to show no major differences between the two species, and investigated its behavior by in vitro studies. Native double-stranded DNA proved to be much more effective as a primer for its activity than did single-stranded DNA. The effectiveness of double-stranded DNA as a primer was enhanced still further when this DNA was degraded very slightly with pancreatic DNAase.

Loeb (1970) made some estimations on the molecular association of the polymerase with chromatin in these species. On the basis of the constant ratio between polymerase activity and amount of DNA, he assumed some sort of constant structural association between the two. He estimated that in these species there is one molecule of the polymerase localized in chromatin for every 2000–3000 nucleotide pairs. His estimates were derived through the progression of computing molecules of polymerase per embryo, cells per embryo, and molecules of polymerase per chromosome. They are based on the haploid number of 19 given by Harvey (1956) for *Arbacia,* rather than the figure of 22 found by Auclair, which may possibly be more accurate. It is doubtful that this would make any serious difference in the significance of his findings. The relationship determined between enzyme and DNA may represent the approximate size of a replicating unit. The proposal by Loeb that "polymerase punctuates the chromosome into functional units of replication" is in harmony with the concept of individual replicating segments arranged in tandem along the DNA molecule, as has been suggested to exist in cells of other animal types.

In 1969 Anderson made an electron-microscope study on the newly fertilized egg of *Paracentrotus lividus* with the use of tritiated thymidine. Within 15–30 minutes after fertilization there was widespread evidence of DNA synthesis. Thymidine was being incorporated into male and female pronuclei, mitochondria, and yolk platelets. In polyspermic embryos, all differentiated male pronuclei were synthesizing DNA simultaneously. He noted that the synthesis of DNA in mitochondria does not follow the phases of DNA synthesis in the nucleus and proposed that the active DNA synthesis in mitochondria might be occurring in anticipation of mitochondrial multiplication. This is not the first report of DNA synthesis in the pronuclei of echinoids. Simmel and Karnofsky, for example, reported DNA synthesis in pronuclei of *Echinarachnius parma* in 1961. Anderson also reported the incorporation of thymidine into bacteria-like structures, presumably endosymbionts. It is probable that such endosymbionts do not appreciably affect the results of analyses, from the evidence of studies made to determine the extent and effect of bacterial contamination of homogenates.

The cycle of cell division, in a sense, turns from generation unto generation. The fusion of the pronuclei to form the zygote may be considered the starting point for the turning of the cycles in the organism. The first cleavage cycle is not completely typical of the cycles that follow it in early development. Its duration in some species of sea urchin, for example, is over twice that of succeeding cycles. Although Nemer (1962) and Ficq et al. (1963) placed DNA synthesis at sea urchin cleavage at interphase, which is the usual time for its occurrence in cells in general, Hinegardner et al. (1964) have found that, at least in this first cleavage, there are two periods of DNA synthesis in *Strongylocentrotus purpuratus,* the first beginning in the pronuclei and lasting until shortly after nuclear fusion, the second beginning in telophase and lasting 13 minutes at 15°C. At the start of the second period of synthesis, the egg has already begun to furrow. Cleavage has terminated and the embryo is in interphase by the time the synthetic period ends.

The general picture for division in most eukaryotic cells involves periods that vary greatly in duration relative to one another from cell type to cell type. At the beginning of interphase there occurs a period designated by Pelc as G_1 (gap 1). This period can often vary considerably in duration within a given cell type. This is not really a resting period, as it sometimes is asserted to be, but rather a period in which the cell is preparing for the periods to follow. The S period occurs next and marks the time of synthesis of DNA. A G_2 period follows the replication of DNA and is probably a time of preparation for mitosis. Mitosis occurs in the M period. Before the daughter cells are produced, the parent cell DNA is in the tetraploid condition for part of the cycle. Interphase is the period from the beginning of G_1 to the end of G_2.

The Hinegardner group state in effect that DNA synthesis occurs for a brief interval during which the cell is still in the M period of the first cleavage. More recent descriptions of the timing of DNA synthesis (see Kedes et al., 1969) simply state that in the first few cleavage cycles G_1 and G_2 are either extremely brief or entirely absent, so that the cell alternates between S and M. During a 20- to 30-minute culturing period, it is possible at some time to find essentially every cell in some stage of S.

As has been mentioned previously, the time required for a given cleavage is predictable for a given species under given physical and chemical parameters, although the durations of successive cleavage periods vary somewhat. This accounts superficially for the synchrony of cell division that is seen in the early cleavage cycles of the embryo. Since large numbers of eggs are fertilized simultaneously, if activation is the mechanism that "punches the stop watch" that starts the sequence of these periods, then it becomes understandable why the embryos of a batch undergo cell division in synchrony.

The actual reason for the phases (the S period, for example) of the cleavage cycle beginning at a predictable time and having a predictable duration is not really understood. It may, of course, be postulated that events in one of these periods trigger the mechanism that starts the next period. Rao and Hinegardner (1965) discovered that low doses of X-irradiation, which delay the onset of mitosis, delay by a comparable interval the onset of the synthetic period. They concluded that some aspect of mitosis must regulate the inception of DNA synthesis. Some workers have suggested that DNA synthesis is triggered by the activity of some participant in DNA synthesis itself, such as exonuclease (Slater and Loeb, 1970) or DNA polymerase (moving into the nucleus as proposed by Fansler and Loeb; see Jansz, 1971). In other types of cell, many workers have found evidence for the synthesis of a protein initiator substance. The existence of such an initiator substance in the sea urchin has not been established.

It is not known that any specific protein or proteins must be synthesized to enable DNA synthesis to occur within a single cleavage cycle. Puromycin will halt cleavage, but the blockage, as has been discussed, occurs at the streak stage, and may be associated with the halting of production of a protein or proteins associated with the formation of the mitotic apparatus. With DNA being synthesized exponentially during early embryogenesis, however, an extensive amount of chromosomal protein is required to sustain its production. DNA synthesis can proceed until blastula in the presence of actinomycin D, which halts transcription. In normal development there is active transcription during the period between fertilization and blastula, and perhaps half of it provides template for the synthesis of nuclear proteins. The synthesis of histones will be discussed below. Given the fact that transcription is not necessary for DNA synthesis during this period, one may ask whether DNA synthesis is necessary for transcription. Kedes et al. (1969a) found that when DNA synthesis is inhibited with hydroxyurea bulk RNA synthesis continues.

The intensive synthesis of DNA in early development must be expected to impose heavy demands on the nucleotide pools of the cell. Metabolic cycles for the *de novo* synthesis of purines and pyrimidines and for the interconversion of nucleotides have been investigated in cells of various organisms, but very little work has been done on this problem in the sea urchin embryo. Much of the work that has been done was done at a time when experimental techniques were much cruder than they are today, and some of the early work calls for reexamination with the use of improved methods. A systematic study of the entire problem of metabolic reactions involving nucleotides, of utilization of nucleotides in DNA and RNA synthesis, and of catabolism of polynucleotides in relation to the acid-soluble pools in the sea urchin embryo is in order. Our present knowledge of the subject is meager.

In 1962, Nemer demonstrated that *Paracentrotus lividus* can utilize exogenously supplied deoxyuridine, dTMP, and dUMP for DNA synthesis. The bulk of exogenously supplied ribonucleotides, however, appeared in the acid-soluble pools, and there did not seem to be much evidence for their interconversion to deoxynucleotides. His experiments presented evidence that the supply of available thymidine in the pools of the egg may not be sufficient to support the synthesis of DNA, without being replenished by thymidine synthesis soon after fertilization. Sea urchin embryos incorporate 5-fluorodeoxyuridine into their nucleic acids, and the false residue interferes with nucleic acid function. Embryos treated with this antimetabolite halt development soon after fertilization. Nemer found that embryos in which development had been so halted would resume development up to blastula upon the addition of exogenous thymidine. The suggestion here that exogenous thymidine might be performing a function that endogenous thymidine could not perform, that is, that an apparent preference for exogenous thymidine over endogenous thymidine exists, led Nemer to believe that thymidine might be exerting a feedback control on its own synthesis. Availability of thymidine has been frequently cited as a control mechanism for DNA synthesis in other cell systems.

Stearns et al. (1962) found that antimetabolites to folic acid interfere with the synthesis of DNA and RNA in *Strongylocentrotus purpuratus,* with development being halted at blastula. They assumed that the principal effect of the antifolates was that of interference with the synthesis of inosine monophosphate, although in unreported experiments they found a decrease of 22–25 percent in the labeling of thymine in DNA. They found a substantial decrease in the label in ribosidic purine nucleotides in the acid-soluble pools.

Scarano and his associates investigated the enzymes associated with the interconversion of pyrimidine deoxynucleotides (see, for example, Scarano, 1958a, 1958b; Scarano and Maggio, 1959; Scarano et al., 1964a, 1964b). They discovered an enzyme, deoxycytidylate aminohydrolase, which catalyzes the deamination of dCMP to dUMP. Thymidine synthetase catalyzes the formation of dTMP from dUMP. The formation of dTMP from dUMP is a methylation process that requires folic acid as a coenzyme. Specific kinases phosphorylate dTMP to dTTP for DNA synthesis.

The aminohydrolase system that this group isolated was not highly purified. They found that it would deaminate methyl deoxycytidylic acid, MedCMP. It was their belief that two separate enzymes were involved here. They ultimately demonstrated the existence of an aminohydrolase specific for dCMP, but appear not to have identified an enzyme specific for MedCMP. Their enzyme system would not deaminate deoxycytidine nor would it deaminate ribosidic derivatives of cytosine. The system was isolated from *Sphaerechinus granularis* and was found in the supernatant of a $16,000 \times g$ differential centrifugation.

The aminohydrolase begins to decrease in amount in the embryo at late cleavage, and it undergoes a striking decrease from late blastula to pluteus. The pattern of reduction of the activity of this enzyme appears to be quite important in development. In abnormal embryos in which the development stops at gastrula, the enzyme content was found to remain constant rather than to drop at blastula. In cells of *Paracentrotus lividus* disaggregated in very early cleavage, the enzyme content of the cells likewise remains at a constant level, demonstrating that cellular interaction may be critical in maintaining the normal pattern of enzyme content.

METHYLATION OF DNA

Very small amounts of methylcytosine and occasionally other rare bases are found in the DNA of cells of various organisms, including the sea urchin embryo. Methyldeoxycytidylic acid (MedCMP) is held to be formed *in situ* on the DNA polymer by the methylation of dCMP. The source of the methyl group is the methyl group of methionine, probably as *S*-adenosylmethionine. The functional significance of MedCMP is unknown. Some confusion surrounds the findings on the methylation of the bases of DNA in the sea urchin embryo. Comb (1965) found that the bases of DNA are not methylated until gastrula and speculated that the methylating enzymes are not synthesized until just prior to gastrula. The Scarano group reported that the methylation of bases of DNA occurs at all stages of development. Vanyushin et al. (1970) have reported the finding of MedCMP in sperm DNA, a fact which implies that the male nucleus entering the egg bears with it some of the rare base.

As mentioned above, the Scarano group were able to achieve deamination of MedCMP with a partially purified aminohydrolase system in vitro. This group formed the hypothesis that MedCMP might be deaminated to TMP on the DNA molecule. This transformation would in effect change the information on the DNA molecule. They envisioned this change as occurring in genes that affect the activities of other genes, as opposed to the structural genes that lead ultimately to protein production through the intermediation of m-RNA. They submitted that this interconversion of bases on DNA might play a role in the polarization of the egg, the formation of morphogenetic gradients, and the process of differentiation.

Scarano et al. (1965 and 1967) and Grippo et al. (1970) have performed experiments in which they report the finding of minor thymine (thymine in TMP produced by the deamination of methylcytosine in MedCMP) in the DNA molecules of sea urchin embryos. Such thymine is difficult to detect because it will be reproduced by normal replication subsequent to its formation. They offer in evidence the finding of (1) a nonrandom distribution of thymine that has incorporated the label from methyl-labeled methionine, suggesting that it has been labeled at the polymer level and (2) changes in the ratio of label between two time periods in development in embryos incubated in thymidine labeled with one label (to detect major thymine originating from endogenous pools) and methionine labeled with another label (to detect minor thymine arising from deamination of methylcytosine). Apart from the difficulty of the experiment due to the ephemeral nature of minor thymine, there appear to be several possibilities of error in this type of experiment, such as the possibility of contamination with organelle DNA and the possibility of differences in the uptake of the precursors relative to one another by the cells at different times during development. Considering the import of the findings, some reservation of judgment, pending further work, is appropriate.

CYTOPLASMIC DNA

Interest in the problem of cytoplasmic DNA has been revived in recent years in terms of its contribution to protein synthesis relative to that of nuclear DNA, and, in particular, relative to that of stable maternal m-RNA made during oogenesis and translated after fertilization. Baltus et al. (1965) raised the question of the contribution of cytoplasmic DNA to protein synthesis in early development when they found that there are significant amounts of cytoplasmic DNA in anucleate half-eggs and that it undergoes synthesis or turnover. It occurred to them that there may be some DNA-directed RNA polymerase activity in these anucleate halves. The existence of organelle DNA was already established at this time. DNA in mitochondria of other cell types was under study in the first half of the 1960s. Di Stefano and Mazia (1952) had observed the incorporation of ^{32}P into nucleic acids of the midpiece of the sea urchin sperm, and were quite probably looking at the activity of mitochondrial DNA before its existence was known. Baltus and Brachet had reported the finding of DNA in association with the yolk platelets of amphibia in 1962.

In 1967, Piko et al. isolated, quantified, and partially characterized DNA from mitochondria and yolk spherules in *Lytechinus pictus*. The melting-point profiles of nuclear and cytoplasmic DNA showed them to have different guanine–cytosine content. Buoyant density values were 1.693 for nuclear DNA and 1.703 for mitochondrial DNA. Piko et al. (1968) examined isolated mitochondrial DNA under the electron microscope (see Fig. 17). They found that it occurs in the form of circles, as has been seen in the mitochondrial DNA of other organisms. Such circles are seen in either a single form or a catenated form, usually with two circles present. Open or nicked forms are seen with some frequency.

Isolated mitochondrial DNA from *Lytechinus pictus* and from *Strongylocentrotus purpuratus* has been reported to act as a primer for RNA synthesis in cell-free systems by Piko et al. (1967) and Tyler (1967). It had been reported even before mitochondrial DNA had been discovered that the mitochondria of sea urchin embryos will support protein synthesis. Nakano and Monroy (1958) demonstrated it in vivo and Giudice (1960) was able to produce it in vitro. These workers estimated that the amount of mitochondrial protein synthesis

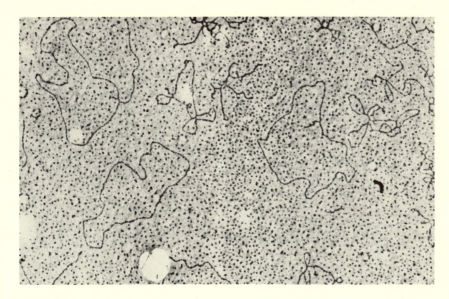

Figure 17
Electron micrograph of DNA from mitochondria of *Lytechinus pictus*. [From Piko et al. (1967); by permission.]

in the early hours of development is very small. Tyler (1967) studied such synthesis with a variety of amino acid precursors. Again, he found the amount of incorporation of amino acids into mitochondrial plus yolk-spherule proteins to represent a very small percentage of incorporation into the total protein of the embryo (6–20 percent). Experiments that show the incorporation of amino acids into mitochondrial fractions must be viewed with caution, however, where the problem of the existence of intramitochondrial protein synthesis is concerned. The presence of label in protein of mitochondria isolated from cells gives no indication as to whether the mitochondria synthesized the protein or imported it. In the early experiments in particular the probability of contamination of mitochondrial preparations used in in vitro studies by extraneous protein-synthesizing machinery may have been rather high. A rigorous program of study is required to demonstrate and describe intramitochondrial protein synthesis with any degree of confidence.

Studies on mitochondria in other organisms demonstrate that they show many similarities to bacteria in such things as the nature of their

DNA (which is ring shaped and innocent of histones), the S-values of their ribosomal RNA, sensitivity to particular inhibitors of protein synthesis, the nature of their t-RNA synthetases, and other features. Such similarities have given rise to the theory that mitochondria may have evolved from primitive bacterial endosymbionts of primitive cells (see Cohen, 1970). Such affinities may offer some clues as to why mitochondria show certain types of molecular and biochemical activity within the cell.

The inheritance of genetic information in mitochondria is completely maternal. DNA replication is semiconservative in nature. A review of some of the findings on mitochondrial information flow is to be found in Attardi and Attardi (1969). Some of the salient points of recent discoveries in other types of cell should be noted here. The intramitochondrial machinery for protein synthesis lacks the ability to synthesize many types of proteins because of the small size of the mitochondrial DNA complement. It is believed that the number of genes in the mitochondrial DNA is much too small for it to be able to produce even the complete protein-synthesizing mechanism itself. The mitochondrion must, therefore, rely heavily upon the nucleus for information. It would appear that nuclear genes provide part of the information for the production of the mitochondrial protein-synthesizing machinery, most, or all, of the enzymes for respiratory cycles, the enzymes for mitochondrial lipid production, and part of the proteins of mitochondrial membranes. Mitochondrial genes are thought to provide information for the production of some of the mitochondrial membrane proteins and for part of the mitochondrial protein-synthesizing mechanism. The problem has not been completely resolved.

Studies on the synthesis of RNA in HeLa cells, in which pulses of varying length of exposure to the radioactive precursor were used, suggest that a heterogeneous population of RNA with S-values ranging from 25S to 50S is transcribed from the DNA and is then processed to produce a final heterogeneous population with S-values predominating in the range of 12S to 25S.

Robberson et al. (1971) have shown that in HeLa cells genes apparently lying quite close together are responsible for the production of a 12S and a 16S ribosomal RNA particle, which are components of the 35S and 45S subunits, respectively, of the 60S mitochondrial-specific ribosome. Aloni and Attardi (1971) have reported that the 12S and 16S particles, as well as 4S mitochondrial RNA are apparently processed from precursors of larger size.

It has been found in other cell systems that message produced on mitochondrial genes is short lived and that some of it is exported to the cytoplasm for translation. The destiny of the protein so produced is not known. Some of it may be expected to be returned to the mitochondrion. Attardi and Attardi (1969) have speculated that some of this protein may be used for production of membrane in structures other than the mitochondrion.

Very little work has been done on the DNA of yolk spherules. We have speculated on its possible function in a previous chapter, but there is not much evidence to support such speculation. If its existence continues to be confirmed, there must be some revision of our thinking about the function of DNA in eukaryotic cells. Intuitively, yolk DNA appears to be something that falls under the aegis of the god of things as they are, rather than the god of things as they ought to be. As opposed to the DNA in the nucleus, in mitochondria, and in chloroplasts, it is not serving through replication to participate in the perpetuation of the organelle that houses it. To all appearances it assumes an identity, serves a function briefly, and then, rather than being duplicated, is recycled. Unless a mechanism of replication and perpetuation is demonstrated, we have here a genetic material that, in the classical sense of the word, has no genetics. As with the little man upon the stair, one is disposed to wish that yolk DNA would go away, but the clarification of its status must await the outcome of further work.

The discussion of mitochondrial RNA and its activities is not completely appropriate to a chapter on DNA. The investigation of mitochondrial DNA and RNA in the sea urchin is still in its infancy, and at this time it is probably more helpful not to consider the two molecular types in separate chapters. Extranuclear RNA synthesis in *Arbacia punctulata* was reported by Chamberlain in 1968 and 1970. He found that the RNA so produced displays a broad peak at about 14–15S with a greater amount of newly synthesized RNA heavier than 15S appearing as development proceeds. The question of whether the change in S-value reflects a processing of transcribed message, as has been discussed above, rather than a change in the species being produced, should probably be investigated. Chamberlain also noted some incorporation of label into 4S RNA (t-RNA).

Both nuclear and cytoplasmic DNA extracted from *Lytechinus variegatus* by Hartmann and Comb in 1969 hybridized with newly synthesized RNA from blastula and prism stages, suggesting that both types of DNA are being transcribed at these stages. Craig (1970) isolated an RNA from anucleate half-eggs of *Strongylocentrotus purpuratus* of which 32 percent hybridized with mitochondrial DNA and virtually none at all with sperm DNA. This RNA showed an elution profile consistent with that for m-RNA rather than for ribosomal RNA.

Selvig et al. (1970) studied the synthesis of RNA in activated anucleate halves of *Arbacia punctulata* relative to that in fertilized nucleate halves and whole embryos. They found the newly synthesized RNA in the anucleate half to be less heterodisperse than that of the other two systems. It showed a broad peak in the region of 17S in density gradient analysis. As compared to the RNA synthesized in nucleate halves and embryos, it showed very little activity above 28S. Selvig (1970) noted that the newly synthesized RNA of the anucleate half did not associate with polysomes, suggesting that it was not participating in the synthesis of proteins in the cytoplasm (see also Raff et al., 1972). The types of experiment performed by Selvig and her associates were not designed to reveal the actual site of synthesis of RNA in the anucleate half.

The Selvig group found that actinomycin D inhibits RNA synthesis in activated anucleate halves by about 70 percent in comparison to an inhibition of somewhat over 90 percent in nucleate halves and embryos. Selvig (1970) reported that ethidium bromide inhibits the synthesis of essentially all RNA above 4S in anucleate halves. This finding was confirmed by Craig and Piatigorsky (1971), who studied the effect of ethidium bromide on protein synthesis in activated anucleate halves. They found that the spectrum of proteins being synthesized was not significantly altered by this agent, and they concluded that all, or at least most, types of protein synthesized in the activated anucleate half are made on stable maternal template.

With the amount of data available, it is difficult to determine what is occurring in the activated anucleate half. If one assumes for the moment that the synthesis of RNA is occurring in the mitochondria as opposed to yolk spherules, it would appear that if this RNA is message it may not be being translated. If it is message and is stable, its synthesis could be designed for mitochondrial activity or mitochondrial replication later in development. Experiments on other types of cell suggest that mitochondrial message is not very stable. Some of the RNA synthesized could be ribosomal and might represent, again, a preparatory type of synthesis, on the assumption that r-RNA in the sea urchin is reasonably stable. The basic question here is that of the normalcy of mitochondrial activity, the question of whether the mitochondrion is doing what it normally does in development or whether it is doing what it can do in the face of changes produced by experimental abuse. There are as yet no data available with which to determine whether the absence of a nucleus causes impairment of function in the apparatus for the synthesis of proteins on mitochondrial template or whether any alteration of physiological conditions in the cells resulting from experimental handling could cause such impairment. There is believed to be a dependence on the nucleus for the production of some components of the mitochondrial machinery for protein synthesis, but whether this is a long- or short-term dependence and whether it is involved here are questions that remain to be resolved. If there is impairment of mitochondrial protein synthesis or normal absence of such synthesis during cleavage, it is really pointless to speculate on the cause until more information has been gained.

PROTEINS ASSOCIATED WITH DNA

The synthesis of DNA in early development is exponential since the production of new cells is exponential, with each new cell containing essentially the same amount of DNA, that is, the complete genome. A given cell at any stage of development or at any phase of differentiation, including complete differentiation, however, needs but a fraction of the genes in the genome to support and direct its activities. In the remainder of the genome, transcription must be suppressed. Proteins associated with DNA have been found to be instrumental in producing and removing such suppression, in other words, in controlling genetic activity.

The histones are the proteins found predominantly in association with DNA, although other proteins are associated with it and influence its function as well as determine its structure to some degree. Histones are basic proteins, soluble in acid. They are lacking in tryptophan and, except for the arginine-rich fraction, are lacking in cystine and cysteine. The function of histones in controlling genetic activity is believed to be complex, and, at the best, it is poorly understood. Histones appear to interfere with the function of RNA polymerase in serving as suppressors of gene action, but the mechanism by which they do so is obscure. As Crane and Villee (1971) have noted, it is particularly difficult to relate them to the *specific* nature of gene activation and suppression. It is doubtful that they can identify specific nucleotides, and the small number of histones known to exist appears to be insufficient to specify the large numbers of individual genes that would require activation or suppression. Histones are not strongly species specific and do not vary greatly among widely divergent species of vertebrates and invertebrates. Calf thymus histones are frequently used as a basis for comparison. At least 13 major histone fractions have been isolated from calf thymus. These histones range from lysine rich at one end of the scale to arginine rich at the other. Histones are frequently described in terms of their lysine content: lysine very rich, lysine intermediate, lysine poor, and so on.

A major responsibility of the histones is to determine the structure of DNA, the configuration that it assumes in chromatin. They reduce its linear dimensions by condensing it into a supercoiled structure. They may position it for proper operation with respect to the enzymes involved in replication and transcription. Under the electron microscope structural changes can be observed in chromatin when certain histones are removed selectively. Reactions occur in the cell that affect the structure of the histones themselves subsequent to their synthesis. These include the methylation, acetylation, and phosphorylation of residues, modifications that an increasing body of evidence shows to be responsible for alteration in structure and function of chromatin.

In various organisms, changes in the composition of histones are frequently observed during development and differentiation. In spermatogenesis in many species, for example, changes occur in the protein composition of chromatin that reduce its ability to be transcribed and that may produce marked alterations in its structure. Depending upon species, such changes may involve changes in histone composition, appearance of new histones or histone-like proteins, or replacement of histones by other proteins.

The histones of sea urchin sperm have been investigated recently by several workers (see, for example, Paoletti and Huang, 1969; Palau et al., 1969; Messineo, 1969; Thaler et al., 1970). These histones generally resemble those of calf thymus, but they have been reported to have a larger very lysine rich fraction, and some of their fractions have been found to have a higher arginine and cysteine content. Paoletti and Huang have reported a new type of basic protein associated with DNA in the sperm of *Arbacia punctulata* and *Arbacia lixula*. In composition this protein shows similarities to both lysine-rich and slightly lysine-rich histones. It is present in substantial amounts. Somewhat similar fractions have been reported in other urchins.

The histone content of the sea urchin sperm differs markedly from that of the egg and from that of the embryo at any given stage in development (see Thaler et al., 1970; Ozaki, 1971). Ozaki has noted, as have other workers, that sperm chromatin has an extremely low ability to support RNA synthesis in vitro as compared to chromatin from embryos. He raises the question as to whether this restriction of template activity prevents the paternal genes from being transcribed in early development and as to when and how sperm histones are replaced, if such a replacement occurs, by embryonic histones so that paternal genes may support protein synthesis. Answers to such questions are not presently available. Johnson and Hnilica (1970) found that the ability of sperm chromatin to support RNA synthesis in vitro can be increased to an astonishing degree if it is treated with trypsin. This finding has been reported in many animal species. Trypsin is purported to remove large amounts of histones from chromatin without damaging the template with respect to its ability to respond to RNA polymerase activity. The increased ability of chromatin to support RNA synthesis upon selective removal of histones is believed by many workers to present very strong evidence for the ability of histones to inhibit transcription in vivo.

The peculiarities of sperm proteins may be speculated to be responsible for structural changes in sperm chromatin. In any event, there is evidence that structural changes have occurred. The chromatin of the sperm head has been condensed into a densely packed mass without any conspicuous structural detail, a circumstance that strongly suggests drastic structural change.

An obvious alternative to removing histones from DNA to study the nature of their function is to add histones to chromatin, nuclei, or cells. Sea urchin embryos were treated with histones by Vorobyev (1969) and Vorobyev et al. (1969b), who found that at any stage from fertilization to early blastula, added histones would halt development at midblastula. The source of the histone was immaterial, although histones from echinoderms were more active than those of other forms. These workers could not produce the effect with acetylated histones, and they concluded that histones inhibit development, not through a polycation effect, but through specific structure. Actually, the effects produced here are similar to those seen when transcription is halted with chemical enucleants, like actinomycin D. The histones inhibited both RNA synthesis and protein synthesis. Protein synthesis was not significantly inhibited at very early development, a time when protein is regarded as being largely synthesized on stable maternal m-RNA transcribed prior to fertilization, as opposed to newly transcribed m-RNA.

Histone inhibition of RNA synthesis has been demonstrated in various organisms from studies with in vitro systems, but there has been considerable controversy attendant upon the interpretation of the results. Inhibitory effects produced by histones in vivo are much more difficult to interpret, and interpretations are equivocal more often than not. Histones have broad adverse effects on respiratory systems, inhibit the activity of transport systems, and generally show a variety of repressive influences not directly related to their effect on transcription, which might individually or collectively impede development. One perplexing question arises from this type of experiment. If one treats cells or embryos with histones of their own type, however inconclusive the results of the experiment may be, the usual result is that some active genes are repressed by these histones. The probability appears to be good that cells so treated may be synthesizing identical histones without causing the repression of those same active genes. One is disposed to wonder what the mechanism is that protects the active genes from those endogenous histones that cannot offer them a safeguard against the repressive effects of the exogenous histones.

Changes occurring in histones during development have been investigated by Repsis (1967), Spiegel et al. (1970), Ord and Stocken (1968, 1970), Vorobyev et al. (1969a), Thaler et al. (1970), and others. This work is continuing, and it promises to produce a large body of data. It is important work and will need to be reviewed in the near future. To explore it in detail here would tend to submerge our overall discussion on development. In general it reveals that some histones increase in amount and others decrease as development proceeds. Repsis has reported that the major bands found in the separation of histones on acrylamide gels at blastula and pluteus are all but lacking in the unfertilized eggs of *Lytechinus variegatus*. Outstanding changes in histone pattern occur in the gastrula and post-gastrula period, a time when the processes of differentiation are beginning to reveal themselves. The arginine-rich histones undergo the most pronounced changes in early embryogenesis and are found to have diminished relative to lysine-rich histones in later development. Despite the striking change that occurs in the pattern of histones in gastrula and later development, the pattern which emerges at that time is reported to be simpler than that seen in earlier development and to bear more resemblance to that found in calf thymus.

Hnilica and Johnson (1970), Johnson and Hnilica (1970), and Orengo and Hnilica (1970) have reported that histones are not present in the unfertilized egg, zygote, and very early cleavage stages. Their position may be summarized as follows:

> 1. Proteins that are histones by definition are not found in nuclei at these stages. Arginine-rich histones appear between the 4- to 8-cell stage and blastula. Lysine-rich histones do not appear until hatching. A typical histone pattern does not appear until gastrula.
> 2. New classes of proteins that are not histones by definition are found in nuclei in these early stages. Hnilica et al. (1971) cite as an example a serine-rich protein found in nuclei of eggs and early cleavage stages.
> 3. The ability to support RNA synthesis of nuclei from the egg (where RNA synthesis is virtually at ground zero normally) and from early cleavage stages is not enhanced by trypsinization, which should selectively remove histones. RNA synthesis is, however, enhanced by trypsinization at blastula and later stages.

Histones are defined primarily in terms of their amino acid composition, which determines certain of their chemical properties. If the existence of a new class of proteins in the unfertilized egg and early developmental stages of the sea urchin, as specified by this type of definition, is confirmed, the problem of basic interest to the embryologist is that of whether the difference in chemical properties between such proteins and the histones signifies a difference in biological function. The insensitivity of the transcription-repressing mechanism in the egg nucleus to trypsin would not appear to demand that the new proteins of Hnilica be assumed to be the repressors of transcription. We know neither what represses transcription in the unfertilized egg nor why the repression is removed so rapidly upon activation. Changes in the conventional histone pattern could be assumed to be required for structural alterations in chromatin as might occur in the conversion from germinal vesicle to the pronucleus. We need to determine whether the proteins described are functionally histones but chemically altered so that the traditional definition no longer applies, and what circumstance in development could call for such a wholesale displacement of conventional histones by these proteins. These findings are somewhat controversial and will need to be resolved.

The site of histone synthesis is a matter of interest. In earlier work on histones in various animals, the nucleus as a site of histone synthesis was not seriously questioned. Kedes et al. (1969a), however, found from the results of electron-microscope autoradiography that essentially all the proteins of the sea urchin embryo are synthesized in the cytoplasm of its cells during early development. They also demonstrated that within a short period of time following its synthesis, much of the protein produced between early cleavage and blastula finds its way to the nucleus. Protein analysis of nucleus and cytoplasm of cells pulsed with radioactive amino acid at the 64-cell stage and chased to mesenchyme blastula furnished them with the estimate that 40–60 percent of the proteins synthesized in cleavage accumulate in the nucleus. The autoradiographs showed much of the radioactivity in the nucleus to be located in the metaphase chromosomes.

Similar autoradiographic studies with cells incubated in actinomycin D at concentrations high enough to eliminate transcription still showed silver grains accumulating in the nucleus, but in lesser amounts. These results suggested that nuclear proteins are produced by synthesis on both maternal templates and transcribed message. Pulse and chase experiments showed a reduction of 20 percent in nuclear proteins in the absence of transcription. It was thought that this figure is somewhat low and that an even greater amount of nuclear proteins may be produced from transcription.

A special class of light polysomes (S-polysomes) with S-values between 100S and 200S was discovered by Nemer and his co-workers, and Nemer and Lindsay (1969) as well as Kedes and Gross (1969) showed that these polysomes are active in synthesizing protein during cleavage, with the latter group demonstrating that not only are these polysomes active from almost the very beginning of postfertilization development, but also that they are primarily engaged in translating transcribed message rather than maternal template.

Kedes et al. (1969a, 1969b) pulse-labeled embryos at the 32- to 64-cell stage with lysine and tryptophan. The region of the polysome spectrum of density gradients that is occupied by the S-polysomes showed a decrease in labeling with tryptophan and an increase in labeling with lysine, relative to the labeling in other regions. This finding indicates that this particular species of polysome is principally preoccupied with the synthesis of basic proteins. Inhibition of DNA synthesis caused a 45 percent reduction in the optical density at 260 nm of the polysome spectrum, most of which occurred in the region of the light polysomes. Actinomycin D reduced a peak with a high lysine/tryptophan ratio in the light polysome region, but these proteins, presumably histones or histone-like proteins, continued to be synthesized, supposedly on maternal template.

In summary, these results imply that

1. Nuclear proteins are synthesized in the cytoplasm.
2. During the period of extremely high DNA synthesis from early cleavage through blastula, half or more of the proteins synthesized in the cytoplasm are accumulated in the nucleus.
3. The synthesis of histones or histone-like proteins at this time depends to a high degree, but not exclusively, on transcription and probably much of the transcription at this time is devoted to such synthesis.
4. The synthesis of histones or histone-like proteins occurs on a special class of light polysomes.

In 1971, Moav and Nemer extracted the nascent peptides from the S-polysomes and purified them by the use of cation-exchange resins and acrylamide-gel electrophoresis. From the incorporation of labeled arginine and lysine into these peptides relative to that of labeled tryptophan, the peptides showed strong resemblance to histones. As these investigators have noted, these nascent peptides cannot be characterized meaningfully, nor do they necessarily resemble the proteins that they ultimately become.

Assuming that active polysomes are fully loaded, the presence of

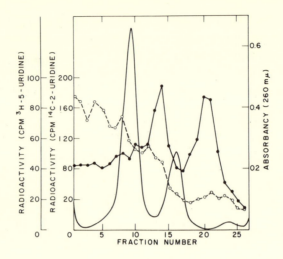

Figure 18

Size classes of new m-RNA at different developmental stages of the sea urchin embryo. Closed circles represent tritium-labeled RNA synthesized by cleavage embryos (32-cell stage). Open circles represent ^{14}C-labeled RNA synthesized by embryos in late blastula. Solid line represents O.D.$_{260}$ pattern with visible peaks at 26S, 18S, and 4S. The 9–10S peak, which has been associated with the production of nuclear proteins, appears only in the curve for cleavage embryos and is the major peak on the right. The other prominent peak in this curve (20S) has not been investigated. [From Kedes et al. (1969b), © 1969 by Cold Spring Harbor Laboratory; by permission.]

a special size class of polysome suggests the possibility that message of a special size class or within a particular size range is being translated. Kedes et al. (1969b) extracted with ethylenediaminetetraacetic acid a newly labeled 9 to 10S RNA from polysomes at midcleavage. This RNA is found almost entirely on the light polysomes. It is produced in cleavage, but not in later development. It is not found in circumstances under which light polysomes do not form or are severely attenuated, as in the inhibition of DNA synthesis with hydroxyurea or in anucleate half-eggs. Their results point to a template that is produced by transcription during cleavage, that is largely responsible for the production of histones, and that is a principal template upon which light polysomes form (see Fig. 18).

Thaler et al. (1970) have reported that in embryos developing in actinomycin D, ^{14}C-valine is incorporated into nuclear protein in early embryogenesis at the same rate as in untreated controls, indicating that the synthesis can proceed on maternal template. They have found the specific activity of cytoplasmic and nonchromosomal proteins to be only about a fourth that of total nuclear proteins. They submit that chromosomal proteins are the most rapidly synthesized cellular component in early development. They have found that the antibiotic inhibits the incorporation of label into lysine-rich proteins, but actually increases the incorporation into arginine-rich proteins. Increases in total protein synthesis have been noted by earlier workers when sea urchin embryos have been treated with actinomycin D. Such increases have occurred in early development, before transcription following fertilization attains a high level of activity. Increases of this type could possibly reflect the activity of some mechanism of translational control attempting to compensate for transcriptional deficiencies.

REFERENCES

Agrell, I., and H. Persson, 1956. Changes in the amount of nucleic acids and free nucleotides during embryonic development of sea urchins. *Nature* (London), *178*, 1398–1399.

Aloni, Y., and G. Attardi, 1971. Relationship between ribosomal 4S RNA and 4S RNA of the fast sedimenting RNA components in HeLa cell mitochondria. *Biol. Ann. Rep., Calif. Inst. Technol., 1970–71,* 140.

Anderson, W. A., 1969. Nuclear and cytoplasmic DNA synthesis during early embryogenesis of *Paracentrotus lividus. J. Ultrastruct. Res., 26,* 95–110.

Attardi, G., and B. Attardi, 1969. The informational role of mitochondrial DNA. In E. Hanley (ed.), *Problems in Biology: RNA in Development.* University of Utah Press, Salt Lake City, 245–281.

Auclair, W., 1965. The chromosomes of sea urchins, especially *Arbacia punctulata;* a method for studying unsectioned eggs at the first cleavage. *Biol. Bull. Mar. Biol. Lab., Woods Hole, 128,* 169–176.

Baltus, E., and J. Brachet, 1962. Le dosage de l'acide desoxyribonucléique dans les oeufs de batraciens. *Biochim. Biophys. Acta, 61,* 157–163.

Baltus, E., J. Quertier, A. Ficq, and J. Brachet, 1965. Biochemical studies of nucleate and anucleated fragments isolated from sea urchin eggs. A comparison between fertilization and parthenogenetic activation. *Biochim. Biophys. Acta, 95,* 408–417.

Bibring, T., J. Brachet, and F. S. Gaeta, 1965. Some physical properties of cytoplasmic deoxyribonucleic acid in unfertilized eggs of *Arbacia lixula. Biochim. Biophys. Acta, 108,* 644–651.

Burgos, M., 1955. The Feulgen reaction in mature unfertilized sea urchin eggs. *Exp. Cell Res., 9,* 360–363.

Carden, G. A., S. Rosenkranz, and H. S. Rosenkranz, 1965. Deoxyribonucleic acids of sperm, eggs, and somatic cells of the sea urchin *Arbacia punctulata. Nature* (London), *205,* 1338–1339.

Chamberlain, J. P., 1968. Extranuclear RNA synthesis in sea urchin embryos. *J. Cell Biol., 39,* 23a.

Chamberlain, J. P., 1970. RNA synthesis in anucleate egg fragments and normal embryos of the sea urchin, *Arbacia punctulata. Biochim. Biophys. Acta, 213,* 183–193.

Chargaff, E., 1955. Isolation and composition of deoxypentose nucleic acids and of the corresponding nucleoproteins. In E. Chargaff and J. N. Davidson (eds.), *The Nucleic Acids*. Academic Press, Inc., New York, 307–371.

Cohen, S., 1970. Are/were mitochondria and chloroplasts microorganisms? *Amer. Scientist, 58,* 281–289.

Comb, D. G., 1965. Methylation of nucleic acids during sea urchin embryo development. *J. Mol. Biol., 11,* 851–855.

Craig, S. P., 1970. Synthesis of RNA in non-nucleate fragments of sea urchin eggs. *J. Mol. Biol., 47,* 615–618.

Craig, S. P., and J. Piatigorsky, 1971. Protein synthesis and development in the absence of cytoplasmic RNA synthesis in non-nucleate egg fragments and embryos of sea urchins. Effect of ethidium bromide. *Develop. Biol., 24,* 214–232.

Crane, C. M., and C. A. Villee, 1971. The synthesis of nuclear histones in early embryogenesis. *J. Biol. Chem., 246,* 719–723.

Di Stefano, H., and D. Mazia, 1952. The role of the midpiece in the incorporation of P^{32} into the ribonucleic acid of *Arbacia* spermatozoa. *Biol. Bull. Mar. Biol. Lab., Woods Hole, 103,* 299–300.

Elson, D., and E. Chargaff, 1952. On the desoxyribonucleic acid content of sea urchin gametes. *Experientia, 8,* 143–145.

Fansler, S., and L. A. Loeb, 1969. Sea urchin DNA polymerase. II. Changing location during early development. *Exp. Cell Res., 57,* 305–310.

Ficq, A., F. Aiello, and E. Scarano, 1963. Métabolisme des acides nucléiques dans l'oeuf d'oursin en développement. *Exp. Cell Res., 29,* 128–136.

Giudice, G., 1960. Incorporation of labeled amino acids into the protein of the mitochondria isolated from the unfertilized eggs and developmental stages of *Paracentrotus lividus. Exp. Cell Res., 21,* 222–225.

Grippo, P., E. Parisi, C. Carestia, and E. Scarano, 1970. A novel origin of some deoxyribonucleic acid thymine and its non random distribution. *Biochemistry, 9,* 2605–2609.

Hartmann, J. F., and D. G. Comb, 1969. Transcription of nuclear and cytoplasmic genes during early development of sea urchin embryos. *J. Mol. Biol., 41,* 155–158.

Harvey, E. B., 1956. *The American Arbacia and Other Sea Urchins.* Princeton University Press, Princeton, N.J.

Hinegardner, R. T., 1961. The DNA content of isolated sea urchin nuclei. *Exp. Cell Res., 25,* 341–347.

Hinegardner, R. T., B. Rao, and D. E. Feldman, 1964. The DNA synthetic period during early development of the sea urchin egg. *Exp. Cell Res., 36,* 53–64.

Hnilica, L. S., and A. W. Johnson, 1970. Fractionation and analysis of nuclear proteins in sea urchin embryos. *Exp. Cell Res., 63,* 261–270.

Hnilica, L. S., M. E. McClure, and T. C. Spelsberg, 1971. Histone biosynthesis and the cell cycle. In D. M. P. Phillips (ed.), *Histone and Nucleohistones.* Plenum Publishing Corporation, New York, 187–240.

Hoff Jørgensen, E., 1954. Deoxynucleic acid in some gametes and embryos. *Colston Papers, 7,* 79–90.

Huberman, J. A., and A. D. Riggs, 1968. On the mechanism of DNA replication in mammalian chromosomes. *J. Mol. Biol., 32,* 327–341.

Jansz, H. S., D. ven der Mei, and G. M. Zandvliet, 1971. DNA biosynthesis. *Int. Rev. Cytol., 31,* 115–167.

Johnson, A. W., and L. S. Hnilica, 1970. *In vitro* synthesis and nuclear proteins of isolated sea urchin embryo nuclei. *Biochim. Biophys. Acta, 224,* 518–530.

Kedes, L. H., and P. R. Gross, 1969. Identification in cleaving embryos of three

RNA species serving as templates for the synthesis of nuclear proteins. *Nature* (London), *223*, 1335–1339.

Kedes L. H., P. R. Gross, G. Cognetti, and A. Hunter, 1969a. Synthesis of nuclear and chromosomal proteins on light polysomes during cleavage in the sea urchin embryo. *J. Mol. Biol., 45*, 337–351.

Kedes, L. H., B. Hogan, G. Cognetti, S. Selvig, P. Yanover, and P. R. Gross, 1969b. Regulation of translation and transcription of messenger RNA during early embryonic development. *Symp. Quant. Biol., 34*, 717–723.

Loeb, L. A., 1969. Purification and properties of deoxyribonucleic acid polymerase from nuclei of sea urchin embryos. *J. Biol. Chem., 244*, 1672–1681.

Loeb, L. A., 1970. Molecular association of DNA polymerase with chromatin in sea urchin embryos. *Nature* (London), *226*, 448–449.

Loeb, L. A., B. Fansler, and R. Williams, 1969. Sea urchin nuclear DNA polymerase. I. Localization in nuclei during rapid DNA synthesis. *Exp. Cell Res., 57*, 298–304.

Loeb, L. A., D. Mazia, and A. D. Ruby, 1967. Priming of DNA polymerase in nuclei of sea urchin embryos by native DNA. *Proc. Nat. Acad. Sci., US, 57*, 841–848.

Marshak, A., and C. Marshak, 1952. Deoxyribonucleic acid in the nuclei of *Arbacia* eggs. *Biol. Bull. Mar. Biol. Lab., Woods Hole, 103*, 295.

Marshak, A., and C. Marshak, 1953. Deoxyribonucleic acid in *Arbacia* eggs. *Exp. Cell Res., 5*, 288–300.

Marshak, A, and C. Marshak, 1954. Biological role of deoxyribonucleic acid. *Nature* (London), 174, 919–920.

Marshak, A., and C. Marshak, 1955. Thymine in the acid soluble fraction of *Arbacia* eggs. *J. Biophys. Biochem. Cytol., 1*, 167–171.

Marshak, A., and C. Marshak, 1956. On the question of DNA content of sea urchin eggs. *Exp. Cell Res., 10*. 246–247.

Messineo, L., 1969. Amino acid analysis of glycerine-extracted deoxyribonucleoproteins (sea urchin sperm). *Arch. Biochem. Biophys., 133*, 92–98.

Moav, B., and M. Nemer, 1971. Histone synthesis. Assignment to a special class of polyribosomes in sea urchin embryos. *Biochemistry, 10*, 881–888.

Nakano, E., and A. Monroy, 1958. Incorporation of S^{35} methionine in the cell fractions of sea urchin eggs and embryos. *Exp. Cell Res., 14*, 236–244.

Nemer, M., 1962. Characteristics of utilization of nucleotides of embryos of *Paracentrotus lividus*. *J. Biol. Chem., 237*, 143–149.

Nemer, M., and D. T. Lindsay, 1969. Evidence that the 3-polysomes of early sea urchin embryos may be responsible for the synthesis of chromosomal histones. *Biochem. Biophys. Res. Commun., 35*, 156–160.

Ord, M. G., and L. A. Stocken, 1968. Variations in the microstructure of histones during early cleavage stages in *Echinus. Biochem. J., 109*, 24.

Ord, M. G., and L. A. Stocken, 1970. Changes in the composition of acid extracts of purified *Echinus* nuclei during cleavage stages and from early embryos. *Biochem. J., 120*, 671–672.

Orengo, A., and L. B. Hnilica, 1970. *In vivo* incorporation of labeled amino acids into nuclear proteins of the sea urchin embryos. *Exp. Cell Res., 62*, 331–337.

Ozaki, M., 1971. Developmental studies of sea urchin chromatin isolated from spermatozoa of *Strongylocentrotus purpuratus*. *Develop. Biol., 26*, 209–219.

Palau, J., A. Ruis-Carrille, and J. A. Subirana, 1969. Histones from sperm of *Arbacia lixula. Europ. J. Biochem., 7*, 209–213.

Paoletti, R. A., and R. C. Huang, 1969. Characterization of sea urchin sperm chromatin and its basic proteins. *Biochemistry, 8*, 1615–1625.

Patterson, J. B., and D. W. Stafford, 1970. Sea urchin satellite deoxyribonucleic acid.

Its large-scale isolation and hybridization with homologous ribosomal nucleic acid. *Biochemistry, 9,* 1278–1283.

Piko, L., D. G. Blair, and A. Tyler, 1968. Cytoplasmic DNA in the unfertilized sea urchin egg: physical properties of circular mitochondrial DNA and the occurrence of catenated forms. *Press. Nat. Acad. Sci., U.S.A., 59,* 838–845.

Piko, L., and A. Tyler, 1965. Deoxyribonucleic acid content of unfertilized sea urchin eggs. *Amer. Zool., 5,* 636.

Piko, L., A. Tyler, and J. Vinograd, 1967. Amount, location, capacity, circularity, and other properties of cytoplasmic DNA in sea urchin eggs. *Biol. Bull. Mar. Biol. Lab., Woods Hole, 132,* 68–90.

Raff, R. A., H. V. Colot, S. E. Selvig, and P. R. Gross, 1972. Oogenetic origin of messenger RNA for embryonic synthesis of microtubule protein. *Nature* (London), *235,* 211–214.

Rao, B., and R. T. Hinegardner, 1965. Analysis of DNA synthesis and X-ray-induced mitotic delay in sea urchin eggs. *Radiat. Res., 26,* 534–537.

Repsis, L. C., 1967. Acid-soluble nuclear proteins in development stages of *Lytechinus variogatus. Exp. Cell Res., 48,* 146–148.

Robberson, D., Y. Aloni, G. Attardi, and N. R. Davidson, 1971. The relative position of ribosomal RNA genes in mitochondrial DNA. *Biol. Ann. Rep., Calif. Inst. Technol., 1970-1971,* 142.

Roels, H., 1966. Metabolic DNA: cytochemical study. *Int. Rev. Cytol., 19,* 1–34.

Rosenkranz, H., 1965. DNA and the embryonic development of the American sea urchin *Arbacia punctulata. Biol. Bull. Mar. Biol Lab., Woods Hole, 129,* 419.

Rosenkranz, H. S., and O. A. Carden, 1967. DNA during the development of the American sea urchin. *Nature (London), 213,* 1024–1025.

Rosenkranz, H. S., B. F. Erlanger, and S. W. Tanenbaum, 1964. Purine- and pyrimidine-specific antibodies: effect on the fertilized sea urchin egg. *Science, 145,* 282–283.

Scarano, E., 1958a. Deaminazione enzimatica dell'ac. 5-deossicitidilico. *Boll. Soc. Ital. Biol. Sper., 34,* 499.

Scarano, E., 1958b. 5'-Deoxycytidylic acid deaminase. Enzymic production of 5'-deoxyuridylic acid. *Biochim. Biophys. Acta, 29,* 459–460.

Scarano, E., B. De Petrocellis, and G. Augusti-Tocco, 1964a. Studies on the control of enzyme synthesis during the early embryonic development of the urchins. *Biochim. Biophys. Acta, 87,* 174–176.

Scarano, E., B. De Petrocellis, and G. Augusti-Tocco, 1964b. Deoxycytidylate aminohydrolase content in disaggregated cells from sea urchin embryos. *Exp. Cell Res., 36,* 211–213.

Scarano, E., M. Iaccarino, P. Grippo, and D. Winklemans, 1965. On the methylation of DNA during development of the sea urchin embryo. *J. Mol. Biol., 14,* 603–617.

Scarano, E., M. Iaccarino, P. Grippo, and E. Parisi, 1967. The heterogeneity of thymine methyl group origin in DNA pyrimidine isostichs of developing sea urchin embryos. *Proc. Nat. Acad. Sci., U.S.A., 57,* 1394–1400.

Scarano, E., and R. Maggio, 1959. The enzymatic deamination of 5'-deoxycytidylic acid and of 5-methyl-5'-deoxycytidylic acid in the developing sea urchin embryo. *Exp. Cell Res., 18,* 333–346.

Selvig, S., 1970. RNA synthesized in enucleated sea urchin eggs. *Amer. Zool., 10,* 530.

Selvig, S. E., P. R. Gross, and A. L. Hunter, 1970. Cytoplasmic synthesis of RNA in the sea urchin embryo. *Develop. Biol., 22,* 343–365.

Shaver, J., 1956. Mitochondrial populations during development of the sea urchin. *Exp. Cell Res., 11,* 548–559.

Simmel, E. B., and D. A. Karnofsky, 1961. Observation on the uptake of tritiated thymidine in the pronuclei of fertilized sand dollar embryos. *J. Biophys. Biochem. Cytol.*, *10*, 59.

Slater, J., and L. A. Loeb, 1970. Initiation of DNA synthesis in eucaryotes. A model *in vitro* system. *Biochem. Biophys. Res. Commun.*, *41*, 589–593.

Spiegel, M., E. S. Spiegel, and P. S. Meltzer, 1970. Qualitative changes in the basic protein fraction of developing embryos. *Develop. Biol.*, *21*, 73–86.

Stafford, D. W., and S. R. Guild, 1969. Satellite DNA from sea urchin sperm. *Exp. Cell Res.*, *55*, 347–350.

Stearns, L. W., W. E. Martin, W. B. Jolley, and J. W. Bamberger, 1962. Effects of certain pyrimidines on cleavage and nucleic acid metabolism in sea urchin, *Strongylocentrotus purpuratus* embryos. *Exp. Cell Res.*, *27*, 250–259.

Sugino, Y., N. Sugino, R. Okazaki, and T. Okazaki, 1960. Deoxynucleosidic compounds. I. Modified microbioassay method and its application to sea urchin eggs and several other materials. *Biochim. Biophys. Acta*, *40*, 417–424.

Thaler, M. M., M. C. Cox, and C. A. Villee, 1970. Histones in early embryogenesis. Developmental aspects of composition and synthesis. *J. Biol. Chem.*, *245*, 1479–1483.

Tyler, A., 1967. Masked messenger RNA and cytoplasmic DNA in relation to protein synthesis and the processes of fertilization and determination in embryonic development. *Develop. Biol.*, *Suppl. 1*, 170–226.

Tyler, A., and B. S. Tyler, 1966a. The gametes: some procedures and properties. In R. A. Boolootian (ed.), *Physiology of the Echinodermata.* John Wiley & Sons, Inc. (Interscience Division), New York, 639–682.

Vanyushin, B. F., S. G. Tkacheva, and A. N. Belozersky, 1970. Rare bases in animal DNA. *Nature* (London), *225*, 948–949.

Vorobyev, V. I., 1969. The effect of histones on RNA and protein synthesis in sea urchin embryos at early stages of development. *Exp. Cell Res.*, *55*, 168–170.

Vorobyev, V. I., A. A. Gineitis, and I. A. Vinogradova, 1969a. Histones in early embryogenesis. *Exp. Cell Res.*, *57*, 1–7.

Vorobyev, V. I., A. A. Gineitis, E. I. Kostyleva, and T. I. Smirnova, 1969b. The effect of histones on the early embryogenesis of sea urchins. *Exp. Cell Res.*, *55*, 171–175.

Whiteley, A. H., and F. Baltzer, 1958. Development, respiratory rate, and content of deoxyribonucleic acid in the hybrid, *Paracentrotus* ♀ × *Arbacia* ♂. *Pubbl. Staz. Zool. Napoli*, *30*, 420–457.

CHAPTER VII

Polysomes in the Sea Urchin Embryo

GENERAL REMARKS

We have discussed the basic template molecule, DNA, which contains the ultimate information on how to synthesize a protein. Before considering individually the three RNA types that are responsible for the direct assembly of the protein molecule, it is appropriate to consider the complete biosynthetic apparatus upon which the protein is assembled, the polysome.

Basic descriptions of polysome structure and function may be found in most general treatises on cell physiology, biochemistry, molecular biology, and cytology. In 1969 Spirin and Gavrilova published a monograph on the ribosome, which presents a detailed analysis of the mechanics of polysome function. Polysomes are usually studied by density-gradient analysis. Since they are rich in nucleotides, they may be detected and quantitated in a density gradient by spectrophotometry at 260 nm, provided they are isolated in sufficient concentration. If the material under study is incubated with radioactive label prior to homogenization and fractionation, polysomes may acquire label if the appropriate synthesis occurs, and they may be detected and quantitated in a density gradient by the use of apparatus for counting radioactive emanations. If labeled uridine or labeled amino acids are used as precursors, one can determine whether polysomes contain newly transcribed message or whether they are actively synthesizing protein.

Since there is a correspondence between the number of nucleotide triplets on an m-RNA molecule and the number of amino acids in a protein molecule, there is also a correspondence between the size of the message and the size of the protein that it produces. The space intervals between ribosomes strung out along an m-RNA molecule that is being read appear to be fairly uniform; therefore, there is expected to be a general correspondence between the size of the messenger molecule and the number of ribosomes it contains. There is thus a rough correspondence between size of polysome and size of message, provided that the polysome contains its full complement of ribosomes. The size of a polysome is most conveniently visualized in terms of the number of individual ribosomes that it contains. S-value reflects roughly the sizes of polysomes since the major contribution to the sedimentation coefficient of a polysome is made by its ribosomes, all of which have essentially the same sedimentation coefficient.

The S-value of a polysome reflects the number of ribosomes that the polysome contains, but not necessarily the number of ribosomes that it can contain. It may be important in studies on development to determine whether polysomes are fully loaded, that is, whether they contain their full complement of ribosomes. The presence of a large number of underloaded polysomes could attest to an impairment of translation activity. The problem of underloaded polysomes in sea urchin development is somewhat controversial at present, as will be discussed below. A polysome that, by acquisition of ribosomes, undergoes a change from an underloaded state to a fully loaded state attains a higher S-value and shifts its position in the polysome spectrum of a density gradient. A means is thus provided for determining whether changes in the loading of polysomes have occurred. The problem is by no means simple, however, since changes in a polysome spectrum can also reflect changes in the pattern of message being translated.

Given the presence of the appropriate enzymes, cofactors, and an adequate supply of precursors, polysomes can be made to function in vitro to support protein synthesis. Under appropriate conditions, they can also be made to form in vitro, not only with native messenger RNA, but also with various synthetic messenger molecules.

Some of the existing concepts of the structure and function of polysomes of eukaryotic cells may prove ultimately to be fallacious in instances where they have been formulated through reference to bacterial polysomes. Although without doubt there are more similarities than differences between the two categories of polysome, differences do exist. Spirin, for example, has pointed out a variety of differences between ribosomes of eukaryotic and prokaryotic cells. It is generally wise to hold reservations on concepts which assume, in the absence of proof, that particular aspects of function in polysomes of eukaryotic cells are identical to those of prokaryotic cells.

EARLY STUDIES ON POLYSOMES
IN THE SEA URCHIN

Shortly after the polysome was discovered, it became the center for investigations in the sea urchin egg and embryo, the work of Monroy and Tyler (1963) and Wilt (1964) being among the pioneer efforts. The first results from studies on sea urchin polysomes were impaired by a lack of resolution in density gradients. Peaks tended to telescope together or to appear as shoulders on other peaks. Yields of polysome material were low, presumably because of degradation. Findings were difficult to interpret and sometimes not very meaningful. The difficulties encountered could be attributed in part to the type of buffer used in experiments. Later investigators, following the lead of Cohen and Iverson (1967), adopted a high ionic strength buffer. The use of this buffer coupled with improved washing techniques has enabled workers to obtain polysome spectra with better yield and resolution than those produced in the past.

A center of interest in early studies on polysomes was the relative status of the polysome in fertilized versus unfertilized eggs. Early studies on protein synthesis (see, for example, Hultin, 1950 and 1952; Hultin and Wessel, 1952; Nakano and Monroy, 1958; and Monroy and Vittorelli, 1962) had shown that there is very little protein synthesis in the unfertilized egg, whereas in a matter of a few minutes after fertilization synthesis begins an exponential rise, which continues until blastula before sloping off. Epel (1967) demonstrated that protein synthesis actually increases several fold in the first half-hour after fertilization. Hultin (1961) and Hultin and Bergstrand (1960) showed that microsome preparations from fertilized and unfertilized eggs would produce in in vitro protein synthesis, a picture essentially parallel to that seen in vivo.

The findings of the early workers on polysomes appeared to confirm this picture. Monroy and Tyler (1963), Wilt (1964), Stafford et al. (1964), and Cohen and Iverson (1967) could not detect the presence of polysomes in the unfertilized egg, although an abundance of ribosomes was found to be present. They showed that polysomes form shortly after fertilization and begin an increase in number forthwith that continues through early development and more or less parallels the increase in protein synthesis. It was revealed by Epel (1967), MacKintosh and Bell (1967), Tyler et al. (1968), and others, however, that there is more protein synthesis in the unfertilized egg than indicated by early reports and that the burgeoning of protein production after fertilization actually represents an increase in, rather than an initiation of, synthesis. It remained, then, to determine whether this low-level synthesis in the unfertilized egg proceeds on polysomes.

Stavy and Gross (1967) found that the region moving faster than ribosomes in a sucrose density-gradient centrifugation of the microsomal fraction of unfertilized eggs of *Lytechinus pictus* could support the endogenous incorporation of amino acids into protein in an in vitro system. The incorporation was low compared to that of the polysome region of the fertilized egg. The experiment demonstrated, however, that either polysomes or some unknown type of apparatus for protein synthesis, which sediments in the polysome region, is present in the unfertilized egg. Rinaldi and Monroy (1969), MacKintosh and Bell (1969a), and Denny and Reback (1970) have reported the presence of polysomes in the unfertilized egg and even made some determinations on their amount, distribution, and activity, relative to those of polysomes of fertilized eggs. In batches of unfertilized eggs within the usual batch-size range used in experimentation, the small population of active polysomes does not show enough absorbance at 260 nm to produce peaks in density gradients that are of sufficient magnitude to be interpreted readily. When labeling with radioactive precursors is employed, the nascent peptide chains on the polysomes of unfertilized eggs show peaks of radioactivity that are of acceptable magnitude for the interpretation of results. These peaks show a distribution which, as far as can be determined, reflects that of the polysomes.

Monroy and Tyler (1963) and Stafford et al. (1964) found that when material in the polysome region of a sucrose density gradient is treated with RNAase there occurs a loss in the 260-nm absorbing material from the polysome region and a correlative increase in size of the monosome (single ribosome) optical density peak. This finding is in accord with findings of other workers in many cell types. If the embryo is given a short pulse with labeled amino acid prior to homogenization or extraction, the label is likewise transferred to the monosome region upon RNAase treatment. It is probably safe to assume that the enzyme ruptures the messenger RNA thread between the ribsomes and that, upon disruption of the polysome, each ribosomal monomer still bears its chain of nascent protein. The conversion of polysomes to monosomes upon treatment with RNAase has come to be used as a test to identify polysomes.

Several early investigators found that some polysomes are bound to membranes, necessitating the use of surface-active agents such as deoxycholate or sodium dodecyl sulfate to release them. The use of such agents may cause a degree of breakdown of polysome material. One would expect the number of free polysomes, that is, polysomes not bound to membranes, to be high in sea urchin embryos during early development, because of the meager endowment of endoplasmic reticulum. There may be some association of polysomes with membrane-enveloped organelles, and the nuclear membrane normally has an abundance of ribosomes associated with it.

Stafford et al. (1964) were able to detect and isolate membrane-bound polysomes in *Lytechinus variegatus* by underlying a 15–30 percent sucrose density gradient with a cushion of 50 or 60 percent sucrose, depending upon the experiment. The membrane-bound material was caught at the interface between gradient and cushion. On the assumption that RNAase will disrupt polysomes without removing them from the membrane, they exposed the material from the gradient–cushion interface to differential treatment with RNAase and deoxycholate to identify and assay that membrane-bound material that is truly polysomal. They estimated that about 10 percent of the polysomes are membrane bound. The rate of amino acid incorporation into proteins appeared to be the same on membrane-bound and free polysomes.

LIGHT AND HEAVY POLYSOMES

On the basis of experiments by other investigators, which will be discussed at a later point and which suggested that the embryo at cleavage synthesizes its proteins on stable maternal m-RNA produced at oogenesis. Spirin and Nemer (1965) turned their attention to the question of whether the embryo in cleavage might also be synthesizing part of its proteins on message transcribed after fertilization. In an analysis of RNA sedimentation profiles from centrifugation in a sucrose density gradient of postmitochondrial supernatants (the supernatant from a centrifugation at $12,000 \times g$ or more, which throws down the mitochondria) from homogenates of embryos of *Lytechinus pictus* previously incubated in ^{3}H-uridine, these workers demonstrated the presence of newly synthesized RNA. The RNA was shown to be neither ribosomal RNA nor 4S RNA (t-RNA). It appeared from its sedimentation characteristics, and its strong tendency to hybridize with DNA, to be m-RNA, transcribed after fertilization. The homogenates in which it was found were prepared from 4- to 16-cell-stage embryos.

Polysome profiles were examined in gradients from the same type of supernatants prepared in the same manner from the same type of embryos, with some preparations included from embryos incubated in ^{14}C-leucine. A series of polysomes was observed that ranged from light to heavy in terms of sedimentation values, in which series the light polysomes appeared to be functionally distinct from the heavy polysomes in that the uridine-labeled newly synthesized message associated itself almost exclusively with the light polysomes, whereas protein synthesis, as evinced by leucine incorporation, occurred primarily on the heavy polysomes with the light polysomes showing little activity (see Fig. 19). The light polysomes ranged from about 100S to 200S or slightly higher, and the heavy polysomes were found in the range of 200S and above. Spirin and Nemer concluded that in early cleavage protein synthesis occurs primarily on the heavy polysomes and utilizes information contained in preformed maternal message. They concluded also that newly transcribed message tends to associate with light polysomes, as opposed to heavy polysomes. They did not assume that all newly transcribed message associates with light polysomes, but proposed rather that some of it forms complexes with protein to which they gave the name *informosomes*. The informosome, which is discussed by Spirin (1966) appears to be a

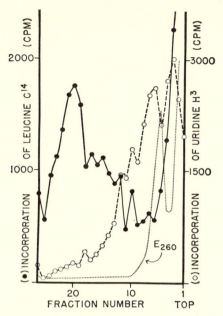

Figure 19

Incorporation of ³H-uridine and ¹⁴C-leucine in the polysomes of cleavage-stage sea urchin embryos. Embryos at the 4-cell stage were incubated in seawater with uridine ³H (10μC/ml; 4.63 C/ mmole) for 2 hours at 19°C. At the end of this period they were given a 2-minute pulse with ¹⁴C-leucine (0.2 μC/ml; 111C/mole). Embryos were homogenized, and the 12,000 × g supernatant was analyzed by sedimentation. The light polysomes are shown here to be relatively inactive in protein synthesis. [From Spirin and Nemer (1965); copyright 1965 by the American Association for the Advancement of Science.]

carrier and/or a storage particle containing message that is awaiting translation.

Actually, Wilt (1964) had demonstrated in the previous year that newly transcribed RNA, presumably m-RNA, associates with polysomes in early development, but his description of the distribution of this message on the polysome spectrum did not delineate the association with a special class of polysome. Historically, the experiments of Spirin and Nemer in 1965 are of considerable interest, yet work in recent years has demonstrated that their conclusions with regard to the function of these two classes of polysome were erroneous. As has been noted in the discussion on histones in a previous chapter, however, the light polysomes have been shown to have an extremely important function in development.

Spirin and Nemer proposed in effect that light polysomes are basically a species of inactive polysome which can withhold newly transcribed message from activity in development until such a time as it is required. The heavy polysomes, by contrast, would constitute the active protein-synthesizing machinery of the cell. Infante and Nemer (1967) carried this thesis one step further on the basis of their findings on the kinetics of formation of the two classes of polysome. They reported that both types of polysome increase in number rapidly to attain a plateau value in the first 2 hours after fertilization, with, however, the heavy polysomes showing a great preponderance in number. At the 16-cell stage the light polysomes begin to increase very rapidly, acquiring a high concentration at the time of blastulation. While the light polysomes are undergoing this rapid increase, the heavy polysomes hold a fairly constant concentration. At blastula, with the light polysomes now far in excess, the heavy polysomes begin a gradual increase, which maximizes at about mesenchyme blastula. As the heavy polysomes start to increase at blastula, the light polysomes begin an inexorable decline in number, which they maintain through mesenchyme blastula into gastrula. The observation that the light polysomes decrease in number while the heavy polysomes increase suggested to these investigators that the light polysomes are converted to heavy polysomes presumably by the acquisition of ribosomes. A light polysome is thus light because it is underloaded. Underloading is seen as symptomatic of interference with the initiation of readout for protein synthesis. Such interference would reflect the activity of a mechanism for translational control. The light polysome would thus hold the translation of newly transcribed message in abeyance until after blastula.

Viewed intuitively, this postulate is somewhat disquieting because it would appear reasonable to expect considerable activity in the light-polysome region in the translation of light message to produce protein in the lower molecular-weight ranges. In any event, within 2 or 3 years after the publication of these results, the findings of other workers demonstrated that the concept of inactive, underloaded polysomes serving to any degree as a mechanism of translational control in development is untenable.

Stavy and Gross (1967) were able to elicit significant amino acid incorporation into nascent protein on both light and heavy polysomes in *Lytechinus pictus*. They worked at an earlier stage (2-cell) than did Spirin and Nemer, albeit with the same animal. They asserted that there existed no evidence in their results that in the panorama of complexes heavier than ribosomes any complex was, or contained, inactive polysomes. Rinaldi and Monroy (1969) reported that newly transcribed message is to be found in association with both light and heavy polysomes.

Kedes and Gross (1969a) made a detailed investigation of the nature of light and heavy polysomes. They found first that in the cleavage period all polysomes are actively engaged in protein synthesis. When 32- to 64-cell embryos were pulse-labeled with radioactive amino acids, the heavy polysomes did indeed have a much greater specific activity than the light polysomes. These investigators assumed that heavier polysomes, however, would have longer peptides than would lighter polysomes, and that these peptides would contain proportionately a greater amount of radioactivity. Heavy polysomes would thus have the superficial appearance of being more active in synthesis than light polysomes. A plot of the estimated number of ribosomes per polysome (which number is correlated to the length of the messenger molecule to an approximate degree, and hence to the length of the polypeptide chain) versus counts per minute showed a linear increase for polysomes with ribosome numbers between 2 and 15. Although such a curve demands certain assumptions, such as the existence of a general symmetry of amino acid content throughout the various size classes of polysome, for example, it does present evidence that light polysomes are not inactive. A region of the polysome spectrum not contributing to the radioactivity of nascent peptides would produce a deviation from the theoretical line of the plot. No such deviation was found.

Second, these investigators were able to effect a disruption of both light and heavy polysomes with puromycin, a phenomenon that appears to occur only when polysomes are engaged in active translation of message. They proposed that newly transcribed message is not being held for translation at a later stage in development but rather is being translated immediately, or at least in a very short time after becoming associated with polysomes.

Third, Kedes and Gross found by treating embryos incubated in ³H-uridine with actinomycin D and comparing the polysome spectra from such embryos with those from controls labeled in a similar fashion that newly transcribed RNA, presumably message, is contained on all size classes of polysome, light and heavy.

Finally, they presented compelling evidence that light polysomes

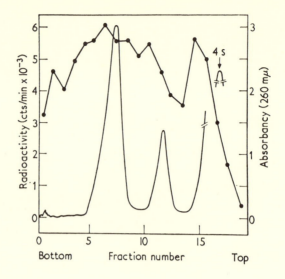

Figure 20

Sucrose-gradient sedimentation profile of phenol-extracted RNA from polysomes of 4-hour-old *Arbacia punctulata* (morulae) labeled with ³H-uridine (100 μC/ml) for 90 minutes. Alternate fractions from the polysome region of a sucrose density gradient were pooled (10 ml) and after the addition of 1 O.D./ml of yeast 4S RNA as a carrier, the RNA was extracted. The RNA was layered over a 10 to 30 percent sucrose density gradient containing dodecyl SO₄ buffer and centrifuged for 16 hours at 22,000 rpm in the SW 25.3 rotor of a Spinco L2 ultracentrifuge at 22°C. Solid lines show absorbency. Filled circles show radioactivity. 840 cpm were recovered from the pellet. The 9–10S peak associated with the production of nuclear proteins is seen at the light end of the profile. [From Kedes and Gross (1969a); by permission.]

are not underloaded. They extracted m-RNA from a polysome gradient from 4-hour *Arbacia* embryos after the embryos had been exposed to radioactive uridine. The spectrum of message was heterodisperse with a broad range of S-values ranging from just above 4S to about 50S (see Fig. 20). A prominent 9S peak, which has been associated with histone production, was present. With this profile of message distribution as a basis for comparison, they isolated RNA from the light region of the gradient (see Fig. 21) and found that the profile of messenger RNA therefrom contained no evidence of any heavy species, which if present would suggest underloading of polysomes.

During cleavage and blastula, newly transcribed message does

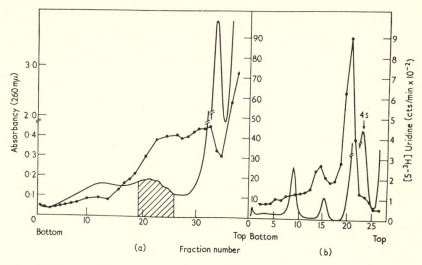

Figure 21

Sucrose-density gradient analysis of radioactive RNA from light polysomes of embryos of *Arbacia punctulata* is shown in (b). Solid lines represent absorbency and filled circles represent radioactivity. Gradient was produced by pooling alternate fractions of the light-polysome region of the density gradient indicated by the shaded region in (a) and extracting the RNA after the addition of carrier yeast 4S RNA. Labeling was performed as in Fig. 20, and Fig. 20 was produced by pooling the entire polysome region of a parallel gradient and extracting its RNA. Figures 20 and 21 may thus be compared. Figure 21 shows no accumulation of heavy messenger in the light region of the gradient as would be predicted if there were underloading of polysomes. [From Kedes asnd Gross (1969a); by permission.]

form on light polysomes to a greater extent than on heavy polysomes, but the explanation for this difference appears to be simple. During early development, the synthesis of nuclear proteins is extensive, and this synthesis has a requirement for the transcription of message of which some species, at least, are small in size. The 9–10S peak reported by Nemer (1963) and Nemer and Infante (1965) and associated with histone synthesis by Kedes and Gross (1969b) and others, reflects the extensive production of such a species of light message. It is highly probably that the increase in numbers of light polysomes in the period from cleavage to blastula as observed by Infante and Nemer (1967) is primarily indicative of an increase in synthesis of nuclear proteins, which occurs during that period to support the increase in number of nuclei.

POLYSOMES BEFORE
AND AFTER FERTILIZATION

The increase in protein synthesis that occurs immediately after fertilization has probably been the focal point of more research than any other single problem in the molecular biology of sea urchin development. The search for mechanisms responsible for the increase is shedding considerable light on the nature of information flow and its control in the sea urchin embryo. A direct approach in investigating the cause or causes for this increase is to examine the behavior and characteristics of polysomes before and after fertilization. Some investigations of this type have been performed in recent years. The majority of these investigations have tended to explore two possible explanations of the manner in which polysomes are involved in the postfertilization increase in protein synthesis: (1) more messenger molecules are accumulating in polysomes after fertilization than before fertilization, and (2) message is being translated on polysomes more efficiently after fertilization than before. The first alternative rests on the concept that there exists in the unfertilized egg a pool of messenger molecules unavailable for translation and that these messenger molecules are activated or in some way made available for translation following fertilization. To this newly accessible message is added newly transcribed message, and the result is a great augmentation in the numbers of polysomes producing protein and in the amount of protein being produced. There is no assumption here that upon fertilization previously unavailable m-RNA immediately becomes available in its entirety. Many experiments by various investigators have shown that when transcription is blocked by actinomycin D the amount of polysomal material continues to increase for as much as 4 hours after fertilization. If this increase reflects availability of message, then the template molecules would appear to become available progressively with time rather than simultaneously although one cannot be completely certain that this is true.

Increases in efficiency of translation can be visualized as arising through a variety of causes. Humphreys (1969) has defined efficiency of translation as the number of protein molecules synthesized per RNA molecule per unit time. A polysome could presumably increase its efficiency by increasing the speed of ribosome attachment and initiation of traverse, if underloaded, or by decreasing the time required for a ribosome to traverse a messenger molecule. In the latter instance, the number of ribosomes making the transit of the messenger strand per unit time would increase and hence more protein would be produced, but the assumption must be made that the ribosomes could also attach more rapidly to the message, initiate traverse more rapidly, and detach more rapidly from the message since hindrance to any of these activities can be seen as decreasing efficiency and negating the advantage of a decrease in traverse time.

There are, of course, other conditions that might lower protein production in the unfertilized egg. The effects of inhibitors or of an unfavorable chemical environment to the polysomes could be predicted to lower the efficiency of translation. The questions of possible shortages of synthetases or of t-RNA and of the inability of ribosomes to function has been investigated and will be discussed in a later chapter. MacKintosh and Bell (1969b) have demonstrated that the availability of energy for reactions is not a limiting factor here.

Both MacKintosh and Bell (1969a) and Humphreys (1969) have calculated the transit time for ribosomes. This calculation of time required for a ribosome to move across the messenger molecule in a polysome amounts to determining the ratio of the radioactivity of amino acids in nascent peptide on the polysomes to the rate of incorporation of these amino acids into the TCA-precipitable protein, which rate reflects the amount of label that emerges from the nascent peptide array per unit time. MacKintosh and Bell found the transit time to be essentially identical in egg and embryo. Humphreys, however, found the time required for transit in the embryo to be twice that in the egg. If either of these two findings is correct, the increase in rate of protein synthesis cannot be attributed to a decrease in time required for ribosomes to make the transit of messenger molecules. Humphreys (1971) made a finding that appears to reinforce the evidence for a longer transit time in the embryo. He found that in the first 2 hours after fertilization the increase in the number of ribosomes on polysomes is about twice that to be expected to account for the increase in amount of protein synthesized. The discrepancy would be explained by the postulate that from the moment of fertilization the rate of translocation of the ribosomes is only half as great in the embryo as it was in the egg.

There have been reports from one group of workers that attribute the increase in protein synthesis following fertilization to the removal of conditions in the unfertilized egg which cause an inefficiency of initiation of peptide chains and a consequent underloading of polysomes. MacKintosh and Bell (1969a) found that by exposing unfertilized eggs to a carbon dioxide-free medium they could cause an increase in protein synthesis which would in time attain a rate of about 50 percent of that of newly fertilized eggs. An increase in polysome content occurred that corresponded roughly to the increase in protein synthesis. Exposure of fertilized eggs to a CO_2-free medium actually depressed the rate of protein synthesis slightly.

Cycloheximide, which is an inhibitor of protein synthesis in many cell systems, causes only a partial inhibition in unfertilized eggs of *Arbacia punctulata*. MacKintosh and Bell found that while causing such a partial inhibition it gives rise to a large *increase* in polysomal material. Somewhat similar effects to those of CO_2 deprivation and cycloheximide treatment could be obtained by making eggs anoxic or by puromycin treatment (see MacKintosh and Bell, 1967).

The basic difficulty involved in interpreting the results of these experiments is the fact that the mechanism of action in this particular instance, of the four agencies used in treating the eggs, that is, a carbon dioxide free medium, anaerobiosis, puromycin, and cycloheximide, is not actually known. The investigators suggest that cycloheximide may increase the amount of polysomal material by interfering with the movement of ribosomes on the messenger molecule. Supposedly, with an inefficient initiation mechanism, the entry of ribosomes and initiation of readout on the polysome does not manage to keep pace with the rate of transit and release, so that the polysomes of the fertilized egg are in an underloaded state. Slowing down transit with cycloheximide would thus increase the numbers of ribosomes on the polysome. There is reason to doubt that this explanation is correct. The experiments do not demonstrtate that an increase in loading actually occurred.

If the polysomes of the unfertilized egg were in an underloaded state, the result should be the existence in the unfertilized egg of a population of small polysomes. An acquisition of ribosomes, which would increase the loading, should cause a shift in size of polysomes toward the heavy end of the polysome spectrum. Such a shift should occur upon fertilization, and such a shift should have occurred in these experiments if the postulate of an inefficient initiation mechanism is valid. If, however, the increase in protein synthesis following fertilization is due to an increased availability of m-RNA, one should expect to observe an increase in numbers of polysomes across the entire profile, but no shift in size classes toward the heavy end. Obviously, such a shift could occur if some control mechanism were to release for translation a large amount of message in a particular size range. Such a mechanism could theoretically cause an increase in any region of the polysome profile.

MacKintosh and Bell did not directly demonstrate the existence of underloaded polysomes in the unfertilized egg. They were unable to obtain evidence that a shift in polysome size class occurred between treated and control embryos. Other workers have failed to observe any bias in the direction of light polysomes in the polysome profile of the egg (see Kedes and Gross, 1969a; Kedes et al., 1969). Humphreys (1971) has shown that there is little change in the size of polysomes between the unfertilized egg and the embryo up to the first hour after fertilization (see Fig. 22). Rinaldi and Monroy (1969) noted some increase in the region of heavy polysomes in the first half-hour after fertilization, but it appears not to be of great magni-

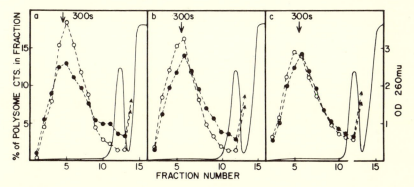

Figure 22

Comparison of sizes of polysomes in eggs with those in embryos at various times after fertilization. Eggs, 3.6×10^5, were incubated 5 minutes with 20 μC/ml ^{3}H-leucine and divided into three aliquots. Embryos, 1.2×10^4, at 20 (a), 60 (b), and 360 minutes (c) after fertilization were incubated 5 minutes with 2 μC/ml ^{14}C-leucine and mixed with an aliquot of eggs. Polysomes were extracted from each preparation and centrifuged on 17.2 ml, 15–35 percent sucrose gradients at 26,000 rpm in a Spinco SW27 rotor. The gradients were monitored for optical density at 260 nm (solid lines), for ^{3}H (eggs represented by closed circles), and for ^{14}C (embryos represented by open circles). [From Humphreys (1971); by permission.]

tude. Humphreys (1969) and Denny and Reback (1970) reported increases in polysomal material after fertilization as being due primarily to changes in numbers of polysomes rather than in size.

Denny and Reback observed, in fact, that the increase in polysomal material after fertilization is far too great to be accounted for on the basis of increased loading of polysomes and proposed that polysomes form after fertilization as a result of m-RNA becoming available. Humphreys (1969, 1971) reached essentially the same conclusions. Humphreys (1971) quantitated some of the changes occurring in polysomes after fertilization. He found that there is a 30-fold increase of ribosomes on polysomes in the first 2 hours after fertilization (from 0.75 to 20 percent of the total ribosomes). He determined that the amount of m-RNA necessary to support this increase amounts to 0.4 percent of the total RNA of the egg. According to his estimates, 15 percent of the m-RNA entering polysomes in this period is newly transcribed and 85 percent is maternal template. Rinaldi and Monroy (1969) have found that the newly transcribed m-RNA begins to enter polysomes within 2 minutes after fertilization.

Piatigorsky (1968) and Piatigorsky and Tyler (1970) investigated polysomal profiles of unfertilized eggs of *Lytechinus pictus* labeled at oogenesis with ^{3}H-uridine. They reported that there was considerable ribosomal-aggregate material in the polysomal region of the unfertilized egg that was not broken down to monosomes upon treatment with RNAase. Such ribosomal aggregates were inactive in promoting protein synthesis. They suggested the possibility that such aggregates might constitute a form of inactive polysome. These results are not reflected in the findings of other workers. Ribosomes, however, do show a tendency to aggregate artificially, particularly in concentrated solutions (see Humphreys, 1971), and it is possible that these workers may have been observing a laboratory artifact, particularly since they were unable to demonstrate m-RNA in association with the aggregates. They acknowledged this possibility.

OTHER ASPECTS OF POLYSOMES

The polysome is the principal component of the protein-synthesizing system, but it is not the sole component. The system entails the participation of a variety of substances, including transfer RNA, amino acids that will associate with it, enzymes, coenzymes, cofactors and so on. The bulk of such substances are normally located in the cell sap and can be found in the 100,000 × g supernatant when homogenates are subjected to differential centrifugation. Those which are actually involved in the synthesis probably exist in some sort of loose association with the polysome. The association is not so loose as to prevent them from being thrown down in the 100,000 × g pellet. Candelas and Iverson (1966), working with homogenates from embryos of *Lytechinus variegatus* and *Echinometra lucuntur* found that if such pellets were washed two or three times these ancillary substances tended to be removed from the pellets. The pellet material (microsomes) then lost its ability for endogenous incorporation of amino acids into protein *in vitro*. Addition of 100,000 × g supernatant (cell-sap fraction) sufficed to restore activity.

It is also noteworthy that they found that the activity of their in vitro amino acid-incorporating system could be enhanced by the addition of an energy-generating system. Hultin (1964a, 1964b) found that in *Paracentrotus lividus* the formation of polysomes is an energy-requiring process, and that uncouplers of phosphorylation, such as dinitrophenol, cause a decrement in both the formation of polysomes and the incorporation of amino acids into nascent protein. The requirement of energy is certainly to be expected for some aspects of protein synthesis, the activation of t-RNA, for example. In recent years it has been shown that there is a requirement of energy, which is obtained by the conversion of GTP to GDP, for the translocation of the t-RNA residue and displacement of the m-RNA chain relative to the ribosome in the readout of the template. This utilization of GTP occurs immediately following the formation of each peptide bond. The mechanics of the processes involved are not completely understood. Spirin and Gavrilova (1969) have discussed the problem in some detail.

REFERENCES

Candelas, G. C., and R. M. Iverson, 1966. Evidence for translational level control of protein synthesis in the development of sea urchin eggs. *Biochem. Biophys. Res. Commun., 24,* 867–871.

Cohen, G. H., and R. M. Iverson, 1967. High-resolution density gradient analysis of sea urchin polysomes. *Biochem. Biophys. Res. Commun., 29,* 349–355.

Denny, P. C., and P. Reback, 1970. Active polysomes in sea urchin eggs and zygotes–

evidence for an increase in translatable m-RNA after fertilization. *J. Exp. Zool., 175,* 133–140.

Epel, D., 1967. Protein synthesis in sea urchin eggs: a "late" response to fertilization. *Proc. Nat. Acad. Sci. U.S.A., 57,* 899–906.

Hultin, T., 1950. The protein metabolism of sea urchin eggs during early development studied by means of ¹⁵N-labeled ammonia. *Exp. Cell Res., 1,* 599–602.

Hultin, T., 1952. Incorporation of N¹⁵-labeled glycine and alanine into the proteins of developing sea urchin eggs. *Exp. Cell Res., 3,* 494–496.

Hultin, T., 1961. Activation of ribosomes in sea urchin eggs in response to fertilization. *Exp. Cell Res., 25,* 405–417.

Hultin, T., 1964a. Factors influencing polyribosome formation *in vivo. Exp. Cell Res., 34,* 608–611.

Hultin, T., 1964b. On the mechanism of ribosomal activation in newly fertilized sea urchin eggs. *Develop. Biol., 10,* 305–328.

Hultin, T., and A. Bergstrand, 1960. Incorporation of C¹⁴-leucine into protein by cell-free systems from sea urchin embryos at different stages of development. *Develop. Biol., 2,* 61–75.

Hultin, T., and G. Wessel, 1952. Incorporation of C¹⁴-labeled carbon dioxide into the protein of developing sea urchin eggs. *Exp. Cell Res., 3,* 613–616.

Humphreys, T., 1969. Efficiency of translation of messenger RNA before and after fertilization in sea urchins. *Develop. Biol., 20,* 435–456.

Humphreys, T., 1971. Measurement of messenger RNA entering polysomes upon fertilization of sea urchin eggs. *Develop. Biol., 26,* 201–208.

Infante, A. A., and M. Nemer, 1967. Accumulation of newly synthesized RNA templates in a unique class of polyribosomes during embryogenesis. *Proc. Nat. Acad. Sci., U.S.A., 58,* 681–688.

Kedes, L. H., and P. R. Gross, 1969a. Synthesis and function of messenger RNA during early embryonic development. *J. Mol. Biol., 42,* 559–575.

Kedes, L. H., and P. R. Gross, 1969b. Identification in cleaving embryos of three RNA species serving as templates for the synthesis of nuclear proteins. *Nature* (London), *223,* 1335–1339.

Kedes, L. H., B. Hogan, G. Cognetti, S. Selvig, P. Yanover, and P. R. Gross, 1969. Regulation of translation and transcription of messenger RNA during early embryonic development. *Cold Spring Harbor Symp. Quant. Biol., 34,* 717–723.

MacKintosh, F. R., and E. Bell, 1967. Stimulation of protein synthesis in unfertilized sea urchin eggs by prior metabolic inhibition. *Biochem. Biophys. Res. Commun., 27,* 425–430.

MacKintosh, F. R., and E. Bell, 1969a. Regulation of protein synthesis in sea urchin eggs. *J. Mol. Biol., 41,* 365–380.

MacKintosh, F. R., and E. Bell, 1969b. Labeling of nucleotide pools in sea urchin eggs. *Exp. Cell Res., 57,* 71–73.

Monroy, A., and A. Tyler, 1963. Formation of active ribosomal aggregates (polysomes) upon fertilization and development of sea urchin eggs. *Arch. Biochem. Biophys., 103,* 431–435.

Monroy, A., and M. Vittorelli, 1962. Utilization of C¹⁴-glucose for amino acid and protein synthesis by the sea urchin embryo. *J. Cell Comp. Physiol., 60,* 285–287.

Nakano, E., and A. Monroy, 1958. Incorporation of S³⁵-methionone in the cell fractions of sea urchin eggs and embryos. *Exp. Cell Res., 14,* 236–244.

Nemer, M., 1963. Regulation of protein synthesis in embryogenesis in the sea urchin. *National Cancer Institute Monograph 13.* U.S. Government Printing Office, Washington, D.C., 141–154.

Nemer, M., and A. A. Infante, 1965. Messenger RNA in early sea urchin embryos. Size classes. *Science, 150,* (Oct. 8), 217–221.

Piatigorsky, J., 1968. Ribonuclease and trypsin treatment of ribosomes and polyribosomes from sea urchin eggs. *Biochim. Biophys. Acta, 166,* 142–155.

Piatigorsky, J., and A. Tyler, 1970. Change upon fertilization in the distribution of the RNA-containing particles in sea urchin eggs. *Develop. Biol., 19,* 73–85.

Rinaldi, A. M., and A. Monroy, 1969. Polyribosome formation and RNA synthesis in the early post-fertilization stages of the sea urchin egg. *Deveop. Boil., 19,* 73–86.

Spirin, A. S., 1966. On "masked" forms of messenger RNA in early embryogenesis and in other differentiating systems. *Current Topics Develop., 1,* 1–38.

Spirin, A. S., and L. P. Gavrilova, 1969. *The Ribosome.* Springer-Verlag New York, Inc., New York.

Spirin, A. S., and M. Nemer, 1965. Messenger RNA in early sea urchin embryos: cytoplasmic particles. *Science, 150,* 214–217.

Stafford, D. W., W. H. Sofer, and R. M. Iverson, 1964. Demonstration of polyribosomes after fertilization of the sea urchin egg. *Proc. Nat. Acad. Sci., U.S.A., 52,* 313–316.

Stavy, L., and P. R. Gross, 1967. The protein-synthetic lesion in unfertilized eggs. *Proc. Nat. Acad. Sci., U.S.A., 57,* 735–742.

Tyler, A., B. S. Tyler, and J. Piatigorsky, 1968. Protein synthesis by unfertilized eggs of sea urchins. *Biol. Bull. Mar. Biol. Lab., Woods Hole, 134,* 209–219.

Wilt, F. H., 1964. Ribonucleic acid synthesis during sea urchin embryogenesis. *Develop. Biol., 9,* 299–313.

CHAPTER VIII

Maternal Messenger RNA
and Its Role in Development

GENERAL REMARKS

We have seen that upon activation of the sea urchin egg there occurs a marked increase in the rate of protein synthesis and a concomitant increase in the amount of polysomal material present in the cytoplasm. Considerable evidence supports the idea that an increase in availability of m-RNA for translation is responsible for much of the increased protein synthesis. Transcription of the nuclear genes and translation of the m-RNA thereby produced occurs during the first cleavage period and thenceforth during development. The bulk of the proteins synthesized immediately following fertilization, however, are produced on maternal template. The relative amount of participation of newly transcribed message in protein synthesis increases with time, but Kedes and Gross (1969) have asserted that even at swimming blastula embryos in which transcription has been blocked by actinomycin D can assemble 50–60 percent of the polysomes accumulated by untreated embryos.

It has not appeared unequivocal to many investigators over the past decade that the increase in protein synthesis following fertilization is attributable to an increased availability of maternal message for translation. Many have proposed, and some still propose, that, following fertilization, the protein-synthesizing apparatus becomes more competent to translate message. The reasons advanced for the increase in competence have included the elimination of ribosomal defects, improvement in the initiation of translation, improvement of transfer factor activity, and the removal of inhibitors that purportedly hold the polysome in an inactive state. A few workers have attributed the increase in protein synthesis to an increased availability of substances other than m-RNA, synthetases and t-RNA, for example. Although the evidence that the acceleration of protein synthesis upon the activation of the egg may be ascribed to an increase in availability of maternal template through an unmasking process is quite convincing, the controversy that has centered on this problem is extremely interesting, and we shall attempt to trace some aspects of its history in the following pages.

Actually, several important questions regarding the nature and behavior of maternal message have become foci for experimental attention in recent years. It is of interest to know what types of protein are specified by maternal template made during oogenesis and to know the extent to which these proteins differ from those specified by template transcribed in the postfertilization period. It is likewise of interest to ascertain whether the molecules of maternal m-RNA are made available synchronously at fertilization and then translated as rapidly as the translating apparatus can cope with them or whether they are made available gradually and selectively through the activity of regulating mechanisms. The nature of the masking mechanisms and of the mechanics of unmasking is a matter of great concern. Few of these and other cogent questions concerning the function of maternal template have been fully resolved as yet. We shall consider some aspects of the experimentation that has been dedicated to them. Some discussions and review of problems associated with maternal message are to be found in the literature (see, for example, Spirin, 1966; Gross, 1967a 1967b, 1967c; Tyler, 1967).

EARLY STUDIES ON THE FUNCTION
OF MATERNAL MESSAGE AFTER FERTILIZATION

Two basic considerations appear to have instigated some of the first studies on maternal m-RNA. One was the finding by Nemer

(1963), Gross and Cousineau (1963), Wilt (1963), and Brachet et al. (1963a) that the amount of RNA synthesized immediately after fertilization appeared to be too insignificant to account for the increase in protein synthesis that occurs at that time. The other was the well-established fact that anucleate egg halves are able to support a certain amount of cell division upon parthenogenetic stimulation, a fact which implies that protein synthesis to implement such division may be occurring in the absence of transcription. A classical embryonic concept holds the mature egg to contain a reservoir of stored material for use after fertilization, a reservoir produced or preserved by such mechanisms as vitellogenesis, the attenuation of metabolic activity during the period before fertilization, and the conservation of materials in the face of mandatory cell division by the extrusion of polar bodies. The hypothesis that the materials stored in the mature egg might well include templates for postfertilization protein synthesis was a logical one to test.

A series of investigations were performed by Gross and Cousineau (1963, 1964) and Gross et al. (1964) in which newly fertilized eggs were treated with actinomycin D. Actinomycin D is an antibiotic isolated from *Streptomyces*. It interferes but little with DNA polymerases, so that DNA synthesis is but mildly depressed on exposure to it. Its effect on RNA polymerase is so powerful that, in many instances, it all but eliminates DNA-dependent RNA synthesis. It becomes, in effect, a chemical enucleant. It is believed to interfere with that segment of the enzyme–substrate system that involves guanine–cytosine association. Actinomycin D regrettably is now officially designated as dactinomycin. It is to be hoped that if this designation heralds a trend in decisions on nomenclature such a trend will be short lived.

The above-mentioned experiments with actinomycin D suggested that the synthesis of new m-RNA after fertilization is not a requirement for the acceleration of protein synthesis which occurs at that time, and that templates for this protein synthesis preexist in the unfertilized egg. The experiments did not demonstrate that new m-RNA is not transcribed in the early postfertilization period, and subsequent work demonstrated that it is transcribed.

The effect of actinomycin D on sea urchin embryos is strikingly apparent from the standpoint of morphogenesis. Gross et al. (1964) showed that embryos of *Lytechinus pictus* treated with actinomycin D cleaved as rapidly as did control embryos. The treated embryos produced a blastocoel, but they did not proceed morphologically beyond the blastula stage. Half the treated embryos developed cilia and exhibited a sluggish rotation; about a third of them hatched. These embryos continued viable, and their cells divided after blastocoel formation, but their destiny was to end their existence as "inert multicellular masses." Gross and Cousineau (1963) described a slightly different developmental picture for actinomycin D-treated *Arbacia punctulata* embryos, including a lag in the rate of cleavage of treated embryos behind that of the controls. They suggested that this lag might result from a mild depressive effect of actinomycin D on DNA synthesis. Cleavage in *Arbacia* is irregular in treated embryos as compared to normal embryos.

The molecular effects of actinomycin D on early development were shown in the work of Gross et al. (1964) with *Arbacia punctulata* and *Lytechinus pictus*. In normal development, the rate of incorporation of amino acids into proteins of *Arbacia* was found to rise sharply until blastula, whereupon it went into a plateau. At late blastula it was seen to rise sharply again through mesenchyme blastula, sloping off somewhat at late gastrula. Gross and his co-workers demonstrated that in actinomycin D-treated embryos the curve did not execute the second rise. Up to blastula, however, the rates of protein synthesis in treated and normal embryos were equal, or, to be more exact, they were equal until the curves approached the plateau at blastula, at which time the rate in treated embryos actually exceeded that in normal embryos, a curious circumstance the cause of which appears never to have been explained completely. At the beginning of the second rise in normal embryos, the rate in treated embryos fell below that of the controls and declined steadily, although it was still substantial at last gastrula (see Fig. 23).

In order to be on safe ground in assuming that actinomycin D is blocking the transcription of message, it is necessary to demonstrate that message is being transcribed in the absence of actinomycin D, to present evidence that the inhibitor has that which to inhibit. Working with *Strongylocentrotus purpuratus,* Wilt (1963) and Nemer (1963) found that within the first hour or two after fertilization there begins a synthesis of nonribosomal, non-4S RNA, which continues throughout the developmental process, with some modifications of the S-values of such RNA as embryogenesis proceeds. Gross and Cousineau (1963) showed both nuclear and cytoplasmic localization for labeled uridine taken up in the early hours after fertilization and

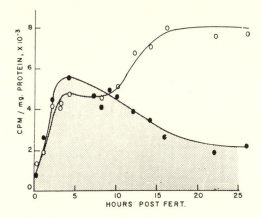

Figure 23

Rates of incorporation of ^{14}C-L-valine into fertilized eggs of *Arbacia punctulata* with and without actinomycin D (20 μg/ml). Filled circles represent 20-minute pulse incorporations for embryos in actinomycin pretreated with actinomycin for 3 hours before fertilization. Open circles represent controls in normal artificial seawater. [From Gross et al. (1964); by permission]

demonstrated that the material incorporating the uridine is RNAase digestible. Gross et al. (1965) demonstrated the synthesis by the time of hatching of a population of RNA molecules that are greater than 12S, are rapidly synthesized, show a heterogeneous profile in density-gradient analysis, and appear on the basis of guanine–cytosine base ratios to be DNA-like.

Glišin and Glišin (1964) reported what, on the basis of rapid incorporation of label and heterogeneity of sedimentation profile, appears to be synthesis of m-RNA in the sea urchin embryo beginning somewhere between the 4-cell stage and the 32-cell stage of *Lytechinus pictus*. Nemer and Infante (1965b) made more or less confirmatory findings on RNA extracted from polysomes of the same species. The earlier experiments show the time of the inception of m-RNA synthesis as being later than that established by more recent experiments, which reveal that transcription begins almost immediately after fertilization (see, for example, Rinaldi and Monroy, 1969). These early investigations, however, did make it clear that transcription is occurring during cleavage and during the time interval encompassed by actinomycin D treatment in the experiments under discussion.

There remained the necessity of determining the actual effect of actinomycin D on RNA synthesis during early embryogenesis of the sea urchin. In 1963 and 1964 Gross and Cousineau showed that actinomycin D has very little effect upon uridine incorporation into RNA during the first few hours of development. After this period of apparent insensitivity to actinomycin D, however, uridine incorporation is brought to a halt by the drug. One could not overlook the possibility that before a block takes effect in the treated embryos, enough *new* message might be synthesized to provide for the metabolic needs of the embryo through cleavage and into blastula. Barring such an eventuality, there appeared every likelihood that the treated embryo is being carried from fertilization to blastula largely by message already present when the egg is fertilized.

The possibility that any extensive transcription of new message could have escaped the actinomycin D inhibition appears to have been eliminated when Gross et al. (1964), working with *Lytechinus pictus* and *Arbacia punctulata,* reexamined that problem of RNA synthesis in the period immediately following fertilization. They gave a 20-minute pulse of ³H-uridine immediately upon fertilization to eggs that had been preincubated with actinomycin D. Density-gradient sedimentation analysis was performed in which the centrifugation technique was designed to spread out the 4–18S region of the spectrum. The results showed that synthesis of RNA in the *control embryos* was occurring in the first few minutes after fertilization. Labeled RNA was found throughout the gradient, with extensive incorporation in the 4S region. With the exception of a 9–10S peak, which has been mentioned above in a different context, the newly synthesized RNA with sedimentation values higher than 4S was heterodisperse. There was no evidence of any synthesis of ribosomal RNA. *The embryos treated with actinomycin D showed incorporation only in the 4S region,* which may be presumed to represent transfer RNA, and here, as in the controls, the incorporation was extensive. The synthesis of new message was apparently being blocked in the early period after fertilization as well as later, and the actinomycin D insensitivity or the uridine incorporation could be ascribed to the labeling of 4S RNA (see Fig. 24).

A plausible explanation for the insensitivity of the labeling of 4S RNA to actinomycin D may be found in the report by Glišin and Glišin (1964) that immediately after fertilization there is a period of extensive terminal addition activity where t-RNA is concerned. A py-

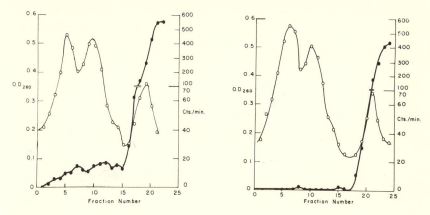

Figure 24

Distribution of labeled RNA in fertilized eggs of *Lytechinus pictus*. Controls are shown in figure on left; actinomycin D-treated eggs are shown in figure on right. Treated eggs were pretreated with actinomycin for 200 minutes. Lighter end of the profile is to the right. Pulse duration: 0–60 minute postfertilization. RNA label: ^{14}C-uridine, 0.5 μC and 4.0 μg/ml in artificial seawater. O.D. peaks of approximately 28S, 18S, and 4S are shown in open circles. Filled circles give counts/minute of each fraction. Shaded area in controls represents newly synthesized non-4S RNA. Activity in treated eggs is seen to be in 4S region. [From Gross et al. (1964); by permission]

rophosphorylase promotes the addition of the terminal pCpCpA group of nucleotides to the molecule. The addition of the terminal group confers a label on RNA of which the primary structure has already been synthesized. Terminal addition, as would be expected, is insensitive to actinomycin D.

The early experiments involving the treatment of sea urchin embryos with actinomycin D were made at a time when polysomes were first being explored in the sea urchin embryo. Malkin et al. (1964) demonstrated that protein synthesis in actinomycin D-treated embryos occurs on polysomes. It might also be noted that early workers noted a slight depression in thymine incorporation into DNA in embryos treated with the antibiotic.

It was apparent then that

    1. The acceleration of protein synthesis after fertilization is not due to synthesis of new m-RNA, even though some may be synthesized at this time in normal development.
    2. Maternal m-RNA can support protein synthesis at a normal rate until blastula (a circumstance that hints of the existence of some special type of translational control, since more recent experiments, such

as those of Kedes and Gross in 1969, have shown that when transcription is prevented by actinomycin D there is a drastic reduction in numbers of polysomes, possibly up to 40–50 percent).

3. Maternal m-RNA does not have the ability, in the absence of transcription, to promote the cellular movements of gastrulation and the formation of organs in morphogenesis.

It is an attractive hypothesis that maternal m-RNA primarily provides information for endowing the embryo with a large supply of cells, which will ultimately be differentiated in the process of organogenesis, but that it does not contain the requisite information to produce the differentiation directly. Such a hypothesis does not imply that newly transcribed message does not likewise support the exponential increase in cells during normal cleavage or that maternal message may not be involved in generating protein that will catalyze reactions of which the products stimulate alterations in gene patterns leading to differentiation.

Another avenue of approach to the demonstration of the presence, adequacy in amount, and stability of maternal message in embryos at the time of fertilization lies in the use of the anucleate half-egg. Parthenogenetic activation of anucleate halves of the egg results in repeated but irregular cleavage with the ultimate formation of something resembling a blastula. These pseudoblastulae may live as long as a month, but show no tendency toward morphogenesis. The phenomenon bears resemblance to that seen with actinomycin D-treated embryos.

The experiments of Hultin (1961a) with puromycin, an inhibitor of protein synthesis, indicate that protein synthesis is a prerequisite to cleavage. Hultin reported that when eggs are treated with puromycin before fertilization, development comes to a halt at the clear-streak stage. The spindle fails to form, and cell division does not occur. Anucleate half-eggs produce cytasters and contain dividing cells after parthenogenetic activation. Reasoning from the findings of Hultin one could form the hypothesis that protein synthesis might be required for cell division in these cleaving anucleate halves, even though the cleavage is decidedly abnormal. In any event, it was desirable to determine whether protein synthesis does occur in cleaving embryos that are completely innocent of any nuclear genes.

Brachet et al. (1963b), Tyler (1963), and Denny and Tyler (1964) showed that, whereas the synthesis of proteins in anucleate halves of unfertilized eggs proceeds at a very low rate, parthenogenetic activation causes an immediate stimulation of rapid incorporation of amino acid into protein. The synthesis actually proved to be somewhat more intense than in comparable experiments in which nucleate halves were used, although such a difference might be expected to arise from a variety of causes, some of which, such as availability of enzymes or cofactors or activity of respiratory cycles, might not reflect the relative amount of template in the two halves. Obviously, maternal template is supporting development, albeit somewhat abnormal, up to blastula in the absence of transcription of nuclear genes in the anucleate half-egg. These experiments do not bar the possibility of some protein synthesis on template transcribed from cytoplasmic DNA, but from the small amount of experimental evidence that is available, it can probably be assumed that the amount of such synthesis is not great and may be virtually absent.

Burny et al. (1965) demonstrated that in both nucleate and anucleate halves, amino acid incorporation into proteins occurs on polysomes formed *after* activation. Tyler (1963) and Denny and Tyler (1964) were able to activate protein synthesis in vitro in homogenates from anucleate halves of *Strongylocentrotus purpuratus* and *Lytechinus pictus,* ruling out the possibility of the increase in protein synthesis being due to an increase in permeability to amino acids caused by activation. Tyler (1966) provided evidence that proteins synthesized by the anucleate fragment appear to be similar in character to those synthesized by the whole egg. This point should be reexamined. There must, at least, be some pronounced quantitative differences in the protein spectrum, since the region of light polysomes responsible for the synthesis of nuclear proteins is starkly reduced. Recent evidence suggests that qualitative differences also exist.

THEORY OF THE INCOMPETENT
OR REPRESSED RIBOSOME

Alberto Monroy appropriately began a chapter of a brief monograph on fertilization, which he wrote in 1965, by quoting a statement made 40 years ago by D. M. Whitaker: "The crux of the problem of fertilization lies in the nature of the inhibition of the unfertilized egg." This idea has motivated an enormous amount of investigation over the years, and many of the problems concerning the causes for the low level of synthetic activity in the egg that are currently being investigated have long histories.

The study of the mechanisms involved in producing the transition from a relatively attenuated protein synthesis in the unfertilized egg to a very active protein synthesis in the fertilized egg was begun before the world knew of the existence of ribosomes, polysomes, or messenger RNA. This change in rate of protein synthesis was recognized as soon as workers began to expose fertilized and unfertilized eggs to radioactive amino acid precursors (see, for example, Hultin, 1950, 1952, 1953). These experiments also revealed that the unfertilized egg has a low permeability to amino acids. As has been noted in a previous chapter, Nakano and Monroy (1958) demonstrated by preloading the egg with radioactive label that amino acids introduced into the unfertilized egg accumulate in the free amino acid pools rather than being incorporated into protein. When Hultin and Bergstrand (1960) showed that homogenates and postmitochondrial supernatants from unfertilized eggs have a much lower capacity to support protein synthesis in vitro than do those from fertilized eggs, workers realized that the cause for the stimulation of protein synthesis upon activation of the egg should be sought in the workings of the protein-synthesizing machinery itself. In 1961 (see Hultin 1961b) Hultin analyzed various cell fractions for their ability to support protein synthesis in vitro. He found the greatest amount of activity in $70,000 \times g$ pellets or microsomal fractions, and he showed that the microsomal fractions of fertilized eggs have anywhere from a tenfold to a fiftyfold greater ability to support protein synthesis than those from unfertilized eggs. In his discussion of the results of these experiments, he made the statement: "the increase in incorporation is largely due to modifications in the ribosomes." This statement has repeatedly been misinterpreted to the effect that Hultin discovered that there exists a defect in the ribosome (as we know the ribosome today) that prevents it from participating in the readout of message in the unfertilized egg. Hultin did this work before the concept of the polysome was known to the scientific world. In 1961, one spoke of proteins as being synthesized on the ribosome. His comment must be interpreted as applying to modifications in the protein-producing machine itself, rather than modifications in one of its components. His experiments had nothing to say about ribosomes as we know them today. His microsome fractions without doubt represented a mélange of polysomes, ribosomes, m-RNA, and t-RNA, and he was unaware of their sedimentation characteristics. He does, however, appear to have believed that the ribosome in the strict sense, the ribosome as a component of the protein-synthesizing apparatus, might be involved in the stimulation of postfertilization protein synthesis, because he speculated on the possibility of its undergoing changes in size between fertilized and unfertilized egg. This speculation is not related to the results of his experiments and does not justify the association of these experiments with the problem of ribosomal competence, or lack thereof, in the unfertilized egg as we view the problem today.

Maggio et al. (1964) explored both the problem of the competence of the ribosomes of the unfertilized egg to participate in protein synthesis and that of the availability of translatable template in the unfertilized egg. They extracted from the unfertilized egg of *Paracentrotus lividus* a template RNA that would stimulate protein synthesis in vitro when added to a rat liver $30,000 \times g$ supernatant test system. The ability so to stimulate was found to be on a par with that of a template RNA extracted from embryos at mesenchyme blastula. Both of these RNA's were tested for ability to support protein synthesis in vitro with ribosome preparations from the unfertilized egg and from embryos at mesenchyme blastula. The level of radioactivity in the control ribosomal preparations from mesenchyme blastula, which contained no added template, was so high that it was patent that these were not pure ribosomal preparations, but rather contained active polysomes. The increase in counts per minute caused by the addition of equal amounts of template to ribosomes from fertilized versus unfertilized eggs was very nearly the same. These particular experiments seem to offer little basis for the assertion by the authors that the ribosomes of the unfertilized egg probably have a structural defect that prevents them from combining with message.

These experiments have been cited as proof that the availability of message is not a limiting factor in protein synthesis. The fact that the template isolated from unfertilized eggs supports protein synthesis readily in vitro cannot be taken as proof that it is avaliable for translation in vivo. The behavior of cell-free systems does not necessarily duplicate the behavior of systems within the cell. There is a distinct possibility that the extraction procedures used in these experiments rendered the template translatable. This is a difficult point to prove or disprove, but it is certainly a point that must be considered. The finding of translatable template in the unfertilized egg, however, was confirmed by Slater and Spiegelman (1966), who actually calibrated this template RNA in *Lytechinus pictus* against RNA of known message content from phage and bacterial systems. Their data indicated that about 4–5 percent of the bulk RNA isolated from the unfertilized egg was translatable, and they calculated that such an amount was adequate to support protein synthesis in the early hours of development after fertilization without there being tandem transcription of new m-RNA. Humphreys (1971), however, has calculated that the actual amount of m-RNA activated at fertilization, that is, which enters polysomes, is only about 0.4 percent of the total RNA of the egg. Humphreys has suggested that the discrepancy between these two figures may reflect the possibility that only a small fraction of the heterogeneous DNA-like RNA isolated by various workers and characterized as template is really m-RNA. Penman et al. (1968) have proposed that such a situation may exist in animal cells in general. At the time of this writing the problem appears not to have been resolved. Some aspects of it will be discussed at a later point.

Monroy et al. in 1965 performed a series of experiments similar to those of Maggio et al. (1964) but with an interesting modification. It had been found by Lundblad (see Lundblad, 1950, 1952, 1954) that immediately after fertilization there is a transient activation of proteases in the sea urchin embryo. Monroy and his co-workers postulated that such proteases might play a role in "ribosomal activation" and hence in the initiation of active peptide synthesis. They worked with *Paracentrotus lividus* in in vitro studies wherein they employed 105,000 × *g* "unpurified" microsomal pellets, which they treated with trypsin and exposed to various types of message, including poly U and RNA, with template activity extracted from unfertilized eggs and blastulae. Poly U is an artificial template containing exclusively uridine nucleotides. Since it possesses the triplet that codes for phenylalanine, it gives rise to a polyphenylalanine when translated in in vitro systems.

Microsomal pellets from unfertilized eggs, when not treated with trypsin, failed to promote amino acid incorporation in vitro either in the presence or the absence of additional message extracted from unfertilized eggs or from blastulae. They would, however, respond to poly U. Upon treatment with trypsin, they would support amino acid incorporation, even in the absence of added message. The addition of message from unfertilized eggs or blastulae enhanced such incorporation. Trypsin treatment also enhanced the effect of poly U. When microsome preparations from blastulae were used, trypsin treatment tended, if anything, to cause a decrease in incorporation.

This was an exciting experiment, and the work is of considerable interest from the standpoint of the history of the problem. There is some reasonably strong evidence against these findings being valid either as an argument for the presence of incompetent ribosomes in the unfertilized egg or, as suggested by the Monroy group in their conclusion, as an argument for the presence of inactive polysomes in the unfertilized egg. The ribosome preparations used in this work may be supposed to have contained polysomes, ribosomes, transfer RNA, message, and ancillary compounds involved in protein synthesis. There can be no certainty as to which particulate or particulates may have been directly affected by the trypsin. On the basis of this study, polysomes and ribosomes have both been purported to be derepressed or activated by the enzyme. It appears reasonable to suggest that repressed endogenous message in their preparations might likewise have been affected and that template might have been released for translation. With the variety of effects that could be conceived to result from trypsinization, it is difficult to be confident about what actually was affected. A problem that remains to be resolved about these experiments is that of why poly U increased incorporation in the controls, whereas exogenous message did not do so markedly.

It is interesting that although the theory that lack of competence of the ribosomes to participate in polysome activity is responsible for the repression of protein synthesis in the unfertilized egg is probably the result of interpretations placed on Hultin's experiments of 1961, Hultin was a co-author of one of several studies which gave rise to a finding that is held to be one of the most powerful arguments against this theory. Several investigators (Wilt and Hultin, 1962; Tyler, 1963; Nemer, 1962; Nemer and Bard, 1963; Stavy and Gross, 1969a) showed that the ribosomes from the unfertilized egg can support protein synthesis with poly U and other synthetic message and can do so as actively as ribosomes from embryos. Wilt and Hultin, as well as Nemer, reported that the rate of polyphenylalanine production is actually somewhat greater with ribosomes of unfertilized eggs.

If one proposes the theory that the lower level of protein synthesis in the unfertilized egg is due to functional shortcomings of the ribosome, one must, of course, explain the nature of the ribosomal deficiency. Three explanations are commonly advanced:

> 1. The structure of the ribosome in the unfertilized egg is such that it cannot participate in protein synthesis, but the structural aberration is repaired upon fertilization.
> 2. The ribosome in the unfertilized egg is under repression by an inhibitor (this theory is inherent in the conclusions of the Monroy group in 1965).
> 3. The ribosome of the unfertilized egg cannot function at full capacity because of deficiencies in transfer factors, the enzymes that are involved in binding t-RNA to the ribosome and in facilitating translocation and the participation of t-RNA in the formation of the peptide bond.

There is no substantial evidence for a structural difference between ribosomes of the unfertilized egg and embryo. Nemer and Infante in 1967 found that the 18S subunit of ribosomes of unfertilized eggs of *Strongylocentrotus purpuratus* would form a 13S particle on being heated to 60°C, whereas that of ribosomes synthesized after gastrula would not. Although this finding reflects a structural peculiarity of ribosomes made during oogenesis, there is no evidence that the ribosome undergoes any alteration upon fertilization, since the 13S subunit can be formed from 18S subunits in embryos. This ribosomal oddity is believed, moreover, to represent a unique species difference in *Strongylocentrotus purpuratus*. Some workers have reported failure to find this particle.

Any structural difference that may exist between ribosomes of fertilized and unfertilized eggs has not revealed itself in differences in physical properties. Wilt (1963) found that as far as sedimentation properties and magnesium dependence are concerned ribosomes of fertilized and unfertilized eggs are identical. Several other authors, most recently Castañeda (1969), have confirmed this finding and extended it to include other physical properties.

The commonest form of the theory that the ribosomes are under repression by an inhibitor in the unfertilized egg is to be found in the concept of the soluble cytoplasmic inhibitor as exemplified by the work of Candelas and Iverson (1966). By washing microsome fractions of fertilized eggs to remove enzymes, cofactors, and the like, these investigators reduced to a very low level the ability of the fractions to support amino acid incorporation. If they then added to these washed microsome fractions cell-sap fractions (105,000 × *g* supernatants) from fertilized eggs, purportedly restoring the substances washed out and adding other soluble cytoplasmic materials as well, normal amino acid incorporation was restored. If, alternatively, comparable supernatants derived from unfertilized eggs were added, incorporation was severely depressed relative to that in preparations containing cell-sap fractions from fertilized eggs. Timourian in 1967 found that, given a microsomal fraction that can support protein synthesis in vitro, its ability to do so is greater in the presence than in the absence of supernatant from either the fertilized or unfertilized egg, although the supernatant from unfertilized egg is much less active in enhancing synthesis than that from the fertilized egg. Stavy and Gross (1967) found, by contrast, that cell-sap fractions from fertilized and unfertilized eggs are essentially equal in their ability to support protein synthesis and are interchangeable in in vitro preparations. From an overview of this work, a series of possibilities present themselves:

    1. A soluble inhibitor of protein synthesis exists in the cytoplasm of the unfertilized egg, but not of the fertilized egg.
    2. t-RNA synthetases, which are found in the cell-sap fractions, may be deficient in the cytoplasm of the unfertilized egg.
    3. Transfer factors, another component of cell-sap fractions, may be deficient in the cytoplasm of the unfertilized egg.
    4. All the preceding explanations are fallacious, since there is no difference in the ability of cell-sap fractions of fertilized and unfertilized eggs to support protein synthesis.

The synthetases, as will be discussed below, can probably be eliminated from consideration. There is, moreover, a widespread reluctance among workers to accept the idea of a soluble cytoplasmic inhibitor, considering that much of the investigation devoted to the problem has suggested either that the inhibitor does not exist or that effects attributed to an inhibitor could be explained by a deficiency of some material critical for protein synthesis. At the time of this writing there has been no clear-cut demonstration that transfer factors in the cytoplasm of the unfertilized egg are deficient to the point of being limiting to protein synthesis. Castañeda (1969) has presented kinetic studies which show that transfer factors of unfertilized eggs of *Lytechinus pictus* are less active in complexing with GTP than are those of fertilized eggs, but has not demonstrated that this difference is responsible for the low level of protein synthesis in the unfertilized egg. Metafora et al. (1971) report that in the presence of saturating concentrations of the T_1 and T_2 transfer factors ribosomal pellets from unfertilized eggs of *Paracentrotus lividus* still support a low rate of protein synthesis relative to those from fertilized eggs. Although without doubt further studies will be made on the effect of the transfer factors, at present it does not appear that the effectiveness of ribosomes in supporting protein synthesis in the unfertilized egg versus the fertilized egg is seriously influenced by soluble cytoplasmic substances.

Soluble cytoplasmic inhibitors aside, arguments have been advanced for the possibility that the ribosome of the unfertilized egg may be under the influence of an inhibitor which is complexed directly with it and restricts some aspects of its activity. A protein inhibitor of the type proposed by Monroy and his co-workers would fall into this category. Metafora et al. in 1971 sought further evidence for the presence of such an inhibitor. Their experiments attempted not only to isolate the inhibitor, but also to clarify to some degree the nature of the inhibition. Using a test system of ribosomal pellets from a centrifugation at 135,000 × *g,* they measured the ability of these ribosomal preparations, derived from both fertilized and unfertilized eggs, to bind poly U on the one hand, and aminoacyl t-RNA, on the other. They found both of these binding capacities to be in the range 35–40 percent lower in ribosomal preparations from unfertilized eggs than in those from fertilized eggs. They then proceeded to extract these ribosomal preparations with 1 *M* NH₄Cl. The extract from ribosomal preparations of unfertilized eggs strongly inhibited the ability of ribosomes of fertilized eggs to bind to poly U and to aminoacyl t-RNA. It also inhibited polyphenylalanine synthesis in in vitro systems utilizing ribosomes from the fertilized sea urchin egg, from rat liver, from rabbit reticulocytes, from pea germ and from *E. coli.* The NH₄Cl extract from fertilized eggs manifested no inhibitory effect. The inhibitor appears from preliminary characterization to be a protein, as might be expected. Since a great deal more of the NH₄Cl extract was needed to produce the inhibition in the presence of the $135,000 \times g$ supernatant from the fertilized egg than in its absence, these workers postulated that when fertilization releases ribosomes from inhibition by this protein, the inhibitor is probably broken down or in some way inactivated by a component or components of the cell sap.

Kedes and Stavy (1969), by contrast, have presented a convincing demonstration that the ribosomes of unfertilized eggs are not different from those of fertilized eggs in their ability to support protein synthesis. They separated large and small ribosomal subunits from fertilized and unfertilized egg homogenates and recombined them reciprocally. Hybrid ribosomes and normal ribosomes all supported poly U-directed peptide synthesis at about the same rate.

The problem of ribosomal competence is thus unresolved and remains controversial after more than a decade of work. The hypothesis that inhibited or structurally modified ribosomes are responsible for the repression of protein synthesis in the unfertilized egg is not appealing, because in the various versions of this hypothesis the element of specificity appears invariably to be missing. The hypothesis envisions a gross control, a generalized mechanism for repression and derepression of translation, that does not possess the ability to make decisions as to what particular message will or will not be translated after fertilization but merely stipulates that message will be translated at that time. Versatility may be expected, on the other hand, in a masked-message system. Since specificity is the outstanding attribute of message, it is not unreasonable to predict some specificity in a system that controls its availability for translation, as opposed to controlling the availability of a system by by which it can be translated. The appeal of an idea to the mind, however, is not a criterion of truth, nor is there any absolute certainty as to how specific and how versatile whichever of these systems that proves to apply may be.

Evidence for repression of ribosomal activity continues to appear in the literature, and it would seem that the time is at hand for a major effort to validate or disprove this evidence to the satisfaction of all concerned. A controversy may become protracted to the extent of wasting human energies. This problem is important, but there is a question as to how long it should occupy center stage, with problems of equal or greater magnitude waiting in the wings. A careful examination in depth of the techniques used in the controversial experiments to determine their sensitivity to various parameters and to determine whether they actually reflect what they report to reflect is in order. Some of the analytical approaches used over the past decade to provide evidence on this problem have been quite superficial. There is little to gain in dwelling on this point, because there are times when superficiality is acceptable. It is important to determine here what will be revealed when superficiality gives way to circumspect, detailed examination.

The stage has been set for such detailed examination by the experiments of Stavy and Gross (1969b). They determined the effect of various parameters on the rate of protein synthesis in cell-free systems in which the fraction containing the translating machinery had been subjected to different degrees of purification (crude extracts versus microsomes versus microsomes freed of membranous material). The parameters included the effects of pH, of varying concentrations of monovalent and divalent cations, of varying concentrations of nucleotide triphosphates, and of using different species of sea urchin as the source of the preparations. They found a single optimum with respect to all variables. Low incorporation in preparations from unfertilized eggs and the postfertilization upsurge in protein synthesis were seen in all instances. Calcium ions were found to exert a powerful inhibitory effect on protein synthesis purportedly because of competition with magnesium ions, which are a prerequisite for protein synthesis. They also found that a mixture of the nucleotide triphosphates of all four common bases inhibits protein synthesis where crude extracts or microsomes are used, with CTP or UTP apparently being responsible for the inhibition. Supraoptimal amounts of ATP are shown to inhibit the systems markedly. It was discovered that ATP is more critical in determining rate of synthesis in purified systems than in crude preparations. Rates of polyphenylalanine synthesis with poly U as template were found to be the same for eggs and embryo systems. There appeared to be no lack of any cofactor nor any evidence of a soluble cytoplasmic inhibitor in the unfertilized egg.

Stavy and Gross found also that different species of sea urchin are not equally reliable as sources for material to be used in in vitro systems, with certain characteristics of some species, such as RNAase activity, exerting a marked effect on the reproducibility of results.

Levels of incorporation in cell-free systems were also shown to vary with the season, suggesting that the maturity of the gametes is an important variable in such systems. The message could not possibly be more explicit. The results of much of the in vitro work done in the past with sea urchin eggs and embryos are suspect. There is a need for an intensive and extensive study of techniques, an improvement of techniques, and a standardization of techniques.

AVAILABILITY OF TRANSFER RNA
AND SYNTHETASES FOR PROTEIN SYNTHESIS
BEFORE AND AFTER FERTILIZATION

The question of whether a swift production of previously limiting activated t-RNA could be responsible for the acceleration of protein synthesis upon fertilization posed itself to the early workers in the field. Such an event would involve the activity of the synthetases, the enzymes that charge t-RNA with amino acids. Comb (1965) reported that the primary structure of t-RNA is not being synthesized in either the fertilized or unfertilized egg.

Working with embryos of *Lytechinus pictus* and *Arbacia punctulata,* Nemer and Bard in 1963 addressed themselves to the problem of t-RNA availability. They made the assumption that incorporation of amino acids into polypeptides could serve as an index of minimal capacity of the system to produce t-RNA needed for the synthesis of such polypeptides. They used in vitro systems, and their approach was, first, to determine how much protein synthesis could be produced with poly U as a template in homogenates from unfertilized eggs and, second, to determine whether the addition of t-RNA from yeast to homogenates from unfertilized eggs would enhance protein synthesis in cell-free systems. Poly U was found to increase phenylalanine incorporation 200-fold in these homogenates. Since this synthesis must be supported by provision of phenylalyl t-RNA through the auspices of activating and transfer enzymes, a large store of such enzymes would appear to be present in the unfertilized egg. A comparable experiment with poly UG and leucine incorporation essentially confirmed these results. The investigators were led to the conclusion that, if there exists any degree of comparability between endogenous protein synthesis and peptide synthesis with artificial messenger, the fact that homogenates from an unfertilized egg can support an increased amount of protein synthesis would suggest that they cannot contain a limiting factor for protein synthesis, and therefore that they are sustained with adequate enzyme facilities where t-RNA is concerned and/or an adequate pool of specific t-RNAs.

These workers found that the addition of t-RNA from yeast has very little effect on the incorporation of amino acid into protein in the unfertilized egg, the 1-hour zygote, the blastula, and the gastrula. They were forced to conclude that "unless yeast t-RNA is lacking in t-RNA specific for the sea urchin, endogenous levels of t-RNA are adequate to all stages to the need of protein synthesis." They ascribed the failure of significant protein synthesis in the unfertilized egg to the unavailability of m-RNA rather than of t-RNA and its enzymes.

Maggio and Catalano (1963) assayed synthetase activity in cell-sap fractions from eggs and embryos of *Paracentrotus lividus* by determining the exchange of radioactive label between ATP and inorganic phosphate in the synthetase-catalyzed activation reaction and by an alternative assay system in which they measured spectrophotometrically the rate of formation of the hydroxamate derivative of the amino acid. They found little increase during cleavage of exchange activity or hydroxamate formation over that found in the unfertilized egg, and they concluded that up until blastula the activity of the amino acid-activating enzymes present in the unfertilized egg is sufficient to meet the requirements of protein synthesis. Other workers in later years (see, for example, Ceccarini et al., 1967) have confirmed this finding at least as it relates to the period immediately before and after fertilization. There appears to be fairly general agreement among investigators at present that the acceleration of protein synthesis after fertilization is unrelated to the availability of activated transfer RNA.

MASKED MESSENGER RNA
AND THE INFORMOSOME CONCEPT

The view that the difference in availability of m-RNA for translation before and after fertilization is the principal cause, if not the sole cause, for the acceleration of protein synthesis upon activation of the egg is being reinforced by an ever-increasing amount of evidence. It is patent that the concept of regulation of availability of message as a means of translational control implies a broader application of the mechanism than that involved in the change of rate of protein synthesis at fertilization and can be extended to include the regulation of the release of message for translation throughout the course of development. We have discussed a variety of experiments which bear witness to the fact that template that is not being translated exists in the unfertilized egg and that such template enters polysomes and is translated following fertilization. If one assumes tentatively that the protein-synthesizing mechanism in the unfertilized egg is fully competent to translate this message, then one must attempt to describe the conditions that prevent translation. The term *masked* as applied to message unavailable for translation is widely held to apply to a template inactivated through complexing with protein. The findings of some studies suggest that masking of message in the unfertilized egg, however, may be produced by compartmentalization of the message through vesiculation.

Some workers are of the opinion that dense bodies or heavy bodies of the oocyte and egg serve to sequester maternal message. There is at present little evidence to substantiate this opinion except for the possibility that heavy bodies are identical to the L-particles of Mano and Nagano (1970), a point upon which these authors have some reservations. Mano and Nagano (see also Mano, 1966, and Mano and Nagano, 1966) extracted an RNA with template activity for protein synthesis from the 12,000 $\times g$ pellets of homogenates of unfertilized eggs of sea urchins from Japanese waters. Fertilization caused this RNA to be transferred from the 12,000 $\times g$ pellets to the microsome fraction. A *trypsin digestion* of homogenates of unfertilized eggs also caused this shift. In the unfertilized egg, the template was found to be associated with specific particles, which were shown by electron microscopy to be membrane-bound vesicles containing electron-dense particles of uniform size. They designated these vesicles as L-particles. The vesicles sedimented in a polydisperse fashion in a range of 300–400S. The released RNA likewise sedimented in a polydisperse fashion in a range of 20–60S, which is the approximate range of bound m-RNA particles found by

Infante and Nemer (1968). The released RNA appeared to combine with ribosomes to form polysomes. The vesicles were reported to contain a trypsin-like protein, which may be responsible for the release of the RNA at fertilization. Mano and Nagano have expressed the belief that some of the results of the trypsinization experiments of Monroy and his co-workers may have been caused by contamination of their preparations with these vesicles.

The picture presented by this study by Mano and Nagano appears, superficially at least, to imply the synchronous release of maternal message for translation upon fertilization. Although these authors propose that the released message is associated with a protein, it has not been determined whether this control system can differentiate qualitatively or quantitatively in the release of various species of message. It is possible that in vivo the rupture of vesicles might proceed over a protracted period of time so that the release of message might be gradual, but such a control would appear to be nonspecific.

The temporal relationships involved in the release of maternal message to the translating mechanism are difficult to determine. Stavy and Gross (1969a) found that in embryos treated continuously from the beginning of fertilization with actinomycin D the increase in rate of protein synthesis, as tested in cell-free systems with samples taken throughout the course of development, followed the rate curve for protein synthesis through the normal course of development. This circumstance reflects an ever-increasing amount of maternal message coming under translation. The authors noted that whereas their results favor the idea of a programmed and continuous exposure of maternal template to the translating machinery the possibility of synchronous release of template cannot be discounted completely.

Humphreys (1971) concludes from his finding of constancy in size of polysomes during the period of protein synthesis following fertilization that part of the maternal message becomes fully loaded with ribosomes while the remainder remains inactive. Since his experiments show that more and more of the inactive message becomes active in the 2-hour period following fertilization, it would appear that messenger molecules become released for translation gradually. Humphreys proposes that this picture of the kinetics of polysome formation cannot be explained by the effect of a limiting component (such as synthetases or transfer factors) or by the release of inhibited ribosomes. It demonstrates, rather, that translational control activity in the time after activation of the egg resides at the level of the template molecule.

In addition to compartmentalization, two other mechanisms for control of message availability have been proposed. One concept suggests a structural change in the m-RNA molecule itself. Humphreys, for example, suggests that fertilization might activate a ribonuclease to rupture a molecule so that its initiation sequence is exposed. The other concept proposes that message is inactivated by an inhibitor, possibly a protein, which is degraded to activate the template. At present there is little evidence, if any, to confirm the existence of the former control system in sea urchin embryos. Some work has been done to indicate that the latter, in one form or another, may be operative in sea urchin development.

In 1964, Spirin et al., described a type of particle in sedimentation gradients from homogenates of the loach, *Misgurnus fossilis* (a freshwater fish resembling the carp), which appeared to be a form of masked messenger RNA, although it was an m-RNA transcribed after fertilization rather than a maternal m-RNA from the egg. It had the earmarks of a carrier particle transporting m-RNA from the nucleus and also of a storage particle functioning to hold the template in an inactive state until the time of translation. A profile of such particles is shown in Fig. 25.

In a sedimentation gradient, particles of this type were fast moving but moved more slowly than ribosomes. Some of them had S-values ranging from 40 to 60S and appeared too heavy to be free m-RNA. They were not formed in cell-free systems, and the time of their formation in the embryo did not correspond to a period when ribosomes were being synthesized. Accordingly, they were judged to be neither breakdown products of ribosomes nor ribosomal precursors. Upon analysis they were shown to contain 15–35 percent RNA and 85–65 percent protein. They were also shown to be able to form polysomes and to support in vitro the synthesis of polypeptides, provided that ribosomes were present in the system. They were present in all stages of development of the loach, from 4 to 14 hours, that were studied, but they appeared not to be able to program ribosomes until the eight-cell stage. Spirin and his associates have given the name *informosome* to such particles. Spirin (1966)

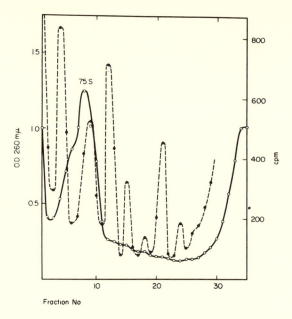

Figure 25

Sucrose-gradient sedimentation of labeled cytoplasmic (nuclei-free) extract of embryos of the loach, *Misgurnus fossilis.* Solid line shows ultraviolet absorption. Dashed line shows radioactivity. Such curves could be produced with either radioactive nucleic acid precursors or radioactive amino acids. [From Spirin (1966); by permission.]

has visualized the informosome as possibly consisting of m-RNA surrounded by a protein capsid or coat to protect it from being read at an inappropriate time and possibly also to protect it from breakdown by enzymes. He also postulated that informosomes should manifest a predominance of protein over RNA and should contain more protein than do ribosomal particles. He reasoned that since there are various sizes of messenger molecule there should also be various sizes of informosome, with the size of the message determining the size of the informosome.

In 1965, Spirin and Nemer separated by differential and sucrose density-gradient centrifugation of homogenates from embryos of *Lytechinus pictus* six distinct size classes of newly labeled RNA with S-values ranging from 20–66S. The fractions showed identical S-values when viewed by either ^{14}C-leucine or ^{3}H-uridine labels, suggesting that they are the result of both RNA and protein synthesis. They showed a high degree of hybridization with DNA, which is a characteristic of messenger RNA. In view of their size and their characteristics with respect to labeling of RNA and protein, they appear to be large message-bearing particles that contain protein. Nemer and Infante (1965a, 1965b) isolated a group of such particles from *Strongylocentrotus purpuratus*. These particles were found in five discrete size classes, ranging approximately in S-value from 30 to 60S. Each sedimenting class of particle or informosome appeared to be represented by m-RNA from a particular size-class region of the polysome spectrum.

If this RNA reflects a system of translational control as is believed by its discoverers, it must be pointed out that these experiments show it only as a possible mechanism for making newly transcribed message available for translation. There have been no experiments on the sea urchin that reveal this type of mechanism for making maternal message available after fertilization, other than the suggestion in the experiments of Mano and Nagano that the message particles released from vesicles at fertilization may be released in the form of informosomes. Informosomes represent a pool of template awaiting translation. A problem which must be resolved is that of how much message is found in informosomes as a function of time in development and how long it remains there. The collective experiments of Infante and Nemer show what appears to be a fairly large amount of template in these particles purportedly awaiting translation, whereas the experiments of Kedes and Gross and their co-workers, which have been discussed previously, tend to show that in cleavage the bulk of newly transcribed message finds its way to polysomes very shortly after being transcribed.

Infante and Nemer (1968) examined the physical characteristics of this DNA-like RNA. They investigated the entire range of subribosomal particles, that is, particles sedimenting more slowly than ribosomes in a density gradient, in early embryos of *Lytechinus pictus* and *Strongylocentrotus purpuratus*. Subribosomal particles in the range of 19–63S, other than ribosomal subunits, could be rapidly labeled with either radioactive uridine or radioactive amino acids. In embryos at the 8-hour late-cleavage stage labeled with ^{3}H-uridine, the 19–63S RNA displayed itself in six fairly discrete peaks (see Fig. 26). When some of these peaks were deproteinized and the derived RNA sedimented, the resulting peaks suggested

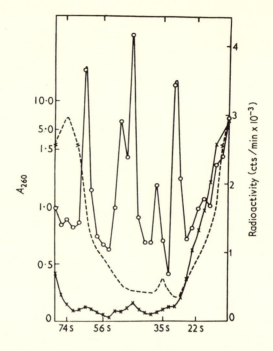

Figure 26

Distribution in a sucrose density gradient of subribosomal, labeled RNA from 8-hour late cleavage embryos of *Strongylocentrotus purpuratus*. Embryos were incubated for 15 minutes with ^{3}H-uridine (100 μC/ml) and homogenzied. A 15,000 × *g* supernatant was centrifuged in a 15–30 percent sucrose gradient in a Spinco SW39 rotor at 39,000 rpm for 4½ hours. Fractions were tested for their ability to pass through membrane filters that pass free RNA but retain ribonucleoprotein. Open circles show radioactivity retained on membrane filters. Crosses show acid-insoluble radioactive material, which passed through membrane filters. Dashed line represents O.D.$_{260}$. Deproteinization of the material in the subribosomal fraction yielded free RNA, which adhered negligibly to the membrane filters. [From Infante and Nemer (1968); by permission.]

that the size of the informosome is a function of the size classes of m-RNA contained within it. The RNA sedimented in broad peaks, of which the average S-values varied proportionately with those of the informosomal peak of origin.

Below 20S was found a large amount of RNA, which was also rapidly labeled with uridine and which showed a polydisperse distribution. These investigators assumed it to be free m-RNA, that is, m-RNA not bound to protein. Ovchinnikov and Spirin (1970) have failed to observe this free m-RNA and have expressed doubts as to its existence, proposing that protein in the cells combines too readily with m-RNA to allow any of it to exist in a free state, an idea with which Nemer now appears to concur (see Fromson and Nemer, 1969).

It might be noted that in these experiments Infante and Nemer determined the S_{20w} of ribosomes and their subunits for these two species of sea urchin, finding the values similar for both species. They found a value of 74S for the ribosome, 56S for the larger subunit, and 35–36S for the smaller subunit. The value for the ribosome is considerably smaller than that of 85S found for *Mellita quinquiesperforata* by Ecker and Brookbank in 1963.

Ovchinnikov and Spirin (1970) have reviewed the informosome problem. They note that in analyses in CsCl density gradients informosomes show characteristically a buoyant density of 1.4 g/cm³, a value which is independent of sedimentation coefficients, that is, of the size of the particle. The major density component contains approximately 20 percent RNA and 80 percent protein. The minor density components have higher percentages of RNA. Sea urchin informosomes, however, show nontypical high buoyant densities, which these workers propose may arise through damage to the particles in extraction procedures. They stress the point that a more rigid proof of the existence of m-RNA in informosomes would be desirable, pointing out that the bulk of efforts to demonstrate m-RNA concentrate on showing that the particles do not contain r-RNA and t-RNA.

They submit that the concept of a "naked" m-RNA molecule being read on the polysome may have to be revised in favor of an m-RNA in some way complexed with protein. They cite as evidence, first, the fact that the traditional concept of the nature of the polysome would call for it to have a buoyant density essentially identical to that of the monosome. Calculations show that t-RNA and m-RNA should not seriously affect its buoyant density. The buoyant density of the polysome, however, is lower than that of the monosome by 0.04 g/cm³. This difference suggests the presence of a molecule (or molecules) on the polysome that is lowering its buoyant density. Second, ethylenediaminetetraacetic acid removes from the polysomes an m-RNA apparently complexed with some other molecule. This complex has S-values higher than those of m-RNA removed from polysomes by deproteination. It does not go through membrane filters, and its buoyant density corresponds closely to that of the informosome.

Some questions are raised about the validity of the informosome theory as a result of theories proposed by Penman et al. (1968), Darnell (1968), and Darnell et al. (1969) from studies made on HeLa cells. A heterogeneous, rapidly labeled DNA-like RNA with S-values ranging from 40 to above 100S is found in HeLa cells. It sediments over a good part of the range in which informosomes sediment and in the higher reaches of its range co-sediments with light polysomes. The authors theorize that this RNA is not m-RNA and is not en route to polysomes. They propose that the only RNA in the cytoplasm that can safely be considered to be m-RNA is that which can be removed from the polysomes by EDTA. They offer two reasons for this view of the heterogeneous RNA: (1) If cells are treated with actinomycin D, the heterogeneous RNA does not "chase" into the polysomes even after a considerable period of time, and (2) if cells are broken up in such a way in isotonic medium as to preserve nuclei from swelling and disruption, the heterogeneous RNA is decreased by a factor of 10, suggesting that it is of nuclear origin and is found in the cytoplasm as a result of nuclear leakage and cannot be classified as a natural resident of the cytoplasm. These authors have as yet no answer as to what the true function of this RNA may be. Should such RNA prove to be identical with the informosomes of Spirin and Infante and Nemer or with heterogeneous, rapidly labeled, DNA-like RNA described by other workers in the sea urchin embryo, and should the postulates of Darnell and the Penman group prove to be valid, a reexamination of concepts of translational control in the sea urchin is in order.

Fromson and Nemer (1969) removed nuclei from cells and after lysing them compared their RNA with that of the cytoplasm. They isolated from the lysed nuclei particles sedimenting in the range 150–250S, which they took to represent an RNA characteristic of the nucleus, but they could find no subribosomal particles that they could designate as informosomes. In the cytoplasm, however, they did find informosomes. This experiment suggests that informosomes are not an artifact produced by nuclear leakage. Kedes and Gross (1969) report that from an examination of m-RNA derived from polysomes in the sea urchin the bulk of newly synthesized

RNA in the cytoplasm after fertilization is m-RNA. It appears to enter all size classes of polysomes and to be translated forthwith. These findings do not exclude the possibility of a part of the new RNA being held in an informosomal storage form, although the authors find that the bulk of the label of newly labeled RNA sediments with the polysomes in early development. Despite the reservations of Humphreys, which we have discussed in a previous chapter, as to whether m-RNA is more than a small subclass of the DNA-like RNA in the cytoplasm, it may well be that the bulk of the cytoplasmic DNA-like RNA of sea urchin embryos is template and is not comparable to the heterogeneous DNA-like RNA of HeLa cells.

The problem of the mechanics of masking of RNA is not yet resolved. The informosome represents a possible mode of holding template until a control mechanism releases it for translation, but whether it is a general mechanism or a special mechanism reserved for certain m-RNA or designed to respond to certain triggers remains to be determined.

SOME CONSIDERATIONS ON
THE BEHAVIOR OF ACTINOMYCIN D

The ability of protein synthesis to proceed in the presence of actinomycin D has been an extremely important element in the body of evidence that has been presented for the proposition that maternal messenger RNA is functional after fertilization. There has been some controversy over the behavior of actinomycin D with respect to the sea urchin embryo. In recent years investigators have undertaken some detailed studies of the activity of this antibiotic to determine how effective it actually is and have examined more circumspectly the effect of treatment with actinomycin D at different times in the course of development.

Giudice et al. (1968) confirmed the finding of earlier workers that when actinomycin D is administered between fertilization and mesenchyme blastula development stops before gastrula. They found that when the drug is administered at mesenchyme blastula the embryos gastrulate but form no skeleton. When the treatment is given at the beginning of gastrula, skeleton formation starts, but does not get beyond the triradiate-spicule stage. This progression in the amount of development attainable as a function of the time of administration of actinomycin D is held to reflect the time at which vital information for certain morphogenetic activity is transcribed. The m-RNA needed for gastrulation appears to be made during late blastula. Transcription for skeleton formation begins at gastrula, but the complete complement of information needed appears not all to be transcribed at that time.

Some workers have suggested that the inhibitory effects on development caused by actinomycin D may not all be due to the prevention of transcription of critical information for the developmental program. Soeiro and Amos (1966) have noted that in other cell systems actinomycin D may inhibit glycolysis and other aspects of respiration and may have certain toxic effects on cells. In 1961, Wolsky and Wolsky had found that actinomycin D may cause cleavage delay and chromosomal aberrations in *Arbacia*. This finding was confirmed in 1969 by Kiefer et al., who reported such mitotic abnormalities as impairment of sister chromosome separation and formation of anaphase bridges. Their explanation for these pathological phenomena is that the failure of transcription causes deficiencies in histone production, which in turn causes the production of abnormal chromatin and, hence, abnormal chromosomes.

The validity of experiments that involve the effect of actinomycin D as a chemical enucleant was challenged by Thaler et al. (1969), who reported from autoradiographic experiments with ^{14}C-labeled actinomycin D that once the fertilization membrane has formed it serves as a barrier to prevent the penetration of the drug, so that actinomycin D does not enter the embryo until after hatching.

The question raised by Thaler and his associates was examined by Summers in 1970. He removed jelly coats and fertilization membranes from embryos of *Lytechinus variegatus* and exposed the embryos to actinomycin D shortly after fertilization. Development of the embryos was halted at mesenchyme blastula, as was development of actinomycin D-treated nondemembranated controls. No treated embryo gastrulated. The treated, demembranated embryos formed normal cilia, swam normally, and elaborated hatching enzyme, but were incapable of further development. This experiment appears to refute the idea that the reason for actinomycin D halting development at blastula is that blastula is the time when the embryo is first exposed to actinomycin D. If one were to assume that removal of the fertilization membrane exposes the embryo to actinomycin D at an earlier time than it would otherwise be exposed, then such "premature" exposure does not change the time at which development is arrested.

Greenhouse et al. (1971) performed autoradiographic studies with tritium-labeled actinomycin D and showed the presence of the drug within cleaving embryos. Their autoradiograms revealed that more radioactivity is located in the nucleus than in the cytoplasm. They reported that treatment with actinomycin D in early cleavage can inhibit RNA synthesis by more than 90 percent and corroborated the findings of Gross and his associates and other early workers with the antibiotic with respect to its efficiency as an inhibitor of transcription. It was the opinion of this group that the difference between these results and those of Thaler and his associates may be attributable to the specific activity of the labeled antibiotic being higher in one instance than in the other.

The toxic effects of actinomycin D were investigated by De Vincentiis and Lancieri in 1970 in experiments in which they compared the effect of actinomycin D with that of desamino-actinomycin C_3, which cannot form complexes with DNA to prevent transcription, but which has approximately the same lethal toxic effect on rats as does actinomycin D. Embryos of *Paracentrotus lividus* exposed to actinomycin D at blastula formed plutei with abnormal gut, abnormal stomodaeal region, a rudimentary skeleton, and no arms. Those exposed at the same developmental stage to desaminoactinomycin C_3 formed plutei which appeared normal except for arms that were somewhat shortened. With due consideration for the fact that the effects described here are for actinomycin D treatment at blastula rather than at or before fertilization, it would appear that nonspecific toxic effects of actinomycin D may not be particularly significant and that its effects on development are primarily those associated with the blockage of RNA synthesis.

REFERENCES

Brachet, J., M. DeCroly, A. Ficq, and J. Quertier, 1963a. Ribonucleic acid metabolism in unfertilized and fertilized sea urchin eggs. *Biochim. Biophys. Acta, 72,* 660–662.

Brachet, J., A. Ficq, and R. Tencer, 1963b. Amino acid incorporation into proteins of nucleate and anucleate fragments of sea urchin eggs: effect of parthenogenetic activation. *Exp. Cell Res., 32,* 168–170.

Burny, A., G. Marbaix, and J. Quertier, 1965. Demonstration of functional polyribosomes in nucleate and anucleate fragments of sea urchin eggs following parthenogenetic activation. *Biochim. Biophys. Acta, 103,* 526–528.

Candelas, G. C., and R. M. Iverson, 1966. Evidence for translational level control of protein synthesis in the development of sea urchin eggs. *Biochem. Biophys. Res. Commun., 24,* 867–871.

Castañeda, M., 1969. The activity of ribosomes of sea urchin eggs in response to fertilization. *Biochim. Biophys. Acta, 179,* 381–388.

Ceccarini, C., R. Maggio, and G. Barbata, 1967. Aminoacyl-s-RNA synthetases as possible regulators of protein synthesis in the embryo of the sea urchin *Paracentrotus lividus. Proc. Nat. Acad. Sci., U.S.A., 58,* 2235–2239.

Comb, D. G., 1965. Methylation of nucleic acids during sea urchin embryo development. *J. Mol. Biol., 11,* 851–855.

Darnell, J. E., 1968. Ribonucleic acid from animal cells. *Bacteriol. Rev., 32,* 262–290.

Darnell, J. E., B. E. H. Maden, R. Soeiro, and G. Pougalatos, 1969. The relationship of nuclear RNA to cytoplasmic RNA. In E. W. Hanly (ed.), *Problems in Biology: RNA in Development,* University of Utah Press, Salt Lake City, 315–329.

Denny, P. C., and A. Tyler, 1964. Activation of protein biosynthesis in non-nucleate fragments of sea urchin eggs. *Biochem. Biophys. Res. Commun. 14,* 245–249.

Ecker, R. E., and J. W. Brookbank, 1963. A ribosome fraction from sand dollar (*Mellita quinquiesperforata*) ova. *Biochim. Biophys. Acta, 72,* 490–493.

Fromson, D., and M. Nemer, 1969. Discussant: Nuclear structures containing heterogeneous RNA. In E. W. Hanly (ed.), *Problems in Biology: RNA in Development,* University of Utah Press, Salt Lake City, 349–350.

Giudice, G., V. Mutolo, and G. Donatuti, 1968. Gene expression in sea urchin development. *Wm. Roux Entwicklsmech. Org., 161,* 118–128.

Glišin, V. R., and M. V. Glišin, 1964. Ribonucleic acid metabolism following fertilization in sea urchin eggs. *Proc. Nat. Acad. Sci., U. S. A., 52,* 1548–1553.

Greenhouse, G. A., R. D. Hynes, and P. R. Gross, 1971. Sea urchin embryos are permeable to actinomycin D. *Science, 171,* 686–689.

Gross, P. R., 1967a. RNA metabolism in embryonic development and differentiation. I. Fertilization and after. *New Eng. J. Med., 276,* 1239–1247.

Gross, P. R., 1967b. RNA metabolism in embryonic development and differentiation. II. Biosynthetic patterns and their regulation. *New Eng. J. Med., 276,* 1297–1305.

Gross, P. R., 1967c. The control of protein synthesis in embryonic development and differentiation. *Current Topics Develop., 2,* 1–46.

Gross, P. R., and G. H. Cousineau, 1963. Effects of actinomycin D on macromolecular synthesis and early development in sea urchin eggs. *Biochem. Biophys. Res. Commun., 10,* 321–326.

Gross, P. R., and G. H. Cousineau, 1964. Macromolecule synthesis and the influence of actinomycin on early development. *Exp. Cell Res., 33,* 368–395.

Gross, P. R., K. Kraemer, and L. I. Malkin, 1965. Base composition of the RNA synthesized during cleavage of the sea urchin embryo. *Biochem. Biophys. Res. Commun., 18,* 569–575.

Gross, P. R., L. I. Malkin, and M. A. Moyer, 1964. Templates for the first proteins of embryonic development. *Proc. Nat. Acad. Sci., U. S. A., 51,* 407–414.

Hultin, T., 1950. The protein metabolism of sea urchin eggs during early development studied by means of ^{15}N-labeled ammonia. *Exp. Cell Res., 1,* 599–602.

Hultin, T., 1952. Incorporation of N^{15}-labeled glycine and alanine into the proteins of developing sea urchin eggs. *Exp. Cell Res., 3,* 494–496.

Hultin, T., 1953. Incorporation of N^{15}-DL-alanine into protein fractions of sea urchin embryos. *Arkiv. Kemi., 5,* 559–564.

Hultin, T., 1961a. The effect of puromycin on protein metabolism and cell division in fertilized sea urchin eggs. *Experientia, 17,* 410–411.

Hultin, T., 1961b. Autoradiographic studies on incorporation of C^{14}-labeled algal hydrolyzate in early sea urchin development. *Exp. Cell Res., 25,* 405–417.

Hultin, T., and A. Bergstrand, 1960. Incorporation of C^{14}-leucine into protein by cell-free systems from sea urchin embryos at different stages of development. *Develop. Biol., 2,* 61–75.

Humphreys, T., 1971. Measurement of messenger RNA entering polysomes upon fertilization of sea urchin eggs. *Develop. Biol., 26,* 201–208.

Infante, A. A., and M. Nemer, 1968. Heterogeneous ribonucleoprotein particles in the cytoplasm of sea urchin embryos. *J. Mol. Biol., 32,* 543–565.

Kedes, L. H., and P. R. Gross, 1969. Synthesis and function of messenger RNA during early embryonic development. *J. Mol. Biol., 42,* 559–575.

Kedes, L. H., and L. Stavy, 1969. Structural identity of ribosomes from eggs and embryos of sea urchins. *J. Mol. Biol., 43,* 337–340.

Kiefer, B. I., C. F. Entelis, and A. A. Infante, 1969. Mitotic abnormalities in sea urchin embryos exposed to dactinomycin. *Proc. Nat. Acad. Sci., U. S. A., 64,* 857–862.

Lundblad, G., 1950. Proteolytic activity in sea urchin gametes. *Exp. Cell Res., 1,* 264–271.

Lundblad, G., 1952. Proteolytic activity in sea urchin gametes. II. Activity of extracts and homogenates of eggs subjected to different treatments. *Arkiv. Kemi., 4,* 537–565.

Lundblad, G., 1954. Proteolytic activity in sea urchin gametes. III. Further investigations on the proteolytic enzymes of the egg. *Arkiv. Kemi., 7,* 127–157.

Maggio, R., and C. Catalano, 1963. Activation of amino acids during sea urchin development. *Arch. Biochem., 103,* 164–167.

Maggio, R., M. L. Vittorelli, A. M. Rinaldi, and A. Monroy, 1964. *In vitro* incorporation of amino acids into proteins stimulated by RNA from unfertilized sea urchin eggs. *Biochem. Biophys. Res. Commun., 15,* 436–441.

Malkin, L. I., P. R. Gross, and P. Romanoff, 1964. Polyribosomal protein synthesis in fertilized sea urchin eggs: the effect of actinomycin D treatment. *Develop. Biol., 10,* 378–394.

Mano, T., 1966. Role of trypsin-like protease in "informosomes" in a trigger mechanism of activation of protein synthesis by fertilization in sea urchin eggs. *Biochem. Biophys. Res. Commun., 25,* 216–221.

Mano, T., and H. Nagano, 1966. Release of maternal RNA from some particles as a mechanism of activation of protein synthesis at fertilization in sea urchin eggs. *Biochem. Biophys. Res. Commun. 25,* 210–215.

Mano, T., and H. Nagano, 1970. Mechanism of release of maternal messenger RNA induced by fertilization in sea urchin eggs. *Biochemistry (Tokyo), 67,* 611–628.

Metafora, S., L. Felicetti, and R. Gambino, 1971. The mechanism of protein synthesis activation after fertilization in sea urchin eggs. *Proc. Nat. Acad. Sci., U.S.A., 68,* 600–604.

Monroy, A., R. Maggio, and A. M. Rinaldi, 1965. Experimentally induced activation of the ribosomes of the unfertilized sea urchin egg. *Proc. Nat. Acad. Sci., U. S. A., 54,* 107–111.

Nakano, E., and A. Monroy, 1958. Incorporation of S^{35}-methionine in the cell fractions of sea urchin eggs and embryos. *Exp. Cell Res., 14,* 236–244.

Nemer, M., 1962. Interrelation of messenger polyribonucleotides and ribosomes in the sea urchin during embryonic development. *Biochem. Biophys. Res. Commun., 8,* 511–515.

Nemer, M., 1963. Old and new RNA in the embryogenesis of the purple sea urchin. *Proc. Nat. Acad. Sci., U. S. A., 50,* 230–235.

Nemer, M., and S. G. Bard, 1963. Polypeptide synthesis in sea urchin embryogenesis: an examination with synthetic polyribonucleotides. *Science, 140,* 664–666.

Nemer, M., and A. A. Infante, 1965a. Informosomes: messenger RNA complexes. *Fed. Proc., 24,* 283.

Nemer, M., and A. A. Infante, 1965b. Messenger RNA in early sea urchin embryos: size classes. *Science, 150,* 217–221.

Nemer, M., and A. A. Infante, 1967. Ribosomal ribonucleic acid of the sea urchin egg and its fate during embryogenesis. *J. Mol. Biol., 27,* 73–86.

Ovchinnikov, L. P., and A. S. Spirin, 1970. Ribonucleoprotein particles in cytoplasmic extracts of animal cells. *Naturwiss., 57,* 514–521.

Penman, S., C. Vesco, and M. Penman, 1968. Localization and kinetics of formation of nuclear heterodisperse RNA, cytoplasmic heterodisperse RNA, and polysome associated RNA in HeLa cells. *J. Mol. Biol., 34,* 49–71.

Rinaldi, A. M., and A. Monroy, 1969. Polyribosome formation and RNA synthesis in the early post-fertilization stages of the sea urchin egg. *Develop. Biol., 19,* 73–86.

Slater, D. S., and S. Spiegelman, 1966. An estimation of genetic messages in the unfertilized echinoid egg. *Proc. Nat. Acad. Sci., U. S. A., 56,* 164–170.

Soeiro, R., and H. Amos, 1966. m-RNA half-life by use of actinomycin D in animal cells—a caution. *Biochim. Biophys. Acta, 129,* 406–409.

Spirin, A. S., 1966. On "masked" forms of messenger RNA in early embryogenesis and in other differentiating systems. *Current Topics Develop., 1,* 1–38.

Spirin, A. S., N. V. Belitsina, and M. A. Aitkhozhin, 1964. Messenger RNA in early embryogenesis. *Zh. Obsch. Biol., 25,* 321–330.

Spirin, A. S., and M. Nemer, 1965. Messenger RNA in early sea urchin embryos: cytoplasmic particles. *Science, 150,* 214–217.

Stavy, L., and P. R. Gross, 1967. The protein–synthetic lesion in unfertilized eggs. *Proc. Nat. Acad. Sci., U. S. A., 57,* 735–742.

Stavy, L., and P. R. Gross, 1969a. Availability of m-RNA for translation during normal and transcription-blocked development. *Biochim. Biophys. Acta, 182,* 203–213.

Stavy, L., and P. R. Gross, 1969b. Protein synthesis *in vitro* with fractions of sea urchin eggs and embryos. *Biochim. Biophys. Acta, 182,* 193–202.

Summers, E. G., 1970. The effect of actinomycin D on demembranated *Lytechinus variegatus* embryos. *Exp. Cell Res., 59,* 170–171.

Thaler, M. M., M. C. Cox, and C. A. Villee, 1969. Actinomycin D: uptake by sea urchin eggs and embryos. *Science, 164,* 832–834.

Timourian, H., 1967. Protein synthesis in sea urchin eggs. I. Fertilization-induced changes in subcellular fractions. *Develop. Biol., 16,* 594–611.

Tyler, A., 1963. The manipulation of macromolecular substances during fertilization and early development of animal eggs. *Amer. Zool., 3,* 109–126.

Tyler, A., 1966. Incorporation of amino acids into protein by artificially activated non-nucleate fragments of sea urchin eggs. *Biol. Bull. Mar. Biol. Lab., Woods Hole, 130,* 450–461.

Tyler, A., 1967. Masked messenger DNA and cytoplasmic DNA in relation to protein synthesis and the processes of fertilization and determination in embryonic development. *Develop. Biol., Suppl. 1,* 170–226.

Vincentiis, M. De, and M. Lancieri, 1970. Observations on the development of the sea urchin embryo in the presence of actinomycin D. *Exp. Cell Res., 59,* 479–481.

Wilt, F. H., 1963. The synthesis of ribonucleic acid in sea urchin embryos. *Biochem. Biophys. Res. Commun. 11,* 447–451.

Wilt, F. H., and T. Hultin, 1962. Stimulation of phenylalanine incorporation by polyuridylic acid (poly U) in homogenates of sea urchin eggs. *Biochem. Biophys. Res. Commun., 9,* 313–317.

Wolsky, A., and M. I. Wolsky, 1961. The effect of actinomycin D on the development of *Arbacia* eggs. *Biol. Bull. Mar. Biol. Lab., Woods Hole, 121,* 414.

CHAPTER IX

Other Aspects of the Nature and Function of RNA

GENERAL CONSIDERATIONS

Our considerations of m-RNA to this point have had to do largely with three concepts:

1. m-RNA made at oogenesis may be translated after fertilization and will support what appears to be normal development up to, and including, blastula in the absence of transcription.

2. The availability of maternal RNA is likely to be the principal cause, if not the sole cause, of the increase in protein synthesis that occurs upon fertilization, although there is some experimental evidence for the existence of other phenomena which may contribute to the increase.

3. A mechanism or mechanisms must exist to hold maternal template in an inactive form pending translation, a mechanism that exerts a control over translation, be the control gross or sophisticated.

We now come to a consideration of the changes that occur in the pattern of message throughout development and of the timing of such changes. Changes in the pattern of message are of interest because they reflect changes in the pattern of active genes on the one hand, and produce changes in the pattern of proteins, on the other. It is not feasible to study changes in DNA directly in the present state of our knowledge. There does not even exist for the sea urchin any substantial amount of information in the realm of classical Mendelian genetics. Genetic change must therefore be viewed indirectly through the study of change in proteins and m-RNA. Even in the study of m-RNA and proteins, we have unearthed little information on definite individual molecular types, and when we detect a change in pattern, we usually do not know what protein or what messenger species has changed. Before considering evidence for changes in proteins and m-RNA, we must look first at some general problems.

Since maternal m-RNA cannot support the production of specialized structures characterizing later stages of development, differentiation at that time must depend upon transcribed information. Unless certain critical information is transcribed at some time after fertilization, the formation of specialized organs, and of specialized cells to constitute the tissues of such organs, will not occur. We cannot say that maternal m-RNA is divorced from differentiation. The statement that it supports the activity of the cells until transcription provides them with the information for their differentiation is without doubt an oversimplification and probably fallacious. Maternal m-RNA may very possibly supply proteins that are critical for differentiation. It is likely also that through reactions which they catalyze some proteins produced on maternal m-RNA might be responsible for the activation of genes that contain information for the elaboration of new structure and the initiation of new function. At the present time it is equivocal as to whether the appearance of new protein species in development, a phenomenon that has come to be recognized as a sign that the process of differentiation is underway, can be attributed to the activity of maternal template. Direct translation control would be a prerequisite for the occurrence of such an event. The experiments of Ellis, discussed below, suggest that such a control is in effect for quantitative protein production on maternal template, and qualitative control cannot be ruled out.

The activation and deactivation of genes in development depends upon intercellular and nucleocytoplasmic interactions. An outstanding reason why these interactions may vary among cells and may thus give rise to divergent pathways of differentiation is that the molecular contents of cells themselves come to vary from one another as development proceeds. This variation occurs under the aegis of events that are characteristic of the cellular level of organization. The molecules of the zygote exhibit organized regional distribution even before the first cleavage, with the selective orientation of the prospective germ layer material being quite apparent. It is clear that the partitioning of cytoplasmic material through the formation of cleavage planes places newly formed nuclei, newly synthesized message, newly synthesized proteins, and reserves or pools of inactive molecules into ever-altering cytoplasmic environments. As cleavage proceeds, the cytoplasm becomes more uniform in molecular content within cells, and more diverse among cells.

During cleavage, cells are undergoing decreases in potentiality, their fates being progressively pointed in a given direction, even before the ultimate characteristic patterns of active genes that will differentiate these cells have actually been formed. It should also be borne in mind that during a time when the number of destinies open to a cell may be decreasing the cells still retain some of the substances that would enable them to attain the destinies that are closing to them. The experiments of Hörstadius (1928 and 1935) clearly demonstrate this. Hörstadius found through the use of the techniques of the experimental embryologist that under a variety of circumstances cells can give rise to structures which they do not normally produce. Whether the substances that allow this flexibility are being actively synthesized is not known.

Intercellular reactions, in which materials are passed from one cell to another, may be viewed as occurring at the cellular level, but producing their effect at the molecular level. It is not certain that all the intercellular reactions in sea urchin development are of an inductive nature. So little is known about this type of reaction in the sea urchin embryo that a meaningful discussion of it is impossible. Studies on reaggregation may be expected to contribute some information on the subject.

The question arises as to how the onset of differentiation can be recognized from a molecular standpoint. Consider a mammalian embryo. It will ultimately give rise, among other things, to a vascular system in which there will be red blood cells. A prerequisite for the production of red blood cells is the production of hemoglobin. Hemoglobin is not being synthesized in the zygote. Sooner or later, then, some cell in the embryo will have to turn on a gene or genes responsible for hemoglobin synthesis. This activation should occur in a cell the fate of which has been resolved. If the cell went on to become a neuron, the result would be disastrous. The cell that turns on the synthesis of hemoglobin will give rise ultimately to a red blood cell. We extrapolate from this sort of situation to the idea that when new species of proteins are detected, their appearance (1) probably signifies that differentiation is occurring, and (2) is probably indicative of the establishment of characteristic patterns of active genes for various cell types. If new species of proteins are detected before cell types are detected, such an event may suggest that such gene patterns are being established gradually.

The appearance of new protein species should probably not *invariably* be considered to be indicative of differentiation of cell types. Perhaps general morphogenetic processes such as gastrulation, for instance, may have a requirement for the production of new protein species. Detection of a new protein species should usually indicate that a change has occurred in the pattern of message being *translated,* if the detection is made in terms of physical or immunological characteristics of the protein. If detected by the sudden appearance of function or activity, a protein species may be new in the sense of newly translated or new in the sense of newly activated, and it is difficult to say what its appearance reflects. There is no implication that a change in the pattern of transcription in later development which will produce a new protein species must be followed *immediately* by the relevant change in pattern of translation. Translational control of protein synthesis on the message produced in such an instance is deemed possible.

STUDIES ON CHANGES IN THE PATTERN OF PROTEIN SYNTHESIS DURING DEVELOPMENT

Some of the earliest attempts to identify new protein species in the sea urchin embryo involved the use of immunological techniques. There is always the remote possibility that the substance against which an antibody employed in such studies is directed may not be a protein, but this is generally unlikely. A variety of methods are available in immunological studies, but one common approach is to obtain an antibody against an antigen or antigens from one developmental stage and then to determine by means of a characteristic antigen–

antibody reaction whether the antigen is present in earlier or later developmental stages. The earliest stage at which an antigen appears ought probably to represent a time very close to that at which its synthesis is turned on. Most of these immunological experiments lacked the reliability that is now attainable with the techniques of biochemistry and molecular biology and failed to produce an equivalent yield in specific information about the appearance of new protein species, but they are of considerable historical importance because they allowed the detection of the appearance of new protein species long before such detection was possible with biochemical techniques.

In 1948, Perlmann and Gustafson demonstrated that "one or several molecular species of new specificity" were to be found in 0.9 percent saline extracts from larvae of *Paracentrotus lividus* at 48 hours after fertilization. These antigens were not present in earlier embryonic stages or in the unfertilized egg. They were detected by the use of rabbit antisera against the 48-hour stage of development and were postulated by the authors to have arisen from a synthesis probably turned on at early gastrula. The 48-hour stage appears to have been the pluteus with the system of culture used by these investigators. Perlmann found in 1953 that the spectrum of saline-soluble antigens for later stages of development is more or less the same as for the unfertilized egg, except that in the pluteus stage at least three antigens are definitely present that were absent in the unfertilized egg.

Through the use of a vertical immunodiffusion technique, Perlmann and Couffer-Kaltenbach (1957) were able to follow from fertilized egg to pluteus the concentration of antigens relative to those found in the unfertilized egg of *Paracentrotus lividus*. These antigens were tentatively identified as proteins with differing physicochemical properties. They showed a decrease in concentration at the onset of the first cell division followed by an increase up to the 16-cell stage. Concentration fluctuated in varying degrees thereafter and fell to a very low level at pluteus. Such measurements can now be made with greater precision through biochemical techniques.

Ranzi (1962) performed immunological experiments wherein rabbit antisera against unfertilized eggs were used to demonstrate antigens still present at the swimming blastula, at gastrula, or at pluteus, or present only in the fertilized or unfertilized egg. Rabbit antisera against adult sea urchin preparations showed antigens present since mesenchyme blastula, since gastrula, since prism, or present only in the adult stage. These experiments give the general picture of new protein species tending more often to appear after gastrula rather than before, and of the synthesis of some proteins being repressed early in development.

Recently, Westin (1969) incubated eggs and embryos of *Paracentrotus lividus* with radioactive amino acids and examined them for the presence of labeled antigens through the use of the combined techniques of autoradiography and immunoelectrophoresis, employing rabbit antisera against sea urchin preparations. Until the time of hatching no changes in the labeling pattern of antigens were observed. At mesenchyme blastula, however, a new labeled antigen was detected, and an antigen that was previously unlabeled became heavily labeled, showing that the synthesis of some protein had been reactivated after a period in which the protein was not being synthesized. The intensity of labeling of other antigens also changed at mesenchyme blastula. Embryos exposed to actinomycin D at about the time of hatching never developed the normal labeling pattern of mesenchyme blastula. The results of these experiments indicate that new templates are needed and produced to permit gastrulation and that some of them may be under translation by the time of mesenchyme blastula. In 1972 Westin prepared through absorption techniques a series of stage-specific antisera and again detected a change in the pattern of labeled antigens at mesenchyme blastula. She also demonstrated the presence of egg-specific antigens, which decreased and disappeared by the time of blastula.

Early attempts to demonstrate changes in protein species under synthesis during development, with the use of analytical, as opposed to immunological, techniques were largely unsuccessful. Working with cellulose ion-exchange columns or with electrophoresis, Monroy et al. (1961) and Spiegel and Spiegel (1959) were unable to detect qualitative differences in the pattern of proteins in stages between the unfertilized egg and pluteus in *Paracentrotus lividus* and *Arbacia punctulata*. Electrophoretic studies by Pfohl and Monroy (1962a, 1962b) showed the same general lack of change in pattern and absence of new species from stage to stage in *Arbacia punctulata*, except that there appeared to be a new band, showing esterase activity, as well as one showing alkaline phosphatase activity, at mesenchyme blastula.

In 1964 Gross anticipated a breakthrough on the problem when he noted that in gradient-analysis studies there looked to be some differences in the profiles of proteins between control and actino-mycin D-treated embryos of *Arbacia punctulata* at blastula. Spiegel et al. (1965), however, found no such differences upon examining protein spectra from 100,000 × *g* supernatants of actinomycin D-treated and untreated embryos of *Strongylocentrotus purpuratus* by disk electrophoresis. The same peaks showed in both treated and untreated embryos, and these peaks showed no significant difference from stage to stage among those stages studied up to prism.

Terman and Gross (1965) performed similar experiments in protein fractionation and analysis, but they were able to obtain somewhat better resolution. In gel electrophoresis studies on *Arbacia punctulata* they found patterns of protein synthesis in normal embryos to be essentially unvaried from fertilization to gastrula in experiments wherein a stain was used to develop the migrating bands. They did find, however, that at pluteus there were easily recognizable changes from the earlier pattern. They also found that there was some decrease in density (suggestive of change in *rate* of synthesis) in one band in particular as development proceeded. In a parallel group of experiments they labeled the protein synthesized by means of incor-poration of radioactive amino acids, and detected the electrophoretic bands by autoradiography. Whereas a stain may reveal protein that is not incorporating label, autoradiography will not do so. It is not surprising that the results from the two techniques varied somewhat, although as development progressed and protein synthesis increased these results became more similar to one another.

In the autoradiographic studies, there occurred considerable change in grain density of certain peaks as the function of time, indicat-ing quantitative variation in the synthesis of some proteins. Embryos treated with actinomycin D showed this type of change also. The electrophoretic bands of treated and control embryos were similar up until hatching, whereafter they varied somewhat. The results suggested that during cleavage and blastula the proteins synthesized on maternal m-RNA and newly transcribed m-RNA are essentially identical. They also suggested that the rate of translation may vary at different times in development where the synthesis of individual pro-teins is concerned, whether maternal or newly transcribed m-RNA is being translated. As the authors pointed out, however, the bands may

represent groups of proteins, and changes in grain density could reflect changes in types of protein within a set, rather than changes in
rate of synthesis of individual species.

Finally, in 1966 Ellis achieved a degree of resolution in his
separation of protein peaks that enabled him to demonstrate that
changes do occur in the protein spectrum even in the early hours of
development. He employed ion-exchange chromatography with
DEAE Sephadex on proteins extractable in 0.5 N NaCl from embryos
of *Arbacia punctulata* and determined the synthetic activity through
the measurement of rate of incorporation of radioactive amino acids.
In terms of extractability and recovery, he estimated that he was
examining about 25 percent of the embryonic protein. His curves
(Figs. 27–29) reveal peaks in the 8-hour hatching embryo that are not
present in the zygote 1 hour after fertilization. The curves also show
that there is differential control over protein synthesis in this early
period, with some peaks increasing in activity while others decrease.
The results of treating embryos with actinomycin D suggest that in
the first 8 hours of development this differential control operates
largely at the translational level and involves stable maternal template.
The curves appear to favor the idea of a controlled, as opposed to
synchronous, release of this template following fertilization. The
activity of some of the minor peaks at the 8-hour stage is shown to be
under direct, gene-level control.

At 18 hours after fertilization, when the embryo is gastrulating,
there is seen to be an increase in complexity of the profile of protein
peaks, with the most prominent peak of earlier development now
severely attenuated and with new peaks emerging. Treatment with
actinomycin D reveals a strong shift toward the transcriptional level in
the control of protein synthesis. By 24 hours, with the embryo at
pluteus, the protein spectrum assumes a less complicated appearance, probably as a result of a loss in resolution due to the emergence
of many new species of protein.

Ellis also found that in actinomycin D-treated embryos, the inhibition of DNA-dependent RNA synthesis and of differentiation beyond
blastula is reversible, at least up to 18 hours into development.
By 24 hours, however, reversibility of the effect of actinomycin D is
lost. If the antibiotic is removed at that time, the embryo cannot free
itself from the effect of the inhibition, and goes into a prism-like
terminal form, which lacks a skeleton. If the antibiotic is removed

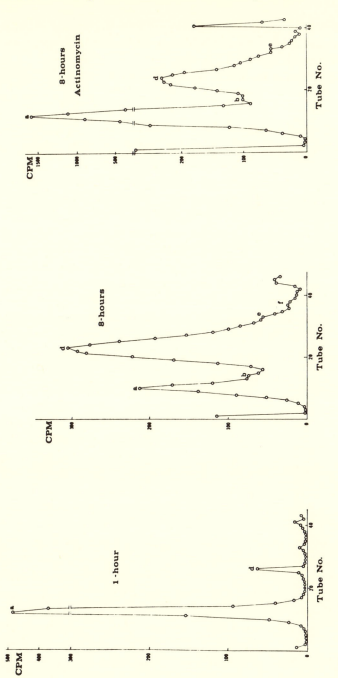

Figure 27

Elution profiles from ion-exchange chromatography of radioactive protein of soluble protein extract of embryos of *Arbacia punctulata* incubated for 1 hour with ^{14}C-protein hydrolyazate during development. Left: control embryos incubated in the first hour. Center: control embryos incubated in eighth hour. Right: embryos grown in actinomycin D incubated during eighth hour. [From Ellis (1966); by permission.]

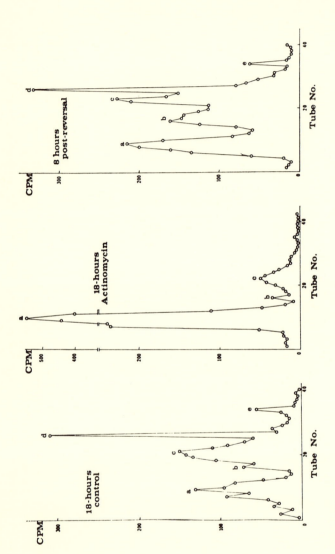

Figure 28

Elution profiles from ion-exchange chromatography of radioactive protein of soluble protein extract of embryos of *Arbacia punctulata* incubated for 1 hour with ¹⁴C-protein hydrolyzate during development. Left: control embryos incubated during eighteenth hour. Center: embryos grown in actinomycin D incubated during eighteenth hour. Right: embryos removed from continuous exposure to actinomycin D at eighteenth hour and incubated with precursor during twenty-sixth hour after fertilization. [From Ellis (1966); by permission.]

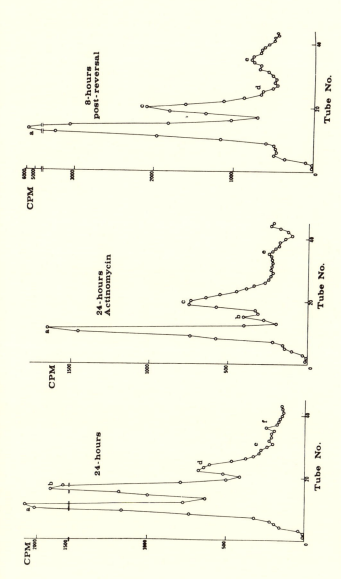

Figure 29

Elution profiles from ion-exchange chromatography of radioactive protein of soluble protein extract of embryos of *Arbacia punctulata* incubated for 1 hour with ^{14}C-protein hydrolyzate during development. Left: control embryos incubated during twenty-fourth hour. Center: embryos grown in actinomycin D incubated during twenty-fourth hour. Right: embryos removed from continuous exposure to actinomycin D at the twenty-fourth hour and incubated with precursor during thirtieth hour after fertilization. [From Ellis (1966); by permission.]

before the 18-hour point, recovery from inhibition occurs in all peaks of protein synthesis, and the normal elution pattern is restored. Ellis found that after the point of irreversibility has been passed, however, only one major peak is able to recover. The point at which irreversibility is lost coincides with a time of increased complexity in the elution profile and of very strong synthetic activity in several of the protein peaks.

Ellis has noted that the capability for reversibility with regard to actinomycin D inhibition demonstrates a flexibility in the requirement for timing of gene expression, as far as transcriptional control is concerned, and demonstrates that in the first 18 hours of development, the period from fertilization to gastrula, *no particular gene-directed synthesis must occur as a* sine qua non *for normal development to proceed.* This is an extremely important point. We have here embryos arrested at blastula as a result of 18 hours of exposure to the inhibitor, embryos that would be gastrulating in normal development. It should not be assumed that upon removal of the inhibitor the transcription of critical genes and the translation of the information thereby produced is not necessary for the recovered embryo to proceed from blastula to gastrula. The concept implies, rather, the absence of a feedback between the products of transcription at an early point in development and the expression of the genome at a later point. The embryo is not prevented from proceeding from blastula to gastrula because, being inhibited, it failed to transcribe some gene at, let us say, the third hour in development. The necessity of transcribing such a gene did not exist. The problem of timing of signals for transcription or translation will be considered further when we come to the subject of reaggregation.

By means of polyacrylamide gel electrophoresis, Terman in 1970 could find no difference in the labeling pattern of proteins from actinomycin D-treated embryos versus normal embryos between fertilization and midcleavage. At hatching blastula the labeling patterns were widely divergent. He proposed that the pattern of protein synthesis before blastula is largely under translational control. Ellis found clear-cut differences in some regions of the profiles of proteins of inhibited versus control embryos in a high-resolution study performed on these embryos in the seventh hour of development, which we would assume to be 1 hour before hatching. As Ellis has noted, it is difficult to make comparisons between analytical studies employing polyacrylamide gel electrophoresis and those employing ion exchange, but these two studies appear to be in essential agreement as to the predominance of translational control prior to blastula.

In contrast to the findings from immunological studies and from hybridization studies, which will be discussed below, the experiments of Ellis demonstrate the appearance of new protein species in the period between fertilization and blastula. This discovery is not surprising. Although cleavage is primarily a time of rapid cell proliferation, many other important developmental events occur during this period. Cells are undergoing changes in developmental capacity, leading to the determination of their fates. This process starts very early in the sea urchin embryo, possibly as soon as the 8- or 16-cell stage. Metabolic gradients are being established that will promote morphogenetic change. Cytoplasmic environments of basic reactions are being altered by the formation of cleavage planes. Such events without doubt produce broad changes in the complexion of reactions within cells, and such changes in the reactions may well be believed to lead to the activation of genes and the appearance of new species of protein. Some recent investigations appear to have confirmed the findings of Ellis. Studies of the synthesis of nuclear proteins, for example, although attended by some controversy, have shown that these proteins undergo changes in spectrum during cleavage which reflect alterations in the pattern of active genes (see Hnilica et al., 1971).

As we have suggested previously, it may be questioned as to whether every new protein appearing upon the developmental scene signals the presence of a differentiative process. A convenient working definition of differentiation is that it is the establishment of the ultimate pattern of active and inactive genes within a cell which imparts to that cell its ultimate structural and functional characteristics. The forming of this ultimate pattern is conceived to be a gradual process bound intimately to the events of morphogenesis. Morphogenesis, however, is a process that builds an embryo, and that process includes events other than differentiative events. It should not be viewed as the sum total of all embryonic differentiative events and no more. Because of the interlacing of the various aspects of morphogenesis with those of differentiation, it is difficult to separate the two, but phenomena such as ciliation, hatching, yolk degradation, some aspects of the rapid cell proliferation of cleavage, and some aspects of cell movement, for example, may be thought to serve the developing embryo as distinct from serving the differentiating cell. Any gene activation that implements such processes by giving rise to new proteins and is not built into the final pattern of genes in the cell in which it occurs should be considered as distinct from the phenomenon of differentiation. Without doubt such activations are infrequent, and some of them may occur at oogenesis. As experimental scrutiny begins to bear down on the process of differentiation, however, it is important to make this distinction.

The number of peaks that represent the appearance of new protein species in the experiments of Ellis is not great. One need not assume, however, that the number of new protein species appearing up to pluteus is small. Even if such experiments looked at all the proteins of the embryo rather than a portion of them, there remain vexatious problems in obtaining good resolution. Gross (1967) suggested that a new species of protein that is produced in development may represent a very small perturbation on the massive background of bulk protein and may pass undetected in electrophoretic or chromatographic analysis. There appears to be, however, no grounds for the idea that enormous numbers of genes are being activated between gastrula and pluteus, as was once thought to be true.

STUDIES ON OTHER FEATURES
OF THE NATURE AND BEHAVIOR OF m-RNA

In the investigation of the activity of transcriptional and translational controls during development, an obvious alternative to a search for changes in the profile of proteins synthesized during development and for the emergence of new species of protein is a search for changes in the pattern of message under translation or awaiting translation. Until recently this approach has not been very successful other than in revealing gross changes in the population of messenger molecules seen between fertilization and pluteus. In the earlier studies on changes in the populations of template, the technique of RNA–DNA hybridization looked to be a promising experimental approach. This experimental method provides no insight into the specific nature of changes in species or size classes of message. It is designed to detect changes in the total population of messenger molecules as reflected by changes in the amount of message that can combine with active transcription sites in a given amount of DNA.

The rationale for the technique of hybridization commonly used in these experiments is simple. If a population of various species of m-RNA molecule is hybridized with DNA, each of its constituent molecules can theoretically be replaced competitively by any identical molecular species within a second population of m-RNA molecules. If the original population is labeled by the use of radioactive precursors to RNA synthesis before it is hybridized, and the competing population is unlabeled, the loss in specific activity by the complex reflects the degree of competition that has occurred. The degree of competition reflects the degree of difference between the two populations of message. The more a population has changed, the less the number of sites at which competition can occur, and the smaller the loss in specific activity. By this technique, one should be able to compare message from different stages of development as to the degree of difference in their populations. Unfortunately, as will be discussed below, some of the predictions of the theory that underwrites this technique have failed to come true.

Two investigations on the m-RNA of sea urchin embryos involving this approach were made in 1966, one by Glišin et al. and the other by Whitely et al. The findings of the two groups tend to corroborate one another. A typical curve of the results may be seen in Fig. 30. The findings are typical of those obtained from the early immunological studies. They show an essential identity in the populations of message in all stages of development from the unfertilized egg through blastula, followed by a progressive increase in competition or progressive change in the species of message in the later stages of development. A serious difficulty arises here in the failure to find differences in the message populations in the early stages of development. First, the findings of Ellis with respect to protein spectra imply that there should be differences. Second, the inherent nature of the hybridization phenomenon is such that when differences in message populations are not revealed in experiments such as these the results should be classified as uninterpretable.

Because there exist in DNA many repetitious sequences or sequences very similar to one another, hybridization does not show complete locus specificity. Species of RNA that are closely similar to one another may form hybrids with sequences on DNA other than those sequences from which they were transcribed. There are, in

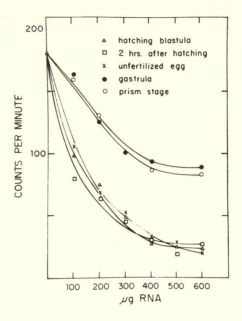

Figure 30

Comparison of RNA's from different stages of development in the sea urchin. Unlabeled RNA samples were compared from different stages of development by the determination of their inhibition of binding of 100 μg of the labeled hatching-blastula RNA. Changes in sequences relative to those of hatching blatula are revealed in the curves from gastrula and prism. See discussion in the text. [From Glišin et al. (1966); by permission.]

other words, cross reactions. About 20 percent of the DNA in the sea urchin is estimated to consist of repetitive sequences, whereas the remaining 80 percent is made up of sequences of which there is one copy each per haploid genome. Hybridization experiments such as those described above reflect the presence of repeated rather than unique sequences. Since the possibility of cross reactions exists, populations of message that show no differences in competition in hybridization experiments cannot be said to be either identical or not identical. The results of such a finding cannot be interpreted. Where differences are found in the amount of m-RNA hybridized, they may reasonably be expected to reveal differences in the populations of messenger molecules. Some sets of repeated sequences of DNA, for example, may be under translation at one time in development and others at another time. With the possibility of some cross reactions, there is always some likelihood that the magnitude of differences in the populations of template will be underestimated.

Differences in unique sequences under translation at different stages of development cannot be determined readily. The incubation time required to effect hybridization is usually so long as to make the determination experimentally unfeasible, although it is sometimes possible to circumvent this difficulty by using high ratios of RNA to DNA in experiments.

Although the function of repeated sequences in DNA is not known, these sequences appear to be ubiquitous among the genomes of higher organisms. There appears to be also a large amount of conservatism in the distribution of families of repeated sequences among the species by the mechanisms of evolution. Many families of repeated sequences are shared by widely divergent species, whereas other families are not shared. It is of interest to determine whether the distribution of related sequences, in terms of degree of difference among them as opposed to identity, can offer a clue to taxonomic relationships among organisms. It is important, in other words, to ascertain whether hybridization studies would serve as an important experimental tool to the taxonomist.

Whiteley et al. (1970) made some comparisons by hybridization experiments of differences in distribution of populations of m-RNA transcribed from repeated sequences among three species of the genus *Strongylocentrotus*, *Dendraster excentricus*, and *Pisaster ochraceus*. These comparisons cross the lines of species, superorder, and class, respectively. Samples of curves for competition may be seen in Figs. 31 and 32. The results of both RNA–DNA hybridization and DNA–DNA annealing experiments are in agreement with those reached by anatomical and paleontological approaches with respect to the nature of the taxonomic relationships of the animals under consideration. It cannot be determined from studies on a small group of organisms whether such agreement will be found in investigations of all the taxa, but in view of the amount of controversy that exists over systematic affinities of organisms, the problem is certainly worthy of continued investigation.

The degree of difference in populations of m-RNA from the unfertilized egg among the organisms studied by Whiteley and his co-workers was small, suggesting considerable conservatism among the families of repeated sequences in the genes being transcribed to pro-

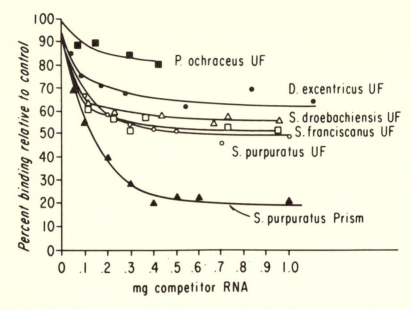

Figure 31

Competition by RNA preparations from unfertilized eggs (UF) of five species of echinoderm in the binding of ^{3}H-prism RNA from *Strongylocentrotus purpuratus* to DNA from *S. purpuratus*. Conditions as described in Fig. 32. [From Whiteley et al. (1970); by permission.]

vide the maternal template stored in the unfertilized egg. By contrast, a wide degree of divergence was seen in the RNA populations of larval stages. The genes activated after hatching appeared to produce a greater amount of species-specific RNA than did those of the unfertilized egg. Such RNA may be associated with differentiation and responsible for species characteristics. This is a picture, however, of divergence in template derived from repeated sequences, and it is to be expected that template produced on unique-sequence regions of the genome might contain a greater amount of m-RNA that is critical in determining species characteristics. Such assumptions are speculative, however, and it must be repeated that the actual function of repeated sequences is unknown. These investigators made some determination on hybridization of unique or infrequent sequences through the use of increased concentrations of RNA. Populations of these sequences were found to be widely divergent in both the unfertilized egg and larval forms among the five animal species

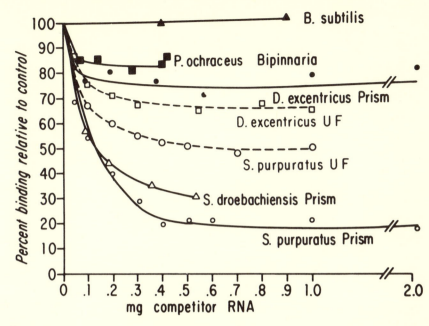

Figure 32

Competition by RNA preparation from prisms and bipinnaria larvae in the binding of *Strongylocentrotus purpuratus* prism ³H-RNA to *S. purpuratus* DNA. ³H-RNA (5 μg) from *S. purpuratus* prisms was incubated with 48 μg of *S. purpuratus* DNA in the presence of indicated amounts of competitor RNA. Curves for competition by RNA from unfertilized eggs (UF) of *Dendraster excentricus* and *S. Purpuratus* from Fig. 31 are shown by dashed lines. [From Whiteley et al (1970); by permission.]

studied. It appeared that the proportion of unique sequences under transcription, however, was much lower in the oocyte than in the larval stages.

The direct analysis of the spectrum of m-RNA in the sea urchin embryo presents more difficulties than does the analysis of the protein spectrum and has sometimes yielded results that are less than gratifying. The analysis of m-RNA profiles, however, yields some types of information about transcription and translation that cannot be obtained by studies of protein profiles. An assortment of difficulties is involved in the analysis of message populations. The amount of message present in the embryo is very small. The use of radioactive labeling is usually required for one to observe it properly. Only newly transcribed message is, of course, labeled in the postfertilization period. Stable maternal template must be labeled at oogenesis, since there is virtually no transcription in the unfertilized egg. Such labeling is possible, but it requires such techniques as injecting radioactive precursor into the perivisceral cavity, and it precludes the possibility of controlled pulse labeling. In the postfertilization period the question arises as to how the labeling picture may be affected by the presence of short-lived RNA. Brandhorst and Humphreys (1971) have reported unstable m-RNA of which one third has a half-life of 5–10 minutes with the remainder ranging in half-life from 60 to 90 minutes. Nuclear DNA-like RNA appears to be characteristically short-lived and is known to leak into the cytoplasmic fraction when some types of extraction procedure are used. Another difficulty involved in labeling in very early development is the fact that methods which label m-RNA tend to label 4S RNA as well. In some gradient analyses, problems arise because peaks of these two species of RNA overlap. There have been other problems of technique. Contamination with RNAase has at times caused difficulties. Some of the early work was marked by troubles with the phenol-extraction procedure, and modifications in this procedure were required before satisfactory results were achieved.

The experimental method most commonly used in investigation of m-RNA of the embryo is density gradient analysis. Within the scope of this technique one has the opportunity for viewing tendencies in message utilization by observing size-class changes in polysome profiles or changes in amount of polysome material in various peaks, of analyzing changes in the spectrum of m-RNA species from different stages in development by examining m-RNA extracted from polysomes, or of studying rapidly labeled DNA-like RNA not located on polysomes, as is found, for example in subribosomal particles. Other approaches involving gradient analysis are sometimes used. The problems are complicated and require considerable versatility in technique.

We have already discussed to this point several experiments that have examined the nature and behavior of m-RNA through such approaches, general and special. Let it suffice here to mention two studies that examined the total spectrum of newly transcribed message through various stages in development. One was made a decade ago by Nemer (1963). He noted the presence of the 9S peak which has since been associated with the production of nucleoproteins. He also made an observation of considerable interest, that is, a progressive increase in labeling of the heavy end of the spectrum of m-RNA as development progresses. Possibly this increase may be attributed to an initial preoccupation of transcription with producing information for the synthesis of nuclear protein, a synthesis that tends to monopolize the template at the lighter end of the gradient, followed by a gradual switchover to the task of providing more message for the production of other protein species, many of which may be made on larger template.

The same phenomenon was observed by Slater and Spiegelman (1970). They used the combined techniques of gradient analysis and electrophoresis in their studies. They reported that from the 4-cell stage through blastula there is an increase in the number of physically distinct m-RNA species and in the average molecular weight of the population of m-RNA being produced. Electrophoresis revealed several species of m-RNA being transcribed between fertilization and the 4-cell stage. The use of this technique, in fact, revealed the presence during cleavage of many more species than are shown by gradient analysis alone. They reported the existence during cleavage of a fairly prominent 20S peak, which has also been reported by Kedes and Gross (1969a) and the nature and function of which has not yet been investigated, as well as a peak with a sedimentation value of 12S. There have been reports of a 12S peak in association with the RNA of both yolk spherules and mitochondria.

These studies provide something of a picture of changes in transcribed m-RNA during early development, but leave unanswered the question of how closely the spectrum of transcribed message resembles that of maternal message. Slater and Spiegelman propose that message transcribed during the cleavage period is largely redundant to maternal template. Their reasoning is based on the fact that maternal message requires no tandem transcription to carry the animal through the developmental stages to blastula. They point out the possibility of such redundancy offering the advantage of a compensatory production of message. It could be expected, for example, to eliminate the danger caused by a fortuitous deficiency of some species of maternal message.

This is a reasonable and interesting hypothesis. The experiments of Ellis do indeed suggest that in the period up to blastula transcribed message may show considerable redundance to maternal message, but it is difficult to assess the function of transcription during cleavage. It does appear to have a functional bias in that much of it is dedicated to the production of nuclear proteins. Ultimately, it may prove to have several categories of function. There may be a possibility that the most critical segment of the profile of transcribed message to the developmental program as a whole is the one not redundant to maternal message, the one represented by the new species of message that are transcribed prior to hatching. It is interesting that in amphibians (see Davidson et al., 1968, and Crippa and Gross, 1969) little, if any, message transcribed in cleavage shows sequence homology to maternal message in hybridization experiments.

From the evidence provided by Kedes and Gross (1969b), it is likely that prior to hatching the bulk of newly transcribed message is being translated within a very few minutes after entry into the cytoplasm. It is an appealing hypothesis that the remainder of this message, which may be stabilized on subribosomal particles or stabilized by some other mechanism, undergoes a programmed release for translation, species by species. It is also an attractive idea, as we have suggested previously, that in lieu of synchronous release at fertilization a similar selective utilization occurs in the instance of maternal message. Evidence for such selective utilization of maternal message in the sea urchin embryo is scant at present. Crippa and Gross (1969) have found through hybridization experiments on *Xenopus* that different species of maternal m-RNA associate with polysomes at different times in development in a situation in which not all maternal m-RNA is on the polysomes at any one time. This finding suggests selective utilization of maternal message, and it would thus appear that programmed availability of maternal message for translation is a reality in at least some developmental systems.

We come now to a consideration of some investigations on information flow that are presently difficult, if not impossible, to interpret from a molecular point of view, but which are extremely fascinating and quite ingenious. These are the experiments of Neyfakh (1960, 1964). They examine the commerce of messenger molecules in the cells in terms of their effect on the whole organism, and they are concerned with what one might term the survival aspect of transcription. The experimental approach in these studies involves the determination of the length of time an embryo can survive if transcription is halted at any given moment in development. Variations in this time period throughout development should theoretically reflect changes in requirement for transcription, should give some idea of the time schedule of transcription operating to meet these requirements, and should reveal the moments in development when further progress is impossible without transcription.

Neyfakh used a technique of radiational inactivation of the nucleus. He determined a radiation dose that would arrest nuclear function but not interfere with embryogenetic activity in the cytoplasm. In the arrest of nuclear function, transcription would theoretically be halted. Supposedly, this effect is parallel to chemical enucleation by actinomycin D, except that the method is much more convenient and that the inhibition can be administered at the exact moment of one's choosing. The rationale of the experiments is as follows: Let us suppose that one irradiates embryos at different moments along the time course of development and then notes the time which elapses before development comes to a halt. If the nucleus is normally inactive during a particular period, and message is not being transcribed, development of an embryo irradiated during that period of inactivity will proceed to a certain definite point before cytoplasmic inadequacies bring it to a halt, regardless of the time within the inactive period at which the embryo is irradiated. If, by contrast, the nucleus is in a period during which it is actively transcribing message, the longer the wait before irradiating during this period, the more time the nucleus is given to provide for future development and the longer the embryo will survive.

Neyfakh (1960), working with *Strongylocentrotus dröbachiensis*, found two such periods of nuclear inactivity. The first lasted 14 hours, from fertilization to early blastula. No matter when the animal was irradiated during this period, development proceeded normally to early blastula. From early blastula to late blastula, a 16-hour period of active transcription occurred during which maximum delay in irradiating the embryo would carry development to advanced gastrula. At late blastula, when this animal was 30 hours into development, this active period terminated. A second inactive period ensued, which lasted 12 hours, carrying the embryo into mesenchyme blastula. Regardless of the time or irradiation in this

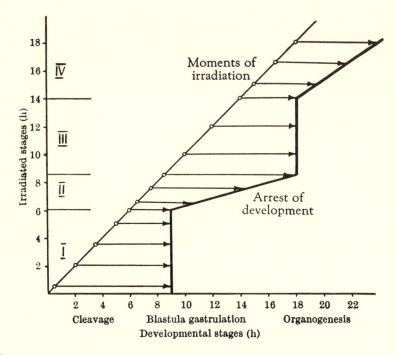

Figure 33

Dependence of developmental arrest on irradiated stages (40,000 R). Each arrow shows the development of the "enucleated" embryo from the moment of irradiation to the event of development. [From Neyfakh (1964); by permission.]

period, the animal would develop to advanced gastrula. At mesenchyme blastula, 42 hours into development, a second and final active period occurred. The degree of coelom formation, gut formation, and skeleton formation that occurred during this period was a function of the time at which the embryo was irradiated. Thus two periods of active transcription, critical for morphogenetic events, alternate with two resting periods in the nucleus.

As it applies to the sea urchin embryo, at least, the interpretation given to the results of these experiments by Neyfakh is unacceptable. During the first proposed rest period, transcription in the sea urchin embryo is not only active, but is increasing the tempo of its activity, nor is it inactive at other times in development. Spirin et al. (1964), working with the loach, employed the irradiation technique of Neyfakh and examined the effect on nucleic acids. They found that

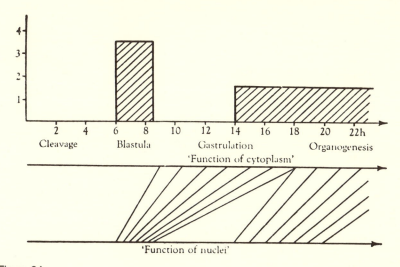

Figure 34

Upper: Periods of morphogenetic activity of nuclei. Time of development, which is predetermined during 1 hour of nuclear activity, is plotted on the ordinate. Lower: Scheme of nucleocytoplasmic interrelations. Stages of development (upper line) are joined with stages of nuclear function that determine these forms. [From Neyfakh (1964); by permission.]

following irradiation m-RNA synthesis continues unabated, whereas DNA synthesis is virtually arrested within 30 minutes after irradiation. The technique used by Neyfakh apparently failed to block transcription. Whether the experiments of Neyfakh did or did not demonstrate what they were intended to demonstrate, they did reveal a very interesting phenomenon, as can be seen from an examination of his graphs in Figs. 33 and 34. His results appear to be predictable, and he showed that they apply in several animals. The phenomenon should be investigated further to seek the causes of the periodicity, particularly as they may relate to the arresting of DNA synthesis and of nuclear replication.

ASPECTS OF RNA
SYNTHESIS AND DISTRIBUTION

In our discussions to the present moment, we have considered RNA primarily in terms of information flow. The role of RNA in cellular activity goes beyond that of providing information to be translated and machinery to implement the translation. RNA is synthesized and degraded. In the process it draws from pools and contributes to pools the components of which serve a variety of functions in the metabolic system of the cell. The mechanisms whereby RNA is produced and degraded and the distribution of RNA are of interest.

Schmidt et al. (1948) and Elson et al. (1954) determined that there is no net synthesis of RNA in the sea urchin embryo. Tocco et al. (1963) and Comb et al. (1965a) have more or less confirmed this finding. In this organism where appropriate nutrients in the surrounding medium may be lacking and where growth up to the time of the formation of the larva is negligible, many molecular types must be synthesized at the cost of degrading others. The RNA resources of the embryo are maintained at an operational level by a balancing of the processes of anabolism and catabolism, and the timing of these processes must in all probability be extremely critical with respect to the developmental process as a whole.

Most of the early studies on RNA synthesis were marked by one species or another of shortcoming, as might be expected inasmuch as many of the techniques used had not reached the state where they could be considered adequate unto the complexity of the problems involved. A good proportion of early studies were of a cytochemical nature. This type of approach may often yield information the value of which is largely qualitative. Such information may be useful in determining such things as large local variations in amounts of RNA in regions of the embryo but is generally of limited value.

Since work on problems of RNA synthesis had been in progress for many years before the existence of three basic types of RNA was discovered, it is apparent that many early studies made measurement on all three types in aggregate, and that thus a loss in the usefulness of such studies was sustained. It is generally true that the bulk of the RNA isolated in these experiments was ribosomal, and that, where measurements by ultraviolet spectrophotometry, the orcinol reaction, and certain other analytical tests are concerned, variations in the quantitative data caused by the presence of m-RNA or t-RNA may not have been large. Where incorporation of radioactive precursors into RNA was involved and measurements on specific activity were made, the validity of results is often questionable. Where the information is valid, it may be useful only in a general sort of way.

The early studies on the RNA content of the embryo reveal fluctuations throughout the course of development, suggesting the alternation of synthesis and degradation of RNA. Such fluctuations were described by Bäckström (1959) in *Paracentrotus lividus*. He found that the RNA content underwent a temporary decrease immediately after fertilization. Such a decrease had been reported in the same species by Elson et al. (1954). Both of these workers, as well Olsson (1965, 1966), found evidence also of long-term fluctuations in RNA content. These were described as a gradual buildup to blastula, a decrease at hatching, and a buildup after mesenchyme blastula or after gastrula. The decrease in RNA reported by Elson and Bäckström to occur after fertilization must be supposed to reflect largely a decrease in ribosomal RNA. Ribosomal RNA not only participates in polysome formation, but serves from fertilization onward as a biosynthetic reservoir. A decrease in ribosomal RNA has been reported following fertilization by Comb and Brown (1964), Slater and Spiegelman (1966), and Nemer and Infante (1967a, 1967b). It is much more difficult to explain the increases of RNA during cleavage reported by early workers than to explain the loss following fertilization. The only RNA being synthesized during this period is m-RNA, according to the findings of most workers. An increase in m-RNA content presumably would be difficult to detect by the techniques used by some of the early workers. Studies by Nemer and Infante (1967a) involving phenol extractions and determinations on the persistence of the 13S particle from egg ribosomes of *Strongylocentrotus purpuratus* give the following picture of the content of ribosomal RNA in the embryo: From fertilization onward there is a very gradual, but continuous, decline in ribosomal content. Up to gastrula the decline reflects the loss of egg ribosomes. Following mesenchyme blastula the loss of egg ribosomes becomes more precipitous. At gastrula the synthesis of new ribosomes begins to compensate for the loss of egg ribosomes. The net result, however, is a continued slow decline in total ribosomal content. As has been noted previously, some workers have failed to detect the 13S RNA.

Comb and Brown (1964) reported a stark loss of ribosomal RNA from the cytoplasm from fertilization through blastula and a concomitant and essentially corresponding increase in nuclear RNA. These experiments should be viewed with some reserve, although they appear to be sufficient unto the time at which they were performed. The RNA was estimated through the use of a lithium chloride precipitation method. The amount of ribosomal RNA was shown to decrease in the cytoplasm by nearly half by the end of swimming blastula. The collective results of more recent work suggest a less severe diminution of ribosomal RNA in the cytoplasm during this period.

Should there be a migration of ribosomes to the nucleus in pregastrula development, as suggested by the work of Comb and Brown, it is reasonable to suspect that some of the ribosomes would be degraded to provide nucleotides for nucleic acid synthesis. Although one can do no more than speculate about it, it is a matter of interest as to whether ribosomes might enter the nucleus to participate in the activity of polysomes. There have been recent reports by Aronson and Wilt (1969) and Wilt et al. (1969) of the presence of polysomes in the nucleus.

The RNA of the nucleus of the sea urchin embryo has received but little experimental attention until lately, and the current work is surrounded by some controversy and confusion. Wilt and his coworkers have established that nuclei of sea urchin embryos contain a class of RNA which resembles the nuclear RNA of other organisms in that it turns over with great rapidity, is neither r-RNA or t-RNA, and, except for a very small fraction entering the cytoplasm from time to time, is a permanent resident of the nucleus. The Wilt group estimate that 90 percent of this RNA turns over in association with the nucleus. The relationship of this RNA to the m-RNA of the cytoplasm with respect to information content has not been established in the sea urchin. What may be a comparable RNA in mammalian cells has been shown to have an overlap in sequences with the m-RNA of the cytoplasm. This mammalian-cell nuclear RNA has been viewed as undergoing a processing wherein the molecule transports a part of its sequences to the cytoplasm and degrades the remainder into the acid-soluble pools, although proof of this concept is lacking (see Darnell et al., 1969).

Wilt et al. (1969) have compared sedimentation profiles of nuclear RNA and cytoplasmic m-RNA in the sea urchin embryo. Both are heterodisperse, but the nuclear RNA is generally of a much larger size than the cytoplasmic m-RNA, as has been reported in other organisms.

Aronson and Wilt (1969) reported that DNA-like RNA exists in the nucleus on membrane-bound polysomes. Their defense of this assertion included the fact that the particles containing this RNA appeared like polysomes under electron microscopy, that they were easily destroyed by RNAase and pronase, that they were sensitive to EDTA, that they sedimented over a range of 150 to 400S, and that 18S and 28S particles could be extracted from them. Their findings indicate that some nuclear RNA on these polysomes is a precursor to cytoplasmic m-RNA, and that in pregastrular development there is a transfer every 15–20 minutes of nuclear RNA to the cytoplasm at a constant rate of about 6 percent of the initial rate of nuclear RNA synthesis. It would appear from their theory that the selected nuclear polysomes are stabilized and move to the cytoplasm to become active in protein synthesis. This concept remains to be resolved against a massive amount of evidence that points to the cytoplasm as the site of formation of cytoplasmic polysomes.

If this finding of the presence of polysomes in the nucleus is confirmed, the function of these particles remains to be established. Wilt et al. (1969) submit that the forming of nuclear RNA on polysomes may represent a scanning or selection mechanism to determine which RNA will be stabilized and exported to the cytoplasm. Polysomes forming in the appropriate immediate nuclear environment will be those selected to undergo this experience. Perhaps the retention in the nucleus and quick degradation of a large amount of RNA stems from the rejection by this system of large amounts of transcribed RNA that is not immediately useful in development. It would appear more probable that such RNA serves some unknown, possibly regulatory, function in the nucleus.

These experiments are controversial. They are representative of the entire picture that is developing in the study of RNA metabolism and utilization. As techniques and methods become more precise, situations show themselves to be infinitely more complicated than they were previously believed to be. The more complicated the problems become, the more difficult it is to evaluate and resolve them. For example, Fromson and Nemer (1969) also report finding particles of polysome dimension in the nucleus. They note that if these particles are first purified and then treated with EDTA they can be shown not to be EDTA sensitive and are not polysomes. The description of the DNA-like RNA of the nucleus that has been provided by Wilt and his associates appears to be in agreement with those given for the nuclear RNA of other organisms. The problem remaining to be resolved is that of the nature of the large particle with which they report the RNA to be associated. Suggestions have been made that it might be a large nuclear ribonucleoprotein particle of undetermined nature or an artifact caused by the binding of nuclear RNA to other particles of the nucleus, although these investigators have performed tests which show that the RNA does not appear to bind to nuclear elements.

The presence of polysomes in the nucleus would seem to imply the need for a pool of intact ribosomes in the nucleus, whether they arise from a cytoplasmic source, as would be implied by the findings of Comb and his co-workers, or are of nuclear origin. At the time of this writing we are aware of no studies that have revealed the presence of such a pool in the nucleus of the sea urchin embryo.

We have discussed various experiments in which the synthesis of RNA has been considered in the light of different phenomena occurring in the embryo. Mention should be made of some experiments that have been devoted to the study of RNA synthesis for its own sake. The rate of synthesis of rapidly labeled RNA was studied and characterized in embryos of *Strongylocentrotus purpuratus* for stages from midcleavage to pluteus by Kijima and Wilt (1969) and for unfertilized and fertilized eggs and early cleavage by Wilt (1970). They determined the kinetics of labeling by measuring the incorporation of guanosine into GTP and GMP of hydrolyzed RNA. In the later stages of development, the increase in synthesis of RNA per embryo with time was exceeded by the increase in number of cells in the embryo, so that a decrease in the rate of synthesis of RNA per genome was apparent. Where labeling periods of some length were used, the incorporation decreased as labeling time was extended. This failure to maintain initial rate of incorporation has also been observed by Comb et al. (1965a) and by Siekevitz et al. (1966). It could indicate that some of the newly made RNA is unstable and is degraded. Kijima and Wilt also demonstrated by autoradiography that in a 2-hour period immediately prior to gastrula the bulk of the newly synthesized RNA remained in the nucleus with very little entering the cytoplasm.

As have earlier workers, Wilt found there to be little or no RNA synthesis in the unfertilized egg, nor would his technique reveal any appreciable synthesis in the period immediately following fertilization. It is recognized from the work of Kedes and Gross (1969b) and of Rinaldi and Monroy (1969) that RNA synthesis does occur almost immediately after fertilization. At the 16-cell stage, Wilt found RNA synthesis to be intensive and suggested that a rate change may occur at that time.

There is broad, but not universal, agreement among investigators that the synthesis of r-RNA, which ceases upon the dissolution of the nucleolus at the end of oogenesis, is resumed after gastrula and not before. The work of Comb and his associates is usually cited as evidence of the timing of the recrudescence of r-RNA synthesis in the embryo, although Nemer (1963) reported that an RNA with sedimentation properties like those of maternal r-RNA is synthesized after gastrula. The Comb group demonstrated the production of new r-RNA at early pluteus in embryos of *Lytechinus variegatus* through the use of labeled methionine on the assumption that ribosomal RNA is methylated immediately following its synthesis (Comb, 1965, Comb et al., 1965a). They also detected the presence of r-RNA after gastrula through the use of pulse and chase experiments with ^{32}P. Wilt et al. (1969) have also noted from unpublished results that methylation of bases of r-RNA does not occur until after gastrula. It is interesting that Comb and his co-workers were quite dubious about there being any significant synthesis of ribosomal RNA in the embryo before the feeding stage (see Comb et al., 1965a; Comb and Silver, 1966).

Comb and Silver (1966) also examined the labeling of basic proteins in development in *Lytechinus variegatus* and noted at early pluteus the first incorporation into proteins that could be identified with ribosomes.

Active incorporation of label into the 45S precursor of r-RNA was reported by Nemer and Infante (1967a) from sedimentation analysis of pulse-labeled RNA from early gastrula of *Lytechinus pictus*. These workers proposed that from late gastrula to pluteus the synthesis of r-RNA overshadows that of all other classes of RNA. Giudice and Mutolo (1967, 1969) placed the time of the inception of active synthesis of r-RNA between gastrula and prism, but intimated that some low-level r-RNA synthesis might occur before that time. From observations of labeling of 18S and 28S RNA in 1969, they inferred that such low-level synthesis might occur as early as blastula. Sconzo et al. (1970) preloaded embryos of *Paracentrotus lividus* with radioactive precursors in the period of development to early blastula to prevent permeability problems and found that the synthesis of 28S RNA is activated at swimming blastula and proceeds at a very low level, although it is synthesized more extensively in later development.

The import of all this work is that significant synthesis of ribosomal RNA occurs only after gastrula. Emerson and Humphreys (1970, 1971), however, assert that r-RNA is synthesized in the cells of the cleaving embryo at perhaps 75–80 percent of the rate of its synthesis in the pluteus. They submit that this synthesis is not detected in sedimentation analysis because the labeled product is obscured by DNA-like RNA. Through the use of methylated albumin kieselguhr columns they were able to separate DNA-like RNA from bulk r-RNA in cleaving embryos of *Strongylocentrotus purpuratus*. They discovered a radioactive peak moving with the bulk r-RNA that appeared from its base ratios to contain a large amount of 28S RNA. They were able to expand this analysis and estimate the amount of such labeled RNA produced.

The question which follows immediately is that of how much r-RNA might manage to be produced in the absence of a nucleolus. Upon examination of cleavage nuclei by phase microscopy, Emerson and Humphreys found that during the cell cycle several minute atypical nucleoli form in each nucleus and manifest a tendency toward fusion that is interrupted by the mitotic cycle. They propose that these nucleoli are functional in RNA synthesis and are prevented by the rapidity of cell proliferation from forming a single large nucleolus. Karasaki (1968) reported small nucleoli in some cells at blastula but did not assess their ability to incorporate label. He did report that nucleoli at gastrula show a positive cytochemical test for RNA.

By the same techniques as those used to demonstrate the synthesis of r-RNA, the Comb group (see, for example, Comb et al., 1965a) reported that the synthesis of t-RNA begins after gastrula. As has been noted previously, t-RNA is believed not to be synthesized during cleavage and blastula, and as has been demonstrated by Glišin and

Glišin (1964), the labeling of t-RNA that is seen following fertilization may be attributed to pCpCpA end labeling. In general, the studies of t-RNA that have been conducted in the sea urchin embryo have concentrated more on its activation than on the synthesis of its primary structure.

The rate, extent, and timing of RNA synthesis, as well as the class of RNA synthesized, although important in development, must actually become truly meaningful in the developmental program only against the background of delicate control machinery that directs the selective utilization of RNA. Perhaps this is illustrated in the experiments of Butros (1969). He developed a technique of inducing the cells of the embryo to take up from the medium any fraction of RNA extracted from fellow embryos. Having so succeeded, he attempted to break an actinomycin D block by introducing into the embryo arrested at blastula template from embryos in early gastrula. The exogenous RNA not only failed to break the block but paralyzed the swimming movements of the blastula and actually prevented gastrulation in normal embryos.

Only a small amount of work has been done on investigating the production of the enzyme, RNA polymerase, in the sea urchin. Roeder and Rutter (1969 and 1970) have isolated three RNA polymerases from embryos of *Strongylocentrotus purpuratus*. These enzymes show different sensitivities to magnesium and manganese ions. The nature of their activities has not been definitely established. One is thought to be associated with the synthesis of r-RNA. It increases in proportion to the amount of cell division throughout embryogenesis so that the amount of enzyme per cell is relatively constant. The other two, one of which is purported to be associated with m-RNA synthesis, increase but little in amount through the course of development, so that the amount of enzyme per cell decreases.

RNA AND PROTEIN SYNTHESIS IN OOGENESIS

The production and activity of RNA have to this point been considered primarily with respect to the unfertilized egg or the postfertilization period. Experimentation on the period of oogenesis has been somewhat scant until recent years, particularly from a chemical standpoint. The bulk of the investigations that have been performed have been of a cytochemical nature. Whereas many of these have obvious cytological merit, they are less informative with respect to the nature and activity of RNA at oogenesis than are experiments of the biochemical type. Rather than to attempt a broad review of the cytochemical and other cytological work that has been done, we shall select samples of this type of work for consideration. Many of these experiments have examined both RNA synthesis and protein synthesis. In view of the intimate association that exists between the two, we shall not attempt to divorce them, even though we are primarily concerned here with RNA.

Immers in 1961 noted that the nucleolus is the site of the first incorporation of ^{14}C algal hydrolysate in the oocytes of *Paracentrotus lividus, Echinus esculentus,* and *Sphaerechinus granularis.* Algal hydrolysates used in this type of work contain a variety of radioactive amino acids. Presumably the label in the nucleolus is associated with the formation of ribosomal protein.

Cowden (1962) made a cytochemical study in *Lytechinus variegatus* on the synthesis of RNA and the formation of yolk during oogenesis. He found the cytoplasm to be only slightly basophilic in the smallest oocytes (basophilia normally being assumed to be an indication of the presence of RNA). There was a steady increase in nucleolar and cytoplasmic RNA production throughout oogenesis. Terminal oocytes showed an intensely basophilic cytoplasm. Cowden also showed an increase in protein synthesis over the same period, with weak reactions of the appropriate stains seen in young oocytes and strong reactions in terminal oocytes. Erb and Maurer (1962) found a proportionality between the size of the oocyte and the rate of amino acid incorporation into its proteins.

Ficq (1964) found that actinomycin D inhibits the incorporation of ^{3}H-cytidine and ^{3}H-uridine into nucleolar RNA of oocytes of *Paracentrotus lividus,* but does not inhibit the incorporation of labeled phenylalanine into nucleolar proteins. Puromycin, as might be expected, was found to produce a heavy inhibition of protein synthesis. Ficq observed an extensive synthesis of r-RNA in young oocytes, which ceases as the oocyte matures and is virtually absent in the unfertilized egg.

Sanchez (1968) examined the effect of actinomycin D on several aspects of development of the oocytes of *Paracentrotus lividus.* His studies involved the use of both staining and autoradiography. His results showed an increase in nuclear metabolism at the end of oogenesis in control embryos. Embryos treated with actinomycin D showed an interference with migration of RNA and basic proteins to the cytoplasm, causing them to accumulate in the nucleus.

Esper (1965) made a histochemical study of oocyte development and noted that the young oocyte appears to be concerned primarily with RNA synthesis and that vitellogenesis gets underway only as oogenesis draws to a close.

Collectively, these studies reflect an intense synthesis of ribosomal RNA, the only aspect of RNA activity that would be expected to reveal itself where staining techniques are used. The interference with migration of RNA to the cytoplasm caused by actinomycin D reported by Sanchez appears to refer to ribosomal RNA. There is no ready explanation for such a phenomenon. The actinomycin D insensitivity of protein synthesis in the oocyte, as noted by Ficq, points to the necessity of extending studies of mechanisms of stabilization of template to include an examination of the situation in the oocyte. The increasing rate of protein synthesis seen as the oocyte matures is not surprising, since vitellogenesis, which has a heavy requirement for protein synthesis, is a terminal event in oogenesis.

Through a modification of the method of Nakano and Monroy (1958) wherein acid-soluble pools could be labeled during oogenesis and later stages by injecting radioactive material into the body of the female, Gross et al. (1965) were able to study RNA synthesis during the later stages of oogenesis. They found that a forced partial spawning of gravid females instigated by the use of an electric current would stimulate the incorporation of label into the RNA of maturing oocytes. Mature eggs with radioactive RNA could then be collected after several days of incubation. Most of the activity in RNA extracted by the hot phenol method was found in the 28S and 18S ribosomal RNA. A smaller, more variable amount was found in material sedimentating in the 4S region. Evidence from distribution of label in density-gradient profiles and from the spectrum of peaks eluted from methylated albumin kieselguhr columns, as well as preliminary hybridization studies, demonstrated that some messenger RNA was synthesized also.

Piatigorsky and Tyler (1967) injected labeled uridine into previously spawned females of *Lytechinus pictus* and *Strongylocentrotus purpuratus* and then obtained batches of mature eggs at various periods up to 3 months after injection. The urchins retained about 95 percent of the label, of which 20–32 percent was recovered in the eggs. They found 70–80 percent of the recovered label in ribosomal RNA in the mature eggs, and 5–10 percent in 4S RNA. Between 10 and 20 percent of the label appeared in heterogeneously sedimenting RNA, which they assumed might be m-RNA.

Piatigorsky et al. (1967) were able to use a technique of artificial shedding to obtain from *Lytechinus pictus* batches of eggs that contained extremely high percentages of (unlabeled) oocytes. They compared these batches with batches of mature unfertilized eggs with respect to their ability to incorporate exogenous ^{3}H-uridine and ^{14}C-valine into RNA and proteins, respectively. Mature eggs incorporated virtually no uridine and very little valine. The batches strong in oocyte content incorporated appreciable amounts of uridine into RNA. They incorporated 15 or 16 times as much valine into protein as did the unfertilized eggs. The valine incorporation into both oocytes and mature eggs occurred on polysomes. The authors found that actinomycin D inhibited uridine incorporation in oocyte batches, although it appears not to have eliminated it completely. Valine incorporation was found to be actinomycin D insensitive. In some instances, actinomycin D was found to be stimulatory to valine incorporation into protein of oocytes, a circumstance that to date has not been explained. These investigators have taken note of the fact that their comparisons on synthesis between oocytes and mature eggs do not take into consideration differences in size of amino acid pools or in permeability to labeled precursors that may exist between the two. This is an appropriate reservation.

SOME CHARACTERISTICS
OF RIBOSOMES AND RIBOSOMAL RNA

The mechanics of ribosome formation and of the elaboration of the ribosomal subunits have been given but little study in the sea urchin embryo. It is to be presumed that the small subunits are formed in much the same way as in other eukaryotic cells. The manner in which these subunits are probably formed in HeLa cells has been described by Darnell (1968). It is believed that a 45S particle is formed in the nucleolus, methylated, and cleaved into a succession of particles, which ultimately give rise to the 18S ribosomal subunit and a 32S particle. The 32S r-RNA particle produces the 28S ribosomal subunit. A 5S r-RNA particle associates itself with the nascent r-RNA particles and is ultimately found in association with the 28S subunit. This 5S particle appears, from the evidence of hybridization studies, to arise from a different locus on the DNA molecule than that which produces the 45S particle. The 45S particle has been identified in sedimentation analysis of sea urchin gastrulae by Nemer and Infante (1967a). Sy and McCarty (1970 and 1971) isolated the 5S particle from embryos of *Arbacia punctulata*. It was found to have an S-value of 5.8S and to be hydrogen bonded to the 28S particle. It contains possibly 140–150 nucleotides. It can be released from the 28S particle by heat and urea solutions, hydridizes to DNA to a small degree, and is not methylated. These investigators were able to effect reassociation of 5S and 28S particles *in vitro*. They propose that this particle may possibly hold the 28S subunit in the correct three-dimensional configuration to allow for the addition of peptide moieties as the mature ribosome is formed. A "t-like" RNA reported by Comb and Katz (1964) and Comb et al. (1965b) and thought to be a possible precursor of t-RNA appears similar to the 5S RNA and may have been mistaken for it.

A good general picture of the structure and properties of ribosomes may be obtained from Spirin and Gavrilova (1969). A perusal of this treatise will show that the bulk of the information that permits a description of the morphology of a ribosome and the formulation of theories as to the manner of its function derives from studies made on bacterial ribosomes. That which is known of the nature of ribosomes of eukaryotic cells is not based to any extent on studies made on the sea urchin embryo. Some work has been done in the sea urchin embryo, to be sure. Sedimentation coefficients (S_{20w}) and buoyant densities of ribosomes and their subunits were determined for *Strongylocentrotus purpuratus* and *Lytechinus pictus* by Infante and Nemer (1968), for example, and an occasional measurement of these values is seen elsewhere. Maggio et al. (1968), for instance, have determined buoyant densities of ribosomes in *Paracentrotus lividus* and *Sphaerechinus granularis*. Perhaps in the future there will be something to be gained by collecting and tabulating all such data, but at present it can be said that such measurements are generally made not to obtain a picture of the nature of the ribosome in the sea urchin embryo, but to demonstrate some point about the function of the ribosome as that function relates to the developmental picture as a whole.

Sea urchin embryologists have been interested for some time in the question of whether ribosomes of the unfertilized egg undergo changes upon fertilization and whether ribosomes of the egg differ from those produced at gastrula. Egg ribosomes have been shown to be identical to those of the embryo as far as most physical properties are concerned. Occasionally, some oddity of the egg ribosome is reported. We have already cited the example of the 13S particle derived from a subunit of the egg ribosomes of *Strongylocentrotus purpuratus* (see Nemer and Infante, 1967a). Maggio et al. (1968) have reported that the ribosomes of the unfertilized egg are much more resistant to dissociation into subunits in a buffer low or lacking in magnesium ions than are those of the embryo at mesenchyme blastula. Since trypsin abolishes this difference, these workers suggest that the reluctance of the ribosomes of the unfertilized egg to dissociate may be due to a trypsin-sensitive substance, presumably a protein, which is complexed with them and which interferes with the dissociation. Presumably, they relate the presence of this substance to the theory that ribosomes of the unfertilized egg are incompetent to participate in protein synthesis because of the activity of a trypsin-sensitive repressor.

Hanocq and Quertier (1967) and Mutolo et al. (1967) have compared electrophoretic profiles of the ribosomal proteins of the unfertilized egg with those found in various developmental stages of the embryo. The experiments imply that if there are differences in the ribosomes of the egg and the embryo those differences do not lie in the nature of the ribosomal protein species.

Mutolo and Giudice (1967) compared 28S RNA from different stages of development with respect to its ability to hybridize with DNA. They reported a slight difference in competition between the subunit at the 2-cell stage and at the prism, suggesting changes in base sequence. The difficulty here is that even a very modest contamination with DNA-like RNA would introduce error that could account for such differences.

Whereas the existence of minor differences between egg and embryonic ribosomes cannot be discounted, it would appear that the continual search for such differences may reflect an overemphasis placed by embryologists on the importance of the ribosome as a control mechanism in developmental information flow.

ASPECTS OF THE
ACTIVATION OF TRANSFER RNA

Transfer RNA has been regarded as a possible mechanism for controlling protein synthesis in some cell systems. In phage infections species of r-RNA are sometimes altered or new species of t-RNA appear, a circumstance that has been inferred to reflect regulatory mechanisms in action. Since several different triplets may code for the insertion of a given amino acid into a peptide chain and since specific synthetases exist to activate different species of t-RNA, it has been thought that selective activity of certain synthetases at various times in development might control the types of protein being synthesized. Evidence for the existence of multiple forms of a given amino acyl t-RNA and for differential activity of synthetases in the sea urchin embryo has been obtained.

The methods used to obtain such data have varied somewhat. Ideally, the t-RNA is extracted from the embryo at a given developmental stage and stripped of its amino acids. Synthetases from the same stage and the appropriate labeled amino acid are added to the stripped t-RNA in a reaction mixture, and the mixture is incubated. The t-RNA's are separated on a methylated albumin kieselguhr column and quantitated. Sometimes the synthetases from a given developmental stage are allowed to charge a standard spectrum of t-RNA, such as yeast t-RNA.

In 1967 Ceccarini et al. demonstrated quantitative changes in synthetase activity in development by showing that valyl t-RNA synthetase is twice as active at mesenchyme blastula as in the unfertilized egg of *Paracentrotus lividus.* Yang and Comb (1968) demonstrated two forms of lysyl t-RNA in the egg and 2-cell stage of *Lytechinus variegatus.* Molinaro and Mozzi (1969) showed that multiple forms of leucyl, tyrosyl, arginyl, and seryl t-RNA exist in embryos of *Paracentrotus lividus.* An examination of synthetase activity at different stages in development of embryos of *Strongylocentrotus purpuratus* by Zeikus et al. (1969) showed quantitative

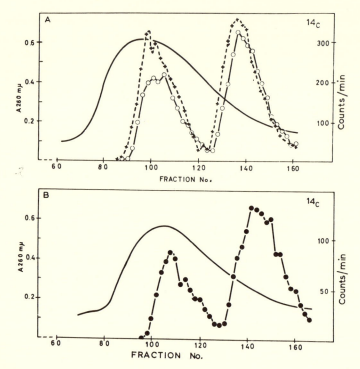

Figure 35

(A) Profile of yeast methionyl-t-RNA charged with activating enzyme extracted from unfertilized eggs (crosses) and plutei (open circles). (B) Enzyme extracted from blastula. Solid lines represent absorbances. Curves suggest that the activity of synthetases for two species of methionyl-t-RNA vary quantitatively and independently throughout the course of development. (From Ceccarini and Maggio. Reproduced from *Biochim. Biophys. Acta, 190,* 1969, p. 558, Fig. 2.)

differences for synthetases of leucyl t-RNA between egg and blastula, the emergence of a new species of lysyl t-RNA at mesenchyme blastula, and shifts in the elution profiles of lysyl and seryl t-RNA between egg and blastula. Ceccarini and Maggio (1969) reported quantitative variations in the activity of synthetases associated with well-defined peaks representing two species of methionyl t-RNA between unfertilized egg, blastula, and pluteus of *Paracentrotus lividus,* as shown in Fig. 35.

Collectively, these findings show clearly that there is differential activity of the synthetases throughout the course of development. This activity cannot at present be construed to imply that the synthetases are serving as a mechanism to regulate protein synthesis. The findings could, for example, reflect the workings of a program of differential activation of synthetases or of changes in the rate of synthesis of these enzymes that serves to ensure that the supply of activated t-RNA's become neither limiting nor excessive at given times in development.

REFERENCES

Aronson, A. I., and F. H. Wilt, 1969. Properties of nuclear RNA in sea urchin embryos. *Proc. Nat. Acad. Sci., U. S. A., 62,* 186–193.

Bäckström, S., 1959. Changes in ribonucleic acid content during early sea urchin development. *Arkiv. Zool., 12,* 339–342.

Brandhorst, B. P., and T. Humphreys, 1971. Synthesis and decay rates of major classes of deoxyribonucleic acid-like ribonucleic acid in sea urchin embryos. *Biochemistry, 10,* 877–881.

Butros, J., 1969. Entry and action of exogenous RNA on protein synthesis in the sea urchin. *Acta Embryol. Morphol. Exp.* (Palermo), *1,* 70–90.

Ceccarini, C., and R. Maggio, 1969. A study of the aminoacyl transfer RNA synthetases by methylated albumin kieselguhr column chromatography in *Paracentrotus lividus. Biochim. Biophys. Acta, 190,* 556–559.

Ceccarini, C., R. Maggio, and G. Barbata, 1967. Aminoacyl s-RNA synthetases as possible regulators of protein synthesis in the embryo of the sea urchin, *Paracentrotus lividus. Proc. Nat. Acad. Sci., U. S. A., 58,* 2235–2239.

Comb, D. G., 1965. Methylation of nucleic acids during sea urchin embryo development. *J. Mol. Biol., 11,* 851–855.

Comb, D. G., and R. Brown, 1964. Preliminary studies on the degradation and synthesis of RNA components during sea urchin development. *Exp. Cell Res., 34,* 360–370.

Comb, D. G., and S. Katz, 1964. Studies on the biosynthesis and methylation of transfer RNA. *J. Mol. Biol., 8,* 790–800.

Comb, D. G., S. Katz, R. Branda, and C. J. Pinzino, 1965a. Characterization of RNA species synthesized during early development of sea urchins. *J. Mol. Biol., 14,* 195–213.

Comb, D. G., N. Sarkar, J. DeVallet, and C. J. Pinzino, 1965b. Properties of transfer-like RNA associated with ribosomes. *J. Mol. Biol., 12,* 509–513.

Comb, D. G., and D. J. Silver, 1966. Synthesis of basic proteins and cellular RNA species during sea urchin development. *National Cancer Institute Monograph 23,* U.S. Government Printing Office, Washington, D.C., 325–326.

Cowden, R. R., 1962. RNA and yolk synthesis in growing oocytes of the sea urchin, *Lytechinus variegatus, Exp. Cell Res., 28,* 600–604.

Crippa, M., and P. R. Gross, 1969. Maternal and embryonic contributions to the functional messenger RNA of early development. *Proc. Nat. Acad. Sci., U. S. A., 62,* 120–127.

Darnell, J. E., 1968. Ribonucleic acid from animal cells. *Bacteriol. Rev., 32,* 262–290.

Darnell, J. E., B. E. H. Maden, R. Soeiro, and G. Pougalates, 1969. The relationship of nuclear RNA to cytoplasmic RNA. In E. W. Hanly (ed.), *Problems in Biology: RNA in Development,* University of Utah Press, Salt Lake City, 349–350.

Davidson, E. H., M. Crippa, A. E. Mirsky, 1968. Evidence for the appearance of novel gene products during amphibian blastulation. *Proc. Nat. Acad. Sci., US, 58,* 152–159.

Ellis, C. H., 1966. The genetic control of sea urchin development: a chromatographic study of protein synthesis in *Arbacia punctulata* embryos. *J. Exp. Zool., 163,* 1–22.

Elson, D., T. Gustafson, and E. Chargaff, 1954. The nucleic acids of the sea urchin during embryonic development. *J. Biol. Chem., 209,* 285–294.

Emerson, C. P., and T. Humphreys, 1970. Regulation of DNA-like RNA and the apparent activation of RNA synthesis in sea urchin embryos: quantitative measurements of newly synthesized RNA. *Develop. Biol., 23,* 86–112.

Emerson, C. P., and T. Humphreys, 1971. Ribosomal RNA synthesis and the multiple, atypical nucleoli in cleaving embryos. *Science, 171,* 898–901.

Erb, W., and W. Maurer, 1962. Autoradiographic studies of the protein metabolism of oocytes and egg cells. *Z. Naturforsch., 17b,* 268–273.

Esper, H., 1965. Studies on the nucleolar vacuole in the oogenesis of *Arbacia punctulata. Exp. Cell Res., 38,* 85–96.

Ficq, A., 1964. Effets de l'actinomycine D et de la puromycine sur le métabolisme de l'oocyte en croissance. *Exp. Cell Res., 34,* 581–594.

Fromson, D., and M. Nemer, 1969. Discussant: Nuclear structures containing heterogenous RNA. In E. W. Hanly (ed.), *Problems in Biology: RNA in Development.* University of Utah Press, Salt Lake City, 349–350.

Giudice, G., and V. Mutolo, 1967. Synthesis of ribosomal RNA during sea urchin development. *Biochim. Biophys. Acta, 138,* 276–285.

Giudice, G., and V. Mutolo, 1969. Synthesis of ribosomal RNA during sea urchin development. II. Electrophoretic analysis and cytoplasmic RNA's. *Biochim. Biophys. Acta, 179,* 341–347.

Glišin, V. R., and M. V. Glišin, 1964. Ribonucleic acid metabolism following fertilization in sea urchin eggs. *Proc. Nat. Acad. Sci., U.S.A., 52,* 1548–1553.

Glišin, V. R., M. V. Glišin, and P. Doty, 1966. The nature of messenger RNA in the early stage of sea urchin development. *Proc. Nat. Acad. Sci., US, 56,* 285–289.

Gross, P. R., 1964. The immediacy of genome control during early development. *J. Exp. Zool. 157,* 21–41.

Gross, P. R., 1967. Protein synthesis, mitosis, and differentiation. *Can. Cancer Conf., 7,* 84–110.

Gross, P. R., L. I. Malkin, and M. Hubbard, 1965. Synthesis of RNA during oogenesis in the sea urchin. *J. Mol. Biol., 13,* 463–481.

Hanocq, F., and J. Quertier, 1967. Etude des proteines ribosomiales au cours du développment de l'oeuf de l'oursin. *Arch. Int. Physiol., 75,* 164–165.

Hnilica, L. S., M. E. McClure, and T. C. Spelsberg, 1971. Histone biosynthesis and the cell cycle. In D. M. P. Phillips (ed.), *Histones and Nucleohistones.* Plenum Publishing Corporation, New York, 187–240.

Hörstadius, S., 1928. Uber die Determination des Keimes bei Seeigeln. *Acta Zool., 9,* 1–191.

Hörstadius, S., 1935. Uber die Determination im Verlaufe der Eiachse bei Seeigeln. *Pubb. Staz. Zool. Napoli, 14,* 251–479.

Immers, J., 1961. Comparative study of the localization in incorporated C^{14}-labeled amino acids and $^{35}SO_4$ in the sea urchin ovary, egg, and embryo. *Exp. Cell Res., 24,* 364–378.

Infante, A. A., and M. Nemer, 1968. Heterogeneous ribonucleoprotein particles in the cytoplasm of sea urchin embryos. *J. Mol. Biol., 32,* 543–565.

Karasaki, S., 1968. The ultrastructure and RNA metabolism of nucleoli in early sea urchin embryos. *Exp. Cell Res., 56,* 163–166.

Kedes, L. H., and P. R. Gross, 1969a. Identification in cleaving embryos of three RNA species serving as templates for the synthesis of nuclear proteins. *Nature* (London), *223,* 1335–1339.

Kedes, L. H., and P. R. Gross, 1969b. Synthesis and function of messenger RNA during early embryonic development. *J. Mol. Biol., 42,* 559–575.

Kijima, S., and F. H. Wilt, 1969. Rate of ribonucleic acid turnover in sea urchin embryos. *J. Mol. Biol., 40,* 235–246.

Maggio, R., M. L. Vittorelli, I. Caffarelli-Mormino, and A. Monroy, 1968. Dissociation of ribosomes of unfertilized eggs and embryos of sea urchins. *J. Mol. Biol., 31,* 621–626.

Molinaro, M., and R. Mozzi, 1969. Heterogeneity of t-RNA during embryonic development of the sea urchin, *Paracentrotus lividus. Exp. Cell Res., 56,* 163–166.

Monroy, A., L. Vitorrelli, and R. Guaneri, 1961. Investigations of the proteins of the cell fluid during the early development of the sea urchin, *Paracentrotus lividus. Acta Embryol. Morphol. Exp., 4,* 77–95.

Mutolo, V., and G. Giudice, 1967. Experiments of hybridization of ribosomal RNA from different stages of sea urchin embryos. *Biochim. Biophys. Acta, 149,* 291–293.

Mutolo, V., G. Giudice, V. Hopps, and G. Donatuti, 1967. Species specificity of embryonic ribosomal proteins. *Biochim. Biophys. Acta, 138,* 216–217.

Nakano, E., and A. Monroy, 1958. A method for the incorporation of radioactive isotopes in the sea urchin egg. *Experientia, 13,* 416–417.

Nemer, M., 1963. Old and new RNA in the embryogenesis of the purple sea urchin. *Proc. Nat. Acad. Sci., U. S. A., 50,* 230–235.

Nemer, M., and A. A. Infante, 1967a. Early control of gene expression. In L. Goldstein (ed.), *The Control of Nuclear Activity.* Prentice-Hall, Inc., Englewood Cliffs, N. J.

Nemer, M., and A. A. Infante, 1967b. Ribosomal ribonucleic acid of the sea urchin egg and its fate during embryogenesis. *J. Mol. Biol., 27,* 73–86.

Neyfakh, A. A., 1960. A study of nuclear function in the development of the sea urchin *Strongylocentrotus droebachiensis* by radiational inactivation. *Dokl. Biol. Sci. Sec., 132,* 376–379.

Neyfakh, A. A., 1964. Radiation investigations of nucleocytoplasmic interrelations in morphogenesis and biochemical differentiation. *Nature* (London), *201,* 880–884.

Olsson, O. A. T., 1965. Changes in the metabolism of ribonucleic acid during early embryonic development of the sea urchin. *Nature* (London), *206,* 843–844.

Olsson, O. A. T., 1966. The ribonucleic acid metabolism during the one-cell stage of the sea urchin development. *Comp. Biochem. Physiol., 17,* 501–507.

Perlmann, P., 1953. Soluble antigens in sea urchin gametes and developmental stages. *Exp. Cell Res., 5,* 394–399.

Perlmann, P., and T. Gustafson, 1948. Antigens in the egg and early developmental stages of the sea urchin. *Experientia, 4,* 481–483.

Perlmann, P., and J. C. Couffer-Kaltenbach, 1957. Quantitative changes in soluble antigens during early development of the sea urchin. *Exp. Cell Res., 12,* 185–188.

Pfohl, R. J., and A. Monroy, 1962a. Changes in some proteins in the course of the development of *Arbacia punctulata. Biol. Bull. Mar. Biol. Lab., Woods Hole, 123,* 477.

Pfohl, R. J., and A. Monroy, 1962b. Electrophoretic and ultracentrifugal analysis of the fractionated extracts of *Arbacia punctulata* eggs and early plutei. *Biol. Bull. Mar. Biol. Lab., Woods Hole, 123,* 477.

Piatigorsky, J., H. Ozaki, and A. Tyler, 1967. RNA and protein-synthesizing capacity of labeled oocytes of the sea urchin, *Lytechinus pictus. Develop. Biol., 15,* 1–22.

Piatigorsky, J., and A. Tyler, 1967. Radioactive labeling of RNAs of sea urchin eggs during oogenesis. *Biol. Bull. Mar. Biol. Lab., Woods Hole, 133,* 229–244.

Ranzi, S., 1962. The protein in embryonic and larval development. *Advances in Morphogenesis,* Vol. 2, Academic Press, Inc., New York, 211–257.

Rinaldi, A. M., and A. Monroy, 1969. Polyribosome formation and RNA synthesis in the early post-fertilization stages of the sea urchin egg. *Develop. Biol., 19,* 73–86.

Roeder, R. G., and W. J. Rutter, 1969. Multiple forms of DNA-dependent RNA polymerase in eukaryotic organisms. *Nature* (London), *224,* 234–237.

Roeder, R. G., and W. J. Rutter, 1970. Multiple ribonucleic acid polymerases and ribonucleic acid synthesis during sea urchin development. *Biochemistry, 9,* 2543–2553.

Sanchez, S., 1968. Effets de l'actinomycine D sur les constituents cellulaires et le métabolisme de l'ARN de l'ovocytes en croissance de *Paracentrotus lividus* (Lmk). *Exp. Cell Res., 50,* 19–31.

Schmidt, G., L. Hecht, and S. J. Thannhauser, 1948. The behavior of the nucleic acids during early development in the sea urchin egg. *J. Gen. Physiol., 199,* 441–446.

Sconzo, G., A. M. Pirrone, V. Mutolo, and G. Giudice, 1970. Synthesis of ribosomal RNA in disaggregated cells of the sea urchin embryo. *Biochim. Biophys. Acta, 199,* 441–446.

Siekevitz, P., R. Maggio, and C. Catalano, 1966. Some properties of a rapidly labeled ribonucleic acid species in *Sphaerechinus granularis. Biochim. Biophys. Acta, 129,* 145–156.

Slater, D. W., and S. Spiegelman, 1966. A chemical and physical characterization of echinoid RNA during embryogenesis. *Biophys. J., 6,* 385–404.

Slater, D. W., and S. Spiegelman, 1970. Transcriptive expression during sea urchin embryogenesis. *Biochim. Biophys. Acta, 213,* 194–207.

Spiegel, M., H. Ozaki, and A. Tyler, 1965. Electrophoretic examination of soluble proteins synthesized in early sea urchin development. *Biochem. Biophys. Res. Commun., 21,* 135–140.

Spiegel, M., and E. S. Spiegel, 1959. The extractable proteins of sea urchin embryos. *Biol. Bull. Mar. Biol. Lab., Woods Hole, 117,* 427.

Spirin, A. S., N. V. Belitsina, and M. A. Aitkhozhin, 1964. Messenger RNA in early embryogenesis. *Zh. Obshch. Biol., 25,* 321–330.

Spirin, A. S., and L. P. Gavrilova, 1969. *The Ribosome.* Springer-Verlag New York, Inc., New York.

Sy, J., and K. S. McCarty, 1970. Characterization of 5.8S RNA from *Arbacia punctulata. Biochim. Biophys. Acta, 199,* 86–94.

Sy, J., and K. S. McCarty, 1971. Formation of a 5.8S–26S sea urchin r-RNA complex. *Biochim. Biophys. Acta, 228,* 517–525.

Terman, S. A., 1970. Relative effect of transcription-level and translation-level control of protein synthesis during early development of the sea urchin. *Proc. Nat. Acad. Sci., U. S. A., 65,* 985–992.

Terman, S. A., and P. R. Gross, 1965. Translational level control of protein synthesis during early development. *Biochem. Biophys. Res. Commun.,* 595–600.

Tocco, G., A. Orengo, and E. Scarano, 1963. Ribonucleic acids in early embryonic development of the sea urchin. 1. Quantitative variations and ^{32}P orthophosphate incorporation studies of the RNA of subcellular fractions. *Exp. Cell Res., 31,* 52–60.

Westin, M., 1969. Effect of actinomycin D on antigen synthesis during sea urchin development. *J. Exp. Zool., 171,* 297–304.

Westin, M., 1972. The occurrence of stage-specific antigens during early sea urchin development. *J. Exp. Zool., 179,* 207–214.

Wilt, F. H., 1970. The acceleration of ribonucleic acid synthesis in cleaving sea urchin embryos. *Develop. Biol., 23,* 444–445.

Wilt, F. H., A. I. Aronson, and J. Wartiovaara, 1969. Function of the nuclear RNA of sea urchin embryos. In E. W. Hanly (ed.), *Problems in Biology: RNA in Development.* University of Utah Press, Salt Lake City, 331–353.

Whiteley, A. H., B. J. McCarthy, and H. R. Whiteley, 1966. Changing populations of messenger RNA during sea urchin development. *Proc. Nat. Acad. Sci., U.S.A., 55,* 519–525.

Whiteley, H. R., B. J. McCarthy, and A. H. Whiteley, 1970. Conservatism of base sequences in RNA for early development of echinoderms. *Develop. Biol., 21,* 216–242.

Yang, S. S., and D. G. Comb, 1968. Distribution of multiple forms of lysyl transfer RNA during early embryogenesis of the sea urchin *Lytechinus variegatus. J. Mol. Biol., 31,* 138–142.

Zeikus, J. G., M. W. Taylor, and C. A. Buck, 1969. Transfer RNA changes associated with early development and differentiation of the sea urchin, *Strongylocentrotus purpuratus. Exp. Cell Res., 57,* 74–78.

CHAPTER X

Some Miscellaneous Problems of Current Interest

We have not attempted to consider all phases of research on the sea urchin embryo in this work. With isolated exceptions, the material omitted represents largely the problems that interested earlier workers in the field, and much of this material has been given more than adequate treatment elsewhere. Among the subjects that we have treated but briefly or have omitted from our discussions are oxygen consumption, glucose and fat metabolism, the activity of certain enzymes, pigment studies, the biochemistry of sea urchin steroids, effects of drugs on development, effects of radiation on development, photodynamic effects, studies on interspecific hybridization, electrical properties of the egg, effects of certain ions on the egg, the permeability of the egg to ions, surface tension properties of the egg, spawning and reproductive periods, and others. Let us make a rough estimate that 70 percent of these studies are covered by bibliographies and brief resumés in Harvey (1956). Boolootian (1966) may be found helpful for bibliographies of more recent work.

We shall terminate our discussion by considering a few selected problems that are currently being given considerable attention and that reveal some interesting aspects of the embryogenetic picture, but which, with the possible exception of reaggregation studies, are probably not destined to develop into major fields of research in sea urchin embryology.

PROBLEMS OF UPTAKE VERSUS
INCORPORATION OF EXOGENOUS PRECURSORS

The common method for the determination of rates of synthesis of molecules in the sea urchin egg and embryo, as with other systems, involves the use of the radioactive precursor. In the experiments on rates of synthesis in an in vivo system, we have recourse only to the exogenous precursor, which must enter the cell before it can be incorporated into the product of synthesis, and hence is subject to the laws and forces governing the permeability of cell membranes. The permeability of eggs and embryos of the sea urchin to ions and to compounds of low molecular weight has been under study for possibly three quarters of a century, and often the egg has been used merely as a system with which to study the phenomenon of permeability itself, as well as the effect on permeability of various parameters and of diverse chemical substances. Permeability of the cells of the embryo to various materials is an important agency in development. It may vary not only in time, with changes observed from one developmental period to another, but also in space, with some regions of the embryo exhibiting high permeability, and others low, to a given material.

In developmental studies, the experimenter usually has two basic types of concern with permeability. At certain times he may wish to determine the extent to which membranes are permeable to materials occurring naturally within the cells under normal physiological conditions or within the medium that the cells inhabit in order to understand either how permeability affects the course of development or how the course of development affects permeability. At other times it is critical that he know the rate at which experimental materials with which he is treating the embryo are entering its cells or being lost from its cells. There is overlap between these two categories of experimental interest, since agents used in experimental treatment may sometimes enter the embryo through normal physiological mechanisms such as active transport systems and since experimental agents such as radioactive precursors are commonly used to study the natural permeability characteristics of the embryonic cells.

An excellent example of the first type of experimental concern is to be found in the early studies on the problem of the increase in rate in protein synthesis following fertilization. The question arose as to whether the increase might be due to an abrupt increase in permeability caused by the activation of the egg. The experiments of Nakano and Monroy (1958a, 1958b), wherein radioactive amino acids were injected into the perivisceral cavity of the adult female urchins, thereby preloading eggs in the gonad with label, offered an approach to the solution of this problem. These workers found radioactivity in the unfertilized egg to be concentrated almost exclusively in the pools of free amino acids. After fertilization there ensues a vigorous incorporation into protein. They could thus offer a reasonably good refutation to the argument that the acceleration of protein synthesis after fertilization is merely a reflection of permeability change. Hultin and Bergstrand (1960) ultimately demonstrated that the postfertilization increase in protein synthesis occurs in in vitro systems, which, of course, do not involve permeability. In forming the hypothesis that an increase in permeability might be responsible for the increase in protein synthesis, the early workers must have assumed that amino acids in appreciable amounts are normally present in the marine environment of sea urchin eggs, unless the increase in protein synthesis is to be considered a laboratory artifact. There appears to be little data as to the availability of precursors of nucleic acids and proteins in spawning beds. We do know that the embryo does not have a requirement for these exogenous precursors between fertilization and pluteus.

An important example of the second category of experimental concern with permeability comes in studies of the relationship between the rate of uptake of precursors to synthesis and the rate of their incorporation into the product of synthesis. Sacher has for many years pleaded the case for more meticulous attention being paid to the relationship between uptake and incorporation. He notes (see Sacher, 1966) that an increase in specific activity of an exogenous precursor can result in an increase in uptake of radioactivity and thus in incorporated activity, and that an additive which affects the rate of uptake of a radioactive substrate may well affect its incorporation into a macromolecule. In 1965 he urged that the determination of the ratio of counts per minute of incorporated label to the counts per minute of total uptake become an established practice, since it is a more meaningful method of comparison of rates of RNA and protein synthesis under varied conditions than is a simple measurement of incorporation. In recent years workers in sea urchin embryology have given considerable attention to uptake–incorporation relationships, whereas earlier workers more often than not ignored them. Uptake studies have repeatedly revealed that despite the fact that the stimulation of protein synthesis at fertilization is independent of permeability there is, nonetheless, a marked increase in the permeability of the sea urchin egg to amino acids and nucleotides following fertilization. These studies have led to a revision of previous ideas on rates of protein synthesis, an increased understanding of the activity of endogenous pools, and some insight into the activity of active-transport systems.

Piatigorsky and Whiteley (1965), working with embryos of *Strongylocentrotus purpuratus* in a study of uptake of ^{14}C-uridine, found that very little precursor could get into the unfertilized egg, but that precursor was taken up readily after fertilization. The time course of uptake after fertilization was characterized by a lag phase, an acceleration phase, and a constant accumulation or plateau phase, the last mentioned of which was attained in the first hour after fertilization. Embryos proved to be very efficient in accumulating label from very low concentrations of the external medium. As the concentration of external uridine was increased, a point was reached where the uptake mechanism appeared to be saturated. A standard uncoupler of phosphorylation, 2,4-dinitrophenol, inhibited uridine uptake, suggesting that the uptake is energy dependent. Free ^{14}C-uridine was found in very low amount in the embryos, and there appeared a good probability that uptake involves a phosphorylation process, which was considered tentatively on the basis of findings from ion-exchange chromatography to convert the uridine to nucleotides, possibly largely uridine triphosphate. The authors have proposed that at fertilization (1) an active-transport system for uridine uptake is activated, and (2) cellular uridine metabolism is initiated and may become a force in uridine uptake.

Mitchison and Cummins (1966) found a similar situation to apply in a study of valine and cytidine uptake in *Paracentrotus lividus*. The rate of uptake of these compounds maximized before the first cleavage and then held at a constant rate, again suggesting the saturation of sites of an active-transport system. The plateau of constant rate of uptake in the instance of valine continued all the way to pluteus. Curves for initial uptake rate versus concentration of valine were similar to Michaelis–Menten curves for enzyme reactions. Uptake of both compounds was inhibited by competitors, and the uptake of valine was shown to be inhibited by the uncoupling of oxidative phosphorylation. Berg (1968) confirmed that the uptake of valine shows a

Michaelis–Menten type of saturation kinetics and reported that it also has a high Q_{10}, a characteristic which would be unexpected if uptake were due primarily to passive diffusion. Bellemare et al. (1968) reported similar evidence for the existence of an active-transport system for leucine.

Although the evidence is compelling that precursors of proteins and nucleic acids are taken into the cells of the embryo by active-transport systems, it appears somewhat unusual that these systems should be present and be activated in an organism during a period in which it has no manifest requirement for exogenous precursors for protein and nucleic acid synthesis. There is some question, however, as to whether their services are directed entirely toward the uptake of exogenous precursors as the embryo progresses through the various developmental stages. As a cleavage furrow forms, the membrane pulls inward between the daughter cells so that arrays of transport enzymes on the surfaces of cells find themselves exposed not only to the external medium but also to the surfaces of adjacent cells. At blastula some of these enzymes also come to lie next to the blastocoel fluid. Such transpositions could conceivably present new situations in which transport enzymes are used. One might suppose that the carriers might, for example, find use in redistributing breakdown products of yolk among cells or in establishing biochemical gradients.

It is becoming clear that descriptions of the activity of transport enzymes in development have in the past been too prone to generalization. Whereas it appears that activity of carriers for uridine in the unfertilized egg may be essentially at ground zero, the same may not be said for transport enzymes for amino acids. Timourian and Denny (1964), Tyler et al. (1966), and Timourian and Watchmaker (1970) have all confirmed the finding of Mitchison and Cummins that there is an increased uptake of amino acids after fertilization, but that many amino acids are accumulated to some degree by the unfertilized egg. It is clear that transport systems for many amino acids, rather than being activated, as in the instance of the carrier for uridine, are merely stimulated to increase their activity upon fertilization. The Tyler group demonstrated that the transport enzymes for several amino acids evince a specificity, so that uptake activity before and after fertilization depends upon the acid involved. Timourian and Watchmaker have reported that the stimulation of the enzyme associated with the uptake of valine does not reveal itself until 5 or

10 minutes after fertilization, and that during that interval the rate of uptake may actually drop below that of the unfertilized egg, although the evidence for this drop is not unequivocal because measurements are rendered difficult by the fact that some valine is lost from the egg at fertilization.

With the complexity of events surrounding the activation of the egg and with the multitude of problems that have hounded those workers who have attempted to discover the cause for the stimulation of protein synthesis following fertilization, it might seem pointless to speculate on the mechanisms involved in the activation of transport enzymes at fertilization. The activity of transport enzymes, however, is commonly found to be linked strongly to the activity of the reactions of oxidative phosphorylation. It is not unreasonable to postulate that the cause for the stimulation or activation of transport enzymes may be sought in the mechanisms (presently unknown) that accelerate respiratory activity at fertilization. The existence of a linkage between mitochondrial activity and activity of transport enzymes, which goes beyond a mere dependence on supplies of ATP, might serve to explain why transport enzymes are turned on when the requirement for them is not immediately apparent.

Although some workers have viewed the presence of active-transport activity following fertilization as simply attesting to the fact that carriers which were synthesized in oogenesis to provide the sex cells with the capability of accumulating precursors from auxiliary cells failed to be degraded when their usefulness ceased and were activated willy-nilly at fertilization, there is some evidence that these carriers are being synthesized almost up to the moment of fertilization. If they are synthesized in the unfertilized egg, the amount synthesized must be small since total protein synthesis in the unfertilized egg is not extensive. Mitchison and Cummins (1966) and Bellemare et al. (1968) have reported that puromycin decreases uptake of valine and leucine, respectively, if administered just before fertilization. If administered at fertilization, there is no inhibition. The obvious reservation to be made here is that these experiments monitor not the synthesis but rather the activity of the enzymes in the presence of the inhibitor. The results could signify that puromycin inhibits the synthesis of some protein (or proteins) that is required for active-transport activity to occur. The same type of reservation applies when experiments involve the use of actinomycin D.

Mitchison and Cummins found that actinomycin D has no effect on the uptake of valine until the time of gastrula, when it lowers uptake severely. This finding implies that no transcription is necessary to maintain the normal activity of the enzyme for the transport of valine prior to gastrula. It need not imply that active-transport enzymes are being synthesized on maternal template during this period. Mitchison and Cummins, in fact, propose that the most plausible explanation for the constant rate of valine uptake in cleavage and the following stages is that new carriers are not being synthesized. An increase in number of carriers would be likely to cause an increase in rate of uptake of valine unless it were to be prevented by controlling parameters, such as metabolic rate or size of the internal pools. With metabolic activity on the increase and pool size relatively constant as far as can be determined from available evidence, it is probable that these parameters do not dispose toward constancy of rate of uptake. Mitchison and Cummins note that if there is no production of new carriers the number of carriers per unit area of cell surface must decrease during cleavage, since there is an increase in surface area of the cells in that period.

A critical problem encountered in the analysis of uptake–incorporation relationships is that of the commerce between the synthesis, the exogenous precursor, and the endogenous pool. The principal question here is that of whether the internal pools are compartmented so that the synthesis may draw precursors either from them or from the exogenous source or whether they are an obligate intermediate for the incorporation of the exogenous precursor into the product of synthesis. Examining this problem in protein synthesis in 1968, Berg was drawn to the conclusion that the endogenous pools of amino acids are compartmented. He was led to this interpretation by two observations in particular. One of these was the demonstration that the time course for incorporation of valine into protein showed a linear relationship. Had endogenous ^{14}C-valine been going into the endogenous pools, some sort of lag due to the difference in rate between entry of label into the pools and incorporation of label into protein would have been expected that would produce a curvilinear relationship. Synthesis appeared to be showing a preference for exogenous valine, which was being incorporated directly, shunting the endogenous pools. The other was the demonstration that in embryos preloaded with ^{14}C-valine, incubation in exogenous "cold" ^{12}C-valine would cause the cessation of incorporation of endogenous ^{14}C-valine into the protein being synthesized. In 1970, Berg reexamined these findings and concluded that both were illusory and could actually be explained in terms of a rapidly expanded endogenous valine pool resulting from a massive influx of the exogenous precursor. He sharpened his time-course curves by the use of scintillation counting with sequential pulses of different duration and found that the curves did show a brief initial curvilinear phase. He postulated that the exogenous valine enters the endogenous pool with great rapidity and quickly raises its specific activity to a level close to that of the external medium. With the two specific activities so nearly the same, the incorporation of endogenous valine gives the impression that exogenous valine is being incorporated directly as manifested by the linearity. He reasoned that if embryos preloaded with ^{14}C-valine are returned to seawater after being incubated in ^{12}C-valine, the rate of incorporation into protein should return to that of controls (preloaded with ^{14}C-valine) in seawater if the endogenous pools are being shunted, but should not return to the rate of the controls if the cold valine is entering the endogenous pools and lowering their specific activity and if the endogenous pools are in turn feeding the synthesis. Figure 36 shows that embryos transferred from a medium containing ^{12}C-valine to seawater at the end of 5 minutes and at the end of 22 minutes both failed to reach the incorporation rate of the controls. The earlier interpretation of the compartmented endogenous pool appeared no longer to be tenable.

The uptake and incorporation of leucine into protein has been studied more recently by Fry and Gross (1970b). In agreement with the findings of Berg on valine, they have shown that internal pools of leucine also are expansible by exogenous precursor and are apparently not compartmented. They have found that, particularly in *Arbacia*, a great deal of leucine in the internal pools is converted into other amino acids. In the internal pools of *Arbacia*, for example, 15 percent of the original leucine label was found in glutamic acid. Because these products of conversion are greatly diluted by their entry into the pools, they appear to have little qualitative effect on the incorporation of label into protein, about 95 percent of which label was found as leucine in these experiments. Berg (1968) reported that approximately 4 to 5 percent of labeled exogenous valine is converted to other low-molecular-weight compounds.

Silver and Comb (1966) and Fry and Gross (1970b) have reported

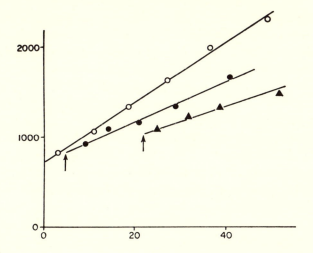

Figure 36

Incorporation of ¹⁴C-valine from the amino acid pool after different periods of time in 20 μg of ¹²C-valine/ml of seawater. Abscissa: min. Ordinate: counts/minute/100 embryos. Early gastrulae of *Lytechinus anamesus* preloaded with ¹⁴C-valine were divided into three batches. One batch in seawater served as controls and is indicated by open circles. A second batch (filled circles) was placed in ¹²C-valine for 5 minutes and transferred (arrow) to seawater. A third batch (triangles) was placed in ¹²C-valine for 22 minutes and transferred (arrow) to seawater. Experiment suggests that as long as exogenous ¹²C-valine is available there is a continued expansion of the pool and a resulting loss in specific activity of the pool [From Berg (1970); by permission.]

a general constancy of size of amino acid pools at various stages in development. Fry and Gross compared the pools of several amino acids at various times up to 2 hours after fertilization with those of the same acids in the unfertilized egg and found no difference as to size, demonstrating that the stimulation of protein synthesis after fertilization is not related to change in size of amino acid pools. They did find striking differences in the composition of amino acid pools between species. This finding confirms the reports of earlier workers, which have been reviewed briefly by Monroy and Maggio (1966). Fry and Gross found, for example, that the free glycine content of *Strongylocentrotus purpuratus* is 96.8 percent of the total amino acid pool as compared with 4.8 percent in *Arbacia punctulata*. It has been known for many years that embryos of certain species of sea urchin have high glycine contents, and several cell physiologists have proposed that glycine may serve an osmotic function in the sea urchin embryo. It is important to consider the possibility that if composition of amino acid pools varies among species of sea urchin, so too may vary the extent to which a given exogenous amino acid is converted to other amino acids upon entering the pools. Fry and Gross have quoted Malkin and Goldschmidt to the effect that the amino acid composition of the pools reflects neither the amino acid composition of the yolk nor that of bulk sea urchin protein, nor does it reflect the amino acid composition of any individual proteins presently known to be synthesized during development.

From their results Fry and Gross were able to work out equations for the specific activity of the internal leucine pools as a function of time, and to develop rate equations for protein synthesis. Their calculations show that the curves for rate of protein synthesis found by many workers, which show a steady and rapid increase in rate during cleavage, another increase during blastula, and on occasion an increase at the onset of gastrula, need to be revised in terms of permeability data. Their results, which do consider permeability, suggest that, at least during cleavage, there is no increase in the absolute rate of protein synthesis.

The experimental methods used by Fry and Gross were subject to error at very low levels of uptake and incorporation, so that they could not make determinations on unfertilized eggs or on eggs immediately after fertilization. Timourian and Watchmaker (1970) report that they can detect an increase in the rate of incorporation of amino acids into protein within the first 2 minutes after fertilization by considering in their calculations the label that is lost from the fertilized egg by back exchange from the endogenous pools. They have accomplished this by using eggs preloaded with ^{3}H-valine and exposing them to ^{14}C-valine at the time of fertilization.

The findings of Fry and Gross that there is no increase in absolute rate of protein synthesis in cleavage, particularly early cleavage, must be resolved against two groups of experiments by other workers. One of these is the finding that the rate at which the cytoplasmic ribosomes become engaged on polysomes suggests that there should be an increase in the rate of protein synthesis. There is no ready explanation for this enigma. The clarification must await the outcome of further study. The other is the fact that in vitro systems have showed tendencies toward an increase in rate in protein synthesis through the cleavage period; but as the authors have observed, in vitro experiments do not necessarily mirror in vivo phenomena. Stavy and Gross (1969), moreover, have reported data from a cell-free system in which, following a rate increase early in the first cleavage cycle, protein synthesis has held a nearly constant rate up to blastula.

Fry and Gross reported that newly synthesized protein is fairly stable with respect to degradation to the pools They found that the loss of label from the acid-insoluble fraction in a 20-hour chase with ^{12}C-leucine was negligible. Berg and Mertes (1970) found that proteins labeled shortly after fertilization undergo an average degradation of 0.8 percent per hour. Their pulse-chase experiments with valine, however, are comparable to those of Fry and Gross in that they show only a small loss of label in newly synthesized protein over a period of 20 hours, with appreciable loss beginning at about 27–28 hours after fertilization. The two groups worked with different species. The thesis of Fry and Gross is that the *de novo* synthesis of proteins is fed from the breakdown of preexisting proteins, presumably yolk proteins, and that there is no rapidly turning over protein fraction that serves as a pool source for new protein synthesis.

It is worthy of note that permeability is not necessarily the only factor to be considered in evaluating rates of incorporation. The volume of the cell may be of importance in considering the extent of synthetic activity. Spiegel and Tyler (1966), for instance, developed a technique for isolating large numbers of micromeres. The ability of the isolated micromeres to incorporate valine was considerably less than that found in a mixture of mesomeres, micromeres, and macromeres. After corrections were made for the volume of the micromeres, however, the incorporation was found to be about the same in each preparation.

FLUCTUATIONS IN THE RATE
OF PROTEIN SYNTHESIS DURING MITOSIS

An interesting problem which has received considerable attention in the past 5 years is that of fluctuations in the rate of protein synthesis during mitotic cycles, particularly the first mitotic cycle. Sofer et al. (1966) observed such fluctuations both in vivo and in cell-free systems derived from 12,000 × *g* supernatants of *Lytechinus variegatus* embryos. The fluctuations were manifested by a drop in the rate of protein synthesis at metaphase and anaphase followed by an increase at about the time of telophase. These workers interpreted these fluctuations as possible examples of regulation of changes in protein synthesis at the translational level. Colchicine, which halts cell division, failed to affect the depression of synthesis, and the changing of the precursor from leucine to valine likewise had no effect. The fact that the phenomenon was observed in vitro suggested that it is unrelated to permeability effects.

In the same year, Gross and Fry (1966) failed to find a depression in protein synthesis in the first cleavage cycle in studies on *Arbacia punctulata* and *Strongylocentrotus purpuratus*. Timourian noted in 1966 both the depression and the absence of the depression in a series of experiments on *Lytechinus pictus* and *Strongylocentrotus purpuratus*. He discounted the possibility that the discrepancy could be due to the precursor used or to fundamental species differences.

The problem was studied in 1968 by Mano. He reported that the phenomenon of cyclic variation of protein synthesis is superimposed on an increasing basal rate of protein synthesis in the first cleavage cycles. He observed the fluctuations in the first three cleavage cycles, but the peak in the first cycle was shown to be much more pronounced than those in the second and third cycles. He also reported that these cyclic variations occur in artificially activated anucleate fragments and in cell-free systems.

Mano examined the problem further in 1970 in three sea urchins from Japanese waters, at which time his experiments revealed that the peaks of the cycles occur in the stage from prophase to metaphase, and the troughs in the stage from anaphase to telophase. If the temperature was lowered, the cycles evinced a longer duration, which was linked to the time required for the cell cycle.

The most crucial problem that must be considered here is the status of the uptake–incorporation relationship during the period in which these fluctuations occur. Mitchison and Cummins (1966) reported minor fluctuations in uptake during the first cell cycle. Fry and Gross (1970a) found fluctuations in both uptake and incorporation curves, with the depression aspect occurring at metaphase (as opposed to anaphase) in *Strongylocentrotus purpuratus* and *Arbacia punctulata*. The curves for uptake and for incorporation showed a remarkable correlation with one another with respect to these fluctuations. The inflections varied from a mild depression (Fig. 37) to a rather sharp notch (Fig. 38). In general, the fluctuations were sharper at higher temperatures, at which cleavage cycles are shorter. With due recognition of the difficulty involved in interpreting these variations, they favored the idea that there are no actual fluctuations in rate of protein synthesis at this time and that probably the variations in incorporation simply reflect variations in uptake. In their experiments they were unable to detect fluctuations in incorporation in the second and third cleavage cycles; hence their results and conclusions reflect a single fluctuation in the first cleavage cycle.

Mano (1970) observed fluctuations in the uptake of label, but asserted that their periodicity was sufficiently different from that of cyclic variations in incorporation for the existence of a cause–effect relationship between the two types of fluctuation to be unlikely. When eggs were preloaded with label before fertilization, the cyclic variations still showed. They were also seen in curves for the percentage of label incorporated versus time.

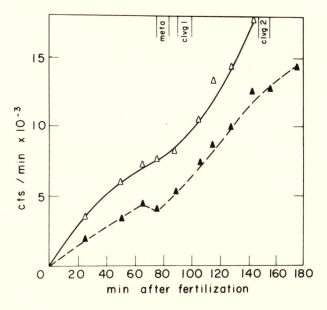

Figure 37

Uptake (open triangles) and incorporation (filled triangles) of ^{14}C-leucine into *Strongylocentrotus purpuratus* embryos that were incubated at 18°C and labeled for 5 minutes at 0.05 μC/ml, specific activity 222 μC/mmole with approximately 2500 embryos/ml. [From Fry and Gross (1970b); by permission.]

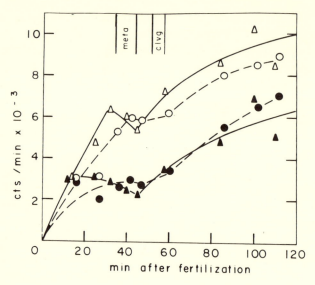

Figure 38

Effect of 10^{-4} M colchicine during the first cleavage. Eggs were taken from a single female and were at the same density in both cultures. Colchicine was added at fertilization. Label was added as 5-minute pulses of ^{14}C-leucine, 0.05 μC/ml. Controls gastrulated, while colchicine-treated cells were arrested at prometaphase. Uptake controls, open triangles; incorporation controls, filled triangles; uptake colchicine-treated cells, open circles; incorporation colchicine-treated cells, filled circles. [From Fry and Gross (1970b); by permission.]

   Although results on the problem of the relationship of cyclic variation in incorporation to fluctuations in uptake are somewhat conflicting, Fry and Gross have produced evidence which offers a convincing refutation to the thesis that the fluctuation in incorporation in metaphase results from a temporary arrest of protein synthesis. Both continuous-labeling experiments and experiments involving preloading the embryos with label after fertilization show no sign of even a brief cessation of protein synthesis.

   A possible explanation that might be considered for the fluctuations is that some species of protein is being synthesized for a brief period and then degraded, possibly becoming a substrate for endogenous proteolytic activity. Fluctuations in in vivo proteolytic activity have been reported in the past (see Kavanau, 1954), but they have never been satisfactorily proved. The problem of lability of newly synthesized protein requires further investigation. Fry and

Gross (1970b) have suggested that newly synthesized protein is quite stable, but studies have generally not been addressed to short-term effects as might be conceived to occur here.

Both Mano and Fry and Gross have concluded that these cyclic changes are independent of the events of karyokinesis and cytokinesis per se. Fry and Gross found that treatment with colchicine to inhibit mitosis had virtually no effect on the fluctuations in uptake and incorporation. Mano, by contrast, found that colchicine partially inhibited cyclic variations in incorporation but did not prevent them from occurring. Both groups found that actinomycin D did not prevent the fluctuations, and Fry and Gross found that when actinomycin D delayed the onset of mitosis there was no comparable delay in the fluctuation in uptake and incorporation curves. When Mano eliminated nuclear division and cytokinesis altogether, with puromycin and cycloheximide, the cyclic variations still occurred. These experiments demonstrate that the control of the cyclic variations is in the cytoplasm.

Cyclic variations in incorporation, in other words, do not require transcription of nuclear genes in the cell cycle in which they occur, and they can exist in the absence of nuclear division. Their timing, however, is normally linked to that of the phases of mitosis when nuclear division does occur. If the variations prove to be caused by fluctuations in uptake, then those fluctuations must be synchronized with the phases of mitosis as well. Fluctuations in uptake are likely to be associated with fluctuations in the activity of active-transport enzymes, which in turn may result from fluctuations in the activity of the respiratory cycles. If, then, the cyclic variations reflect changes in uptake, the command center may perhaps be sought in some aspect of respiratory metabolism which facilitates the events of mitosis or in some unknown agency which controls that aspect. Such a thesis is purely speculative, however.

In 1968 and 1969 Mano reported the induction of cyclic variations in incorporation in cell-free systems. If the findings are confirmed, these experiments would appear to preclude the possibility that these variations are due to fluctuations in uptake. The fluctuations were induced in the $12,000 \times g$ supernatant of unfertilized eggs by the addition of small amounts of the $12,000 \times g$ supernatant from fertilized eggs. Mano isolated from the latter three factors that showed activity in the induction. One appeared to be a translatable m-RNA and another a mixture of low-molecular-weight compounds, possibly providing coenzyme or energetic facilities for protein synthesis. The third was identified with a "proteinous" type of molecule containing SH groups. This factor was postulated to exert a pacemaker function on the cycle, to determine the moment when each cycle begins. Mano believed that the other two factors stimulated protein synthesis in the unfertilized egg supernatant where it is normally low.

Mano (1970) examined the polysome spectra of cell-free systems evincing fluctuations in incorporation and found that they showed a periodicity, corresponding approximately to that of the cycles, in the appearance and disappearance of polysomes in a sedimentation range between 150 and 180S. The range falls within that of the S-polysomes, which have been discussed in a previous chapter. In the basal phase of the synthesis (between the cycles) the average S-value of the polysomes was about 250S. This finding suggests that the protein synthesized in the cycles is different from that synthesized in the basal protein synthesis upon which Mano originally reported the cycles to be superimposed.

ISOZYMES IN THE SEA URCHIN EMBRYO

Attention has been given to the activity of various enzymes in the sea urchin embryo from time to time, but more work needs to be done on the role of enzymes in controlling developmental events. A voluminous literature exists on transcriptional control and translational control of protein synthesis in terms of their possible relationship to the developmental program. Only a scant amount of study, however, has been devoted to the question of whether important developmental events can be initiated and directed by the activation of enzymes. Some work has been done on RNA and DNA polymerases, on proteolytic enzymes that may be involved in liberating substances inhibited through the formation of complexes with proteins, on enzymes possibly involved in yolk utilization, on RNAases, and on some of the respiratory enzymes, but not enough work has been done on the whole to afford a meaningful picture of how much of the control of development may be exercised by enzyme activity.

An important aspect of enzyme regulation of respiratory metabolism, which may be found to be crucial in the control of some events in embryogenesis, is the function of multiple molecular forms of enzymes, or isozymes. This problem has been given considerable study by C. A. Villee and his co-workers. The work has not progressed to the point where the actual activities of isozymes in development can be described in detail. Enough knowledge on the nature and function of isozymes in other systems has been gained, however, to point up the fact that this work in the sea urchin is of considerable importance.

Isozymes are enzymes that exist in multiple forms and catalyze the same general reaction at different rates. Some forms of the enzyme may encourage the reaction to proceed in a forward direction, whereas others may promote its reversal. The best-known isozymes are associated with the reactions of respiratory metabolism. Isozymes of lactate dehydrogenase, for example, vary in their ability to drive pyruvate to lactate and thus to promote anaerobic metabolism or to facilitate the entry of pyruvate into the citric acid cycle and thus to promote aerobic metabolism. The catalytic propensities of respiratory isozymes in a given tissue tend to harmonize with the respiratory requirements of the tissue, and since such respiratory requirements vary among tissues, so too may the isozyme pattern. It is thus generally assumed that the elaboration of different patterns of isozymes in different cell types represents an important aspect of differentiation.

In the process of development in many animal types, isozyme patterns may undergo considerable change. Such change may play an important part in the formation of fully differentiated cells of various types, but it may possibly have other significance, particularly when it occurs in early embryogenesis. The control of respiratory reactions may be of considerable importance in facilitating or regulating rates of some of the very basic reactions of development. Changes in curves for rates of synthesis of proteins and nucleic acids and for other reactions have been observed by various investigators to be paralleled by changes in oxygen consumption or in the activity of various respiratory enzymes, although the extent to which respiratory activity represents a cause versus a prerequisite, or in some instances an effect, of synthetic activity in most findings of this type has not been established. Isozymes known to be regulators of respiratory metabolism should be explored further to determine precisely what roles they play in development.

Isozymes are often the result of combinations of monomers, which monomers are determined by more than a single gene. The monomers of lactate dehydrogenase, for example, are thought to be determined by two genes, and since the lactate dehydrogenase isozymes are tetramers, five combinations are possible.

Isozymes of malate dehydrogenase have been of primary concern to workers in sea urchin embryology. Malate dehydrogenase (MDH) is a potentially critical enzyme in the regulation of respiration, since in the presence of a hydrogen acceptor such as NAD, it converts L-malic acid to oxaloacetic acid to terminate a turn of the citric acid cycle. Oxaloacetic acid, the product of the reaction catalyzed by L-MDH may be considered a portal of entry to the citric acid cycle, since its condensation with acetyl coenzyme A initiates a new turn of the cycle.

Villee (1960) and Kaplan et al. (1960) demonstrated the existence of isozymes of malate dehydrogenase in echinoderms and noted that they display characteristic rates of reaction with NAD and its analogs. Moore and Villee (1962 and 1963a) studied some of the properties of malate dehydrogenases of sea urchin embryos, and their work may be consulted for data on electrophoretic mobility, rate of reaction with analogs of NAD and with D- and L-malate, sensitivity to heat, and differential solubility in ammonium sulfate. Early studies with isozyme preparations from the unfertilized egg showed five bands on starch gel electrophoresis. Two bands disappeared a few hours after fertilization. One band reappeared a few hours after its disappearance. The concept that MDH isozymes in the sea urchin represent five possible tetramers of two monomer types had to be modified, however, when it was found that this picture applies primarily to NAD L-malate dehydrogenases. There were shown to be seven acetylpyridine-adenine dinucleotide L-malate dehydrogenases and five APAD D-malate dehydrogenases in echinoderms. This may be somewhat unusual among cell systems. Cells of vertebrates, for example, appear on preliminary examinations to have much simpler isozyme patterns in the instance of MDH.

A convenient mechanism for demonstrating fundamental differences among isozyme patterns, beyond the use of zymograms (resolution into bands by electrophoresis), was found to be the calculation of the ratio of the rate of reaction with APAD to that with NAD at any given period or in any given location. Moore and Villee (1963b) dissociated 64-cell embryos and separated large blastomeres and small blastomeres by centrifugation. (There are actually three categories of blastomeres as to size in the 64-cell embryo. Although the investigators did not so specify, it would appear that macromeres constituted the large blastomeres and mesomeres, the small, with the status of micromeres uncertain.) The electrophoretic patterns and APAD/NAD ratios were found to differ between large and small blastomeres. Small blastomeres showed three bands of pronounced activity with NAD and two with APAD. Large blastomeres showed two bands with NAD and one with APAD, a smaller number of bands overall. The APAD/NAD ratio was higher in the large blastomeres. It is patent that even at this stage the pattern of isozyme distribution is showing variations in different regions of the embryo, and the number of different isozymes in a region of the embryo is showing a reduction relative to the total number in the unfertilized egg. These regional differences may be postulated to relate to the animal–vegetal polarity of the embryo, inasmuch as they represent a differential distribution of respiratory enzymes along the animal–vegetal axis of the embryo. Patton et al. (1967) demonstrated that a somewhat similar differential distribution is already present in fertilized and unfertilized eggs.

The Patton group found that the isozyme pattern of nucleate half-eggs is identical to that of whole eggs before and after fertilization, although the number of isozymes is reduced from the seven in the unfertilized egg to four in the fertilized egg by 90 minutes after fertilization. The anucleate halves, however, contain a reduced number of bands in polyacrylamide gel electrophoresis relative to the number in the unfertilized and fertilized egg. The APAD/NAD ratio is higher in anucleate halves of both fertilized and unfertilized eggs than in nucleate halves and whole eggs. These workers also investigated the MDH isozymes of the sperm and found three bands. These bands correspond in electrophoretic mobility to three of the bands in the unfertilized egg. They centrifuged homogenates of unfertilized eggs at 22,000 × g to throw down mitochondria and found that five of the seven bands of the unfertilized egg were located in the soluble fraction. Four were found in a particulate fraction, and it is reasonable to assume that they may have a mitochondrial location. Two of the bands, of course, were common to both fractions. The results of their experiments are shown in Fig. 39.

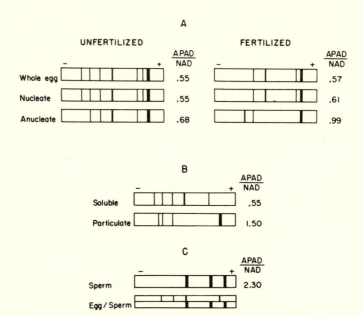

Figure 39

Bands of L-malate dehydrogenase activity separated by disk microelectrophoresis on polyacrylamide gel and stained with nitro blue tetrazolium. (A) Unfertilized and fertilized sea urchin eggs and their nucleate and anucleate halves. (B) Particulate and soluble fractions from unfertilized eggs. (C) The sperm and a split-tube pattern of egg and sperm. The latter shows that the most cathodal sperm band is identical with a band in the egg, but that the most anodal bands of sperm and egg are not identical as to electrophoretic mobility. [From Villee (1968); by permission.]

In commenting on the work of his group, Villee (1968) has suggested that the dichotomy here may indicate that there are two basic MDH systems in the sea urchin, one soluble and one particulate. The particulate system would appear to be characterized by fewer bands in its electrophoretic profile and by a higher APAD/NAD ratio than the soluble system. He assumes the anucleate half-eggs, which show particulate system characteristics, to be rich in mitochondria. The isozyme bands of the sperm show particulate fraction characteristics, and there is little probability of MDH isozymes having a location other than in mitochondria in sperm.

In terms of soluble-isozyme characteristics versus particulate-isozyme characteristics, the small blastomeres correspond to the nucleate half-egg and the large blastomeres to the anucleate half. If it can be assumed that the large blastomeres are primarily macromeres, the mitochondrial MDH isozymes would appear to be more heavily represented in the vegetal half of the cleaving embryo. Where half-eggs are concerned, some investigators (see Harvey, 1956, and Selvig et al., 1970) have reported that mitochondria show a propensity for migrating to the nucleate half, although some are found in the anucleate half. Selvig observed that mitochondria move centripetally in a centrifugal field, although she described the concentration of mitochondria in the anucleate half as "significant." In the illustrations that Villee (1968) presents of nucleate halves, there appears to be an accumulation of mitochondria, along with some yolk. It is curious that anucleate halves should, under these circumstances, show more pronounced characteristics of the particulate population of MDH isozymes than do nucleate halves unless this population is more active within the mitochondria of anucleate halves. If it is more active, it is interesting that evidence of such differential activity should be preserved if there is a significant redistribution of mitochondria in the centrifugation used to produce the anucleate halves.

Billiar et al. (1965 and 1966) reported that neither puromycin nor actinomycin D treatment seriously affects the patterns of isozymes of *L*-MDH after fertilization, indicating that the enzyme is rather stable in early development and suggesting that the bands seen in early embryogenesis may have survived from the fertilized egg rather than have been synthesized *de novo*.

Ozaki and Whiteley (1970) have reported that there may be species differences in MDH isozyme patterns, with *Strongylocentrotus purpuratus* having perhaps as few as two isozymes after fertilization as compared with the several isozymes of *Arbacia*. They have given some clue also as to the nature of the differential activity of MDH isozymes. They have reported that the soluble fractions produce substrate inhibition with high concentrations of *L*-malate, whereas the particulate fractions produce substrate inhibition with high concentrations of oxaloacetate. The activity of the isozymes of both fractions increases as development proceeds.

These studies represent a good beginning in the investigation of malate dehydrogenase activity. There are still many questions to be answered about these isozymes. There appear to be an inordinately large number of them in *Arbacia,* and there might be some merit in reexamining the older studies to determine whether any of these isozymes might be artifacts. The question of what role MDH isozymes play in controlling specific developmental events such as differentiation has not been answered, and it is still only inferential that they do play such a role. Three basic arguments with which a case may be made for their involvement in control of development are first that their individual variation in kinetics suggests a control mechanism, second that they show regional distribution that may correspond to the morphogenetic gradient pattern in the embryo, and third that they vary in number and appear or disappear at different times in development. The third argument needs further experimental examination. Francesconi and Villee (1968) have indicated that shifts in numbers of isozymes observed in the first several hours after fertilization may have resulted from the observation of transitory changes and that the pattern may stabilize as early as 2 hours after fertilization.

Several respiratory enzymes or enzymes indirectly associated with respiratory cycles are likely to have the capability to control the course of development, whether or not they be isozymes. Among these the transaminases in particular must be mentioned. Changes in oxidative metabolism and changes in the rate of protein synthesis may be linked through these enzymes. Substrates in the respiratory cycles, such as pyruvate, α-ketoglutarate, and oxaloacetate, may be converted to amino acids through the activity of these enzymes, and the conversion may serve as a mechanism of controlling the rates of synthesis of proteins. Observed changes in the activity of transaminases, however, may not be interpreted, in the absence of firm evidence to sustain the interpretation, as heralding changes in development, on the one hand, or resulting from changes in development on the other, although it is reasonable to expect that both possibilities exist. Black (1964) has made some investigations into the activity of transaminases in development. He has found that in *Lytechinus variegatus* embryos the activity of glutamic aspartic transaminase decreases somewhat during development up to prism and then nearly doubles between prism and pluteus. Glutamic alanine transaminase increases slowly in activity up to prism and then increases sharply until pluteus. These increases do not follow closely the general curve for the activity of respiratory enzymes. They do, however, occur at a time of both visible and functional differentiation.

REAGGREGATION OF DISSOCIATED CELLS
IN THE SEA URCHIN EMBRYO

The study of the reaggregation of dissociated cells is an important field where both tissues and embryos are concerned. In embryos it may be specifically expected to yield information on the inductive processes; on the extent to which reactions are dependent upon, or independent of, cell interaction; on forces involved in contact and adhesion between cells; and hopefully on mechanisms of cell movement.

Studies on reaggregation in the sea urchin were conducted as early as 1900 by Herbst. The problem of reaggregation did not receive a great deal of attention, however, until the early 1960s, when a group of workers associated with Giudice began a study of the subject in depth. Giudice and Mutolo (1970) have reviewed some of the work of this group. Giudice (1962a) developed refinements in technique and made preliminary observations on some of the cytological aspects of reaggregation. Cells are usually dissociated in buffered calcium-free seawater to which sucrose has been added to protect them from possible harmful mechanical effects. They may be dispersed by the use of a glass homogenizer, obviously with the gentlest of manipulations. Once dispersed, the cells may be held in a dissociated state for study or be allowed to reaggregate under the appropriate experimental conditions. Reaggregation can be promoted by the traditional method of rotating the culture. Cells can also be allowed to reaggregate by forming a layer on the bottom of a Syracuse dish. The latter method, known as self-aggregation, allows continuous observation by the microscopist.

Reaggregation is a very rapid process. Cells begin to clump together almost immediately. Each cell usually has an active pseudopod for motility. Some cells may have a cilium. Upon dissociation cells undergo a variety of cytological changes, depending on their nature and the site of their origin in the embryo. Cells may become spherical, microvilli may disappear, nuclei may shift their position in the cell. The average size of the final aggregate is usually quite similar to that of a normal embryo, although there is often a fair amount of variability in aggregate size. The aggregates normally develop a cavity resembling a blastocoel. The ultimate nature of the "organism" that develops from the aggregate depends to a high degree on the stage of development attained at the time of dissociation. If, for instance, the formation of a skeleton is underway at the time of dissociation, a new skeleton may not be formed. Cell interactions of a specific nature are impossible when cells are in a dissociated state. When development is interrupted by dissociation, structures may be destroyed that require cell interactions to be restored. The inability for the interactions to occur will then lead to the failure of the structure to form. If cells are in a dissociated state at the time in development when a chemical command for morphogenetic or differentiative change is normally given, the command can be effective only if it is of an intracellular, rather than an intercellular, nature. If the command is not received and acted upon by cells in the dissociated state, the evidence indicates that the cells usually do not have an opportunity to have the command repeated for them upon reaggregation. They cannot execute a command they have not received, and the result is the failure of some step in development to occur.

Embryos dissociated up to early prism may develop a larva that has the general appearance of the pluteus (see Fig. 40). It may be kept alive several days by feeding. The Giudice group have not yet determined whether this larva is capable of metamorphosis. Abnormally large aggregates give rise to giant larvae which appear to be polyembryonic in that they may develop several guts or an abnormal number of skeletal spicules.

Knowing the remarkable propensity for filopodal activity that exists when cell contacts are made in invagination and when skeletal formation is in progress and knowing that embryos whose cells are slightly separated from one another in early development appear to exhibit a degree of filopodal activity, one would not be surprised to see this type of activity manifested in the reaggregation process. Millonig and Giudice (1967), however, report from an electron microscope study that it does not occur and that reaggregation involves the contact of smooth surface with smooth surface.

Cells in the process of reaggregation combine ultimately in patterns that are not random and that have meaning, and they undergo visible differentiation, which means that they must also undergo a high degree of chemical differentiation. It becomes important, therefore, to describe the nature of the specificity that prompts their association

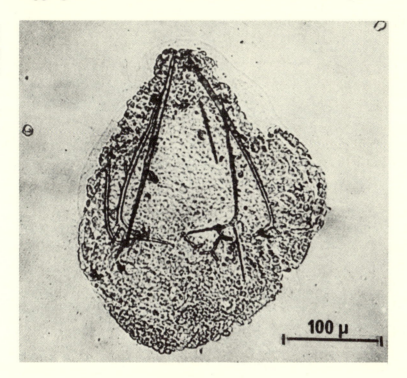

Figure 40
Pluteus-like larva developed from reaggregates of cells of embryos of *Paracentrotus lividus* dissociated at mesenchyme blastula. The larva has been flattened to show details of the skeleton. [From Giudice and Mutolo (1970); by permission.]

with one another and to determine whether they dedifferentiate in reaggregation, after the manner seen in blastema formation in regenerating embryonic amphibian limbs. Giudice (1962a) demonstrated that dissociated cells from *Arbacia lixula* and *Paracentrotus lividus* when mixed together will segregate and reassort themselves to form reaggregates whose cells belong to a single species. It is apparent then that, as has long been known to be true of sponge cells and as has often been demonstrated to be untrue in vertebrate cell systems, the sea urchin embryo shows species specificity in reaggregation.

As Giudice and Mutolo (1970) have pointed out, organ specificity has not been demonstrated in the sea urchin embryo and may be difficult to demonstrate, because of the problem of identifying the territories from which dissociated cells originate. Giudice (1963) was able to demonstrate, however, that cells of the sea urchin do retain their animal or vegetal characteristics upon reaggregation. Embryos that had been animalized or vegetalized chemically and dissociated before the treatment could express itself formed aggregates that assumed the general form of chemically animalized or vegetalized embryos. These experiments suggest, moreover, that reaggregation may not proceed from dedifferentiation but may rather represent a sorting out of cell types by some mechanism such as selective adhesion between cells, possibly involving contact-mediated reactions between specific substances on the cell surface.

Curiously enough, reaggregation does not appear to involve developmental stage specificity. Giudice et al. (1969) have found that radioactively labeled cells from the blastula appear in aggregates along with unlabeled cells from the prism stage. This finding, by contrast, could imply that dedifferentiation does occur in reaggregation and that these cells could associate because they had lost some of the specificity that must accompany differentiation. It could also imply that specific substances on the surface of the cells involved, which substances are capable of promoting cell association, have not changed the pattern of their specificities significantly between blastula and prism.

In sponge cells, in some cells of vertebrate tissues, and in neoplastic structures of embryoid character from mice, the existence of extracellular substances that promote aggregation either has been demonstrated indirectly or has been definitely demonstrated to the point of isolation and at least partial characterization. Such reaggregation factors were not reported in the sea urchin until 1971, when Kondo and Sakai found that a substance was extracted from sea urchin embryos by urea solutions used in the dissociation of these embryos that has the power to accelerate reaggregation. The substance requires the addition of divalent cations to produce its effect, and the manner of treatment that must be used when adding the cations varies with the species in the three species of sea urchin tested.

The reaggregating factor shows the same characteristics in elution from hydroxyapatite columns as does hyalin, the calcium-precipitable protein from the hyaline layer. It can be shown to react to antisera prepared against hyalin. Hyalin, in turn, shows the ability to promote reaggregation. The analysis of the reaggregation factor shows that it has a similar amino acid sequence to hyalin, but some hexosamines are found to be present. While conceding that the hexosamines could be contaminants, the investigators postulated that the reaggregating factor is a glycoprotein with a protein motiety that is similar or identical to hyalin. They propose that it may function under normal conditions as an intercellular cement.

Dissociated cells of sea urchin embryos appear to continue to divide, but their DNA synthesis proceeds at a rate somewhat slower than in intact embryos (see unpublished results of Mutolo et al. in Giudice and Mutolo, 1970).

An extremely interesting picture is presented by experiments on the synthesis of r-RNA by Giudice et al. (1967). With appropriate reservation for recent studies, which have been discussed previously, that suggest that r-RNA may be synthesized throughout development, it may be noted that many investigators including Giudice and his co-workers have found the synthesis of r-RNA to be activated, or at least strongly accelerated, after gastrulation. Giudice et al. (1967) reported this activation to occur in cells dissociated between hatching blastula and midgastrula, dissociated at a time just shortly before the activation would have occurred had the cells remained housed in intact embryos. The cells were reaggregating at the time when the activity was switched on, but they contained at that time no structures characteristic of the morphogenesis of a normal embryo. These results imply that cell interaction is not necessary for the initiation of r-RNA synthesis. Since there would be a considerable delay before the reaggregating cells produced the morphological structures seen in intact control embryos at the moment r-RNA synthesis was switched on in the reaggregating cells, another interesting way of looking at the picture suggests itself. It would appear that the activation of the synthesis of r-RNA depends on the developmental age of the cells of the embryo rather than on the developmental age of the embryo itself, considered in terms of its morphological development. Stated in another fashion, activation of r-RNA synthesis occurs in a cell when that cell reaches a given time in hours after fertilization rather than when the embryo which houses it reaches a certain morphological stage in development. It should be noted that intact control embryos are embryos fertilized at the same time as those which gave rise to the dissociated cells and cultured under comparable conditions.

Sconzo et al. (1970) found that there is an incorporation of label into r-RNA in dissociated cells that is characteristic of that seen after gastrula in intact embryos. This incorporation occurs whether cells are reaggregating or are kept in a dissociated state. They conclude, again, that cell interaction is not necessary for the activation of r-RNA synthesis.

The rate of protein synthesis in dissociated cells of *Paracentrotus lividus* was examined at different developmental stages by Giudice (1962b). Rates of amino acid incorporation determined immediately after dissociation showed that cells were continuing to synthesize protein, albeit more slowly than in the intact embryo. The curve for rate of incorporation immediately following dissociation versus developmental stage at which dissociation occurred was parallel to that found for incorporation through progressive developmental stages in intact embryos. The conclusion that dissociated cells synthesize protein at a rate characteristic of the stage at which they were dissociated appears reasonable.

It has not been determined unequivocally whether dissociated cells synthesize their proteins on the same molecular types of message as the cells of intact control embryos. Giudice and Mutolo (1970) have performed hybridization experiments in which they found that m-RNA from dissociated cells was incapable of increasing the amount of m-RNA bound to DNA that had previously been saturated with messenger molecules from intact control embryos. This type of experiment generally does not offer a very firm proof.

Giudice (1965) followed the aggregation of cells of *Paracentrotus lividus* embryos dissociated at mesenchyme blastula under conditions that normally inhibit protein synthesis. He found that the normally reaggregating cells underwent an increase in protein synthesis over a period of 3 hours, but that reaggregating cells from embryos treated with puromycin underwent a sharp decline in rate of protein synthesis, as might be expected. The reaggregation process, however, proceeded normally for a time, then, after 2 hours, the cells suddenly disaggregated. At the time of this disaggregation, protein synthesis was down to about 20 percent of that of the controls.

The picture with actinomycin D was similar to that with puromycin. It is to be recalled that mesenchyme blastula is a time when there is considerable transcription of genes and that protein synthesis is actinomycin D sensitive at this stage in development. Protein synthesis in reaggregating cells from embryos treated with actinomycin D showed an 80 percent drop from that of the controls in a period of 6 hours. Aggregation was nearly normal up to the time of epithelial differentiation, whereupon occurred a disaggregation, proceeding at a somewhat slower rate than with puromycin and affecting most, but not all, aggregates. Giudice noted, however, that the inhibition of protein synthesis by puromycin and by actinomycin D was accompanied by a sharp drop in respiration. He formulated the hypothesis that the attenuation of respiratory activity, rather than the inhibition of protein synthesis, might be responsible for the failure of aggregation to continue. When cells were allowed to reaggregate in ethionine, which inhibits protein synthesis without seriously affecting respiration for a period of about 5 hours, the reaggregation proceeded normally until the respiration rate dropped. Giudice concluded that protein synthesis is probably not a prerequisite to reaggregation.

Pfohl and Giudice (1967) discovered that cells dissociated shortly before early pluteus undergo the same characteristic increase in the activity of alkaline phosphatase as occurs at that period in development in intact control embryos. If, however, cells are dissociated at mesenchyme blastula, the reaggregating cells do not experience an increase in their alkaline phosphatase activity at the time when intact control embryos have reached early pluteus. They do, however, undergo some increase in the activity of the enzyme when the *aggregate* is achieving a pluteal form (see Fig. 41).

The interpretation which they gave to this phenomenon is that the *commitment* to increase the activity is made at some time shortly after mesenchyme blastula, and that cell interaction is necessary (through the activation of transcription?) to effect the commitment. The *command* to increase enzyme activity is executed (through the activation of translation?) at early pluteus. If the cells are in a dissociated state when the commitment should be made, they cannot make it. When the time in hours after development arrives for the execution of the command, they cannot execute it. When, however,

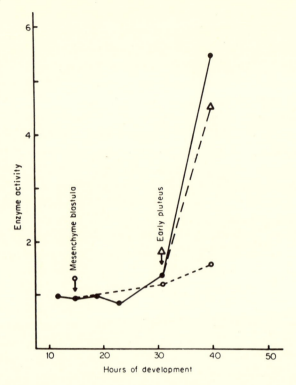

Figure 41
Alkaline phosphatase activity in normal embryos and reaggregating cells. The values
have been normalized on the basis of a value of 1.0 for swimming blastulae. Control
embryos, filled circles; cells dissociated from mesenchyme blastulae, open circles;
cells dissociated from early plutei, triangles. The arrows point to the moment of cell
dissociation. (From Pfohl and Giudice. Reproduced from *Biochim. Biophys. Acta*,
142, 1967, p. 265.)

the reaggregating cells produce the morphological form normally
characteristic of this time in development, some form of cellular
interaction enables the restitution, to a degree, of the activity lost
through failure to commit at the proper time.

FINAL REMARKS

The history of sea urchin embryology shows, despite the not
inconsiderable accomplishment of workers in the field, a panorama
of not quite solved problems and a plethora of experimental results

that state or suggest questions without making any appreciable headway in the direction of obtaining answers. As new problems arise and become the focus of active endeavor, work on older problems is seen less frequently. This is a normal, healthy situation in research. As each new beachhead is made it is extended, and previously occupied territory is vacated in the interests of expansion into new fields of study. Many of the new problems are more intricate, more demanding on resources of technical skill, more basic to the understanding of development as a whole, and perhaps more exciting than some of the older ones. Some of these new fields of inquiry may remain active for a long time to come. Most of the problems of the past that have become inactive as foci for research have not so become because they achieved the status of solved problems. We do not abandon partially solved problems; we simply neglect them. It would be most fortunate if there were a recrudescence of attention to some of the older work. We have more accurate, more sensitive, and more sophisticated techniques with which to examine it. Most of the major problems of the past that are currently receiving only a minor amount of attention are sufficiently important in their own right to justify reinvestigation or continued investigation, although the blind alley is an eternal reality in science. The plea that such reinvestigation might lead to a windfall of knowledge that could conceivably enable a more meaningful interpretation of some of the findings of current work, however, is not without merit.

We need to take a second look at the activity of respiratory cycles in sea urchin development and to attempt to assess more rigorously and more realistically their relationship to the biosynthesis of macromolecules and other synthetic activities. Work in sea urchin enzymology cannot truly be characterized as an older problem, but it has often come in fits and spurts and has varied to a degree in its thoroughness. A massive coordinated effort in this area ought to be given a high priority on the agenda of future research. It is difficult to determine whether extensive research on gradient theory per se ought to be given high priority in future research or not. The theory still holds a dominant position in the thinking of experimental embryologists, and there is certainly little question as to the validity of the theory. The information that it yields is largely quantitative in nature, and there is some question as to how it can be interpreted to explain many of the qualitative aspects of morphogenesis. It is perhaps more critical to concentrate on certain molecular phenomena to see how the gradient theory may reflect them, in other words, to come in from the opposite direction. Some of the work of Villee and his group with malate dehydrogenase isozymes suggests that such an approach is feasible.

The problems of yolk formation and yolk utilization have been given some study in the past, but the time is ripe for an intensive exploration of the discrete mechanics of both these phenomena, particularly in the light of recent findings on yolk spherule DNA. Although the problem of sperm–egg interaction has received an enormous amount of attention in the past, the nature of the interactions has never been fully resolved, particularly as they relate directly or indirectly to the phenomena of activation. A reexamination of the problems associated with activation itself, one that involves a molecular approach, is long overdue and would appear to call for a vast amount of work. The role that hormones may play in activation ought in particular to be thoroughly investigated, in fact, the mechanism of action of hormones in the egg should be studied to reveal whether, and to what extent, they may be implicated in the activation of genes or the triggering of cellular reaction, particularly through the mediation of cyclic AMP. The discrete differences between activation by fertilization and activation by artificial parthenogenesis are in need of study, and the actual mechanism of action of artificial parthenogenesis has yet to be resolved, particularly with respect to the explanation for artificial parthenogenesis being elicited by a wide variety of agencies that appear, superficially at least, often to be unrelated to one another.

Knowledge of intermediary metabolism, particularly the intermediary metabolism of the nucleotides, lacks both breadth and depth where the sea urchin embryo is concerned. The available information is sketchy, and much of it was obtained at a time when techniques were inadequate and often inaccurate relative to those which exist today. There is much to be said for an all-out effort to explore the small-molecule biochemistry of the sea urchin embryo.

Among the newer problems, it is expected that the problem of the activation of the increase in protein synthesis at fertilization will continue to represent a major focus of attention for some time, but it is to be hoped that the controversy over which mechanism is responsible for the activation will be resolved and that attention can be concentrated on determining the details of the operation of the applicable mechanism. The status of the timing of r-RNA synthesis is presently in a confused state and will probably command attention for some time. The molecular aspects of r-RNA, moreover, need to be resolved against the background of the cytology of the nucleolus. Questions associated with the methylation of bases of DNA and RNA and with the possible role of the synthetases in differentiation, or more explicitly in the qualitative and quantitative control of protein synthesis, call urgently for solution. One can cite other instances of similar urgency. Beyond the press of immediate problems, there are three major problems before the sea urchin embryologist today which are truly monolithic, which may have large areas of overlap and interdigitation, and which will doubtlessly occupy the middle ring of the research circus, if one will pardon the metaphor, for many years to come.

Of these, the most significant problem is that of molecular and cellular mechanics of differentiation. This problem perhaps may be considered the central problem of the present age of biology. The major work that has been done on this problem in the sea urchin in recent years has involved hybridization studies on m-RNA at various developmental stages and analysis of patterns of protein production in the search for the emergence of new protein species as indices of changes in the spectrum of active genes, changes that might represent preliminary events in the process of differentiation. Most of the answers to problems on the nature of differentiation still lie behind the veil.

The second problem is that of the mechanisms of control of elaboration of genetic information for protein synthesis. This involves the study of control and timing of transcription and translation of template for protein synthesis. It may be extended to include the control and timing of the activation of the protein so produced. It includes also the investigation of the chemical and physical nature of the participating macromolecules, in the interests of a greater understanding of the mechanisms involved in their activity. Among the three big problems under discussion, the principal gains have been made on this problem of the molecular and cellular mechanics of information flow in protein biosynthesis. The successes that have been achieved are doubtless due in part to the fact that a vast amount of work is being done on related problems in many cell systems by investigators in many fields, resulting in considerable exchange of information.

The third problem is of awe-inspiring magnitude. It involves the exploration of the chemical and cellular events that trigger and coordinate all the complicated reactions of development, the study of the nature of the tape which contains the command sequences that program development. This problem would appear to be of dimensions such that it must await developments in the exploration of the other two problems before it can become an object of serious study. It does, however, appear to involve nucleocytoplasmic interactions and cellular interactions and the manner in which they operate and are programmed to produce changes in gene activity. Although no breakthroughs of any significance have been made in either of these areas, the latter at least appears to be experimentally approachable with the techniques of the present day.

The problems facing the molecular embryologist are sometimes difficult, but he is by no means engaged in an exercise in futility. It is the hope and expectation of embryologists in general that the molecular embryologist will put together a picture of the events of development at the molecular level that will be at least as coherent as the picture of morphogenesis that presently exists at the level of descriptive biology, even though it may turn out to be a picture of much greater dimensions and much greater complexity and take much longer to delineate. It is further to be expected that the picture which he elaborates will go a long way toward explaining the visible aspects of morphogenesis. Thirty years ago, biologists debated interminably over the problem of mechanism versus vitalism. Many asserted, with what may have been an undue boldness in view of the state of knowledge in that day, that the phenomena of life could be explained adequately and completely in terms of the laws of chemistry and physics. It is somewhat ironic that at a time when science is in a position to put the assertion to the test of extensive experimentation, interest in the problem of mechanism versus vitalism has waned considerably. Neither the sea urchin embryologist nor any other species of embryologist can be said truthfully to be laboring to prove the contentions of the mechanist. The sea urchin embryo, however, does represent an admirable system with which to determine the readiness with which that complicated, organized series of events which constitute development will submit to being described in terms of the interaction of various laws and principles of chemistry and physics. The attempt so to describe is likely to be the main thrust of sea urchin embryology for many years to come.

REFERENCES

Bellemare, G., J. Inard, and A. Aubin, 1968. Uptake and incorporation of leucine and thymidine in developing sea urchin eggs. The effects of hexahomoserine. *Exp. Cell Res., 51,* 406–412.

Berg, W. E., 1968. Kinetics of uptake and incorporation of valine in the sea urchin embryo. (*Lytechinus anamesus*). *Exp. Cell Res., 49,* 379–395.

Berg, W. E., 1970. Further studies on the kinetics of incorporation of valine in the sea urchin embryo. *Exp. Cell Res., 60,* 210–217.

Berg, W. E., and D. H. Mertes, 1970. Rates of synthesis and degradation of protein in the sea urchin embryo. *Exp. Cell Res., 60,* 218–224.

Billiar, R. B., J. B. Billiar, C. A. Villee, and L. Zelewski, 1965. The effect of puromycin and actinomycin on cell divison, protein synthesis, and malate dehydrogenase in embryos. *Biol. Bull. Mar. Biol. Lab., Woods Hole, 129,* 399.

Billiar, R. B., L. Zelewski, and C. A. Villee, 1966. L-malate dehydrogenase activity and protein synthesis in sea urchin embryos. *Develop. Biol., 13,* 282–295.

Black, R. E., 1964. Transaminase activity in homogenates of developing eggs of the sea urchin *Lytechinus variegatus. Exp. Cell Res., 33,* 613–616.

Boolootian, R. A. (ed.), 1966. *Physiology of the Echinodermata.* John Wiley & Sons, Inc. (Interscience Division), New York.

Francesconi, R. P., and C. A. Villee, 1968. Changes in malate dehydrogenase patterns in *Arbacia* embryos during early development. *Comp. Biochem. Physiol., 25,* 747–750.

Fry, B. J., and P. R. Gross, 1970a. Patterns and rates of protein synthesis in sea urchin embryos. I. Uptake and incorporation of amino acids during the first cleavage cycle. *Develop. Biol., 21,* 105–124.

Fry, B. J., and P. R. Gross, 1970b. Patterns and rates of protein synthesis during the first cleavage cycle. II. The calculation of absolute rates. *Develop. Biol., 21,* 125–146.

Giudice, G., 1962a. Restitution of whole larvae from disaggregating cells of sea urchin embryos. *Develop. Biol., 5,* 402–411.

Giudice, G., 1962b. Amino acid incorporation into proteins of isolated cells and total homogenates of sea urchin embryos. *Arch. Biochem., 99,* 447–450.

Giudice, G., 1963. Aggregation of cells isolated from vegetalized and animalized sea urchin embryos. *Experientia, 19,* 83–84.

Giudice, G., 1965. The mechanism of aggregation of embryonic sea urchin cells, a biochemical approach. *Develop. Biol., 12,* 233–247.

Giudice, G., and V. Mutolo, 1970. Reaggregation of dissociated cells of sea urchin embryos. *Advances in Morphogenesis,* Vol. 8. Academic Press, Inc., New York, 115–158.

Giudice, G., V. Mutolo, G. Donatuti, and M. Bosco, 1969. Reaggregation of mixtures of cells from different developmental stages of sea urchin embryos. *Exp. Cell Res., 54*, 279–281.

Giudice, G., V. Mutolo, and A. A. Moscona, 1967. The role of cell interactions in the control of RNA synthesis. *Biochim. Biophys. Acta, 138,* 607–610.

Gross, P. R., and B. J. Fry, 1966. Continuity of protein synthesis through cleavage metaphase. *Science, 153,* 749–751.

Harvey, E. B., 1956. *The American Arbacia and Other Sea Urchins.* Princeton University Press, Princeton, N.J.

Herbst, C., 1900. Über das Auseinandergehen von Furchungs und Gewebzellen in kalkfreien Medium. *Wm. Roux Entwicklsmech. Org., 9,* 423–463.

Hultin, T., and A. Bergstrand, 1960. Incorporation of C^{14}-leucine into protein by cell-free systems from sea urchin embryos at different stages of development. *Develop. Biol., 2, 61*–75.

Kaplan, N. O., M. M. Ciotti, M. Hamolsky, and R. E. Bieber, 1960. Molecular heterogeneity and evolution of embryos. *Science, 131,* 392–397.

Kavanau, J. L., 1954. Amino acid metabolism in early development of the sea urchin. *Exp. Cell Res., 7,* 530–537.

Kondo, K., and H. Sakai, 1971. Demonstration and preliminary characterization of reaggregation promoting substances from embryonic sea urchin cells. *Develop. Growth Differ., 13,* 1–14.

Mano, Y., 1968. Regulation of protein synthesis in early embryogenesis in the sea urchin. *Biochem. Biophys. Res. Commun., 33,* 877–882.

Mano, Y., 1969. Factors involved in cyclic protein synthesis in sea urchin cells during early embryogenesis. *Biochemistry (Tokyo), 65,* 483–487.

Mano, Y., 1970. Cytoplasmic regulation and cyclic variation in protein synthesis in the early cleavage stage of the sea urchin embryo. *Develop. Biol., 22,* 433–460.

Millonig, G., and G. Giudice, 1967. Electron microscope study of the reaggregation of cells dissociated from sea urchin embryos. *Develop. Biol., 15,* 91–101.

Mitchison, J. M., and J. E. Cummins, 1966. The uptake of valine and cytidine by sea urchin embryos and its relation to the cell surface. *J. Cell. Sci., 1,* 35–47.

Monroy, A., and R. Maggio, 1966. Amino acid metabolism in the developing embryo. In R. A. Boolootian (ed.), *Physiology of the Echinodermata.* John Wiley & Sons, Inc. (Interscience Division), New York, 743–756.

Moore, R. O., and C. A. Villee, 1962. Malic dehydrogenase in sea urchin eggs. *Science, 138,* 508–509.

Moore, R. O., and C. A. Villee, 1963a. Multiple molecular forms of malate dehydrogenase in echinoderm embryos. *Comp. Biochem. Physiol., 9,* 81–94.

Moore, R. O., and C. A. Villee, 1963b. Malate dehydrogenase: multiple forms in separated blastomeres of sea urchin embryos. *Science, 142,* 398–390.

Nakano, E., and A. Monroy, 1958a. Some observations on the metabolism of S^{35}-methionine during development of the sea urchin egg. *Experientia, 14,* 367–371.

Nakano, E., and A. Monroy, 1958b. Incorporation of S^{35}-methionine in the cell fractions of sea urchin eggs and embryos. *Exp. Cell Res., 14,* 236–244.

Ozaki, H., and A. H. Whiteley, 1970. L-malate dehydrogenase in the development of the sea urchin *Strongylocentrotus purpuratus. Develop. Biol., 21,* 196–215.

Patton, G. W., L. Mets, and C. A. Villee, 1967. Malic dehydrogenase isozymes: distribution in developing nucleate and anucleate halves of sea urchin eggs. *Science, 156,* 400–401.

Pfohl, R. J., and G. Giudice, 1967. The role of cell interaction in the control of enzyme activity during embryogenesis. *Biochim. Biophys. Acta, 142,* 263–266.

Piatigorsky, J., and A. H. Whiteley, 1965. A change in permeability and uptake of (14C) uridine in response to fertilization in *Strongylocentrotus purpuratus* eggs. *Biochim. Biophys. Acta, 108,* 404–418.

Sacher, J. A., 1965. Senescence: hormonal control and protein synthesis in excised bean pod tissue. *Amer. J. Bot., 52,* 841–848.

Sacher, J. A., 1966. Dual effect of auxin: inhibition of uptake and stimulation of RNA and protein synthesis: assessment of synthesis. *Z. Pflanzenphysiol., 56,* 410–426.

Sconzo, G., A. M. Pirrone, V. Mutolo, and G. Giudice, 1970. Synthesis of ribosomal RNA during sea urchin development. 3. Evidence for an activation of transcription. *Biochim. Biophys. Acta, 199,* 435–440.

Selvig, S. E., P. R. Gross, and A. L. Hunter, 1970. Cytoplasmic synthesis of RNA in the sea urchin embryo. *Develop. Biol., 22,* 343–365.

Silver, D. J., and D. G. Comb, 1966. Free amino acid pools in the developing sea urchin *L. variegatus. Exp. Cell Res., 43,* 699.

Sofer, W. H., J. F. George, and R. M. Iverson, 1966. Rate of protein synthesis during first division cycle of sea urchin eggs. *Science, 153,* 1644–1645.

Spiegel, M. and A. Tyler, 1966. Protein synthesis in micromeres of the sea urchin egg. *Science, 151,* 1233–1234.

Stavy, L., and P. R. Gross, 1969. Protein synthesis *in vitro* with fractions of sea urchin eggs and embryos. *Biochim. Biophys. Acta, 182,* 193–202.

Timourian, H., 1966. Protein synthesis during first cleavage of sea urchin embryos. *Science, 154,* 1956.

Timourian, H., and P. Denny, 1964. Activation of protein synthesis in sea urchin eggs upon fertilization in relation to magnesium and potassium ions. *J. Exp. Zool., 155,* 57–70.

Timourian, H., and G. Watchmaker, 1970. Protein synthesis in sea urchin eggs. Changes in amino acid uptake and incorporation at fertilization. *Develop. Biol., 23,* 478–491.

Tyler, A., J. Piatigorsky, and H. Ozaki, 1966. Influence of individual amino acids on uptake and incorporation of valine, glutamic acid, and arginine by unfertilized and fertilized sea urchin eggs. *Biol. Bull. Mar. Biol. Lab., Woods Hole, 131,* 204–217.

Villee, C. A., 1960. Comparative studies on malic and glutamic dehydrogenases. *Biol. Bull. Mar. Biol. Lab., Woods Hole, 119,* 298–299.

Villee, C. A., 1968. Multiple molecular forms of L-malate dehydrogenase in sea urchin eggs and embryos. *Ann. N.Y. Acad. Sci., 151,* 222–231.

Author Index

Subject Index

A antigen (*see* Surface antigens of egg)
Acetylcholine and filopodal contraction, 129
Acid phosphatase in yolk spherules, 35–36
Acrosomal filament (*see* Acrosomal process)
Acrosomal granule, 16–19
Acrosomal process
  fibrous axial core, 16–19, 21
  formation, 16–19
Acrosomal process membrane
  formation, 16–19
  plasmalemma, union, 17
Acrosome in *Echinocardium cordatum*, 12
  origin from Golgi apparatus, 16
Acrosome reaction
  calcium ion, effect, 19–20
  described, 16–19
  loss of activity with age, 19
  midpiece, effect, 20
  nonspecific eversion, 21
  role in fertilization, 20–21
  stimulus, timing, 58
Actin filaments
    in cleavage furrow formation, 108–109
    response to myosin and relaxing factor in glycerinated cells, 108–109

  ultrastructure, 107–108
Actinomycin D
  active transport, effect, 284–285
  animalizing and vegetalizing propensities, effect, 139
  autoradiographic localization in embryo, 227
  ciliation, effect, 117
  DNA synthesis, mild suppression of in cleavage, 203
  exogenous RNA, failure to break actinomycin block, 265
  fertilization membrane barrier, controversy over, 226–227
  histone synthesis, effect, 168–171
  later stages of development, effect of administration, 225–226
  light and heavy polysomes, effect, 185
  mechanism of action, 199
  microscopical studies on effects during cleavage, 199–200
  migration of RNA and basic proteins to cytoplasm, inhibition in oocyte, 267
  mitotic abnormalities produced, 226
  nucleolus, inhibition of nucleotide incorporation, 266
  point of irreversibility of effect on development in *Arbacia*, 240–244